Himmler

OPPOSITION TO PAUL
IN JEWISH CHRISTIANITY

GERD LUEDEMANN

OPPOSITION TO PAUL IN JEWISH CHRISTIANITY

Translated by
M. Eugene Boring

FORTRESS PRESS   MINNEAPOLIS

OPPOSITION TO PAUL IN JEWISH CHRISTIANITY

First English-language edition published 1989 by Fortress Press.

This book is a translation of *Paulus, der Heidenapostel*, vol. 2: *Antipaulinismus im frühen Christentum* (FRLANT 130) by Gerd Luedemann, with emendations and additions by the author. Copyright © 1983 by Vandenhoeck & Ruprecht, Göttingen, Germany.

Unless translated directly from the original languages by the author or translator, biblical quotations are from the Revised Standard Version of the Bible, copyright © 1946, 1952, 1971 by the Division of Christian Education of the National Council of Churches of Christ in the U.S.A., and are used by permission.

Library of Congress cataloging in Publication Data

Luedemann, Gerd.
  Opposition to Paul in Jewish Christianity.

    Translation of: Paulus, der Heidenapostel. Bd. 2,
  Antipaulinismus im fruhen Christentum.
    Includes bibliographical references.
    1. Paul, the Apostle, Saint—Adversaries. 2. Jewish
  Christians—History—Early church, ca. 30–600. I. Title.
  BS2506.L8313 1989   225.9′2   89–23414
  ISBN 0–8006–0908–5

The paper used in this publication meets the minimum requirements of American National Standard for Information Science—Permanence of Paper for Printed Library Materials, ANSI Z329.48–1984.   ∞™

Manufactured in the U. S. A.   AF 1–908

93   92   91   90   89   1   2   3   4   5   6   7   8   9   10

*To W. D. Davies
Teacher and Friend*

CONTENTS

CONTENTS

CONTENTS

PREFACE

The present work represents volume 2 of my trilogy on Paul. I first became interested in the subject of this volume in the winter semester of 1968–69, when Georg Strecker, whose influence can be traced throughout the volume, entrusted me with the task of preparing the index for the Pseudo-Clementine *Homilies*. The present work, which makes grateful use of what I have learned from my teachers and from contemporary scholarship, attempts to appropriate the insights of the Tübingen school and to develop them in some detail, though with a different manner of formulating the questions and thus with different results. In the process, the insight has been confirmed for me that there exists a continuity of critical scholarship which spans the centuries and the continents. This book is indebted to that continuity of critical scholarship.

Preliminary work for the following study goes back to my two-year participation (1977–79) in the McMaster University project "On Normative Self-Definition in Judaism and Christianity," which was financed by the Social Sciences and Humanities Research Council of Canada. It is with both great joy and a sense of obligation that I express my thanks to the Council and my friend, Professor E. P. Sanders, who was then the Director of the project, for the invitation to Canada.

The work itself was written during my tenure at Vanderbilt University (1979–82).

The accurate and careful translation was done by my friend and colleague Professor M. Eugene Boring, with bibliographical assistance provided by Raymond F. Person, Jr. I had the opportunity to confer with both of them about their work. Proofs were checked and the indexes were made by Dr. Edward J. McMahon and Lana N. Byrd. New literature has been incorporated into this translation, and minor adjustments have been made. The English translation is therefore a new edition of the German original.

During the writing of this project I have had the good fortune of being supported by helpful critiques from several directions. An earlier version of the manuscript was read by Professor Hans Dieter Betz (Chicago), Ulrich Luz (Bern), Georg Strecker (Göttingen), and Eugene TeSelle (Vanderbilt). Professor Morton Smith (Columbia) provided almost every page of the manuscript with annotations, which he has graciously permitted me to cite. My thanks to all of these teachers, colleagues, and friends.

Earlier versions of two chapters were presented at separate annual meetings of the Society of Biblical Literature: chapter 1 at the October 1978 meeting in New Orleans and chapter 11.1 at the November 1980 meeting in Dallas (both within the framework of the Seminar on Jewish Christianity led by H. D. Betz and me). I presented an outline of the whole work to the Seminar on Jewish Christianity of the Studiorum Novi Testamenti Societas during its annual meeting in August 1979 in Durham, England. I here publicly express my thanks to Professor Nils Dahl, whose critique on all three occasions I found to be helpful.

Dr. Jürgen Wehnert (Göttingen) has also given me much help during this project. To him, as well as to Professor F. Stanley Jones and Larry Welborn, I offer my sincere thanks for suggestions that have improved both the content and the form of the manuscript.

The concluding third volume will follow. In the meantime, my essay "Paulus und das Judentum" (*TEH* 215 [Munich, 1983] provides something of a preview of it.

The publications indicated in the bibliography by an asterisk appeared too late for me to take them into consideration in the preparation of this work. I will, however, discuss them in forthcoming issues of *Theologische Rundschau* in which I will regularly discuss reports of research on the history of early Christianity.

The English-language edition of this work is dedicated to my teacher and friend, W. D. Davies, as whose assistant I was privileged to spend an unforgettable year at Duke University (1974–75). His wisdom had a decisive effect on my theological development, and his humanity means very much to me and my family.

Gerd Luedemann
Georg-August University
Göttingen, West Germany

ABBREVIATIONS

The abbreviations are generally the same as those in Siegfried Schwertner, *Internationales Abkürzungsverzeichnis für Theologie und Grenzgebiete* (New York and Berlin: Walter de Gruyter, 1974), and Gerhard Kittel, ed., *Theological Dictionary of the New Testament*, trans. and ed. G. W. Bromiley, 10 vols. (Grand Rapids: Wm. B. Eerdmans Publishing Co., 1964–76), 1:xvi–xl. The following list is provided for reference.

The reader is advised to consult also the bibliography.

AAWG.PH	Abhandlungen der Akademie der Wissenschaften in Göttingen, Philologisch-historische Klasse
AB	Anchor Bible
AGJU	Arbeiten zur Geschichte des antiken Judentums und des Urchristentums
AJBA	*Australian Journal of Biblical Archaeology*
AnBib	Analecta Biblica
ANF	*Ante-Nicene Fathers*
ANRW	Aufstieg und Niedergang der römischen Welt
Ap. Const.	*Apostolic Constitutions*
ARW	*Archiv für Religionswissenschaft*
BA	*Biblical Archaeologist*
Barn.	*Letter of Barnabas*
BBB	Bonner biblische Beiträge
BEThL	Bibliotheca ephemeridum theologicarum lovaniensium
BEvTh	Beiträge zur evangelischen Theologie
BFChTh	Beiträge zur Förderung christlicher Theologie
BGBE	Beiträge zur Geschichte der biblischen Exegese
BHTh	Beiträge zur historischen Theologie
BJRL	*Bulletin of the John Rylands Library*
BNTC	Black's New Testament Commentaries
BU	Biblische Untersuchungen
BWANT	Beiträge zur Wissenschaft vom Alten und Neuen Testament

BZAW	Beihefte zur Zeitschrift für die alttestamentliche Wissenschaft
BZ NF	*Biblische Zeitschrift*, Neue Folge
BZNW	Beihefte zur *Zeitschrift für die neutestamentliche Wissenschaft*
Can. Mur.	The Muratorian Canon
CB	Coniectanea biblica
CB.NT	Coniectanea biblica—New Testament Series
CBQ	*Catholic Biblical Quarterly*
ChH	*Church History*
CIJ	*Corpus inscriptionum Latinarum*
I Clem.	*First Letter of Clement*
CMC	*Cologne Mani Codex*
CNT (N)	Commentaire du Nouveau Testament. Neuchâtel
Cont.	*Contestatio* (prefix to *The Kerygmata Petrou*)
CSEL	Corpus scriptorum ecclesiasticorum latinorum
CThM	Calwer theologische Monographien
CTL	Crown Theological Library
Did.	*The Didache*
Diogn.	*Letter to Diognetus*
EeT	*Église et Théologie*
EHPhR	Études d'histoire et de philosophie religieuses
EHS.T	Europäische Hochschulschriften. Series 23: Theologie
EKK	Evangelisch-katholischer Kommentar
Enc.Jud.	*Encyclopedia Judaica*
Epiphanius	
De Mens.	*De Mensuris et Ponderibus (On Measures and Weights)*
Pan.	*Panarion (Refutation of All Heresies)*
EpPetr.	*Epistula Petri* (prefix to *The Kerygmata Petrou*)
ET	*Expository Times*
EtB	Études bibliques
Euripides	
Hec.	*Hecuba*
Eusebius	
Hist. Ecc.	*Historia Ecclesiastica*
EvTh	*Evangelische Theologie*
FGLP	Forschungen zur Geschichte und Lehre des Protestantismus
FKDG	Forschungen zur Kirchen- und Dogmengeschichte
FRLANT	Forschungen zur Religion und Literatur des Alten und Neuen Testaments

xviii

FSÖTh	Forschungen zur systematischen und ökumenischen Theologie
FTS	Frankfurter theologische Studien
GCS	Die griechischen christlichen Schriftsteller der ersten drei Jahrhunderte
Gn.	*Gnomon*, Munich
GNT	Grundrisse zum Neuen Testament
GTA	Göttinger theologische Arbeiten
GThW	Grundriss der theologischen Wissenschaft
Herm. Vis.	*Shepherd of Hermas, Visiones*
HeyJ	*Heythrop Journal*
Hippolytus	
Ref.	*A Refutation of all Heresies*
HMANG.A	Handbuch der mittelalterlichen und neueren Geschichte—Abt. 1: Allgemeines
HNT	Handbuch zum Neuen Testament
HNTC	Harper's New Testament Commentaries = BNTC
HSCP	Harvard Studies in Classical Philology
HThK	Herders theologischer Kommentar zum Neuen Testament
HThR	*Harvard Theological Review*
HThS	Harvard Theological Studies
HZ	*Historische Zeitschrift*
ICC	International Critical Commentary
IDBSup	*Interpreter's Dictionary of the Bible, Supplementary Volume*
JAC	Jahrbuch für Antike und Christentum
JDTh	Jahrbücher für deutsche Theologie
JEH	*Journal of Ecclesiastical History*
Jerome	
De Vir.Ill.	*De Viris Illustribus*
JETS	*Journal of the Evangelical Theological Society*
JJS	*Journal of Jewish Studies*
Josephus	
Ant.	*Antiquities of the Jews*
JPTh	Jahrbücher für protestantische Theologie
JR	*Journal of Religion*
JSJ	*Journal of the Study of Judaism in the Persian, Hellenistic, and Roman Periods*
JSNT	*Journal for the Study of the New Testament*
JThS	Journal of Theological Studies
KBANT	Kommentare und Beiträge zum Alten und Neuen Testament

KEK	Kritisch-exegetischer Kommentar über das Neue Testament begründet v. Heinrich August Wilhelm Meyer
KuD	*Kerygma und Dogma*
LCL	Loeb Classical Library
LexTQ	*Lexington Theological Quarterly*
LingBibl	*Linguistica biblica*
Mart. Pol.	*Martyrdom of Polycarp*
MPTh	*Monatsschrift für Pastoraltheologie*
MThSt	Münchener theologische Studien
NC(C)	Nouvelle clio, Collection, Paris
NGWG.PH	Nachrichten von der königlichen Gesellschaft der Wissenschaften zu Göttingen. Philologisch-historische Klasse
NovTest	*Novum Testamentum*
NPNF	*A Select Library of the Nicene and Post-Nicene Fathers*
NTA	Neutestamentliche Abhandlungen
NTA NF	Neutestamentliche Abhandlungen, Neue Folge
NTApo	*Neutestamentliche Apokryphen in deutscher Übersetzung*
NTD	Das Neue Testament Deutsch
NTS	*New Testament Studies*
PCB	Peake's Commentary on the Bible
PDVHL	Palästinahefte des deutschen Vereins vom Heiligen Lande
Philo	
Migr.	*De Migratione Abrahami*
Plato	
Apol.	*Apology*
PrM	*Protestantische Monatshefte*
Ps.-Clem.	
Hom.	*Pseudoclementine Homilies*
Recg.	*Pseudoclementine Recognitions*
RAC	*Reallexikon für Antike und Christentum*
RB	*Revue biblique*
RBen	*Revue bénédictine de critique, d'historie et de littérature religieuses*
RE	*Realencyklopädie für protestantische Theologie und Kirche*
Recg.	Recognitions
Ref.	Reformatio, Zurich
RestQ	Restoration Quarterly

RHE	*Revue d'histoire ecclésiastique*
RGG3	*Religion in Geschichte und Gegenwart*
RHPhR	*Revue d'histoire et de philosophie religieuses*
RITh	*Revue internationale de théologie*
RM	Die Religionen der Menschheit
RSR	*Recherches de science religieuse*
RVV	Religionsgeschichtliche Versuche und Vorarbeiten
SBFA	Studii Biblici Franciscani: Liber Annus
SBB	Stuttgarter biblische Beiträge
SBLDS	Society of Biblical Literature Dissertation Series
SBLMS	Society of Biblical Literature Monograph Series
SBS	Stuttgarter Bibelstudien
SBT	Studies in Biblical Theology
Schol.	*Scholastik*, Freiburg
SJ	Studia Judaica
SJLA	Studies in Judaism in Late Antiquity
SJTh	*Scottish Journal of Theology*
SNTSMS	Society for New Testament Studies Monograph Series
SPAW.PH	*Sitzungsberichte der preussischen Akademie der Wissenschaften. Philosophisch-historische Klasse*
SPB	Studia patristica et Byzantina
SSAW	Sitzungsberichte der sächsischen Akademie der Wissenschaften
StANT	Studien zum Alten und Neuen Testament
StEv	*Studia evangelica*
StNT	Studien zum Neuen Testament
StPatr	Studia patristica
StTh	*Studia theologica.* Lund, etc.
StUNT	Studien zur Umwelt des Neuen Testaments
SyBU	Symbolae biblicae Uppsalienses
TB	Theologische Bücherei
TDNT	*Theological Dictionary of the New Testament*
TEH	*Theologische Existenz heute*
Tertullian	
Adv. Vul.	*Adversus Valentinianos*
Praescr.	*De Praescriptione Haereticorum*
TF	Theologische Forschung
ThHK	Theologischer Handkommentar zum Neuen Testament
ThJb	Theologisches Jahrbuch. Gütersloh
ThJb(T)	Theologische Jahrbücher. Tübingen

ThJber	Theologische Jahresbericht. Leipzig
ThLZ	Theologische Literaturzeitung
ThR NF	Theologische Rundschau, Neue Folge
ThSt	Theological Studies
ThStKr	Theologische Studien und Kritiken
ThZ	Theologische Zeitschrift. Basel
TRE	Theologische Realenzyklopädie
TS	Theological Studies. Woodstock, Md.
TSAJ	Texte und Studien zum Antiken Judentum
TThSt	Trierer theologische Studien
TU	Texte und Untersuchungen zur Geschichte der altchristlichen Literatur
TZTh	Tübinger Zeitschrift für Theologie
UB	Urban-Bücher
UNT	Untersuchungen zum Neuen Testament
USQR	Union Seminary Quarterly Review
UTB	Uni-Taschenbücher
VF	Verkündigung und Forschung
VigChr	Vigiliae Christianae
WdF	Wege der Forschung
WMANT	Wissenschaftliche Monographien zum Alten und Neuen Testament
WUNT	Wissenschaftliche Untersuchungen zum Neuen Testament
ZBK	Zürcher Bibelkommentar
ZBK.NT	Zürcher Bibelkommentar, Neues Testament
ZDMG	Zeitschrift der deutschen morgenländischen Gesellschaft
ZKG	Zeitschrift für Kirchengeschichte
ZNW	Zeitschrift für die neutestamentliche Wissenschaft und die Kunde der älteren Kirche
ZPE	Zeitschrift für Papyrologie und Epigraphik
ZPK NF	Zeitschrift für Protestantismus und Kirche, Neue Folge
ZRGG	Zeitschrift für Religions- und Geistesgeschichte
ZThK	Zeitschrift für Theologie und Kirche
ZWTh	Zeitschrift für wissenschaftliche Theologie

1

A SURVEY OF THE RESEARCH ON JEWISH CHRISTIANITY AS A MEANS OF FORMULATING THE PROBLEM

1.1 FERDINAND CHRISTIAN BAUR AND HIS PREDECESSORS

It is generally agreed that F. C. Baur was the first to direct the attention of scholarship to Jewish Christianity as the key for understanding the Christianity of the first two centuries. A summary of previous research could thus justifiably report concerning Baur that the modern investigation of Jewish Christianity began with him.[1] It is thus appropriate to introduce our own survey of research with the Old Master of the Tübingen school.

In 1831 Baur published an essay with the title "The Christ Party in the Corinthian Church, the Opposition Between Petrine and Pauline Christianity in the Ancient Church, and the Apostle Peter in Rome."[2]

In the context of a study of the Corinthian letters Baur came to the conclusion that the relationship between Gentile Christians and Jewish Christians had not been so harmonious as had been commonly supposed. Rather, the existence of the Corinthian parties reflect a conflict between the older apostles and Paul. The Christ party and the Cephas party, which together formed one group,[3] stood in opposition to the Pauline party.[4] They placed Paul's authority in question by explaining that their own leader, Peter, was superior to Paul in that he had actually seen Jesus.[5] The same anti-Pauline Jewish Christians are also encountered in Philippians and Galatians. Thus Phil. 3:2–11 struggles against false teachers "who place great importance on circumcision and everything else that is native to Judaism,"[6] which has a parallel in 2 Cor. 11:22–29. This is clear in that in both passages Paul brings the same personal qualifications to bear in the argument.[7] Galatians would then offer a first-rate parallel to

1

the polemical parties of the Corinthian letters which would further illuminate the nature of the opposition to Paul, for in Galatia the opponents had not been so hesitant concerning their demands with regard to the law as in Corinth.[8] Still, Baur supposed that the attack on the apostolic status of Paul was identical with that in Corinth, and the objection posed by the opposition was thus, "What kind of authority can there be for an 'apostle' who, unlike the other apostles, had never been prepared for the apostolic office in Jesus' own school but had only later dared to claim the apostolic office on the basis of his own authority?"[9]

It was thus clear for Baur that already in the earliest period "two opposing parties with a very definite clash of viewpoints had developed."[10] Of course it became clear at the same time that the anti-Pauline Jewish-Christian party operated without the sanction of the original apostles (see below, n. 34).

Baur's evidence for the existence of an anti-Pauline Jewish-Christian party was strengthened by the reports concerning the Ebionites in the church fathers (especially Irenaeus, *Heresies* 1.26 and Epiphanius, *Pan.* 30), who report their rejection of Paul, and by the Pseudo-Clementine *Homilies*[11] from the late second century, in which the apostle to the Gentiles is attacked in the disguise of Simon Magus.[12] These sources further prove that an anti-Pauline stream of Christianity had not disappeared in the second century. Rather, in Baur's view a genetic connection becomes visible between Paul's opponents and the anti-Paulinism of the second century.

There was, of course, one unresolved problem in Baur's bold hypothesis of a historical connection between the anti-Paulinists of the first and second centuries: the great chronological gap of at least 120 years between the Pauline letters on the one hand and the Pseudo-Clementines and Irenaeus's *Heresies* on the other. Baur was aware of this problem and attempted to bridge this chronological distance by proposing to describe the *development* of anti-Pauline Jewish Christianity[13] and its relation to Gentile Christianity during this period.

This task was carried out with reference to the Roman church in the last part of his essay of 1831, in the section entitled "The Apostle Peter in Rome" (pp. 137–206). Baur here regards the tradition that Peter visited Rome and died there—first[14] documented by Dionysius of Corinth (in Eusebius, *Hist. Ecc.* 2.25.8) as unhistorical—and ascribes its origin to a strong Jewish-Christian party in Rome.[15] Baur thus used this one item of evidence to point out the continuity of Jewish Christianity during the time between the composition of the Pauline letters and the Pseudo-Clementine *Homilies* as well as the references in Irenaeus mentioned above. The influence of that party could be further inferred from the following: from Suetonius's report of the expulsion of the (Jewish) Christians from Rome (*The Lives of the Caesars* 5.25) which would document the presence of Jewish Christians in Rome already in the forties of the first century,[16] from Paul's letter to the Romans,[17] and from the existence of such figures as Aquila and Priscilla,[18] who had become Christians in Rome. In addition, Hermas[19] would document the continued existence of that group interested in attacking the apostle to the Gentiles by appealing to Peter.[20]

The essay from 1831 just referred to leaves no doubt that the author was an original scholar who was able to combine New Testament and patristic expertise and to venture boldly toward new critical knowledge. Baur's conclusions, however, did not lead to a revolution in the disciplines of New Testament and church history. Particular points of his conclusions did find acknowledgment and agreement, even from so conservative a scholar as A. Neander,[21] who adopted Baur's denial of Peter's residence in Rome and his death there.[22]

The same scholar had originally called Baur's attention to the Pseudo-Clementine *Homilies*, as is indicated in Baur's own writings.[23] At the same time, it should be noted that independently from Baur not only Neander[24] but already J. K. L. Gieseler[25] and K. A. Credner[26] had pointed out the significance of the Pseudo-Clementine literature for early Christianity and had offered suggestions concerning the literary relationship of the sources[27] and the history-of-religions background of the Ebionites. Thus, since the work of Credner the question of a possible connection between the Essenes[28] and the Ebionites has been raised again and again. Gieseler introduced an issue that has been just as hotly disputed as it is unanswered: the question of different types of Ebionites, namely, the "popular" and the "gnostic." The former he identified with the Nazareans, the more tolerant Jewish Christians (without a high Christology—thus the designation "popular"), who stood in a direct line of descent from the earliest Jerusalem church, while the "gnostic" Ebionites were the heretical anti-Pauline group.[29]

Baur's own work stood in critical continuity with the research prior to him. This becomes completely clear from an essay that was written in the same year as his study of the parties in Corinth discussed above. It bears the title "De Ebionitarum origine et doctrina, ab Essenis repetenda."[30] In accord with the program of this developing school of interpretation, Baur, like Neander, primarily used the reports of Epiphanius and secondarily those from the Pseudo-Clementine *Homilies* as sources for the theology of the Ebionites.[31] Following in the wake of Credner, he saw the historical origin of the Ebionites in the time after 70 C.E. in the region of Pella, which was near the settlement of the Essenes, and specified the following similarities between the doctrines of the Essenes and those of the Ebionites of Epiphanius and the Pseudo-Clementines: (1) the ideal of poverty, (2) retaining the rite of circumcision, (3) the rejection of sacrifice, oaths, and eating of blood, (4) the veneration of Moses, (5) emphasis on the importance of ritual baths of purification, and (6) a different attitude toward the prophets and the Old Testament in general.[32] It is to be emphasized that Baur, in the essay of 1831, did *not* regard the Ebionites as belonging to the period before 70 C.E.[33] Although he emphasized the opposition between the parties of Peter and Paul, highlighted the Jewish-Christian influences in Rome, and pointed to the anti-Pauline parties in the Pseudo-Clementines, Baur saw no fundamental difference between Paul and the original apostles and thus had no hesitation about lumping together the anti-Paulinists in Corinth, Galatia, and Philippi as *pseudo*-apostles.[34] Among other factors, this is related to the fact that Baur at that time treated the New Testament canon with greater respect than other sources.[35] This is the reason why in this period Baur neither expressed doubts concerning the historical reliability of the Acts[36] nor had any second thoughts with regard to the authenticity of the Pastorals.[37, 38]

But the positions just mentioned would of course soon be abandoned. Baur's 1835 book on the Pastorals,[39] which he also thought "could justifiably be regarded as a contribution to the still not ... concluded critical study of the canon,"[40] undertook on the one side the negative goal of showing the inauthenticity of the Pastorals,[41] in order to carry through on the other side the positive goal of indicating their true historical setting in early Christianity. Baur argued that the Pastorals were properly to be understood as part of the contemporary opposition to Marcion (1 Tim. 6:20!) and represented the attempt of a Roman Paulinist to effect a rapprochement with the older Roman Jewish Christians by adopting some of the older Judaizing doctrines,[42] "as soon as this party agreed to acknowledge the authority of the apostle and to exchange what the Marcionites wanted to make of him for what he was in reality."[43]

Using methods similar to those he had applied to his work on the Pastorals, Baur wrote several essays on Acts. He destroyed the assumption that Acts had been composed by a companion of Paul (a church tradition that had enjoyed unqualified trust in the scholarly work on Acts prior to Baur), in order to indicate the book's true place in early Christianity, which turned out to be remarkably similar to that of the Pastorals.

Baur's new views on Acts first came to extensive expression in his great 1845 monograph on Paul.[44] His introduction declared:

> Between the Acts of the Apostles and the Pauline Epistles, as far as the historical contents of the latter can be compared with the former, there will be found in general the same relationship as that between the Gospel of John and the Synoptic Gospels. The comparison of these two sources leads us to the conclusion that, considering the great difference between the two statements, historical truth must be entirely on one side or entirely on the other.[45]

But since Acts presents, among other things, an account of the number of trips to Jerusalem[46] that cannot be harmonized with the letters, as well as different pictures of the Apostolic Council[47] and of Paul's attitude toward Judaism,[48] there can be no doubt as to how the decision on the above-mentioned question is to be made: the life and theology of the apostle to the Gentiles must be reconstructed solely on the basis of the letters. (For the implementation of this program, cf. Luedemann, *Paul, Apostle to the Gentiles*.)

On the other hand, the apologetic tendencies of Acts opened up the possibility of determining its time and place of composition: the goal of the work, first recognized by Baur in 1838,[49] is indicated by the tendency of Acts to portray Paul in a Petrine manner and Peter in a Pauline manner.[50] He thus understood

Acts to be the product of a Paulinist in Rome who wanted to present a Judaizing portrayal of Paul to guard him from the objections of Jewish Christians and at the same time to minimize the differences between Paul and Peter as insignificant.[51] Thereby Acts, like the Pastorals, would contribute to a rapproachement with the Jewish-Christian faction in Rome.

√

From that point on, this hypothesis, derived from Acts and the Pastorals, namely, that in the second and third generations the earliest Christian groups found themselves drawing closer to each other, became more and more important for Baur's theory of the origin of the catholic church at the end of the second century. The catholic church would derive, in fact, from this synthesis of Paulinism and Ebionism (=Jewish Christianity), and the conciliatory gestures found in Acts and the Pastorals would have their counterparts on the opposite side, for example, in the fact that James no longer insists on circumcision.[52]

One often reads that Baur's works on early Christianity were nothing else than a prejudiced reconstruction on the basis of Hegel's philosophy.[53] But here distinctions are needful that most of those who make such accusations are unfortunately either not in a position to make or not willing to do so. The sketch offered above of how Baur really came to his conclusions may be sufficient to refute these allegations, which only prove that Baur's exegetical works are unknown territory[54] to a sector of the present generation of scholars.[55] The fact of the matter is that Baur achieved most of his results on the basis of purely historical exegesis which had made a decisive break with the older supernatural orientation of biblical exegesis.[56] Henceforth Baur, after initial hesitation, abandoned making side glances at Acts and discovered on the basis of the letters alone the fundamental difference between the older apostles and Paul. He thus saw himself compelled to modify his earlier view, according to which the opponents of Paul were pseudo-apostles and the author of the Pseudo-Clementines an outsider, and to regard their anti-Paulinism as a general characteristic of Jewish Christianity. It thus seemed a natural inference to classify both the opponents of Paul and the Ebionites of the second century more closely with the original apostles. On the other hand, there is an element of truth in the accusation mentioned above, namely, that Baur, in his striving to explain the origination of the catholic church at the end of the second century did allocate early Christian texts too one-sidedly to Pauline or Jewish Christianity. Here the Hegelian schema was in fact a hindrance to recognizing the variety in early Christianity and its texts (see further on this below).

In conclusion we must once again note that most of Baur's detailed analyses referred to above have nothing to do with a preconceived theory and, as we shall show below, prove themselves thoroughly superior to subsequent critics.

1.2 ALBERT SCHWEGLER

In 1847 Albert Schwegler,[57] a close disciple of Baur, published the first history of early Christianity to be written from the perspective of the Tübingen school.[58] He based his views on Baur's exegetical results, which he also defended against criticisms that had arisen in the meantime, and attempted to provide additional support for Baur's thesis that a fundamental conflict existed between Paul and the original apostles. But, beyond this, Schwegler strove to present a theory of the origin of the catholic church that departed from Baur's and distinguished itself by a more thorough use of the sources. (At that time Baur had not yet treated the issue of the origin of the catholic church thematically, although the main outlines of such a study were already clear to him.) It was precisely Schwegler's ambitious execution of Baur's plans that was to become the point of contact for the later critique.

Like Baur, Schwegler acknowledged only one class of Ebionites[59] and ably disputed A. Schliemann's view that the Ebionites began in 136 C.E. when the Jewish Christians had to choose whether they should unite with the Gentile church of Aelia, tolerate it, or withdraw and become the (heretical) Ebionites.[60] Since Schliemann too was an advocate of the opinion that a genetic relationship existed between Jewish Christians in the periods before and after 136 C.E., there could be only one question: "At what point had the Jewish Christians (=Ebionites) begun to be regarded as heretics?" —and not: "When did Ebionism begin?"[61] Thus, like Baur, Schwegler reconstructed the course of Ebionism's development and distinguished three phases:

1. The Nazareans as representatives of pre-Pauline Jewish Christianity.

2. The Essenic Jewish Christians (=Paul's opponents in his churches).

3. The Jewish Christians of the Pseudo-Clementine *Homilies*. It is clear from the manner in which Schwegler speaks of the different phases of Ebionism that he thinks more of a logical than a chronological sequence. According to Schwegler, Essenic teachings had already been transmitted to the earliest Christians in Galilee.[62] He can thus summarize his view as follows:

> Whenever in the apostolic and postapostolic age we meet Jewish Christianity, from the earliest time on, in all parts of the Christian world—in Jerusalem, in Corinth, in Rome—we always find it mixed in varying degrees with those elements which in the current discussion are usually called by the summarizing label "gnosticizing Ebionism."[63]

The *Gospel of the Hebrews* was supposed to be the oldest gospel[64] and the midpoint of the Jewish-Christian gospel literature, which was precipitated out into the canonical Gospels. The use of the *Gospel of the Hebrews* can be demonstrated in the fragments of Papias and Hegesippus as well as in the Pseudo-Clementines and the letters of Ignatius.[65] The *apomnemoneumata* of Justin preserved it especially completely.[66]

Schwegler conceived the origin of the catholic church differently from Baur. The church of the first two centuries can be equated with Ebionism: Hermas, and also the writings of Justin and Hegesippus, are considered to be important Ebionite texts for the history of the Roman church. As witnesses for the Ebionism of the church in Asia Minor in the so-called Johannine period,[67] Schwegler presents the Galatian opponents of Paul, the Apocalypse, the Papias fragments, the opponents in Hebrews, Colossians, and Ephesians, as well as the Montanist literature.[68]

Although Schwegler describes the history of the Pauline party as part of the line of development in Rome,[69] he considers its influence on the Ebionite party to have been insignificant. The catholic Christianity of Rome and Asia Minor goes back primarily[70] to developments within Ebionism[71] and not, as Baur had assumed, to a synthesis of Paulinism and Ebionism.

A critical discussion of Schwegler's theses must be careful to distinguish two issues:

1. How are Schwegler's analyses of the texts to be evaluated?

2. Is his understanding of the origin of the catholic church correct? The latter question is answered in the negative even by scholars who belong to the Tübingen school.[72] L. Georgii,[73] K. Planck,[74] and K. R. Köstlin[75] point out two weak points of Schwegler's position: (a) His concept of Ebionism is too broad (especially in the second century) and (b) he underestimates the influence that Paul and his disciples had in the second century.

On the other hand, these same scholars affirmed Schwegler's agreement with Baur's thesis that there was opposition between Paul and the original apostles and that the Ebionite party continued to be strongly influential even in the second century. Thus both the author of James and Hegesippus were anti-Pauline and stood in a genetic relationship to Paul's opponents and the pillar apostles. The Pseudo-Clementine *Homilies* are thus important evidence regarding two different parties at the very roots of Christianity.

To be sure, just as the Tübingen school was not united on the question of the stream of development to which some texts from the second century were to be assigned, so sooner or later the question had to be raised of whether the categories "Paulinism" and "Ebionism" are at all appropriate categories by which to understand the Christianity of the first two centuries and whether or not new categories are now required. Before we pursue these questions, which were also addressed in the Tübingen camp, we must describe how the individual analyses presented by Baur and his school were evaluated in the ensuing reaction.

1.3 REACTION TO THE TÜBINGEN APPROACH

The general approach of the Tübingen school was sharply criticized, especially its exegesis of the sources. In the following, we will *not* discuss those critics who continued to assert only the harmonious character of the apostolic age against the Tübingen criticism[76] but will deal with the reaction only to the extent that it advocated a different exegesis of particular texts.[77] Was it possible to dispute Baur's results on the basis of a more thorough exegesis of the relevant texts?

Baur's critics[78] reconstructed a picture of the apostolic age that could not be harmonized with the results of Baur's work: a genuine agreement was worked out at the Jerusalem Conference, and the report of it in Acts 15 stands in no contradiction to Galatians 2.[79] It is simply clear that—on the basis of such a utilization of the sources—Paul's opponents were not justified in appealing to the Jerusalem apostles and the agreement worked out in Jerusalem[80] The incident in Antioch was only a brief disturbance of the apostolic peace. Acts is a reliable witness for the history of the earliest church and is never found contradicting the Pauline letters. The Pastorals were written by the historical Paul.[81] James is a letter from the Lord's brother and not directed against Paul or his theology:[82] James 2:14ff. attacks either a pre-Pauline Jewish view[83] or a misuse of Pauline theology.[84] Hegesippus was no Ebionite, and the fragment from Book 5 of the *Hypomnemata*[85] transmitted by the monophysite Stephanus Gobarus is not to be used as an indication of Hegesippus's purported anti-Pauline stance.

The saying from 1 Cor. 2:9 which Hegesippus attacks in this fragment is not from Paul himself but is a quotation used mostly by Gnostics.[86] Since Hegesippus wrote that he had found sound doctrine in Rome and Corinth, where the Pauline letters were respected in the period around 165 C.E., Hegesippus is not to be considered an anti-Paulinist in any case.[87]

So how did Baur's critics evaluate the Pseudo-Clementines? In the opinion of these critics, the Pseudo-Clementines do not have the significance for the understanding of early Christianity that the Tübingen school attributes to them. Although they do derive from the second century, they are the work of an outsider,[88] and they contain only sporadic anti-Pauline passages, as for example *Hom.* 17.19.[89] Besides, their claim to represent the apostolic authority of Peter[90] and James is unjustified.[91] Their views resembled those of the Elkesaites, whose origin lay in the second century. The Jewish Christians of the Pseudo-Clementines thus represented only the views of a certain group, which is to be distinguished from other Jewish-Christian parties. In the wake of Gieseler and Credner,[92] critics were accustomed to distinguish at least two different Jewish-Christian factions:[93]

1. The anti-Pauline, gnostic Ebionites, whose heretical teaching is preserved in the Pseudo-Clementine *Homilies* and in Epiphanius, *Pan.* 30.

2. The Nazareans, who lived in peace with Gentile Christians, acknowledged the authority of the apostle Paul, and traced their origin to the earliest Jerusalem Christianity.

A survey of the reactions to the works of Baur and his disciples leads to the following summary:

a. The Tübingen school provided much stimulus for research into the history of early Christianity. Many books and articles were written in direct response[94] to the theses[95] argued by Baur and his students, in which the critics of Baur were directly or indirectly indebted to the beginnings made by Baur.

b. These studies led to renewed investigation of almost every Christian document from the time before 180 c.e., and that not only from the point of view of literary-historical criticism but also with the question in mind of whether it should be attributed to the Pauline or Ebionite stream in early Christianity.

c. In many cases the critics of the Tübingen school returned to positions that had first called forth Baur's criticism, such as the view that the apostolic age had been harmonious (see above) or the assumption of the authenticity of all canonical writings.

In my opinion, the only works of lasting value that derive from this stream of scholarship are those of J. B. Lightfoot, which— although impaired by a certain theological approach[96] —contain a rich treasury of material that is indispensable[97] for every student of Jewish Christianity.[98]

A real challenge to Baur's analyses could, however, proceed only from the following kind of works:

a. Those which had abandoned a supernaturalistic perspective.

b. Those which were able to dispute Baur's theory on the basis of the exegesis of particular texts.

c. Those which understood the need for developing new, appropriate categories that made the formation (or nonformation) of the catholic church out of earliest Christianity more understandable than did those of Baur.

This difficult assignment was executed by one of Baur's closest students, Albrecht Ritschl.

1.4 ALBRECHT RITSCHL AND HIS DISCIPLES

In the second edition of his work *The Formation of the Old Catholic Church*,[99] Albrecht Ritschl devoted considerable attention to the subject "Jewish Christianity."[100] After offering a critique of the manner in which Baur had dealt with Judaizing Christianity on the basis of a combination of the traditions preserved in the Pseudo-Clementine *Homilies* and in Epiphanius, *Panarion*, with the teachings of Paul's opponents and the Jerusalem apostles,[101] Ritschl proceeds to a definition of what is to be understood by his term "Judaizing Christianity." This is well described in *Barn.* 4.6, where the author warns his readers against people who say "The covenant belongs to them [i.e., the Jews] and us." Thus the following is a Judaizing Christian statement: "The law which God gave through Moses is also the essence of Christianity."[102] that is, Christianity is identical with Judaism.[103] Such a definition of Judaizing Christianity would fit the theology of Paul's opponents. Of course, such an understanding of the term "Judaizing Christian(-ity)" (*judenchristlich*) is to be distinguished from the concept "Jewish" (Christian) (*judaistisch*), which only indicates Jewish influence but does not express an identity of Judaism and Christianity.[104]

Ritschl next treats James, 1 Peter, and Revelation as authentic writings of the three "pillars" whom Paul met at the Jerusalem Conference.[105] Neither the three documents nor the attitude of their authors can be regarded as Judaizing, as is clear from Galatians 2. Paul's opponents in Galatia falsely appealed to them to support their claims.[106] Although the "pillar apostles" undertook no mission to the Gentiles, they had nonetheless (according to Galatians 2/Acts 15) acknowledged the freedom of the Gentile churches from the law. The only difference between James and Paul would have consisted in the fact that Paul understood the division of the mission work geographically (Gal. 2:7ff.), while James understood it ethnographically.[107] Thus Paul had understood the Apostolic Decree to be valid only in Palestine, where Gentile Christians were in the minority anyway,[108] not outside this area. It was only because of this different understanding of the manner in which the church's evangelistic mission was to be divided that the conflict in Antioch was possible, and this was only an episode, in any case.

Thus in Ritschl's understanding, Judaizing Christianity had no apostolic authority at all, and its existence is no occasion to suppose that there was a split between the apostle to the Gentiles, Paul, and the personal disciples of Jesus at the roots of Christianity,[109] for they had always acknowledged Paul as an apostle. Their Jewish Christianity was represented in the post-apostolic age by the Nazareans, who—first described by Jerome(!)—acknowledged Paul's authority and are to be distinguished from the Pharisaic Judaizing Christians.[110] This latter group had not been able to come to terms with the destruction of the temple and thus hoped for a renewal of the temple cult.[111] The attitude of the Nazareans is preserved in the letter to the Hebrews, which is directed to the Jerusalem church[112] and is clearly determined by the view[113] that the offering of animal sacrifice cannot be reconciled with the Christian confession.[114] The *Testaments of the Twelve Patriarchs*[115] was considered by Ritschl to be a document of the Nazareans,[116] who remained true to the original teaching of the "pillar apostles" until at least the fourth century.

In Ritschl's view, a further type of Judaizing Christianity (alongside the Pharisaic type) was represented by the Essenes who came to faith in Jesus after the Jewish War. Their Christianized views are preserved in Epiphanius, *Pan.* 30, and in the Pseudo-Clementine *Homilies* and manifest noticeable similarities with Essenic doctrines:[117] the Essenic Judaizing Christians refrain from eating meat, purify themselves in running water, renounce marriage,[118] and forbid the taking of oaths. In addition, they reject the Mosaic institution of sacrifice.[119] Their meal of bread and salt is nothing else than the continuation of the daily sacrificial meal of the Essenes.[120] This Essenic type of Judaizing Christianity was related to the Pharisaic type. To be sure, it was distinguished from it through its genetic connection with the Elkesaites,[121] who themselves manifested some Essenic characteristics.[122]

Not long after the official church took up the struggle against

13

Gnosticism, both Judaizing Christians and Jewish Christians (=Nazareans) were regarded as heretics.[123] This fact and the further circumstance that most of the so-called Judaizing Christian documents (1 *Clement*, the Papias fragments, Justin's *Dialogue with Trypho*) were, in Ritschl's view, to be ascribed to Gentile Christianity[124] exclude Baur's view that Judaizing Christianity played the dominant role until the middle of the second century.[125] Even Hegesippus, who according to Ritschl obviously still belonged to the Judaizing wing of Christianity,[126] witnesses to the non-Judaizing character of the church of his time, when he writes: "In each list [i.e., of bishops] and in each city things are as the law, the prophets, and the Lord preach" (Eusebius, *Hist. Ecc.* 4.22.3). For that triad—"the law, the prophets, and the Lord"—is also documented elsewhere in it[126a] as "*authorities* of the catholic church, which the church directed against Gnosticism precisely in the time of Hegesippus."[127]

We may summarize Ritschl's contribution to the investigation of what he termed "Judaizing Christianity" as follows:

1. Ritschl narrowed Judaizing Christianity down to a fraction of the available texts, distinguished it from Jewish Christianity generally, and divided the witnesses to Judaizing Christianity between at least two different groups.

2. Ritschl gave support to the old thesis of a harmonious relation between Paul and the "pillar apostles," whose views were supposedly preserved by the Nazareans.

3. After imposing such a limitation on the influence of Judaizing Christianity, Ritschl directed his attention to the significance of Gentile Christianity, to which the majority of sources from the second century belong. *It was precisely this Gentile Christianity which was responsible for the formation of the catholic church.*

Ritschl's work signified a turning point in the history of scholarship on this issue. In the following sixty years almost every critic of the Tübingen school referred to Ritschl, since he was supposed to have disposed of Baur's view of Jewish Christianity once and for all. Although modifications were made in the details of Ritschl's exegesis of individual texts, his results were by and large repeated in the publications of succeeding scholars. Before we give a survey of the contribution of Ritschl's following, we will first attempt a critique of the work of Ritschl himself in regard to the Tübingen school.

Let us first turn to the particulars of Ritschl's exegetical work. To a considerable extent, Ritschl advocated positions that were first called forth in reaction to Baur's critical studies: the harmonious relationship between Paul and the original apostles; the authenticity of James, 1 Peter,[128] and the Apocalypse; and the historical reliability of Acts.[129] We need not spend much time on this issue. In the light of modern critical study, Baur's positions on all these points have turned out to be more reasonable: none of the above-mentioned texts is authentic, and "Luke" is by no means a companion of Paul.[130] Thus "the break with the Tübingen scholars [meant] a return to a standpoint that could not be fruitful for scholarship with regard to most of the questions with which historical-critical study of the New Testament is concerned."[131]

Ritschl's effort to develop a more precise terminology for dealing with the history of early Christianity was, however, a praiseworthy accomplishment. To be sure, it was, on the one hand, somewhat artificial not to use the term "Judaizing Christians" for the earliest apostles and their successors, the Nazareans,[132] and one can only suppose that this procedure was adopted because of Ritschl's understanding of the canonical nature of the New Testament, which prescribed for him that any group that stood at the beginning of Christianity be excluded from the Judaizing heresy. On the other hand, Ritschl's "reminder that unreflective Gentile Christianity[133] would obviously flourish, while Judaizing Christianity, thanks to the unsuitability of its environment, would naturally die out, represents a fruitful historical insight."[134] In this regard Ritschl strengthened the objections against the understanding of early Christianity as a whole advocated by Baur, and especially of Schwegler, which had already been expressed by Planck, Georgii, and Köstlin.[135] In addition, by his analysis of the sources available for the study of early Christianity he was able to construct an effective and somewhat persuasive counterposition on the question of the origin of the catholic church.[136]

We indicated above that Ritschl's followers portrayed Jewish and Judaizing Christianity in essentially the same manner as had Ritschl himself. It thus appears unnecessary to examine each work individually. Instead, we will refer in a thematic fashion to certain topics important for the study of Jewish Christianity, reviewing the views of various scholars in the process.[137]

A. von Harnack emphatically agrees with Ritschl on the importance of defining the term "Jewish Christianity" (=Ebionism).[138]

> It should be applied exclusively to those Christians who really maintained in their whole extent, or in some measure, even if it were to a minimum degree, the national and political forms of Judaism and the observance of the Mosaic law in its literal sense, as essential to Christianity, at least to the Christianity of born Jews, or who, though rejecting these forms, nevertheless assumed a prerogative of the Jewish people even in Christianity (Clem., *Homil.* XI.26: *ean ho allophylos ton nomon praxē. Ioudaios estin. mē praxas de Hellēn* ["If the foreigner observe the law he is a Jew, but if not he is a Greek"]). To this Jewish Christianity is opposed, not Gentile Christianity, but the Christian religion, in so far as it is conceived as universalistic and anti-national in the strict sense of the term . . . , that is, the main body of Christendom in so far as it has freed itself from Judaism as a nation.[139]

Contra Ritschl, Harnack regarded earliest Christianity as Judaizing (while for Ritschl it had only belonged to "Jewish Christianity") and rejected Ritschl's distinction between Nazareans and Ebionites.[140]

On the other hand, practically all scholars followed Ritschl in his classification of Judaizing Christians. F. J. A. Hort distinguished the more liberal Judaizing Christians of Pella and Jerusalem from the Ebionites.[141] A. C. McGiffert distinguished the Ebionites from the more tolerant Judaizing Christians in that he assigns the latter group to the period before 70 c.e., while the Ebionites did not originate until the second and third centuries.[142] W. R. Sorley[143] follows Ritschl in distinguishing three groups: Nazareans, Ebionites, and Essenic Christians. As indicated above, Harnack appears to have been the only scholar who recognized a continuity between Jewish Christianity (=Ebionism) before and after 70 c.e.[144]

It is clear that the opinions of the various scholars concerning how many different Jewish Christian groups there were are closely related to their respective views concerning the outcome of the Jerusalem Conference, concerning Paul's relation to the "pillar apostles," and concerning the origin of Paul's opponents. Most authors pointed out the criticism of the original apostles against Paul's opponents[145] and further emphasized that these opponents were not justified in claiming the authority of the "pillar apostles."[146] These scholars generally supposed that a real accord was reached at the Jerusalem Conference,[147] and the dispute in Antioch was only a temporary episode.[148]

Most of the authors who are here discussed have the tendency to harmonize Paul's autobiographical account in Galatians 2 with Acts 15 and, in addition, for the most part (Harnack explicitly), presuppose that the author of Acts was Luke the companion of Paul.[149] Some consider James to be genuine.[150] In this case, James 2:14ff. is considered either not to be directed against Paul[151] or merely opposes a false understanding of the theology of the apostle to the Gentiles.[152] On the other hand, McGiffert does not consider James to have been written by the brother of Jesus and even thinks that James 2:14ff. is an attack on Pauline theology. But it is still not an attack against the apostle to the Gentiles himself (!).[153]

Nor was Hegesippus an anti-Paulinist. Since the fragment transmitted by Stephanus Gobarus does not contain the *name* of Paul, it was not directed against Paul.[154] The other fragments found in Eusebius's *Ecclesiastical History* prove that Hegesippus was in agreement with the doctrines of the catholic church,[155] that is, with the thinking generally current in common Gentile Christianity.[156] The Pseudo-Clementines, the main evidence of the Tübingen school for a Jewish Christianity which continued through the second century, were usually dated somewhat late,[157] their significance was minimized, or their polemic against Paul was even called into question.[158] Sometimes these works took into consideration the intensive research on the Pseudo-Clementines which had been proceeding in the meantime,[159] which had resulted in the establishment of an anti-Pauline source document (= the *Kerygmata Petrou*). Hort believed, however, that neither the *Kerygmata Petrou* nor the Elkesaites belonged to the second century.[160]

Any influence of Jewish Christianity on the formation of the catholic church was generally denied. It degenerated to an insignificant group and disappeared[161] from the stage of church history. Usually it did not find a place in the histories of dogma.[162]

It thus appeared that the old Tübingen standpoint had been refuted once and for all, until finally the last adherent of the Tübingen school in the last century began to speak up,[163] name, Adolf Hilgenfeld.

1.5 ADOLF HILGENFELD[164]

Adolf Hilgenfeld's numerous works on Jewish Christianity span a period of about sixty years.[165] There is hardly a volume of the ZWTh (which he had founded in 1858 and edited until his death in 1907) in which he did not advocate some position regarding this subject—often polemically against others. He strove in all his works to emphasize the significance of Jewish Christianity, as understood by the Tübingen school over against the Ritschlian school.

With regard to the Jerusalem Conference and Paul's opponents in his churches, Hilgenfeld had the same opinion as Baur: the conference and the incident in Antioch revealed grave differences between Paul and the original apostles, to whom Paul's opponents justifiably appealed in their critique of him.[166] Ritschl's acceptance of the authenticity of James and of 1 Peter thereby became the subject of critical investigation. The Apocalypse, which Hilgenfeld too supposed to have come from John the son of Zebedee, he considered to be anti-Pauline and Jewish-Christian because, among other reasons, it deliberately left no room for Paul's apostleship (Rev. 21:14).[167]

The period after 70 c.e. and the place of Jewish Christianity from the perspective of the history of religions became the subject of a monograph dedicated to Eduard Zeller, *Judenthum und Judenchristenthum* (1886). The polemical purpose of this small book can be seen already in the introduction (pp. 9–20), which cast a critical light on the works of Ritschl and Harnack. In the following sections Hilgenfeld analyzed the reports of the church fathers concerning the Jewish-Christian groups and the pre-Christian Jewish sects with the additional question in mind of whether they were genetically related to each other.

Hilgenfeld's treatment of the second century differs from that of Ritschl and Harnack in the following points:

a. The Roman church was Jewish-Christian (cf. Hermas!).[168]

b. That Justin belonged to Jewish Christianity can be seen especially from the tolerance he exercised toward Jewish Christians (*Dial.* 47).[169]

c. The Hegesippus Fragment in Stephanus Gobarus has clear anti-Pauline traits.[170] In addition, it is not clear whether Hegesippus acknowledged *1 Clement*, which mentions Paul positively in chap. 5. From Eusebius, *Hist. Ecc.* 4.22.2, we may only infer that Hegesippus *mentioned 1 Clement*. The other argument against the Jewish-Christian character of Hegesippus's theology, namely, his approval of the church of his time, is not convincing, since Hegesippus's attitude could just as well derive from that tolerant Jewish Christianity described by Justin, *Dial.* 47, which, despite its criticism of Paul (and *1 Clement*), need not necessarily have regarded Paul as a heretic.[171]

d. Contra Harnack, the Pseudo-Clementine *Recognitions* and *Homilies* are to be placed in the second century.[172]

After attributing a greater importance to Jewish Christianity, including the period after 70 C.E., than had his contemporaries, Hilgenfeld expressed himself regarding the history of Jewish Christianity as follows:

The members of the earliest Jerusalem church—also called Nazareans—were the original Jewish Christians. These Nazareans are to be regarded as hostile to Paul for the reason (among others) that in Acts 21:20f. they are called "Zealots for the law." During the Jewish War they fled to Transjordan.[173] Their Gospel was the original Hebrew version of the Gospel of Matthew.[174] In their new location, they came in contact with a heterodox Mosaism which was hostile to the sacrificial cultus as practiced by the Nazareans (Epiphanius, *Pan.* 18). Other Jewish-Christian groups were formed at the beginning of the second century through the preaching of the prophet Elkesai, who proclaimed the Adam-Christ doctrine to the Nazareans and the Ossaeans.[175] Each of the groups was hostile to Paul.

Thus Ebionism, strictly speaking, only began at this point, since Ebion (whom, strangely enough, Hilgenfeld regarded as a historical person[176]) only then appeared on the scene. In contrast to a Gentile Christianity which taught the deity of Jesus and was growing larger and larger, Ebion, who worked on Cyprus and in Asia Minor and Rome, advocated a Mosaic version of Christianity. He thus insisted on the rejection of Paul and moderated the fantastic speculations of Elkesai. (In the course of his pursuit of the historical Ebion, Hilgenfeld discovered fragments of Ebion's writings in the appendix to the "Antiquorum patrum doctrina" of the Presbyter Anastasius [seventh century]).

Thus according to Hilgenfeld, Jewish Christianity was a complex phenomenon. In the first two centuries it consisted of a variety of groups, and finally in the last half of the second century, as part of the defense against Gnosticism, it blended in with a moderated Paulinism to form the catholic church.[177]

Any evaluation of Hilgenfeld's work must hold fast to the following points:

1. Hilgenfeld's detailed critique of Ritschl's reconstruction of the Jerusalem Conference and acceptance of the authenticity of James and 1 Peter was completely justified.

2. His protest against the late dating of the Pseudo-Clementines or their sources had turned out to be correct.

3. He was first scholar to pursue comprehensive literary-critical studies of the Pseudo-Clementines,[178] which later became the absolutely necessary presupposition for any serious work on Jewish Christianity.

4. Like Credner, Baur, Neander, and Ritschl before him, Hilgenfeld pointed out the similarities between Epiphanius's reports concerning Jewish and Jewish-Christian sects and directed renewed attention to the problem of how Jewish Christianity should be categorized from the perspective of the study of the history of religions.

5. At the same time, Hilgenfeld was not critical enough with regard to the reports found in the church fathers and adopted from them the idea that a historical[179] person, "Ebion,"[180] had actually existed, as well as the distinction between Nazareans and Ebionites. But Harnack's objection could not be simply set aside, namely, that this distinction[181] had been made on the basis of witnesses from the fourth century, that is, Epiphanius and Jerome, who in fact differ in the manner in which this distinction is made.

6. Hilgenfeld had to resort to extremely forced arguments in order to regard figures such as Justin and Hermas as Jewish Christians. Here it became apparent that the schema adopted from Baur was of little help in investigating the details—despite the way he related Gnosticism to the general history of the church (in which he deviated from Baur).

1.6 HANS-JOACHIM SCHOEPS

Although there was no lack of cursory treatments of Jewish-Christian texts in the church histories which continued to appear[182] and a few individual studies were written,[183] on the whole interest in the study of Jewish Christianity as it had been pursued in the Tübingen school suffered a noticeable decline in the following period.

This situation was suddenly changed by the work of Hans-Joachim Schoeps.[184] Schoeps saw it as his task to write the history and theology of those groups which were regarded by the church fathers as heretics,[185] that is, of that party described by Justin (*Dial.* 47) which demanded complete obedience to the Jewish law from Gentile Christians.[186]

Schoeps's reconstruction rests primarily on the Pseudo-Clementine literature. By making critical use of the results that had been produced in the meantime, and by developing them further himself, Schoeps was able to appeal to two Ebionite sources:

1. The *Kerygmata Petrou*.[187]
2. The *Anabathmoi Jakobou* (the Ebionite Acts of the Apostles = AJ), which are preserved in Book 1 of the Pseudo-Clementine *Recognitions* (=R).[188]

Both sources are characterized by a sharp anti-Paulinism and derive from the middle of the second century. Schoeps even supposed the Ebionite Acts of the Apostles to be in part older than the canonical Acts, since, in his view, Acts 7 is dependent on it. Schoeps drew upon all the available patristic sources[189] relating to the Pseudo-Clementines and reconstructed from them the following history of the Ebionites:

They left Jerusalem before the Jewish War and settled in the environs of Pella.[190] Their theology was characterized by two peculiarities: their *Christology*[191] was adoptionistic (cf. Acts 2:36; 13:33), and Jesus was the true prophet (Deut. 18:15–18). By means of their doctrine of the prophet Jesus, the Ebionites defended the law and attacked Paul. Their *teaching concerning the law*[192] was based entirely on the Mosaic law, which had been purified by them from non-Mosaic additions made later. These later additions dealt with the sacrificial cultus and passages from the prophetic books that did not readily harmonize with the Pentateuch.

According to Schoeps, these Ebionites maintained an ongoing dispute with Marcion over the Old Testament.[193] Thus Schoeps surprisingly stood the idea on its head that the Jewish Christians who had fled to Transjordan had been absorbed in gnostic syncretism and had been rejected along with it.[194] The Ebionites did not become the victims of the Gnostics but defeated them (especially the Marcionites) with their own weapons.[195] They thus had nothing to do with the (gnostic) Elkesaites.[196]

From the point of view of the history of religions, Schoeps sees the Ebionites as an offshoot of the Essenes, who themselves derived from the Rechabites, and also integrates Jesus of Nazareth into this line of development.[197]

A review of Schoeps's contribution to the investigation of Jewish Christianity would be incomplete without mentioning his thesis concerning the translation of the Old Testament made by Symmachus. Schoeps's point of departure was the tradition current in early Christianity[198] that Symmachus had been an Ebionite, a tradition he attempted to support by pointing out typical elements of Ebionite doctrine in Symmachus's translation.[199] For it was clear to Schoeps that "the Greek-speaking Ebionites read the Old Testament in the translation made by one of their own scholars."[200] In addition, behind the *Hypomnemata* mentioned by Eusebius is to be found nothing less than a commentary on the *Gospel of the Ebionites* written by Symmachus himself, the remnants of which can be reconstructed from the *Kerygmata Petrou*.[201] Thus Symmachus, who had previously not received enough attention from scholarship, was, in Scheops's view, in fact an important witness for Ebionism.

How is Schoeps's contribution to our theme to be evaluated? Schoeps's works are characterized by extensive use of the material from primary sources as well as comprehensive use of secondary literature, and for this reason alone they will be indispensable for all future research. Many of his individual suggestions deserve serious consideration—for example, his view that the gnostic elements in Pseudo-Clementine doctrine were conditioned by an ongoing debate with Gnosticism. On the other hand, it is questionable whether the sharp separation that Schoeps attempts to make between the Ebionites and the Elkesaites can be convincing (see below, pp. 136).

Schoeps's reminder that Essenes and Ebionites have some elements in common is doubtless important. That observation has been made rather often, as we have seen from the preceding history of the study of Jewish Christianity. Schoeps, however, has in my opinion, placed it on a broader foundation.

On the other hand, some of Schoeps's theses float too much in the air, so that they cannot be accepted in their present form, for example, the all too quick extraction of Jewish-Christian sources from the Pseudo-Clementines, the anti-Pauline Acts of the Apostles (which are supposed to be older than the canonical Acts), and the *Kerygmata Petrou*.[202] Further work and a refined method are called for here.

Finally, Schoeps's arguments concerning Symmachus must meet with a skeptical response, for (a) Eusebius's understanding of Symmachus as an Ebionite is not beyond all doubt,[203] (b) the hypothesis that Symmachus wrote a commentary on the *Gospel of the Ebionites* runs aground on the fact that the Pseudo-Clementines apparently use only the canonical Gospels,[204] and (c) the attempt to find characteristic elements of Ebionite doctrine in Symmachus's translation of the Bible has not succeeded.[205]

Schoeps intentionally dealt only marginally with one period, namely, the time before 70 c.e. Although, as our review has made clear, Schoeps from time to time expresses his views concerning earliest Christianity, he devotes himself to a thematic treatment neither of pre-70 c.e.[206] Christianity nor of the issue of whether the more tolerant Jewish Christians[207] (the other group mentioned by Justin in *Dial.* 47) belong to the same group as the original Jerusalem church. It is thus not unexpected that other scholars would in one way or another deal thematically with these questions.

23

1.7 JOHANNES MUNCK[208]

We have seen above that the point of departure for the approach of Baur and his school was the historical continuity of Jewish Christianity before and after 70 C.E. In the scholarship of the following period, this thesis, taken as a whole, was widely disputed but really never thematically treated. Whatever the real reasons for this may have been, in any case criticism of Baur's position was carried on primarily in terms of source criticism, namely, by denying one source after another to the Jewish Christianity to which Baur had attributed it and assigning it to Gentile Christianity in accord with the Ritschlian perspective. At the same time, some scholars such as Harnack could freely acknowledge the continuity of several Jewish-Christian groups before and after 70 C.E.[209]

It was thus overdue when the question of the genetic relationship of Jewish Christianity before and after the war finally was explored thematically, answered in the negative, and used against Baur. The leading advocate of this approach is Johannes Munck. His line of argument proceeds in two directions:

1. Munck proposed the thesis that the opposition against Paul in Galatia had nothing to do with the Jerusalem Jewish Christians. It was, rather, a Gentile Christian phenomenon,[210] just as was the case with the opposition against Paul reflected in the Corinthian correspondence.[211] Paul and James would have had no fundamental differences that they needed to settle.

2. Munck justifiably points out the great chronological gap between the clearly documented Jewish Christianity of the second century and that of the period before 70 C.E.,[212] a difficulty that Baur had already clearly recognized[213] and had sought to overcome by the means described above. In addition, Munck believed that the event supposed to form the historical connection between Jewish Christianity before and after 70 C.E., namely, the purported flight of the Jerusalem church to Pella reported in Eusebius, *Hist. Ecc.* 3.5.3, could be demonstrated to be unhistorical.[214]

With this line of argument—which included a relatively extensive handling of the period before 70 C.E., which was still missing in Schoeps—Munck banished Jewish Christianity as understood by Baur to the second half of the second century and made traces of Jewish Christianity in the period before 70 C.E. even more difficult to identify than had the Ritschlian school.

The results of Munck's works were generally rejected by scholarship.[215] It was in fact clear that the opposition to Paul in Galatia came from outside and stood in some relation to the Jerusalem Christians. In addition, no one could fail to see that Paul's self-defense in Galatians 2 reported tensions between the apostle to the Gentiles and the Jerusalem apostles. And finally, it is a short circuit in the argument to infer the complete destruction of the Jewish Christianity of Jerusalem based on the view that the Pella tradition was unhistorical. This sort of logic would also have to argue that the Jewish community in Jerusalem also completely perished in the Jewish War, since we possess no traditions concerning its flight.

On the other hand, it is to Munck's credit that in his works, written from a kind of love-hate relationship with regard to the Tübingen school, with the intent of being the ultimate refutation of Baur, he saw the problems in bold relief and in many respects was much more critical than either his predecessors or his followers.[216] His thesis that "as regards method, this modern Pauline research suffers from having broken the Tübingen School's literary theory, but not with its historical theory"[217] is in fact an appropriate judgment. It could have pointed to the course that must henceforth be pursued by studies of Paul and Jewish Christianity, namely, either to continue further work along the lines marked out by Munck or to pursue a critical appropriation of the results of the Tübingen school. Unfortunately, so far neither has occurred.

1.8 JEAN DANIÉLOU[218]

According to Daniélou, Schoeps had dealt only with the syncretistic Jewish Christians. The subject matter to be dealt with in a theology of Jewish Christianity thus needed to be expanded considerably, for nonsyncretistic Jewish Christianity must also be included. Scholarship must therefore explore and reconstruct the conceptuality which Christianity took over from Judaism during the whole period up to the middle of the second century. And this means that every extracanonical Christian document written during this period belongs to the realm of

Jewish Christianity (cf. below, n. 219). How does Daniélou carry out his program when dealing with specific cases?

In his book *The Theology of Jewish Christianity*, after a survey of the sources (pp. 7–54) and an introduction to the intellectual milieu of Jewish Christianity (pp. 55–115), Daniélou summarizes the doctrines of those writings of the first and second centuries which in some way or another manifest Jewish-apocalyptic traits, under such rubrics as "The Trinity and Angelology" (pp. 117–46), "The Son of God" (pp. 147–72), "The Lion and the Star: The Theology of the Incarnation" (pp. 205–31), "The Theology of Redemption (I)" (pp. 233–63), "The Theology of Redemption (II): Mysterium Crucis" (pp. 265–92), and so forth. Without grounding his procedure methodologically, Daniélou thus presents an outline of that kind of theology in the Christian church which used a Jewish conceptuality for the period between the New Testament and the beginnings of Hellenistic-apologetic theology.[219]

Both the goal and its manner of execution have weighty considerations[220] against them:

1. Daniélou's presupposition that the Judaism of this time was apocalyptic is an inappropriate generalization.

2. The separation of the New Testament from the real subject matter of a theology of Jewish Christianity, for reasons both of chronology[221] and of subject matter,[222] cannot be maintained.[223] This is related to the next objection.

3. Daniélou works in an unhistorical manner. The Jewish Christianity that he deals with in this work never existed historically. It is an artificially constructed product[224] and no longer describes, as in earlier scholarship, a type of Christianity that could be identified by historical methods, but is an abstract entity which the author imagines existed in a certain period.

4. A further important objection against Daniélou, which at the same time is directed against the previous scholarship on this subject, was raised by M. Simon. He raised the question whether it was appropriate and adequate to describe Jewish Christianity on the basis of its doctrinal characteristics or the conceptual categories which it used (Daniélou). Must not the same have been the case for Jewish Christianity as for Judaism in general, namely, that it was distinguished primarily by its observance of the law and not through (theological) doctrines?

26

This was the guiding question in Simon's own studies of the Jewish-Christian phenomenon, to which we must now direct our attention.

1.9 MARCEL SIMON

Marcel Simon's contributions to the study of Jewish Christianity are scattered through numerous works.[225] Although he never dealt with this theme in a monograph, a rather unified and impressive picture is nevertheless visible. Simon's point of departure for his work is the correct observation that when the church fathers refer to the Jewish Christians they generally classify them with the other "heretics."[226] If Harnack had lamented the fact that Justin communicated so little to us concerning the Jewish Christians (*Dial.* 47), Simon on the contrary considered Justin's reference to have been appropriate and to have emphasized the essential point.[227] In fact, it is from the content of Justin's report that we first learn the category which is adequate for the description of Jewish Christianity: the observance of the Jewish law. This includes the contents of the ritual law and goes beyond the requirements of the Apostolic Decree.[228]

Further, the concept of Jewish Christianity should be used, argued Simon, primarily in the *religious* sense, particularly since the Jewish mission at the turn of the century had registered considerable success in winning proselytes.[229] Thus talk of a "Jewish Christianity which has no commitment to the ceremonial law"[230] only generates confusion.[231]

As mentioned in the introductory comments above, Simon considered the manner in which the question had been posed by previous scholarship to be inappropriate and inadequate, namely, in terms of Jewish-Christian doctrine or conceptuality (Daniélou), since in Jewish Christianity as in Judaism orthopraxy is of incomparably higher significance than is orthodoxy.[232]

Historically, Jewish Christianity assumed concrete form as an anti-Pauline movement.[233] Simon does not hesitate to speak of James as "a notorious adversary of the apostle to the Gentiles,"[234] to regard the anti-Paulinism in the Pauline churches as a continuation of the debate at the Jerusalem Conference,[235] and in an explicit criticism of Munck to emphasize the genetic relationship between Jewish Christianity before and after 70 c.e.[236] We may thus be grateful that Simon directed our attention to the complexity of the phenomenon of Jewish Christianity. Simon thus includes the Stephen group in Jewish Christianity and on this basis can regard the passages in the Pseudo-Clementines that are critical of the cult as ramifications of the theological views of the Stephen group.[237]

The historical connection between Jewish Christianity before and after the Jewish War is, for Simon, the flight of the Jerusalem church to Pella reported by Eusebius (Hist. Ecc. 3.5.3), the historicity of which he sought to establish in an extensive 1972 essay (cf. below, pp. 200ff.). He here reaffirms and elaborates his previous[238] argument for the distinction between the Nazareans (successors of the original Jerusalem church) and the Ebionites, the latter group having split off from the former in the Transjordan, then coming into contact with the pre-Christian sect of the Nazareans.

Quite apart from the facts that the historicity of the tradition of the Jerusalem church's flight to Pella is subject to serious doubt and that the distinction between Nazareans and Ebionites has an inadequate basis in the sources, it is to be affirmed nonetheless that Simon's contribution to the investigation of Jewish Christianity is of the highest significance. His methodological approach to the problem is in a class by itself and deserves unqualified endorsement. It is regrettable that his work has been neglected by some recent scholarship.[239]

1.10 PRESENT TENDENCIES IN THE STUDY OF JEWISH CHRISTIANITY. THE FORMULATION OF THE PROBLEM FOR THE PRESENT WORK

The following section attempts to integrate the results of the preceding analysis into an approach to the problem that will avoid the weaknesses of previous studies, critically appropriate their results, and develop them further. With this goal in mind, I will then propose my own definition of Jewish Christianity, which is in conflict with that definition usually adopted in the works discussed above as well as with other possible understandings of the phenomenon.

We will begin with the present tendency (tendencies) in the

study of Jewish Christianity as the basis for translating the goal just mentioned into reality.

Unless my impression is mistaken, at the moment Daniélou's understanding of the matter, despite some sharp criticisms, enjoys the greatest success.[240] Thus A. F. J. Klijn could write in his programmatic essay:

> Daniélou took a step which had to be taken sooner or later. It is impossible to isolate the Jerusalem Church, Palestinian or Syriac Christianity from the rest of the Church in the Graeco-Roman world. We are dealing with one Christian movement in which the Jewish ideas and practices and the Jews themselves played their part in Jerusalem and Rome, Ephesus and Alexandria. For this reason it is impossible to define the term "Jewish Christian" because it proved to be a name that can readily be replaced by "Christian."[241]

A disciple of Daniélou's, R. N. Longenecker, composed a book with the title *The Christology of Early Jewish Christianity*, in which he dealt with the Christology of those Christian communities between 30 and 135 C.E. which either are to be located in Jerusalem or considered Jerusalem their mother church, so that they used only christological titles of Jewish origin. In this way he was in the situation of being able to draw a unified picture of early Christian Christology.[242]

Likewise G. Quispel, also in Daniélou's wake, could classify the beginnings of Christianity in Syria, Alexandria, and North Africa as Jewish-Christian by applying the term "Jewish Christianity" very broadly.[243]

These essays, all written by followers of Daniélou, have a common denominator in that they all speak of Jewish Christianity wherever they find Christian texts that make use of ideas of Jewish origin. But such a concept of Jewish Christianity is too broad to facilitate a precise historical understanding of early Christian texts and groups, all the more so since it can only lead to such broad generalizations as Klijn's, that early Christianity was a Jewish-Christian phenomenon.

Other scholars used—and some still use—the term "Jewish Christianity" in an ethnic sense.[244] In this case, the adjective "Jewish" in "Jewish-Christian" is simply a more precise designation of those members of the Christian community who were born of Jewish parents. But in such an approach, the term does

29

not take into account the religious sense that Judaism had among Gentiles, a point especially emphasized in the relevant contributions of M. Simon. It would then hardly be meaningful to consider figures like Paul, who intentionally did not observe the Torah in his associations with Gentiles, to be "Jewish Christians."

Another definition of Jewish Christianity is oriented to the schema of orthodoxy and heresy.[245] In this case, the categories of the early Christian heresiologists are accepted as fundamental, and the (heretical) Ebionites of the second century are distinguished from the (orthodox) Jewish Christians of the earliest Jerusalem church on the basis of this a priori decision. In addition, for such an understanding the New Testament canon plays an important role—for it contains not a single Ebionite writing. It is apparent, however, that such an approach must be rejected; its unreflective nature (the question of what actually constitutes Jewish Christianity is seldom raised) is no less amazing than the boundless success it has enjoyed since the time of Eusebius.

As is well known, the definition proposed by M. Simon (see above, p. 27) avoids the weaknesses of the previous definition: "Jewish Christianity" is used to describe those Christian groups which practice a (ritual) *observance* of the law.[246] Jewish Christianity, understood to be so constituted, is not simply identical with early Christianity. But it includes the Gentile Christians who observe the law, just as it excludes Jews who do not observe the law. In this connection, Simon's earlier incidental comment, that Jewish Christianity is characterized by a rejection of Paul, points back to the understanding of Jewish Christianity held by Baur (and the Tübingen school), according to which anti-Paulinism was an essential characteristic of Jewish Christianity (see above, p. 2). Jewish Christianity so understood was, for Baur, the key to grasping what transpired in the first two Christian centuries, for the catholic church at the end of the second century developed dialectically from the synthesis of anti-Pauline Jewish Christianity and Pauline Gentile Christianity. However, it was precisely Baur's speculative application of his understanding of Jewish Christianity that was, from a historical-critical point of view, his greatest weakness. It was only by forcing the evidence that he was able to bridge the great chronological gap between the anti-Pauline witnesses from the periods before and after 70 C.E., by setting forth as the connecting links texts that either mentioned Paul not at all (Hermas, Papias) or only incidentally (1 Clement).

Baur was vigorously and rightly challenged by later scholars concerning the legitimacy of such a procedure (see above, pp. 9–11). The Christianity of the first two centuries was too variegated to permit each of its elements to be assigned schematically to either the Jewish-Christian or the Gentile Christian stream. As Ritschl's historical studies pointed out, Gentile Christianity after 70 C.E. had an incomparably greater significance than did Jewish Christianity. At the same time it must be added that even Jewish Christianity (as defined by M. Simon) is by no means to be limited to anti-Pauline groups. There certainly existed a Jewish Christianity that was not influenced by Paul at all—either positively or negatively.[247]

To be sure, after these critical comments with regard to Baur and his school we must point out that the master of Tübingen, despite his misleading theory concerning the origin of the catholic church, was thoroughly superior to his opponents in the field of historical criticism and that he, like no other before or since, recognized the fact of an anti-Pauline attitude in the sources of the first and second centuries as a problem. This historical survey of studies devoted to the investigation of Jewish Christianity points to the need again to take up the task of the historical-critical analysis of anti-Paulinism in early Christianity and at the same time to ask whether the term "Jewish-Christian" is appropriate in the sense of the definition of Jewish Christianity given by M. Simon.

In this process we will, on methodological grounds, restrict ourselves to such texts as unambiguously presuppose an anti-paulinism, as indicated by the fact that they contain attacks on Paul or Pauline letters or that they permit an attack against Paul or his theology to be clearly inferred.[248] This restriction is necessary, because the Baur school—as is clear from the above survey—was too often impelled by its speculative-historical interests to assign such figures as Papias or Justin, or texts such as the Apocalypse, Hermas, and others, to an anti-Pauline[249] category on the basis of an argument from silence, just as they were impelled primarily by their hermeneutical interests to assume that an anti-Pauline movement was the background for several

Pauline passages in which Paul engages in debate with his opponents. In regard to the first point, our self-imposed restriction may in fact cause us to omit important witnesses to an anti-Pauline attitude, since it cannot be excluded that these authors might have explicitly polemicized against Paul in writings now lost to us. Nevertheless, methodological reasons compel us to use only unambiguous sources as the basis for our argument. And, in regard to the polemical passages in Paul's letters, we need to remember that not everyone whom Paul attacks had first attacked Paul. Thus also here it is necessary to use only those passages which without any doubt reflect an attack on Paul.

Our primary point of contact must of course be the life of Paul himself and not the later stories about the apostle, although these continue to be an important field of investigation.[250] The following presentation thus has two major parts: I. Anti-Paulinism during Paul's Lifetime, and II. Anti-Paulinism in the Post-Pauline Period.

In order to take into account the chronological problem rightly emphasized by Munck, we will deal with the relevant events and texts in their presumed chronological order (which is to be established in each case in the analysis itself). The antiheretical work of Irenaeus is chosen as the chronological boundary for our investigation, since it signified the official proscription of the anti-Pauline groups and since Paul's writings by this time formed a constituent part of the canon.

Each section will usually be concerned to clarify four different questions (although the order in which they are treated can vary, depending on the specific problems presented by each text): (a) Why is anti-Paulinism in evidence? (b) What relationship does it have to the theology of its advocate? (c) Is it Jewish-Christian? (d) How may it be understood historically? We must then at the end draw these individual analyses together to ask comprehensively whether the manifestations of anti-Paulinism of the first two centuries are to be seen as isolated phenomena or whether they belong together genetically. In any case, it is hoped that the present work will contribute to placing the investigation of Jewish Christianity[251] on a firm foundation and ultimately contribute to the interpretation of Paul.

PART I
ANTI-PAULINISM
DURING PAUL'S LIFETIME

2

THE OLDEST RECOGNIZABLE CASES
OF ANTI-PAULINISM[1]

The oldest available criticism of Paul comes to light in connection with the Jerusalem Conference and the related incident at Antioch. For both events we possess primary sources, that is, reports of an eyewitness.[2] The following qualification should of course be kept in mind: Paul in Galatians is struggling against his opponents, and his letter reports events lying several years in the past. Thus the possibility exists that Paul transferred some of the disputed issues with which he was currently engaged to the context of the issues that were debated at the Jerusalem Conference and thus does not give an exact report of what happened there. For this reason it is advisable to begin with *traditional material* that is clearly related to the conference or with issues that were unquestionably dealt with at the conference.

2.1 ANTI-PAULINISM
AT THE JERUSALEM CONFERENCE

The Jerusalem Conference was called in order to debate the question of whether Gentile Christians must be circumcised as a prerequisite to membership in the Christian community (Gal. 2:3). This impossible demand[3] was directed against the Pauline practice of accepting Gentiles into the community without circumcision. The demand was not first made at the time of the conference itself but previously, namely, in the mixed congregation at Antioch, where the "false brethren" (Gal. 2:4) had already sneaked in.[4]

Paul then goes to Jerusalem with Barnabas and takes also the Gentile Christian Titus along, in order thereby to get from the Jerusalem Conference a clear agreement concerning his own practice.

Two series of proceedings may be distinguished in Paul's

account. One takes place within the framework of the assembly of the whole congregation (Gal. 2:2a), the other within the limited circle of distinguished leaders, the "pillars" (Gal. 2:2b, 6ff.). The temporal relationship of these talks is unclear. Is "the special discussion with the leadership . . . perhaps presented in vv. 6–10 as chronologically later than the public deliberations? Or was it chronologically prior but mentioned later by Paul for practical reasons (because it contains the positive results)? Or should it be located during the public deliberations?"[5]

Paul is able to wrest agreement from the "pillars" that the Gentile Christians need not be circumcised. In any case, this was not demanded of Titus, who had accompanied Paul to the conference (Gal. 2:3). Nevertheless this agreement was vigorously disputed, and we must assume that the "false brethren" had considerable support within the Jerusalem congregation for their demand that Titus be circumcised and at the beginning probably had the "pillars" on their side.[6] "How could they, in Jerusalem, under the very eyes of the most respected apostles, have possibly thought that they could *compel* the circumcision of Titus, unless the original apostles and the Jerusalem church already supported this view?"[7] At least a majority of the congregation must have supported the "false brethren," for otherwise they could never have made the demand for circumcision so effectively.[8]

It is clear, however, that Paul was able to overcome this demand and to obtain a fundamental agreement from the "pillars" to continue his Gentile mission in full freedom from the law. The basis for their unity[9] on this matter, sealed with a solemn handshake, was obviously the success of the Pauline mission to the Gentiles, to which the Jerusalem leadership could not close its eyes, and the readiness of the Gentile Christians to support their interest in fellowship with a gift of money.[10] On the other hand, it must be pointed out that the "false brethren" remained members of the Jerusalem church despite the concordat of the Jerusalem leadership with Paul and will have continued vigorously to oppose it. Their open anti-Paulinism is, in any case, to be presupposed as an influential factor at the conference and in the period following.

If the above reconstruction is essentially correct, then we should assume that the "false brethren," despite their defeat on the issue of circumcision, must still have had (indirect) influence on the results of the transactions. This hypothesis is confirmed by a careful examination of the formula of concord in Gal. 2:9, which has a legal character:[11] hēmeis eis ta ethnē, autoi . . . eis tēn peritomēn. The mission field is divided into allotments.[12] From then on, the Gentile mission is the responsibility of Paul and Barnabas, the Jewish mission that of the Jerusalem leadership, James, Peter, and John. The choice of vocabulary in the expressions eis ta ethnē and eis tēn peritomēn, respectively, permit only an exclusive interpretation[13] with regard to the groups to which they refer.[14] That means that ethnē and peritomē have an ethnographic meaning.[15] The formula given above assures Paul of an unlimited right to carry on the Gentile mission. On the other hand, it could also be used to cancel the validity of a mission to Gentiles and Jews. That is, this regulation does not exclude that in the future Jews who lived in a Gentile Christian congregation could be compelled to keep the Jewish law. Thus it is clear that at least a potential anti-Pauline element became a part of the agreement worked out at the Jerusalem Conference, for Paul did not expect Jewish Christians who lived in association with Gentile Christians to live in compliance with the Jewish law (Gal. 2:11ff.).

An additional virtually anti-Pauline element in the Jerusalem agreement concerns Paul's apostolic office: the regulation as communicated in Gal. 2:9 contains no acknowledgement of Paul's apostleship but speaks merely of Paul's Gentile mission.[16] Note that the paralleling of Peter and Paul (v. 8) speaks only of the apostolē of Peter but does not speak of Paul's apostleship.[17] These are unexpected phenomena to find in this text, for (a) the awareness of being the "apostle to the Gentiles" was formed very early in Paul's consciousness (Gal. 1:16—at his call) and was a constituent part of his self-understanding[18] and (b) in view of Paul's interest in refuting the objections of his opponents in Galatia, Paul would hardly have failed to mention a tradition from the conference that included his own apostleship.

The tension between the stated results of the conference and the two considerations just mentioned requires one of the following two explanations: either Paul's apostleship was rejected in Jerusalem or Paul considered it inadvisable for strategic reasons to make his apostleship an issue,[19] since it could have endangered the desired formula of concord.[20] The first possibility would have been a clear action against Paul. If the second possibility is the correct one, then Paul would have avoided an overt anti-Pauline action in the conference. In either case, it is clear that the lack of reference to a Pauline apostolic office in the proceedings of the Jerusalem Conference is the result of anti-Pauline opposition in Jerusalem

2.2 ANTI-PAULINISM
AT THE INCIDENT IN ANTIOCH[21]

On the basis of Gal. 2:11ff., the course of events can be reconstructed as follows: In the integrated Christian church at Antioch, those who were Jews by birth[22] had participated in table fellowship with Gentiles. Peter jointed in this practice while in Antioch. During a visit to Antioch by some Christians associated with James, the Jewish Christians in Antioch, including Peter and Barnabas, withdrew from this table fellowship because of their fear[23] of the circumcision group (*hoi ek peritomēs*).[24] Thereupon Paul brought the charge especially against Peter that by this action he was compelling the Gentile Christians to adopt the Jewish way of life (*ioudaïzein*), a procedure that could not be united with the truth of the gospel.[25]

The proceedings reported in Gal. 2:11ff. permit the following inferences.

1. The *tinas apo Iakōbou* were sent by James the Lord's brother and came to Antioch under his authority.

2. They[26] advocate[27] the separation of the Jewish Christians from the Gentile Christians and are identical with the "circumcision group." The basis for the demanded separation would be the Jewish legal prescriptions that forbade Jews to eat from non-Jewish tables.[28] To explain the incident as a matter of tactics[29] or politics,[30] in order to play down its theological implications, is not convincing. Just as at the Jerusalem Conference, the issue at stake was the theological significance of the law. Both at the conference and with regard to the Antioch Christians, James was an advocate of the view that Jews must keep away from the ritually unclean tables of Gentiles, while Paul expected Jewish Christians not to abide by the Jewish dietary restrictions in their

38

associations with Gentile Christians. The incident at Antioch must therefore be classified as an anti-Pauline[31] action on the part of James the Lord's brother.[32]

Thus the two earliest examples of anti-Pauline actions or attitudes in early Christianity come to light. They belong *chronologically* to the first two decades of the Christian movement, and their subject matter deals with the standing of Gentile Christians within the Christian congregations. The anti-Paulinists were willing to accept them into membership only on the prior condition that they had agreed to keep the law. The anti-Pauline opposition was thus Jewish Christian in the sense defined above (pp. 29–30). The examples stand in direct *geographical* relationship to Jerusalem and concern *personally* Paul's preaching and practice. From Gal. 2:11ff. we see a surprisingly direct participation in anti-Paulinism by James the Lord's brother, in view of which both Peter and Barnabas decide to back off. But even the agreement worked out in Jerusalem bears in part the fingerprints of the inexorable anti-Paulinists and was far from being a victory for Paul.

The two last points form a transition to the task of the next chapter. There we must deal with that Jerusalem Christianity which was involved in anti-Pauline activities from a certain time onward, glimpses of which we have seen in the highlights discussed above. That chapter will have as one of its tasks to throw some light on the problem of how James, brother of the Lord, came to the leadership of the Jerusalem church and why he could have participated in the actions against Paul discussed above. To that extent, the next chapter will be able to clarify the emergence of anti-Paulinism *in retrospect*. On the other hand, we will also give a *preview* of the history of the Jerusalem church from the conference to the Jewish War, in order to provide a sound basis for the subsequent chapter.

3

ANTI-PAULINISM IN JERUSALEM AND JAMES THE LORD'S BROTHER[1]

3.1 JERUSALEM CHRISTIANITY BEFORE
PAUL'S FIRST VISIT

Although the Acts account of the earliest beginnings of Christianity in Jerusalem is certainly incorrect,[2] there can be no doubt that not long after the crucifixion of Jesus a considerable number of his followers, after having left the capital temporarily, established a church in Jerusalem which was of decisive importance for Christianity in and outside Palestine up to the time of the Jewish War.

Before we turn our attention to the history of the Jerusalem church, we must first report the real beginning of the (post-Easter) Christian movement, that is, its earliest beginnings in Galilee, especially since that will be significant with regard to the authority of the Jerusalem church in its relations with other Christian groups.

The first resurrection appearances occurred in Galilee (Mark 16:7; Matt. 28:16ff.; John 21), where Jesus' disciples had returned—or rather, fled.[3] Here the risen Lord first appeared to his disciple Simon Peter. This conclusion can be supported by the following observations: (a) Both in Mark 16:7[4] and in John (Luke 5),[5] Peter plays the principal role and is set off from the other disciples. (b) Other traditions, though they no longer mention Galilee as the location, report the *first* appearance to Peter: Luke 24:34 ("The Lord has risen indeed, and has appeared to Simon"); 1 Cor. 15:5 (Jesus appeared "to Cephas, then to the twelve"). (c) The four extant lists of the Twelve (Mark 3:16ff.; Matt. 10:2ff.; Luke 6:14ff.; Acts 1:13) are unanimous in listing Peter in the first place,[6] although they are independent of one another.[7]

Probably a *second* christophany also occurred in Galilee, when Jesus appeared to Peter and the other members of the Twelve (1 Cor. 15:5).[7a]

40

Regarded historically, the above reconstruction means that Peter reorganized the circle of the Twelve in Galilee and with them returned to Jerusalem,[8] Thus with Peter as leader the Twelve—whether or not an original circle of Twelve was established by the historical Jesus[9]—assumed a position of leadership in the Jerusalem church, for which especially the ancient formula in 1 Cor. 15:5 provides evidence (cf. below, p. 48).

The appearances continued to occur in Jerusalem. We know of Jesus' appearance before five thousand brethren,[10] of the appearance to the women,[11] and of the appearance to James and all the apostles (1 Cor. 15:7). Strangely enough, the circle of the Twelve seems not to have held together for very long. At the time of Paul's first visit to Jerusalem (the visit to Cephas), it appears not to have existed at all.[12]

But other incisive developments in the early life of the Jerusalem church need to be mentioned. Soon after the return of the Jesus community from Galilee, it was joined by a group of Greek-speaking Jews (the "Hellenists"), who soon were having their own Greek-language worship services. They shortly separated from the mother community, primarily for linguistic reasons, and elected their own leadership group, the Seven.[13] The list transmitted in Acts 6:5 is probably traditional and historically reliable. Members of the circle of Seven concerning whom additional traditions are available are Philip, Nicolaus, and Stephen:

Philip later resided with his four prophet daughters in Caesarea on the sea and was host to Paul and his companions just before the decisive trip to Jerusalem (Acts 21:8). Traditions about Philip that have been further elaborated appear in Acts 8.[14]

Nicolaus appears in Irenaeus, *Heresies* 1.25, and probably also in Rev. 2:6, 15, as the forefather of the Nicolaitans. The question of a genetic relationship between the members of the Hellenistic circle and the later Nicolaitans must remain open.[15]

Stephen's martyrdom is reported by Luke in Acts 7. Although the speech attributed to him hardly fits the situation in which he is accused[16] and is to be regarded as the composition of Luke on the basis of older material, Acts 6:11 still goes back to tradition[17] and could reflect the historical Stephen's critique of the law.

The exodus of the Hellenists from Jerusalem was mainly due to their critique of the law,[18] the direct reason for their departure being provided by the violent death of one of the Seven, namely, Stephen.

The closest analogy within the sphere of Jewish history for an exodus from Jerusalem is provided by the withdrawal of the group to Leontopolis[19] in the second century B.C.E. and the withdrawal of another group to "Damascus"[20] at about the same time. These separations may have been called forth[21] by different attitudes toward the cult.[22] If Acts 6:13f. rests on tradition, then for the Hellenists too a critique of the cult is to be presupposed (see above, n. 17).

Having left Jerusalem, the Hellenists began a mission to the Gentiles and carried the gospel to Phoenicia, Antioch, and Cyprus (Acts 11:19). Their preaching in the Syrian-Cilician territory, which was characterized by a critique of the law, evoked their persecution by Paul, citizen of Tarsus,[23] until he "saw" the resurrected Jesus near Damascus (1 Cor. 9:1). The news of his conversion was celebrated in the churches of Syria-Cilicia, just as it was received with gratitude by the congregations in Judea (Gal. 1:22).

The "Hellenistic" phase of Jerusalem Christianity was thus only an episode in the life of the earliest congregation. When Paul came to Jerusalem for the first time, the reasons discussed above make it clear that he certainly did not meet any Hellenists there.

But, as mentioned above, it is also probably the case that the original leadership group of the early Jerusalem church, the Twelve, no longer existed at the time of Paul's visit with Peter in Jerusalem. Paul does not mention the Twelve but speaks rather of those in Jerusalem "who were apostles before me" (Gal. 1:17). To these apostles Peter certainly belonged, and most probably James as well. Galatians 1:19 states: *heteron de tōn apostolōn ouk eidon ei mē Iakōbon ton adelphon tou kyriou*. It has been suggested that the *ei mē* be translated as "but rather": "I saw none of the other apostles, but rather I did see James."[24] That would mean that James is not considered an apostle. But linguistically it is just as possible to translate[25] *ei mē* as "except,"[26] which would indicate that James was one of the apostles. A further argument for the latter translation is provided by 1 Cor. 15:7[27] (cf. below, p. 48); and in addition, the context[28] in Galatians seems to speak for it: in Galatians 1, Paul is making clear his relationship to Jerusalem, and that means in particular to those who were apostles before him (v. 17). When he adds the final clause in v. 19 it is thus readily understandable that in addition to the apostle Peter he had also seen James, the context making it more likely that James is here considered an apostle than the opposite.[29]

For all that, Peter still seems to have been the leading authority among the apostles at the time of Paul's first visit to Jerusalem. That is suggested in the first place by his role as the reorganizer of the circle of the Twelve which in part became the group of apostles (Peter himself being the best evidence of this). In the next place the above conclusion can be drawn from the purpose of Paul's trip, which understandably was to get acquainted with the leading figure of the earliest church.[30]

Our subject requires that in concluding this section we raise the question whether there are texts or traditions, available from the time of Paul's visit to Peter or before, that in any way contain a negative reaction to Paul's (Christian) preaching. The answer requires consideration to the following points:

a.. In Gal. 1:20 Paul reports a positive reaction of the Jewish Christians to his conversion and to his preaching.

b. During this first visit it appears that an agreement concerning the missionary procedure with regard to Jews and Gentiles was worked out, an agreement that was presupposed and acknowledged at the later Jerusalem conference (Gal. 2:7): "When they saw that I had been entrusted with the gospel to the uncircumcised, just as Peter had been entrusted with the gospel to the circumcised . . . ." Of course it is hardly conceivable that Peter would have acknowledged Paul as an equal partner. Still, there can be no doubt that Gal. 2:7 reflects a positive judgment from Peter concerning Paul, and the tradition contained in Gal. 2:7 clearly comes from the time before the conference. Since Paul had not seen Peter between his initial visit and the conference visit, the tradition must derive from the initial visit.[31]

Ernst Haenchen, however, has raised the following objection: "If this subject [i.e., the allocation of the respective missions to the Jews and to the Gentiles] had previously been discussed for fourteen days,[32] then it remains completely inconceivable that after another fourteen years this issue had neither been resolved nor disappeared."[33] Haenchen's argument is hardly persuasive, since the circumstances of the two visits were different. At the conference the issue was whether or not the law was required as a constituent part of the Gentile mission, while the first visit to Peter dealt with the Gentile mission as such.[34]

Given this defense of our understanding of Paul's first Jerusalem visit, we may continue to maintain with regard to a possible anti-Paulinism in Peter or the Jerusalem church that no anti-Pauline tradition from that period is associated with the person of Peter. Paul was welcomed by him and by the Jerusalem Christians as a new member of the community.

It now became a question of how long the Gentile gospel of Paul would be appreciated in Jerusalem, whether and how long Cephas would maintain a positive attitude toward Paul, and finally how the power structures of the Jerusalem church would work themselves out with reference to Paul.

With this, we come to the history of Jerusalem Christianity in that period between Paul's first visit to Peter and the conference visit.

3.2 JERUSALEM CHRISTIANITY BETWEEN PAUL'S FIRST AND SECOND VISITS

Some significant event occurred in the life of the Jerusalem congregation, with the result that Peter left Jerusalem. Acts 12 reports a persecution in Jerusalem under Agrippa[35] which involved Peter and in which James the son of Zebedee was killed.[36] With regard to where Agrippa's action is to be located chronologically, it is to be noted that as a rule Luke accurately reports the information that came to him in the *tradition*.[37] That is hardly helpful in this case, however, since Agrippa is not an integral character in the legend worked into Acts 12:3ff., which Luke only uses as a foil for the story of the miraculous punishment of Agrippa[38] in Acts 12:20ff.

On the other hand, the following considerations speak in favor of the view that the legend reported in Acts 12:3ff. contains *historical* reminiscences: In Jerusalem, Agrippa attempted to give the impression of promoting a strict Judaism.[39] James the son of Zebedee was obviously no longer alive at the time of the Jerusalem Conference a few years later (otherwise he would have been named in Paul's report). And of course there is the *vaticinium ex eventu* of the martyr death of both Zebedee brothers (Mark 10:39),[40] which James may have suffered during the time between Jesus' death and the conference, and Agrippa's opportunism may have been responsible for it. If the report in Acts 12:3ff. is correct (Agrippa "killed James the brother of John with the sword"), it would be reasonable to infer that he also planned measures against Peter, who as the leading personality in the Jerusalem church would have been a victim happily sacrificed by Agrippa. If Peter had wanted to escape this threat, the safest way would have been simply to leave Jerusalem (Acts 12:17).[41]

In addition, it is of great importance that, in the period between Paul's first visit to Peter and the conference, Jews with a stricter observance of the law joined the Jerusalem church. "It is impossible that they can have belonged to it at any time during the period in which the Jewish churches looked with satisfaction on Paul's work in Syria and Cilicia."[42] We have noted in the previous chapter that the Christians devoted to a strict observance of the law had resisted the apostle to the Gentiles both in Syrian territory and in Jerusalem at the conference. It was simply the case that they failed to win a majority of the Jerusalem Christians, especially the leadership, to their side. All the same, that they had an influence on the proceedings is more than clear.

Nor can we fail to notice that a change took place with regard to the leadership of the Jerusalem church. If Peter had been the principal authority up to the time of Paul's first visit to Jerusalem, it appears that James had become the decisive person in the period prior to the conference, partly because of the departure of Peter from the city. For in the "unity formula" which derives from the conference (Gal. 2:9) he appears at the head of the college of "pillars."[43] (Peter had obviously returned to Jerusalem.[44])

The sources simply do not provide enough data for us to determine the nature of the office and function of the "pillars" more precisely. In my opinion it even goes too far if we compare the concept of "pillars" in an ecclesiological sense with the "foundation" on which the church is built,[45] since we do not know enough about the doctrine of the church of the early Jerusalem congregation. All that we can be sure of is that the expression *styloi* was applied in a metaphorical sense[46] to the leadership function exercised by the persons described by this title, but the sphere of influence of the individual "pillars" and their relationship to one another remain unknown.

All the same, the order of names in Gal. 2:9 allows the assumption that at the time of the conference James was the *primus inter pares*.[46a] That such an assumption is in fact correct is seen from James's action against the situation in Antioch (Gal. 2:11ff.) when the second-ranking "pillars" had to give in when confronted by the circumcision group. This argument is independent of the chronological relationship of the conference and the Antioch incident. In either case, the power play illustrates the dominant influence of James the Lord's brother just before or just after the conference.

Finally, form-critical and tradition-critical observations on 1 Cor. 15:3ff. support the above reconstruction of the development of the leadership in the Jerusalem church and throw some light on the growing anti-Paulinism in Jerusalem.

In 1 Cor. 15:3-7 Paul presents a series of witnesses to the resurrection, and as a part of his apologetic includes himself as the final member of the group. In order to clarify the issue of whether 1 Cor. 15:3-7 can give any information on the history of the Jerusalem church, the following questions must first be answered:

a. What is the extent of this formula which Paul communicated to the Corinthians at the time of the establishment of the church?

b. What form-critical relationships exist between individual elements of the tradition in vv. 3-7?

On *a:* The following considerations support the view that the tradition communicated to the Corinthians during Paul's initial mission in Corinth extends through *eita tois dōdeka*: (1) After *eita tois dōdeka* a new structure begins.[47] (2) The words *ex hōn hoi pleiones* certainly do not belong to the tradition. "But then it is much simpler to assume that here he [Paul] is no longer quoting at all, but writing his own words."[48] (3) "The three concluding clauses (*epeita . . . epeita . . . eschaton*) are just as formally

46

identical with each other as are the four previous clauses introduced with *hoti*; but the third of these concluding clauses is
certainly not a part of the tradition . . . , so neither are the first
two to be considered a part of the tradition."[49]

To sum up, the formula communicated by Paul at the time of
the founding of the church extended only through v. 5.[50]

It is clear, however, that this formula communicated initially
to the Corinthians, vv. 3–5, in itself contains disparate elements.
For example, elsewhere the statements about Jesus' resurrection
and Jesus' death for our sins are not found alongside each other
and have thus been placed together in the pre-Pauline redactional phase. The *hoti*-recitativum formula,[51] which appears four
times, is also an indication that *different* kerygmatic formulae
have been brought together in a series. Nonetheless, the disparate character[52] cannot shake the thesis presented above that
Paul transmitted this complex unit of tradition[53] to the Corinthians at the time of the establishment of the Corinthian church.

This brings us to the question of the form-critical interrelationship of the traditions contained in vv. 3–7. Since our
approach to the issue is oriented to the issue of the power structure of the Jerusalem church, we will limit our consideration to a
comparison of the passages that deal with Cephas and James.

On b: An analysis of the tradition delivered to Paul at the time
of the founding of the church indicates that the clause *hoti
ōphthē Kēfa, eita tois dōdeka* was originally an independent
fragment of tradition. This is supported by an argument from the
analysis of the history of the tradition: The appearance to Peter
is reflected in Luke 24:34,[54] independently of 1 Cor. 15:5: *ontōs
ēgerthē ho kyrios kai ōphthē Simōni*. Although the "Twelve" do
not appear in Luke 24:34, they can still be considered a traditional element in 1 Cor. 15:5, for *hoi dōdeka* is a hapax legomenon in Paul. Against the idea that *Paul* added *eita tois dōdeka*[55]
stands (in addition to the traditional character of *hōi dodeka* in
Paul) the observation made above that a new sentence structure
does not begin until v. 6. This element in the tradition taken by
itself allows us to itemize two specific points: (*a*) it contains the
claim that the first appearance was to Peter and (*b*) it expresses
the exceptional position that Peter had in the circle of the
Twelve.

47

This brings us to the following analysis of 1 Cor. 15:7.

From the point of view of the history of traditions, one notes a parallel to the appearance to James in the *Gospel of the Hebrews*.[56] Although there is no reference here to an appearance to all the apostles, it is nonetheless likely that a pre-Pauline formula is found in v. 7, and all the more so, since v. 7b goes back to tradition (see below, n. 57).

The tradition in v. 7 can be itemized into two specific points: (a) it contains the claim of the first appearance to James (cf. the parallel in the *Gospel of the Hebrews*!) and (b) it expresses the exceptional position of James over against all the apostles.

The thesis proposed here, that traditional formulae are present in v. 5 and v. 7, is completely confirmed by a comparison of v. 5 with v. 7. Both traditions are constructed in the same way, so that except for "Cephas"/"James" and "the Twelve"/"all the apostles" the same expressions are used:

compare *ōphthē Kēpha, eita tois dōdeka*
with *ōphthē Iakōbō, eita tois apostolois pasin.*

If we exclude the assumption that Paul himself formulated v. 7 analogously to v. 5,[57] then the parallelism is best explained by the hypothesis of a pre-Pauline formula in v. 5 and v. 7. The following discussion is concerned with additional form-critical considerations.

The formula quoted in 1 Cor. 15:5 and 7 contains a terse expression of the claim that a certain limited group of Christians had experienced an appearance of the Risen One. The possible *function* of such a formula becomes evident from a glance at the Pauline corpus: in his struggle against his opponents, Paul repeatedly points to his having seen the Risen One (1 Cor. 9:1; Gal. 1:15) and does it in order to legitimize his authority. In my view, the formula in 1 Cor. 15:5 and 7 has a similar function, and we should thus follow U. Wilckens in calling it a "legitimizing formula."[58] The formulae in 1 Cor. 15:5 and 7 are distinct from the Pauline parallels in that in each case they attribute to one witness an authority superior to the others in the group and base this presumed superior authority on the claim to have received the initial appearance of the Risen One.

The formula concerning Peter and the (rest of the) Twelve, and the claim inherent in it, have a historical basis in that Peter

48

in fact was the first (in Galilee) to see the risen Lord[59] and for this reason as the head of the circle of the Twelve was the leading authority of the earliest Jerusalem church.

How is the formula cited in 1 Cor. 15:7 related to this? If the determination of its form and function presented above is correct, then this formula would stand in contradiction to that in 1 Cor. 15:5, since Jesus could not have made his first appearance to both Cephas and James (I).

Then comes the related question of the relation of "the Twelve" to "all the apostles" (II).

And finally, if the form and function of the clause presented above is the proper solution to the problem, the question emerges of how Paul could possibly have juxtaposed two competing traditions to each other. Does not the chronological enumeration of the witnesses of the resurrection immediately exclude the possibility that Paul could have quoted two rival formulae (III)? We will deal with these three questions one at a time.

I. If one inquires after the most appropriate location(s) in the development of the Jerusalem church during its first two decades where these two formulae might most appropriately have played a role, in my opinion their competing nature can be seen all the more specifically:[60] from the historical point of view, the first appearance was in fact to Peter. The "legitimizing formula" for him and the Twelve is older than the formula of 1 Cor. 15:7. It derives from the time of the existence of the circle of the Twelve and belongs to the same pre-Pauline layer of tradition as the christological kerygma.

The formula in 1 Cor. 15:7 grew out of the fact that disciples of James claimed for their leader the primacy that Peter enjoyed by virtue of having received the initial resurrection appearance. To support this claim they constructed the formula of 15:7, patterned after that of 15:5.[61] Although Paul in 1 Cor. 15:3ff. is reporting in chronological order,[62] it is still questionable whether this development had occurred prior to Paul's first visit to Jerusalem. In any case, at that time James already had a group of disciples in Jerusalem, although Cephas was still the leading figure. Still, the process of a gradual shifting of authority from Peter to James can be traced in the life of the Jerusalem church prior to the conference. The formula in 1 Cor. 15:7 is helpful in understanding that process and is itself a further argument for the shifting of influence.

II. A. von Harnack,[63] who, so far as I am aware, was the first to recognize 1 Cor. 15:5 and 7 as a reflection of a shifting of authority within the Jerusalem church,[64] at the same time advocated the view that "the Twelve" in 1 Cor. 15:5 were identical with "all the apostles" in 1 Cor. 15:7.[65] This view of Harnack's is still under the spell of Luke's understanding that "the Twelve" are to be identified with the apostles.[66] This view has now properly been generally abandoned, although it remains a possibility that the circle of "the Twelve" became a part of the larger body of apostles.

What, then, was the relationship between "the Twelve" and "all" the apostles"?

We are proceeding from the conclusion to which we came above, namely, that Peter, along with the rest of "the Twelve," constituted the original and recognized leadership of the Jerusalem church.

A second firm conclusion may also be brought into consideration, namely, that the apostles here discussed were a fixed, exclusive group that belonged to the Jerusalem church.[67] It should not be questioned that *pantes* is a traditional[68] element in the expression *tois apostolois pasin*, for in 1 Cor. 15:7ff. Paul has to struggle to maintain his claim that he belongs to an apostolic group that had already been closed (see below, p. 73).

> The *apostoloi ekklēsiōn* (2 Cor. 8:23; Phil. 2:25) are to be distinguished from this exclusive Jerusalem group of apostles.[69] Here it is only a matter of delegates from congregations, to whom the term "apostle" applies only while they are performing this particular duty, that is, their "apostolic" office disappears as soon as they have completed the assignment.[70] This use of the term also probably comes in view in Acts 14:14 ("the apostles Barnabas and Saul"): Barnabas and Saul were delegates of the congregation in Antioch and during the time of this commission were "apostles."[71]

The above discussion leads to the following conclusion concerning the relationship between "the Twelve" and "all the apostles": the latter group includes the former but also no doubt embraces a larger circle including James, the other brothers of Jesus, Andronicus, Junia(s), and others. In relation to this enlarged group,[72] James had the same significance as Cephas in the circle of the Twelve.

One final observation is to be noted with regard to 1 Cor. 15:7: its exclusive understanding of the apostolic circle is a strong argument that it has been preserved intact. Since this fragment of tradition comes from Jerusalem, we may ask whether the program of James's disciples which is perceptible in it had already made its appearance at the conference. If this were the case, the peculiar avoidance of the issue of Paul's apostleship at the conference no longer appears so strange, and we would have discovered a further argument (a) for a strong anti-Pauline element at the conference and (b) for a proximity of the anti-Pauline group in Jerusalem to James.

III. The understanding of the two texts 1 Cor. 15:5 and 7 can be thoroughly integrated into the thrust of the Pauline argument in 1 Corinthians 15. To the kerygmatic formula that Paul had transmitted to the Corinthians at the time of the founding of the church, the formula that speaks of the death and resurrection of Christ as well as the appearance to Peter and the Twelve, Paul adds the other resurrection appearances of which he was aware. The original formula was probably transmitted to him by the Hellenistic congregations in Syria. Except for v. 6b, the other information came from oral tradition, with v. 7 coming from Jerusalem.

Whether Paul was aware of the rival character of the formulae in vv. 5 and 7 can hardly be decided. Presumably he had little interest in the matter. He was, rather, concerned to present the *paradosis* which he had initially delivered to the Corinthians and extend it to the point where it included himself. This made it necessary to include those appearances which had occurred chronologically prior to his own, in order to make clear that he had himself received the same sort of appearance as *all* (v. 8) those in the series.[73] The formulae in vv. 5 and 7 thereby lose, of course, the function they had at the traditional level. They are now used by Paul to testify precisely to the *fact* of the appearances (cf. especially the redactional v. 6b[74]), while originally they had functioned to emphasize the legitimacy of the claims of both Cephas and James to have experienced the first resurrection appearance.

It should now have become clear that the manner in which Paul uses the formulae in 1 Cor. 15:5 and 7 cannot be used as an argument against their original character as legitimization formulae. One must attend to the difference between tradition and redaction also when studying the epistolary literature.[75]

3.3 JERUSALEM CHRISTIANITY BETWEEN PAUL'S SECOND AND THIRD VISITS

It is clear from Paul's report in Galatians 1 that by the time of the conference at the latest, a sector of the Christian community considered circumcision to be a requirement for Gentile Christians. This came to expression in the demand for the circumcision of Titus, whom Paul had taken along to Jerusalem to document that fact that the existing eschatological community consisted of Jews *and Gentiles*. In the above discussion we pointed out that Paul was able to ward off this demand, but this does not mean that sector of the Jerusalem church immediately ceased to exist. Quite the contrary! It continued to be a part of the congregation as a whole, and its members certainly acknowledged James as their authority, as indicated by some observations regarding Paul's third visit to Jerusalem (in addition to what was already pointed out above, p. 51).

The source for our knowledge of what happened during that visit is Acts 21, supplemented by a few hints from Paul's letters.

3.3.1 The Structure of Acts 21

Our text may be divided into the following sections:

1. Acts 21:1–9		The Journey from Miletus to Caesarea
II. Acts 21:10–14		Agabus's Prophecy and Paul's Reaction
III. Acts 21:15–16		The Journey to Jerusalem; Lodging in Mnason's House
IV. Acts 21:17–20a		Paul's Reception by the Brethren; Report to the Elders and James on the Success of the Gentile Mission
V. Acts 21:20b–21		The Christian Zealots and the Rumors They Had Heard about Paul
VI. Acts 21:22–26		The Advice Given Paul concerning the Nazirite Vow and His Paying the Expenses of the Four Nazirites; Paul's Compliance with this Advice; Reminder to the Reader about the Apostolic Decree
VII. Acts 21:27–40		Uproar in the Temple at the Instigation of the Jews from Asia; Arrest of Paul

3.3.2 The Train of Thought and
the Lukan Redaction of the Text

I. Paul is on his final journey to Jerusalem. After he said farewell to the Ephesian elders (20:38), the apostle and his company sail by way of Cos and Rhodes to Patara.

With no transition, the "we" which we had seen earlier in Acts 16:10–17 and 20:5–15 reappears abruptly in 21:1. It then extends from here through 21:18 and then is taken up again in 27:1—28:16 (the journey from Caesarea to Rome).

The next stop after Patara is Tyre, where Paul and his company stay for seven days with disciples of the Tyrian congregation. The disciples warn Paul about the danger of going to Jerusalem (21:4), but of course without being able to change his resolution. After they pray together on the beach, the journey continues via Ptolemais to Caesarea on the sea. Here Paul and his companions lodge at the home of the Hellenist Philip.

II. The prophet Agabus predicts that in Jerusalem, Paul will be handed over by the Jews to the Gentiles. Paul is consequently warned by his companions and the Christians in Caesarea against going to Jerusalem. But Paul is willing to die in Jerusalem for the name of the Lord Jesus.

The warnings repeatedly communicated to Paul against going to Jerusalem (21:4b; 21:12) spring from Luke's own editorial work.[76] They are closely related to the Spirit motif: while on the one hand the warnings originate with the Holy Spirit, on the other hand it is precisely the Holy Spirit who prescribes that Paul must go to Jerusalem (cf. 20:22: "As one bound by the Spirit I go to Jerusalem"; and cf. 19:21).[77] The prayer motif also is an extensive redactional feature of the description of Paul's last journey to Jerusalem (cf. 20:36; 21:5).[78]

III. Disciples from Caesarea bring Paul and his company to his quarters in Jerusalem, where they lodge with the old disciple Mnason.

IV. Paul and his companions are welcomed by the brethren in Jerusalem, and on the following day Paul reports the success of his mission among the Gentiles to James and the presbyters.

Since the vocabulary of 21:19 is clearly a reflection of Acts 15:4, 12,[79] it derives from Lukan redaction.[80] But the other verses too bear a redactional stamp. Examination reveals the following data:

a. *Apodechomai*[81] and *adelphoi*[82] are favorite words of Luke's.

b. Verse 18 represents the Jerusalem congregation as having the same leadership structure as in Acts 15: the presbyters.

c. A redactional seam is visible in v. 17. Although Paul and his company are already in Jerusalem (v. 16), with the help of a participial construction in the genitive absolute, a construction that occurs frequently in Acts,[83] Paul and his companions are conducted there again.

d. Verse 17 stands in an irresolvable tension with v. 22. In v. 17 the congregation (=the "brethren") already greets Paul, while according to v. 22 (the) members of the congregation *will* hear that Paul is visiting in the city. If v. 22 represents traditional material, then v. 17 can only be understood as redactional.

This brings us to the redactional meaning of vv. 17–20a: Luke wants to show that a good relationship existed between Paul and the Jerusalem congregation to the very end. (This theological interest makes him willing to put up with the awkwardness of first having all the "brethren" greet Paul, although most of the "brethren" have yet to hear of Paul's arrival in the city.)

V, VI. The presence of numberless Christian zealots for the law in Jerusalem and the existence of rumors that Paul teaches the Jews of the Diaspora to abandon the law provokes James and the presbyters to ask Paul to perform an act that will demonstrate his own loyalty to the law. He is himself to go through the sacred rituals with four Nazirites, and himself pay the expenses of having their hair cut, so that it will be clear to all that Paul is loyal to the law and fulfills it himself.

When Paul complies with this request, he only does what the Jerusalem leadership had expected from the beginning, for they had never had any doubts about his observance of the law.

The Lukan meaning of the section is clear: Paul lived his life to the end as a faithful Jew. He was not guilty of transgressions against the law. On the contrary, he circumcised Timothy (Acts 16:3) and observed the prescriptions of the law during his last visit to Jerusalem.

It is of course noteworthy that any rumors at all circulated about Paul in Jerusalem, for in the previous rather Jewish descriptions of Paul in Acts there has been no reason for such rumors to grow. It must then necessarily be the case that these rumors were part of the tradition taken over by Luke, which the author of Acts strives to correct in the light of his own picture of Paul. (For additional discussion of the traditional materials in sections V and VI, see below, pp. 56f.).

VII. As Paul is completing the Nazirite ceremonies in the temple, he is discovered by Jews from Asia. They seize him and accuse him of teaching against the holy people, the law, and the temple. They charged him also with having brought a Greek, Trophimus, into the temple. Paul was saved by the Roman soldiers from the tumult that followed.

The significance of all of this from the redactional point of view is that the prophecy is fulfilled: Paul is handed over to the Gentiles by the Jews (Acts 21:11). Thereby the stage is set for the following apologetic speeches by Paul, which place all the blame in the quarrel between Christians and Jews on the latter and urgently commend Christianity to the Romans. The Lukan character of 21:28 can be seen in particular from the fact that (a) Paul's preaching against people, law, and temple is parallel to that of Stephen's (Acts 6:13) and (b) the civil authorities intervene to save Paul from the attacks of the Jews in accordance with the familiar schema (cf. Acts 18:14ff.).

3.3.3 Traditional Elements in Acts 21

I. The report has an itinerary as its source. The "we" style itself is not the evidence for this, however, but the summary character of the report. The details of the stay at the house of Philip probably formed a part of this source. Luke does not invent stories from whole cloth but elaborates his traditions. The report of the four prophetic daughters of Philip in all probability derives from tradition, for it is merely an interesting sidelight.

II. The Agabus story was also probably an element of the tradition that came to Luke. Redactional features are of course not to be overlooked: thus the form of the introductory participial construction (cf. v. 17!) and the content of the announcement that in Jerusalem Paul would be bound and delivered over to the Gentiles (see above, p. 53). In addition, the language of v. 10 is Lukan.[84] Still, the name Agabus and his prophetic activity were items that Luke received from the tradition. Of course the question immediately arises whether the story has been inserted at the correct chronological point, for in Acts 11:27ff. Agabus likewise appears in connection with a journey of Paul to Jerusalem, but this, however, should be regarded as an ideal, model journey[85]—constructed by Luke using individual traditions related to Paul's trips to Jerusalem. Thus the Agabus tradition is to be connected either with the conference journey (=Paul's second trip to Jerusalem) or with his last journey to Jerusalem.

III. The trip from Caesarea to Jerusalem and his lodging in the house of Mnason[86] derive from tradition. The following items of evidence support this hypothesis:

a. The redactional character of vv. 17ff. (see above)

b. The name Mnason

c. The interesting detail that Christians from Caesarea arranged for Paul's lodging in Jerusalem.

IV. The redactional character of this section was discussed above (pp. 53f.). The report, which can be verified from other sources,[87] that James was the leader of the Jerusalem church at the time of Paul's third visit to Jerusalem (v. 18)[88] also comes from tradition.

V, VI. The traditional character of this section was pointed out above. On a closer look, the following traditions become visible:

a. The Jerusalem church is composed of many (*myriades*) Jews[89] who are zealots for the law. This information stands in tension with Luke's previous description of the Jerusalem church.

b. Rumors are in circulation that Paul is teaching the Jews to abandon the law of Moses and dissuading them from circumcising their children (v. 21). In view of the (Jewish) picture of the apostle which Acts has so far provided the reader, these rumors are totally unexpected.[90]

c. Paul participates in a Jewish ceremony. The fact that the present form of the Lukan account contains contradictions indicates the presence of tradition. One could easily surmise that Luke has misunderstood his source.

If one takes the story as it stands, then it reports, first, of Paul's own Nazirite vow (vv. 24a, 26)[91] and, second, of his paying the ceremonial expenses of four Nazirites who are completing their vows (v. 24b; cf. v. 27).

But the Nazirite vow lasts at least thirty days, not seven, as Luke seems to assume (v. 27). The report of Paul's own Nazirite vow is probably a misunderstanding on the part of the author of Acts.[92] On the other hand, the report concerning paying the expenses for terminating the vows[93] of the four Nazirites probably does go back to tradition. Such an undertaking was regarded as an act of piety (cf. Josephus, *Ant.* 19.294) and had nothing to do with making a Nazirite vow as such. Finally, the specification of "seven days"[94] may go back to tradition. One could readily agree with E. Haenchen's placing this statement on the same level of tradition as that of Paul's visit to the temple: Paul had to make the necessary arrangements with the appropriate priests for assuming the expenses of the concluding sacrifices and, at the same time, since he had come from outside the holy land, had to be restored to cultic purity himself. "Paul accordingly . . . went with the four Nazirites to the Temple and there reported first his own purification (*hagnizesthai*) and secondly the *ekplērōsis tōn hēmerōn tou hagnismou* (of the Nazirite of the four). The date could then be fixed on which the appropriate sacrifices—for which Paul paid—were to be presented: it was the seventh day, on which he himself was to be cleared from guilt."[95]

VII. On "seven" as a traditional element, cf. the discussion immediately above.

The only remaining traditional element in our section is that of the name of Paul's companion Trophimus in v. 29 (cf. the list in Acts 20:4), where it must remain an open question whether the name was included in the source that Luke used for Paul's last visit to Jerusalem or was simply known to Luke from the list in Acts 20:4. Luke could have inferred everything else from the reports available to him. He thus knew of the arrest of the apostle in Jerusalem, the basis in tradition for which needs a more detailed investigation,[96] as does that of Paul's assumption of the expenses of the Nazirites in the temple (see above under V, VI). He could thus readily use that report as the occasion in his narrative for the tumult in the temple and the arrest of Paul. We thus come to the limit of the traditional materials that we can recover from this section.

After reconstructing the traditional elements in Acts 21, we must next ask whether they belong to a continuous source and, further, whether they can be regarded as historically reliable.

3.3.4 The Source Underlying Acts 21

When the redactional elements indicated above are taken into account, a source with the following outline appears:

Paul and his companions travel from Miletus via Caesarea to Jerusalem. He is provided lodging in Caesarea by the Hellenist Philip and in Jerusalem by the Hellenist Mnason.[97] In the Jerusalem congregation, which lived loyal to the law with James as its leader, Paul was a disputed figure, for rumors circulated that Paul was an antinomian and spoke against the circumcision of Jewish boys. Paul responded to such rumors by assuming the expenses of the four Nazirites. The source ends with Paul in the temple, where he had gone to purify himself.[98]

The train of thought just described is the best argument for accepting a connected source, for the report proceeds in a straight line, with no internal tensions or gaps.

3.3.5 The Historical Reliability of the Source

If we inquire concerning the historical reliability of the source, the answer must be unconditionally positive. The individual elements are confirmed as probable or at least possible by other reports independent of Acts 21.

Other sources confirm that during the decade of the fifties the Jerusalem church was led by James and was characterized by its Jewishness and commitment to the Torah.[99]

Paul's participation in a cultic act[100] is to be considered probable, on the basis of his understanding of Christian freedom.[101]

That the apostle was hospitably lodged by a Hellenistic Christian is quite possible because of his previous connection with Hellenistic circles.

Finally, the accusation against Paul expressed in v. 21 may also be historical and appropriately express the reservations of the Jerusalem Christians concerning Paul. In any case, it had a point of contact with what had happened in the Pauline churches. To be sure, in accordance with his own calling and the agreement worked out at the Jerusalem Conference, Paul preached primarily to Gentiles. In addition, none of his extant letters contains the kind of statement he is charged with in Acts 21:21.[102] It must, however, be immediately pointed out that the apostle expected Jewish Christians to forgo their observance of the dietary laws in their associations with Gentile Christians (cf. Gal. 2:11ff.) and in his letters several times teaches the unimportance of the law in comparison to the new creation in Christ (1 Cor. 7:19; Gal. 6:15). Could it fail to occur, then, that as a result of such praxis Jews were alienated from the law and ceased to circumcise their children?

Verse 21 thus certainly gives historically reliable information concerning the results of the Pauline preaching and its praxis among Jews and concerning the reservations that the Jerusalem church had concerning him.[103]

Our analysis of the traditions underlying Acts 21 can then be summarized as follows: Luke uses a connected source,[104] which in fact does deal with Paul's last trip to Jerusalem[105] and which is of great historical value.

The last observation, however, raises an issue to which we must direct our attention in the next section. The above discussion which indicates that a valuable historical source is reworked in Acts 21 forced the question: Why do we hear nothing in this chapter of the collection, which according to Paul's own testimony (Rom. 15:25f.) was delivered precisely at that time?

3.3.6 The Rejection of the Collection

Before we give the evidence for the thesis expressed in the title of this section, we will continue the outline of the events begun above up to the time of the delivery of the collection.

At the time of the Jerusalem Conference, Paul and Barnabas had promised in behalf of their churches to keep the poor of the Jerusalem church constantly in mind. In fulfillment of this agreement, Paul immediately began to organize a collection in his churches (Gal. 2:10b). For Paul, this economic support of the Jerusalem church by the Gentile churches had an ecclesiological significance, for it is a tangible demonstration of the (eschatological) unity of the one church composed of Jews and Gentiles. If the collection were to fall through, in Paul's understanding the theological existence of the Gentile churches would be endangered. It is thus no wonder that the (Jewish-Christian) opposition to Paul was eager to have the collection fail. There are indications that they were able to succeed in their intention:[106] thus the collection partly failed in Corinth and completely in Galatia. In Corinth, Paul was able to push the collection through, while in Galatia he seems to have lost the collection along with the churches.

We possess a priceless report concerning the collection from Paul's own hand from the time shortly before his departure for Jerusalem:

> Rom. 15:25f.: At present, however, I am going to Jerusalem with aid for the saints. For Macedonia and Achaia have been pleased to make some contribution for the poor among the saints at Jerusalem. Rom. 15:30f.: I appeal to you, brethren, by our Lord Jesus Christ and by the love of the Spirit, to strive together with me in your prayers to God on my behalf, that I may be delivered from the unbelievers in Judea, and that my service for Jerusalem may be acceptable to the saints.

Paul not only considers himself personally endangered by the unbelieving Jews but also considers the acceptance of the collection by the Jerusalem church to be threatened.[107] "Shortly before the project was completed, the danger that the collection would be refused in Jerusalem became so acute that Paul felt compelled to urge a congregation that had not even participated to pray that the collection would be well received."[108]

It is thus only consistent with this when Paul changes his original plans (1 Cor. 16:3: delegates from the churches will take the collection to Jerusalem) and decides to go to Jerusalem himself—a possibility that he had already pondered in 1 Cor. 16:4—in order to be sure that the collection[109] is accepted.[110]

After these considerations of the history leading up to the delivery of the collection we come to the real question relevant to our subject: If the only purpose of the final journey of the apostle to Jerusalem was to deliver the collection, why do we learn nothing of this in Acts 21?[111] In view of the results obtained in the previous section, we must immediately add that it appears that we must exclude the possibility that the source used in Acts 21 contained no reference to the collection,[112] which forces the question: Why did Luke *eliminate* any reference to the collection in this chapter?[113] (The urgency of this question becomes all the greater if—as is likely—a note concerning the purpose of Paul's last trip to Jerusalem is found in Acts 24:17.[114]) The only possible answer to this question is that Luke intentionally avoided any reference to the collection in Acts 21 because the source that he used reported the failure of Paul's attempt to deliver the offering, that is, that it was refused. For if the source had reported its acceptance, Luke would certainly have included this report (in this chapter!), since his primary purpose (21:17f.!) is to show the good relationship[115] between Paul and the Jerusalem church.[116] Instead, he removes the collection motif from Acts 21, where he had been afraid to report it, and combines it with other individual traditions into the narrative in 11:27ff., thus constructing a model trip of Paul to Jerusalem in the course of which Paul and Barnabas bring a collection to Jerusalem. (Of course even there nothing explicit is said about an *acceptance* of the collection!)

> For additional support of the above hypothesis[117] we may point out that in Acts 21 there is never a trace of any support for Paul from the Jerusalem church.[118] This obviously means that Luke had no such traditions available (cf., however, Acts 23:16), for if he had, he certainly would have made use of them. That leads one to suppose that, regarded historically, Paul found no support from the Jerusalem church, which fits in with the thesis argued above that the collection Paul had raised was rejected.

It thus appears from an analysis of Acts 21, especially with a view to the organization and delivery of the collection, that at the time of Paul's last trip to Jerusalem the church there stood completely within Judaism and had tolerated no abrogation of the law. Their passivity at the time of Paul's arrest and their rejection of the offering presented by the apostle to the Gentiles are, *on the one hand*, an expression of the fact that they considered the agreement struck between the Jerusalem church and the Pauline churches no longer to be valid. The basis for this may be tersely expressed in the rumor described in Acts 21:21: the Pauline preaching means the destruction of Judaism (cf. above, pp. 58–59, with n. 103). *On the other hand*, the attitude described above expresses the continuing relationship of the Jerusalem church to the Jewish people, which is confirmed by the fact that the community remained in the capital city until the time of the Jewish War.

In summary, only one answer is possible with regard to the question of the possible anti-Paulinism of the Jerusalem church under the leadership of James: from the time of the conference, at the latest, the Jerusalem church assumed a preponderately anti-Pauline attitude.[119] Their rejection of the collection, which only a few years before had been a bond of unity between the two churches, was a clear public indication of the hostility to Paul[120] of the Jerusalem church, from which James cannot be excluded.[121]

A concluding glance at the circumstances of the martyrdom of James can only strengthen the case already made above.

3.3.7 The Martyrdom of James

The martyrdom of James the brother of the Lord[122] occurred in the year 62 C.E., thus approximately five to ten years after the arrival of Paul in Jerusalem with the intention of delivering the collection. The report of Josephus, *Ant.* 20.197–203, provides a source[123] for the events which is probably quite reliable. (Hegesippus's account [in Eusebius, *Hist. Ecc.* 2.23] is a source for the way the event was understood by a later generation who looked back to James as their patriarch.)

The circumstances of the death of James were as follows: After the death of the procurator Festus, Nero appointed Albinus as his successor. In the interim, anarchy prevailed in Jerusalem. The younger Ananus[124]—a sympathizer with the Sadducees—took advantage of this situation to have James and a few others[125] brought before the Sanhedrin, charged them with violation of the law,[126] and had them stoned.[127] This act was to be the last in his three-month career as high priest. Residents of the city who, according to Josephus, were faithful to the law and highly respected (*epieikestatoi tōn kata tēn polin . . . kai peri tous nomous akribeis*, *Ant.* 20.201) took offense at Ananus's activities and brought secret charges against him to King Agrippa. Some of them even went to meet Albinus, who was on the way from Alexandria to Jerusalem, and told him that Ananus had not had the authority to call an assembly of the Sanhedrin without his permission. As a result, Albinus threatened to punish Ananus, while Agrippa deposed him.

In addition to theological reasons[128] (which, however, are not quite clear to us), Ananus's action against James and the others was based primarily on personal motives.[129] The view repeatedly expressed, that the measures taken against James were directed against his critique of the law, is incorrect if for no other reason than that James had the Jews who faithfully kept the law on his side.

If Josephus's comment that Ananus was a sympathizer with the Sadducees (*Ant.* 20.199) is trustworthy, then the protest can only have come from the other influential group,[130] the Pharisees.[131] Precisely the indignation that James's martyrdom evoked from them is additional evidence for his blameless[132] conduct within Judaism and—since James was the leading figure in the Jerusalem church—for the nomistic character of the Jerusalem Christians of that time.

Thus what we may infer from the martyrdom of James fits well into our observations on Acts 21.

Before we pose the question of whether the possibility of the Jerusalem church's having carried on an active opposition within the Pauline churches was also an actuality, as the conclusion of this chapter we must raise the question of what happened to this sort of Jerusalem Christianity during the Jewish War.

In the Appendix, I have argued that the tradition preserved in Eusebius's *Ecclesiastical History* which recounts the flight of the Jerusalem Christians to Pella tells us nothing about the destiny of the original Jerusalem congregation but—analogous to Hegesippus's legendary report of the martyrdom of James—throws light on the views of a later group of Jewish Christians.

What really happened to the Jerusalem church during the Jewish War? I consider it probable that the majority opposed the rebellion against Rome.[133] But that by no means implies a flight from Jerusalem, especially in view of the fact that the majority of the "peace party" likewise remained in Jerusalem. This means that we must seriously consider the possibility that the members of the Christian community, just like the Pharisees and the Sadducees who wanted peace, perished[134] in the war, in solidarity with their nation.[135]

4

ANTI-PAULINISM IN
THE PAULINE CHURCHES

The following discussion presupposes the results of my analysis in *Paul, Apostle to the Gentiles* on the order of Paul's letters written after the Jerusalem Conference: 1 Corinthians; 2 Corinthians; Galatians; and Romans. Philippians is discussed in conjunction with 2 Corinthians, although its chronological setting remains questionable. 1 Thessalonians is not analyzed, since it has no indications of anti-Paulinism,[1] nor is Philemon.

It would be helpful to remember at this point what was said earlier (pp. 31f.) concerning the method of reconstructing Paul's opponents: not everyone assailed by Paul had previously launched an attack on the apostle.[2] In order to arrive at results that may be controlled, we may use as data for the reconstruction of the views of Paul's opponents only those passages in which their views are unambiguously reflected. The ideal case is when Paul directly quotes his opponents' statements and indicates that they are directed against him. However, with all due caution we may also use, in a supplementary fashion, those passages which are of an apologetic nature and thus are in response to what can be regarded with some confidence as an attack on him.

In the following, both kinds of texts will be used[3] as the basis for our reconstruction.[4]

It should be clear that on methodological grounds the anti-Paulinism of each individual letter[5] is first to be reconstructed and analyzed on its own terms, that is, a reconstruction that will be oriented to the questions discussed above (pp. 31f.) with reference to the theology of its bearers and its possible Jewish-Christian character. At the same time, we need to note (a) possible interrelations between the individual attacks against Paul (in the same letter and between the different letters) and (b) possible parallels between the results obtained in chapters 2 and 3, all of this in carrying out the assignment of making the anti-Paulinism of each letter historically understandable.

4.1 1 CORINTHIANS[6]

In the following, we will analyze every passage in 1 Corinthians that unambiguously reflects an attack on the apostle and permits a reconstruction of the nature of the attack. After that, we will turn to those passages which, judged by the two criteria named above, are not so clear in what they allow us to see concerning the attacks made against Paul, in the hope that they can be illuminated by the unambiguous passages.

4.1.1 1 Corinthians 9

The abrupt beginning of v. 1 ("Am I not free?" [cf. below, n. 23]) has often given rise to literary-critical operations[7] on the text or sharpened the question of the connection of 1 Corinthians 9 with 1 Corinthians 8. However, before we turn to the latter question, it would be advisable, because of the subject matter, to ascertain what attacks against Paul are reflected in 1 Corinthians 9.

4.1.1.1 ANTI-PAULINISM IN 1 CORINTHIANS 9

In v. 3 Paul himself writes that people criticize (*anakrinein*) him and characterizes his response to them as an apology (*apologia*), which from v. 4 on[8] is developed in several rhetorical questions: Paul affirms that he has the authority/right (*exousia*)[9] (*a*) to eat and drink (v. 4), (*b*) to be accompanied by a Christian sister as his wife[10] (like the other apostles, the brothers of the Lord, and Cephas [v. 5]), and (*c*) to refrain from working (v. 6).

The final point is more carefully grounded in vv. 7–13.[11] In v. 12 we incidentally learn that Paul has not made use of his right not to work, in contrast to others who have claimed this *exousia* and have been supported by the Corinthian congregation (v. 12a; see below, p. 70). That right (=authority) is established by a dominical saying: *ho kyrios dietaxen tois to euangelion katangellousin ek tou euangeliou zēn* ("The Lord commanded that those who proclaim the gospel should get their living by the gospel"). All the same, Paul had not exercised his authority, in order not to "put an obstacle in the way of the gospel of Christ" (v. 12b) and because a necessity is placed upon him (vv. 16ff.).

In what relation do the series of rights and expressions of authority listed in (*a*) to (*c*) stand to each other?

All three rhetorical questions deal with the same issue, which is then broadly elaborated on from v. 6 on, namely, the support of the missionary by the congregation.[12] The items in (a) and (b) above should then each be supplemented with the understood phrase "at the expense of the congregation."[13]

Thus the following question arises: Why does Paul so emphatically point to his right to be supported by the congregation as his defense against his critics?

It seems to me the circumstances are to be described as follows: Paul's opponents correctly point out that Paul had not permitted himself to be supported by the Corinthian congregation—in contrast to themselves. Precisely for this reason, his status is inferior to theirs. Paul answers that he has the same *right and authority* to such support as do his critics, but he had, for his own good reasons, not exercised this right.[14] But this should be no reason at all for regarding him as of lesser status.

Thus this passage immediately raises the further question: What status was the dispute about?

The following reasons indicate that it was Paul's apostolic office that was in dispute:

1. Verses 4–6 contain two rhetorical questions and thus in fact make two affirmations: (a) Paul has the right and authority to be accompanied by a Christian wife as a sister on his missionary journeys and (b) Paul and Barnabas have the right and authority not to work. It should also be noted that these two statements are closely related to each other and in fact have a chiastic structure. Thus the groups mentioned in vv. 5c and 6a correspond to each other, just as do the statements that claim the right to be accompanied by a wife (v. 5a–b) and not to work (v. 6b). The chiastic structure indicates that Paul wants to compare the groups named in v. 5c and v. 6a with each other.

This is also pointed up by the emphatic *monos* (v. 6). What is the point of comparison? In my opinion, the key is given by *loipoi* of v. 5c: "*loipoi* makes a contrast with Paul (and Barnabas)."[15] That is, it is used from the perspective of Paul and intends to say: "the *rest of* the apostles besides me and Barnabas."[16]

2. Verse 2 already reflects a criticism. Since v. 3 continues without the introduction of a new theme, it is easy to suppose

that in vv. 4ff. the same point at issue is to be presupposed, namely, Paul's apostleship.

Thus if it is clear that Paul's apostolic office is the point at issue in vv. 4ff.,[17] then we may turn to vv. 1ff., where the same theme is dealt with.

Paul here poses the questions, "Am I not free? Am I not an apostle? Have I not seen Jesus our Lord? Are not you my workmanship in the Lord?" Probably the last two rhetorical questions are to document the claim of Paul to be an apostle expressed in the second one (on the first question, see below, p. 68). Paul's apostleship follows from his vision of the resurrected one and from the existence of the Corinthian church, of which he is the founder.

Now the final rhetorical question is added on, with the qualification: "If to others I am not an apostle, at least I am to you" (v. 2a). Then Paul emphasizes once again the significance of the existence of the Corinthian church for his apostleship: hē gar sphragis mou tēs apostolēs humeis este en kuriō (v. 2b).

The decisive sentence for the reconstruction of the opponents' statements is contained in v. 2a: ei allois ouk eimi apostolos, alla ge hymin eimi. "Ei, 'if,' can in itself be taken in a purely conditional sense. But the reality of the supposition is presumably included: 'if, as is in fact the case.'"[18]

One might at first be inclined to understand the preceding sentence to mean merely that Paul was not an apostle to others because they—in contrast to the Corinthians—had not received the Christian message from him. Over against this reading of the sentence stands the interpretation which is often advocated that 1 Cor. 9:2 reflects a blanket rejection of the Pauline apostleship as such (by "others").[19]

The possibility just named is the correct understanding, because the immediately following sentence speaks of critics of Paul (v. 3) and incites the apostle to apologetic (developed in vv. 4ff.).

The results of this section may now be summarized: Paul defends himself in 1 Cor. 9:1–18 against the attack that he is not an apostle. Against this, Paul appeals to his vision of Jesus and then to the existence of the Corinthian church founded by him. Finally—reaching rather far for the materials for his defense—

he neutralizes his critics' argument against his apostolicity occasioned by his renunciation of financial support from the Corinthian church.[20]

After this reconstruction of the position of the opponents, we now come to the question of the context of 1 Cor. 9:1b–18.

4.1.1.2 THE CONTEXT OF 1 CORINTHIANS 9:1b–18

As mentioned above, the relation of the question, "Am I not free?" (1 Cor. 9:1a), to that which immediately follows has been a difficult riddle for interpreters. At the same time, however, there has been unanimity that there is some sort of general connection between v. 1a and 1 Cor. 9:19ff., since vv. 19ff. have apostolic freedom as their theme. Cf. only v. 19: *Eleutheros gar ōn ek pantōn pasin emauton edoulōsa, hina tous pleionas kerdēsō.* It is only a step from the above analysis to discover with J. Jeremias that there is a chiastic structure in 1 Corinthians 9: Before Paul develops the ideas expressed in the first rhetorical question ("Am I not free?"), a second question is inserted, *ouk eimi apostolos?* which brings another idea into the foreground. Paul shares Christian freedom with all Christians, but beyond that he has a special position which gives him special prerogatives; he is a commissioned messenger of Christ. It is these prerogatives of the apostolic office and Paul's renunciation of them which Paul deals with in vv. 1c–18 (the third and fourth questions in v. 1 introduce these arguments). Only after this (vv. 19ff.) does he picture his voluntary renunciation of Christian freedom,"[21] which then leads back to 1 Corinthians 8. In the light of these considerations, 1 Corinthians 9 is then to be understood as an illustration of the idea expressed in 1 Corinthians 8 of consideration for the weak brother,[22] for Paul here gives two examples of his readiness to renounce his own rights for the sake of the other: (1) He renounces his freedom (cf. the concretization of this in vv. 20ff.), although it is precisely he who is the free man (vv. 1a, 19)[23] and (2) he renounces his right to support by the church(es), although he is an apostle.

4.1.1.3 THE THEOLOGY AND HISTORY OF THE ANTI-PAULINISM REFLECTED IN 1 CORINTHIANS 9

We have seen that in his own defense Paul introduces the theological arguments of his accusers in order to silence them by affirming that he has the *right* to support by the congregation. If we can now locate these arguments more precisely in terms of their history and the stream of tradition to which they belong, we will be able to obtain important information concerning the historical and theological context of the anti-Paulinism of 1 Corinthians 9.[24]

The views of the opposition reflected in 1 Corinthians 9 have an interesting parallel in the *commissioning traditions:*[25] 1 Cor. 9:4 (the authorization to eat and drink at the expense of the church) corresponds to Luke 10:7f.: *en autē de tē oikia menete esthontes kai pinontes to par' autōn . . . kai eis hēn an polin eiserchēsthe kai dechōntai hymas, esthiete ta paratithemena hymin.*[26] 1 Cor. 9:(4–6)14, the command of the Lord that the preacher of the gospel should live by the gospel, corresponds to Matt. 10:10b/Luke 10:7b: *axios gar ho ergatēs tēs trophēs/tou misthou autou.*

It is often assumed, in my opinion correctly, that the passages[27] introduced above derive from Q.[28] Of course, one will have to be careful not to identify the "theology of Q"[29] with that of the Pauline critics in 1 Corinthians 9. Q is too multilayered an entity, and the parallels between 1 Corinthians 9 and Q are too much a matter of individual detail to enable such an identification to be justified. All the same, we should continue to maintain that the traditions reflected in both Q and 1 Corinthians 9 indicate that there was a mission to Israel at the command of the exalted Lord, which was perhaps the continuation of a pre-Easter mission now carried out within an apocalyptic context. As has just been said, in its earliest phrase this mission was directed to the Jewish people.[30] Although there can be no doubt that the tradents of the Q materials later opened their mission to the Gentiles, it is difficult to decide whether the same can be said for the missionaries who stand in the background of 1 Corinthians 9 (see below, p. 113).

A critique of the law is not to be presupposed for the bearers of this mission. They are therefore to be designated as Jewish Christians in the sense defined above. In Corinth their views collided with those of Paul.

Thus at least a sketch of the theology of the anti-Paulinists of 1 Corinthians 9 can be presented—no more is possible because of the paucity of source material. In the following we will thus inquire whether it is possible to locate them more precisely in the general (church) history otherwise known to us.

In 1 Cor. 9:5b Paul contrasts two groups of missionaries:

1. The rest of the apostles, the brothers of Jesus, and Cephas.
2. Paul and Barnabas.

Paul classifies his critics with the first group, for he sets himself and Barnabas in contrast to them: $\bar{e}$ *monos egō kai Barnabas* (v. 6). This does not mean that the anti-Paulinists are identical with the persons named in group 1.[31] But they probably appealed to this group against Paul in the following way: Paul has no apostolic status, since he does not claim the right to support by the church as is done by the legitimate apostles, the brothers of the Lord, and Cephas. It thus appears that this right has also been claimed in Corinth by Paul's critics, as can be inferred from 1 Cor. 9:12a: "If others share this rightful claim upon you, do not we still more?" (see further on this below, pp. 74f.).

Additional historical light is thrown on the two groups of missionaries named in v. 6 by the observation that they have a parallel in the "agreement" reached at the Jerusalem Conference: compare the formula given in Gal. 2:9, "We [Paul, Barnabas] to the Gentiles // they [James, Cephas, John] to the Jews," with 1 Cor. 9:5f.: the rest of the apostles, the brothers of Jesus, Cephas // Paul, Barnabas.[32]

Because of the partial verbatim agreement of the names cited in both texts and the identical arrangement of their grouping, I consider it certain that Paul has the conference agreement in view in 1 Cor. 9:5f. The difference between "James and Cephas and John" (Gal. 2:9) and "the other apostles and the brothers of the Lord and Cephas" (1 Cor. 9:5) is of little weight, since the triad of Gal. 2:9 doubtless is representative of other missionaries who carried on their evangelistic work under their banner. It must be considered probable that after the leadership of the Jerusalem church was taken over by James, it was to be expected that other brothers of Jesus would have assumed prominent leadership roles. The only difficulty in relating the formula in Gal. 2:9 with that of 1 Cor. 9:5 consists in the lack of the name "John" in 1 Corinthians. But he could still, of course, be included in the group of the "other apostles."

In addition, this group also possibly included the anti-Pauline missionaries whose arguments Paul resists in 1 Corinthians 9.

They were present in Corinth, allowed themselves to be supported by the congregation there, and attacked Paul's apostolic status because he did not do so (see further on this below, p. 80).

4.1.1.4 QUESTIONS THAT REMAIN OPEN

After the above historical and theological classification of the anti-Paulinism of 1 Corinthians 9, in conclusion we will look once again at the attacks against Paul reflected in that chapter, which, in my opinion, denied apostolic status to him because of his renunciation of his claims to support by the church. The vocabulary of 1 Cor. 9:5 and Gal. 2:9 places the interpreter before the following two problems:

a. Gal. 2:9 mentions neither the apostleship of the Jerusalem leaders (James, Cephas, John) nor that of Paul (and Barnabas).

b. 1 Cor. 9:5 appears to attribute apostleship neither to the brothers of Jesus nor to Cephas.

These two observations could lead to the conclusion that 1 Cor. 9:4ff. is not at all concerned with apostleship but with missionary strategy or the like.[33]

Concerning *a:* That the apostleship of the Jerusalem leaders does not explicitly appear in the "formula of concord" does not prove that they did not claim the apostolic title for themselves. Rather, it is to be presupposed as something assumed (cf. for Cephas Gal. 2:8; for James 1 Cor. 15:7), although they did not wish to attribute the apostolic title to Paul (see above, pp. 37–38).

Concerning *b:* 1 Cor. 9:5 excludes neither the brothers of Jesus nor Cephas from the apostolic office.[34] The opposite assumption (which at first glance might seem more nearly correct) is unlikely if only because Cephas, according to other statements from Paul (Gal. 1:18f.; 2:8), was an apostle. Thus an explanation needs to be sought for the fact that Peter's apostleship is not specifically mentioned in this passage. It seems to me that Lietzmann was exactly on target when he discovered that 1 Cor. 9:5 is the climactic point of a series and explains the emphatic place of Peter at the end of the triad on the basis that "Peter's conduct is emphasized, since he had obviously been used as the counter-example of an 'authentic' apostle over against Paul."[35] If Peter is thus to be reckoned among the apostles on the basis of our passage, then the brothers of Jesus cannot be excluded from this group by appealing to 1 Cor. 9:5.[36]

In any case, the objection that 1 Cor. 9:4ff. could not be concerned with apostleship is to be dismissed.

Parenthetically we may note that the preceding dismissal of an objection at the same time provides a point of contact for our understanding what concerned *Paul* in his defense. To be sure, the opponents had not (yet) attacked Paul with regard to the agreement worked out at the Jerusalem Conference. All the same, we observe that Paul so understood the Jerusalem "formula of concord" that his apostolic status was there acknowledged. One indication of this is the expression *hoi loipoi apostoloi* (cf. above, pp. 70f.). When Paul writes, "Do we not have the right to be accompanied by a wife, as the *other* apostles . . . ?" the expression "the *other* apostles" is obviously used from Paul's own standpoint so that one can appropriately add: "the other apostles except *me* [and Barnabas]."[37]

Apart from the attack against Paul's apostleship on the basis of his renunciation of his right to support by the church, no further attack against him can be verified in 1 Corinthians 9. (Still, this passage remains important as a Pauline indication of the historical origins of the opposition to Paul, and we will have occasion to look at it again.) Whether this passage indicates that his opponents already disputed the validity of his vision of Christ (cf. 1 Cor. 9:1) cannot be decided, since in this chapter the apostle discusses only his renunciation of support.

These comments may form a transition to the second passage in 1 Corinthians that reflects anti-Pauline arguments.

4.1.2 1 Corinthians 15:1–11[38]

The results obtained above (pp. 46ff.) in the discussion of 1 Cor. 15:1–11 from the point of view of the history of traditions are here presupposed.

4.1.2.1 ANTI-PAULINISM IN 1 CORINTHIANS 15:1–11

The following consideration speaks in favor of an anti-Pauline tradition in this text and its use in Corinth: Paul defends his apostleship in vv. 8ff. That the subject of debate in Corinth and the object of Paul's proof by means of the list of witnesses[39] was Paul's apostleship, and not the resurrection of Jesus, is already to be inferred from the extent to which Paul speaks about his apostolic office (seven Nestle lines in comparison to eight Nestle lines for the whole traditional unit plus its additions). The apolo-

72

getic character of the section is further confirmed by the apologetic character of the declaration, "I have worked more than all others" (v. 10b).[40]

In v. 7b there is the statement that Jesus had appeared to James and *all* the apostles. In flat contradiction to this stands the statement of Paul's which follows, that last of all Jesus had appeared to him, the least of the apostles. It is not "still quite innocently" that Paul here calls himself the *elachistos tōn apostolōn*,[41] for he is seeking to assert his apostleship over against a tradition according to which the apostolic circle was already closed *before his own conversion*. In fact, he even indirectly strengthens this tradition, in that he describes himself as the "miscarriage" (*ektrōma*) among the apostles.[42]

The question is immediately raised whether Paul is only defending his apostleship over against the tradition expressed in v. 7 or whether his apology is also formulated with the previously mentioned persons (Cephas, the Twelve, the five hundred brethren) in view. The answer to this question is dependent on the referent of *pantōn* in v. 8 and v. 10: v. 8: *eschaton de pantōn ōphthē kamoi . . . perissoteron autōn pantōn ekopiasa*. U. Wilckens refers to *pantōn* in both cases to the *pasin* of v. 7 because of their mutual proximity.[43] That can hardly persuade. Over against the suspicions and challenges, Paul wants to affirm in 1 Cor. 15:1–11 that his vision of the risen Christ was of the same quality as that of the other witnesses and thus extends the list that had been delivered to them as a part of the traditional formula at the time of the founding of the church up to his own time, including himself.[44] Thus it is better to see the *pantōn* of vv. 8 and 10 as referring to the whole list of witnesses.

But Wilcken's thesis has an element of truth in that Paul in 1 Cor. 15:1–11 must make his affirmations over against *apostles*. But this includes all the persons[45] mentioned[46] in vv. 5–7 for each of them had seen the Lord, and the formula of 1 Cor. 15:7, which includes each of them, had regarded the apostolic circle as closed. Thus Paul could not have seen the Lord.

4.1.2.2 ON THE THEOLOGY AND HISTORY OF THE ANTI-PAULINISM REFLECTED IN 1 CORINTHIANS 15

Historically, it is worthy of note that the anti-Paulinism of 1 Corinthians 15 is related to Jerusalem personages (Cephas, the five hundred brethren, James). Two possibilities of relating the anti-Paulinism and the Jerusalem figures immediately present themselves: either they, or some of them, are attacking Paul or others are attacking Paul under the authority of the Jerusalem authorities.

The second possibility is probably to be preferred, because in 1 Cor. 15:11 Paul includes himself harmoniously in the group of witnesses: "Whether then it was I or they, so we preach and so you believed."

Thus with regard to the advocates of the anti-Paulinism reflected in 1 Cor. 15:1–11, no exact statement can be made on the basis of the passage itself. Of course we do have some basis for assuming that the anti-Paulinism of 1 Corinthians 15 belongs with that of 1 Corinthians 9 and that it was carried on by the same people.

4.1.3 A Comparison of the Anti-Paulinism Reflected in 1 Corinthians 9 and 15

A comparison of the anti-Paulinism reflected in these two passages reveals the following noteworthy items:

1. In both instances Paul sees himself as dealing with people who dispute his apostolic authority. The arguments are different in each case: the basis of the objection in 1 Corinthians 9 was his refusing to accept support from the church, while in 1 Corinthians 15 it was argued that the apostolic circle had already been closed before Paul was converted.

2. The disputing of Paul's apostleship occurs each time with some reference to the Jerusalem authorities (1 Corinthians 9: the rest of the apostles, the brothers of Jesus, Cephas; 1 Corinthians 15: Cephas, the five hundred brethren, James, all the apostles).

3. In both cases Paul uses the same arguments to defend himself: (a) he appeals to his vision of Christ (9:1; 15:8) and (b) he introduces his missionary work as confirmation (9:1f.; 15:10).

In my opinion, these three points make the conclusion necessary that the anti-Paulinism of 1 Corinthians 9 and the anti-Paulinism of 1 Corinthians 15 belong together and thus that its advocates belong to one and the same group.

After these observations we may now turn to a further (and final) complex of texts in 1 Corinthians.

4.1.4 Anti-Paulinism in 1 Corinthians 1—4

It was shown above that for F. C. Baur the party slogans in the first four chapters of 1 Corinthians were an important aspect of the evidence that an anti-Pauline party had developed in Corinth. We have reserved treatment of these chapters until here, however, since they reflect no explicit polemic against Paul and because the reconstruction of the opposition movement—if possible at all—meets with incomparably greater difficulties.

Paul had heard from Chloe's people (1:11)[47] that in Corinth some described themselves as belonging to Paul, others as belonging to Apollos, and still others as belonging to Peter.[48] In 1 Cor. 3:22 the triad appears again, while in 1 Cor. 3:4 and 4:6 the apostle speaks only of himself and Apollos. These party slogans did not lead to real divisions[49] within the congregation or to groups splitting off from it[50] but merely reflect the special esteem in which the respective leaders were held by groups within one and the same congregation.[51]

Can these party slogans be brought into relationship with anti-Paulinism? If so, which?

It should be clear from the beginning that the slogan "I belong to Paul" reflects no attack against Paul. But one must immediately add that the slogan "I belong to Paul" is conceivable only as a reaction to other members of the congregation who expressed their solidarity with someone else regarded as the founder of the congregation.[52]

We are thus left with only two slogans as possible candidates for anti-Paulinism: "I belong to Apollos" and "I belong to Cephas."

The problem is now to obtain controllable results on the issue of whether these formulae can be brought into relation to anti-Paulinism in Corinth, even if they themselves do not positively reflect it. This question can be answered affirmatively only if criticism against Paul can be demonstrated in the rest of Paul's statements in 1 Corinthians 1—4 which are bound up with these slogans.

We will thus now make an exploratory examination to inquire after possible anti-Pauline reflections in the context of the slogans mentioned above.

These slogans are in part taken up again in 3:4. Paul here thematically discusses his relation to Apollos and describes it as reciprocal: he himself planted, Apollos watered (3:6). In view of this common service in the cultivation of God's vineyard, the church, slogans that magnify Paul or Apollos at the expense of the other are inappropriate.

In 1 Cor. 4:6 Paul once again speaks of himself and Apollos: the example of Paul and Apollos should teach members of the congregation not to "be puffed up in favor of one against another." Both Paul and Apollos have faithfully accepted their assigned tasks as servants of Christ and stewards of the mysteries of God. Paul is thus unconcerned with whatever judgment the Corinthians may make concerning him, for he is obligated to the Lord alone, to whom he will be responsible in the last judgment.[53]

It seems to me that the (positive) manner in which Paul speaks of Apollos and himself in both passages already casts doubt on the assumption that followers of Apollos had attacked Paul.[54] The ultimate objection, of course, can first be seen in 1 Cor. 16:12: the question as to when Apollos would return to Corinth is supposed to have come from the Apollos party. If this presupposition is correct, then the assumption of hostility to Paul from the Apollos group falls apart internally: one hardly inquires from an opponent when the "real" leader will return to Corinth.[55]

If hostility to Paul is excluded from the Apollos party, there remains the question of whether the Cephas party was anti-Pauline.[56] The question is all the more urgent, since Paul in no passage in 1 Corinthians 1—4 emphasizes his agreement with Cephas, which has caused many scholars to conclude that Paul did not appeal to Cephas because they were not (any longer) in agreement. Rather, it is supposed that in 3:11f. Paul indirectly polemicizes against Cephas, for the saying about the only foundation, Christ, is a polemic against the "rock," Peter. This interpretation is supposed to be confirmed by the fact that the immediate context sets forth Paul and Apollos as the true servants of Christ. But if Cephas was in opposition to Paul at the time of 1 Corinthians, it follows that the Cephas party would have had a similar attitude.[57] If the theses just described were correct, then

76

the origin of the Paul and Cephas parties could be explained as a reaction to the founding of the Cephas party.[58]

Is the hypothesis expressed above historically correct?

It seems to me difficult to avoid the conclusion that Paul is in fact polemicizing against Cephas. This interpretation is supported in the first place, as just mentioned, by the connection between Cephas and *themelios* (v. 11). It can be further supported by form-critical and literary arguments:

Verses 6–9 are parallel to vv. 10–17:[59]

Verse 6 speaks of Paul's founding the church at Corinth and of Apollos's subsequent constructive work on the foundation laid by Paul. Verse 10, which speaks of "another" who builds on Paul's foundation, fits Apollos exactly, though speaking only indirectly of him.

Verse 7 emphasizes the unity of the founder and the one who builds on his work. The negative counterpart to this is found in vv. 10bff., which emphatically warn those who build on Paul's work.

Verse 8 contains an eschatological perspective: both the founder and the one who builds on his work will receive their respective rewards. Verses 12–15 then correspond to this. Here, however, the eschatological perspective is developed further, as the threat of punishment is placed parallel to the promise of reward (although here too the person subject to the threat will finally be saved). Again in vv. 12ff. there appears an anonymous person who builds on the work of the founder of the congregation.

Verse 9 describes Apollos and Paul as co-workers with God and the church at Corinth as God's building. The parallel to this is found in vv. 16f., where the congregation is named God's temple. It is characteristic of this section that it lacks any statement about the unity of founder and builder such as is made in v. 9. In its place is the shrill warning against those who destroy the temple of God.

The preceding comparison between vv. 6–9 and vv. 10–17 confirms the judgment of H. Lietzmann: "The discussion in vv. 10–15 is parallel to what is said in vv. 6–9, only somewhat elaborated."[60] It is elaborated by the pronouncement of judgment on those who do not carry forward the work of Paul in an appropriate manner. It should be mentioned in addition that vv. 16–17 belong with vv. 10–15 as one unit, contrary to Lietzmann (see above).

I consider it probable that vv. 10ff. contain a veiled polemic against Cephas. After Paul has described his relation to Apollos, he naturally turns to address his relation to Cephas, since obviously some Corinthians described themselves as belonging to him. The best indication that he is speaking about a definite person is given by the parallel structure between vv. 6–9 and vv. 10–17. The definite person is in all probability Cephas, since Paul again (after 1:14) deals with the factions, and the triad Paul, Apollos, Cephas again appears in the immediate context (3:223). Thus P. Vielhauer is, in my opinion, correct when he argues that in 1 Cor. 3:10ff. Paul polemicizes against Cephas and thereby against the Cephas party which had been formed in Corinth after Paul's departure (Vielhauer, "Kephaspartei," pp. 348f.).

If, after this long prolegomenon, we now ask whether the Cephas party had polemicized against Paul, the answer must be a cautious "yes." To be sure, 1 Corinthians 1—4 does not permit any reconstruction of the content of this polemic. But the existence of a Petrine polemic against Paul can scarcely be doubted, because, to express it briefly: (1) Paul does not appeal to his unity with Cephas, and (2), instead, Cephas is subjected to a veiled attack.

But in conclusion it must be admitted that of the three passages analyzed above, 1 Corinthians 1—4 provides the weakest indications of anti-Paulinism.[61]

Because of the paucity of data concerning anti-Paulinism in the first four chapters of 1 Corinthians, it is hardly possible to pose more precise questions dealing with its theology and history.[62] It can, however, be affirmed that the greatest probability lies with seeing the anti-Paulinism of the Cephas party in a genetic connection with that of 1 Corinthians 9 and 1 Corinthians 15, for in all three instances appealing to Peter while criticizing Paul plays an important role. This observation provides an interesting clue to the question to be posed next concerning the origin and occasion of the anti-Paulinism in Corinth and its bearers.

4.1.5 Concerning the Occasion and Origin of
Anti-Paulinism in Corinth. Its Bearers

Thus far the questions of how, when, and why anti-Paulinism arose in Corinth have been left open. Dealing with them can no longer be postponed.

According to H. Conzelmann,[63] it is unnecessary to presuppose outside influence to account for the slogan "I belong to Cephas." Since in fact the person of Peter had been an integral part of the (foundational) kerygma of 1 Cor. 15:5, those who paid special honor to Peter could have come together spontaneously. But if this had been the case, the acceptance of an anti-Paulinism among the advocates of Cephas, as argued above, would be superfluous. Conzelmann's thesis may remain as a wholesome corrective over against studies that are overzealous in their use of the category "influence"[64] in the scholarly debate over the identity and nature of "opponents" in the New Testament. But this thesis is finally to be considered unlikely, since there is good evidence for an anti-Pauline attitude of the advocates of Cephas[65] and because the anti-Paulinism behind 1 Corinthians 1—4 is integrally related to that of 1 Corinthians 9, where influence from outside is clearly visible.[66]

The Cephas party thus appears to have been the bearer of the anti-Paulinism[67] in Corinth at the time of 1 Corinthians.[68]

This thesis receives some support through the fact that in 1 Corinthians 9 Cephas is conspicuously named in the last place, although he belongs to the apostolic group previously mentioned (see above, p. 75).

How did the Cephas party originate? Paul provides a hint in 1 Cor. 9:12 (cf. the discussion above, p. 70): this verse stands in the context of Paul's defense of his right to support by the church. Just because Paul does not exercise the right does not mean that he does not have it. This practice of Paul's should not be used as an argument against his apostleship. Paul writes in v. 12a: *ei alloi tēs hymōn exousias metechousin, ou mallon hēmeis?* "Thus in fact others . . . have made use of the apostolic claim to be supported by the church."[69] Since the cited verse stands in the context of anti-Pauline, Jewish-Christian (see above, p. 69) objections to Paul, the *alloi* are Jewish-Christian missionaries[70] who use Cephas's example against Paul and make apostolic claims for themselves (they let the congregation support them!) and challenge Paul's apostolic status. They had of course already left Corinth at the time of the writing of 1 Corinthians. But their advent in Corinth had led to the formation of a Cephas party among the Gentile Christians, who from then on represented a nucleus of Jewish-Christian criticism of Paul in Corinth.[71]

The anti-Pauline Cephas party was of some considerable significance for the group dynamics at work in the following period of the life of the Corinthian church. Its existence led to the formation of other parties. It will have then contributed to the partial alienation between the founder of the congregation and the congregation itself, as becomes visible from such passages as 1 Cor. 4:18; 7:40, and from Paul's criticism of Corinthian enthusiasm (1 Cor. 4:6ff.; 5:2; 8:1; chaps. 12—14).[72] To be sure, the enthusiasts were not anti-Paulinists. On the contrary! They adopted Paul's ideas and developed them further.[73] But once an anti-Pauline faction had arisen in Corinth, and once Paul had reacted negatively to individual features of the Pauline enthusiasts, then the danger was present that sooner or later both factions would unite against Paul.

These observations thus form the transition to the issue of anti-Paulinism in 2 Corinthians.

4.2 2 CORINTHIANS

4.2.1 Literary Criticism (Source Analysis) and Its Significance for the Subject

It would hardly be meaningful to give here a detailed report of the literary-critical problems of 2 Corinthians. They would be discussed here only if they were important for the subject at hand and if they would have decisive effects on the results of our study. That appears, however, not to be the case, for independently of partition theories of every sort,[74] the extent text of 2 Corinthians derives from a period of a year at the most, so that it is to be presupposed at the outset that the letters or letter fragments that comprise our 2 Corinthians more or less belong to the same complex of materials. This indicates that we should proceed from the text as we have it and to analyze it in accord with the method presented above, without side glances at literary-critical theories. In addition, we shall in the process discuss those events which betray anti-Paulinism, to the extent that they can be reconstructed from the prehistory of 2 Corinthians, even if they are not dealt with directly in 2 Corinthians.[75]

4.2.2 The *Adikēsas*[76]

After Paul had received unfavorable reports concerning the circumstances in the Corinthian churches, he changed the travel plans he had already declared in 1 Corinthians 16 and sailed immediately for Corinth.[77] During this visit (en *lupē*) Paul discovered circumstances in Corinth that were very distressing for him, and after only a brief stay he rushed precipitously back to Ephesus. Here he wrote the famous tearful letter, which brought the church back to his side again.

With this we arrive at the question whether some anti-Pauline action occurred during this intermediate visit of the apostle, and if so, why?

In 2 Cor. 1:23 and 2:4f., Paul describes, in reference to the tearful letter, what had happened: during his brief visit, a member of the congregation was guilty of some *adikia* against Paul and had offended and distressed the apostle (and the whole congregation, in reality). After receiving the tearful letter, the congregation had punished the offender, upon which Paul besought the congregation to forgive him and, even more than that, to treat him with Christian love (2:6–8).

There can be no doubt that the *adikēsas* had carried on agitation against Paul. But we cannot determine any details concerning the incident. In any case, the *adikēsas*[78] is not the incestuous person of 1 Corinthians 5,[79] and it is *certain* that the *adikēsas* has nothing more to do with the opposition against Paul which comes to light elsewhere in 2 Corinthians. For in Paul's perspective, that incident is over and settled, but the other opposition is still in full swing at the time 2 Corinthians is written.

At the end of this section we need only add that it is unlikely that the *adikēsas* was of Jewish-Christian origin. Since the congregation was predominately Gentile Christian, it is more likely that the offending party was also a Gentile Corinthian Christian.

4.2.3 Paul's Vacillation with Regard to His Travel Plans

Additional anti-Pauline charges derive from the period between 1 and 2 Corinthians, or were still held up to Paul at the time of the writing of 2 Corinthians: in 2 Cor. 1:15ff. Paul defends himself against the charge that his alteration of the travel plans[80] announced in 1 Corinthians 16 betrays vacillation on his part (2 Cor. 1:17). The following data speak for the fact that the expression "vacillation" (elaphria) was a Corinthian charge against Paul:

a It stands in an apologetic context.

b It is a hapax legomenon in the Pauline corpus and in the New Testament.

The additional circumstances connected to the charge are unfortunately not available. Of course this charge has nothing necessarily to do with Jewish Christianity.

4.2.4 Defrauding the Corinthian Church
by Means of the Collection

In 2 Cor. 7:2b Paul emphatically states that he has not corrupted or taken advantage of anyone (oudena ephtheiramen, oudena epleonektēsamen). It is hardly possible to infer anything with regard to anti-Pauline charges on the basis of this passage alone. But since the key word pleonektein recurs in 2 Cor. 12:17f.,[81] it may throw light on 2 Cor. 7:2b: Paul asks rhetorically whether he has taken advantage of the church through Titus and those sent with him. This charge of being cheated and taken advantage of refers to the collection, in the service of which the apostle had already sent Titus once before—Titus, whom he was ready to send to Corinth with the same service at the time of the writing of 2 Corinthians (see chap. 8—9).

In 2 Cor. 8:20 Paul expresses his fear that he might become suspect in Corinth because of the large sum of money he is administering (mē tis hēmas mōmēsetai en tē hadrotēti tautē tē diakonoumenē hyph' hēmōn) and thus takes precautions to ward off any such charge: he sends a tried-and-true brother with Titus to Corinth. In addition, delegates from other churches[82] accompany Titus (8:23), one of whom is the brother already mentioned, to make it clear that no misuse of the funds in the collection will take place.

Here too, in this charge that Paul has taken advantage of the church by means of the collection, no Jewish-Christian influence can be detected. Nor can any decision be made as to whether the charge is a result of influence from outside. But it appears more probable that the charge had a Corinthian origin.

4.2.5 Paul's Deficiency as a Pneumatic

There is a series of passages in 2 Corinthians that more or less clearly reflect criticism against Paul for his lack of spiritual powers:

2 Cor. 10:1 (probably a quotation):[83] Paul is "humble (*tapeinos*) when face to face with you, but bold to you when absent." The assumption that the sentence is a direct quotation is confirmed by 2 Cor. 10:10: "For they say, 'His letters are weighty and strong, but his bodily presence is weak, and his speech of no account,'" for it is clear that Paul here quotes a slogan directed against him.[84]

The same theme is taken up again in 2 Corinthians 13:

> 2 Cor. 13:1–3: "This is the third time I am coming to you. Any charge must be sustained by the evidence of two or three witnesses. I warned those who sinned before and all the others, and I warn them now while absent, as I did when present on my second visit, that if I come again I will not spare them—since you desire proof that Christ is speaking in me. He is not weak in dealing with you, but is powerful in you."

The last sentence shows that those addressed are pneumatics (Christ is mighty in them). They demand proof that the same is also true for Paul. Until it is brought forward, they must hold up the objection that he is lacking in spiritual power.

Finally, 2 Cor. 12:1–10[85] also belongs to the topic "Paul's lack of spiritual powers." With the statement *eleusomai de eis optasias kai apokalypseis kyriou* (2 Cor. 12:1), Paul here turns to a new subject in the letter, but a subject occasioned by the Corinthian situation.[86] In 2 Cor. 12:2–8 he wants to show that he also is capable of boasting of visions and revelations of the Lord. Obviously this had been denied in Corinth. It would have been an aspect of the charge of "weakness" (2 Cor. 10:10, see above) that Paul could produce no visions and revelations.[87]

All of the passages introduced above thus reflect the same charge against Paul: he did not possess the Spirit. When this is recognized as the content of the anti-Pauline position, then other passages such as 2 Cor. 10:7, 11; 11:6 come to light. In addition, one passage from 1 Corinthians is illuminated (7:40), for it possibly reflects the earliest beginnings of Corinthian criticism against Paul because of his lack of possession of the Spirit (to be discussed immediately below).

We now come to the question of whether this anti-Pauline charge is Jewish-Christian and how it can be understood historically. For the moment, neither a positive nor a negative answer can be given to the first question, for it is dependent on how the historical origin of the charge is regarded. Two possibilities must be taken into consideration: (a) the possibility of internal Corinthian origin and (b) the possibility of an external origin.

4.2.5.1 CORINTHIAN SOURCE OF THE CHARGE

At the time of the writing of 1 Corinthians, a considerable element in the Corinthian church could already be addressed as "spiritual." Paul resists some aspects of this fascination with spiritual powers in 1 Cor. 4:6ff.; 5:2; chap. 8; chaps. 12—14. But there is no reason to suppose that when 1 Corinthians was written, there was a connection between anti-Paulinism and the Corinthians' interest in spiritual powers,[88] while it is the case that these two had been united by the time of the writing of 2 Corinthians. On the one hand, it can be understood entirely as an inner-Corinthian phenomenon, for already in 1 Corinthians the first signs of an alienation between Paul and the Corinthians begin to appear (cf. 4:18: "Some are arrogant, as though I were not coming to you"). If the tines had thought "Paul does not dare to show himself in Corinth again because of his own consciousness of his inferiority,"[89] this comes rather close to the charge reflected in 2 Corinthians that Paul lacked the powers of the Spirit. If we take account of Paul's countercriticism to such an attitude, and the other changes in the relationship of the Corinthians to Paul (see the formation of the Cephas party), then a sharpening of the situation is imaginable and the explicit criticism of Paul on the points mentioned above could readily be understood.

4.2.5.2 EXTERNAL SOURCE OF THE CHARGE

The citation mentioned above (2 Cor. 10:10: "His letters are weighty and strong, but his bodily presence is weak") is found in a context that refers to persons outside the congregation, persons who commend themselves. With such people Paul does not wish to compare himself (v. 12). The same group is envisaged in 2 Cor. 3:1.[90] From these passages it is clear that members of this group had come to Corinth with letters of recommendation and that Corinth had equipped them with additional such letters. 2 Cor. 10:10 thus appears to document the case that this (external) circle of persons had directed attention to the weakness of Paul's public appearance and had used it as an argument against him.

This verse casts some light on 2 Cor. 12:1–10 which is part of the larger unit of 2 Cor. 10:12—12:18, all of which is related to the charge found in 2 Cor. 10:10. In this section Paul defends himself against the claims of the external anti-Paulinists (cf. 2 Cor. 12:19) and sets forth his meaning of "boasting" in a positive manner. Thus 2 Cor. 12:1–12 shows that Paul had also received visions and revelations (although he would prefer to boast in his weaknesses, 2 Cor. 12:9).

This conclusion is strengthened by 2 Cor. 12:11. Here Paul affirms that he is in no way inferior to these superlative apostles (*hoi hyperlian apostoloi*). "The signs of a true apostle were performed among you in all patience, with signs and wonders and mighty works" (v. 12). Independently of the group to which the "superlative apostles" may be assigned (see below), it is clear that Paul's claim to "the signs of an apostle" is a response to external claims from others. His statement that he should rather be commended by the Corinthians probably refers to the letters of recommendation that the Corinthians had provided for the external anti-Paulinist, already mentioned in 3:1 and 10:12. Thus the reference to Paul's deficiency in the signs of an apostle derive from an anti-Pauline group outside the Corinthian church.[91]

Finally, one additional passage in 2 Corinthians throws light on the issue discussed here and confirms the conclusions already drawn. In 2 Cor. 11:5f. Paul writes that he is in no way inferior to these superlative apostles and continues: "Even if I am unskilled in speaking, I am not in knowledge" (v. 6). The expression *idiōtēs tō logō* is too strongly reminiscent of the phrase *logos exouthenēmenos* of 10:10 to be independent of it— both phrases have the same origin. In addition, the claim to stand on the same plane as the "superlative apostles" appears in both 11:5 and 12:11.

We can thus say by way of summary that Paul was also attacked from outside with the charge that he lacked spiritual powers. At the time of the writing of 2 Corinthians, inner-Corinthian and extra-Corinthian opposition to Paul were in agreement. In fact, this provides a partial explanation of how it could happen at all that the external opposition could conduct such a successful agitation against Paul at the time he was writing 2 Corinthians. In the following section we will attempt to determine the identity of this external opposition more precisely. We are presupposing only that the external anti-Paulinism visible in 2 Corinthians all belongs to *one* party.

4.2.6 Historical-Theological Evaluation of the External Anti-Pauline Opposition of 2 Corinthians

We will first list the characteristics and traits that can be assigned to the opponents with certainty, and immediately after each item we will raise the question of how it is to be evaluated historically and theologically.

4.2.6.1 THE HONORIFIC TITLES OF THE ANTI-PAULINISTS

The opponents are Hebrews, Israelites, seed of Abraham, servants of Christ[92] (2 Cor. 11:22f.). The first three predicates point to the Jewish origin[93] of the anti-Paulinists, the final one to the fact that they belong to the Christian movement. It is not possible to infer a Jerusalem or even a Palestinian origin for these anti-Paulinists on the basis of these three self-designations, because they were current also in extra-Palestinian Judaism[94] —with a view to emphasizing the separateness of the elect people (cf. Bauer, *Lexicon*, s.v.).

4.2.6.2 THE ANTI-PAULINISTS AS APOSTLES OF CHRIST

The anti-Paulinists call themselves apostles of Christ. But Paul can refer to them only as false apostles (2 Cor. 11:13). The fact that they positively claimed to be apostles of Christ also can be seen from Paul's involuntary concession that they had trans-

86

formed themselves into apostles of Christ (*metaschēmatizome-noi eis apostolous Christou*, 11:13b). Then Paul continues: "And no wonder, for even Satan disguises himself as an angel of light. So it is not strange if his servants also disguise themselves as servants (*diakonoi*) of righteousness" (vv. 14–15). Since his opponents describe themselves as servants of Christ (*diakonoi Christou*; see above, n. 92), it is easy to surmise that Paul here intentionally takes up their self-description in a polemical manner: in reality they are servants of Satan, not servants of Christ!

The claim of the opponents to apostleship also follows from the use of the expression "superlative apostles" in 2 Cor. 11:5 and 12:11.

For the purpose of clarifying the identity of the "superlative apostles," we must go back to a previous point: in 2 Cor. 10:12 Paul explicitly rejects the practice of comparing himself with others who commend themselves. Paul nonetheless does precisely this a few verses later, but of course in the form of a fool's speech (11:1, 16, 21), which the Corinthians had forced him to do. This fool's speech is Paul's means of boasting in response to the opponents who had invaded Corinth and comparing himself with them, in order to show to the Corinthians that he had at least the same qualifications as they (cf. 11:18: *epei polloi kauchōntai kata sarka, kagō kauchēsomai*). The commentary on this is provided by 2 Cor. 5:12:[95] "We are not commending ourselves to you again but giving you cause to be proud of us, so that you may be able to answer those who pride themselves on a man's position and not on his heart."

On the other hand, Paul cannot concede the legitimacy of the opponents' claim to apostleship (see above). They are in fact for him servants of Satan (11:15). One must keep this dialectic procedure of Paul with regard to his opponents in view in the exegesis of 11:5 and 12:11. To this task we now turn.

2 Cor. 11:5: In 11:1 Paul ironically pleads with the Corinthians to bear with his fool's speech. He does not begin with it immediately, however; rather, the apostle emphasizes his sincere concern for the church (v. 2). He then expresses his fear that the Corinthians could be led astray from Christ. For if someone comes and preaches another Jesus than the one proclaimed by Paul, or if the Corinthians receive a different spirit from the one they have already received (through Paul's preaching), or if they accept a gospel different from that which they had already accepted, they submit to it readily enough (v. 4).

Paul is not thinking here of a hypothetical case[96] but of a real event in the recent past. That follows from the context (vv. 12ff.) and from the expression in v. 20 parallel to v. 4, which certainly reflects a real event: "for you bear it if a man makes slaves of you, or preys upon you."

The "fools speech" as such begins in v. 5. Paul affirms that he is not the least behind these superlative apostles (*mēden hysterēkenai tōn hyperlian apostolōn*). If one keeps in mind what was said above concerning Paul's dialectical manner of expression, then v. 5 "explains that Paul is not inferior to the interlopers named in 11:4,"[97] and the thesis becomes probable that the opponents in view in v. 4 are identical with the superlative apostles named in v. 5.

The same conclusion follows from 2 Cor. 12:11. Paul writes in 12:11a that the Corinthians had forced him to indulge in foolishness. He (and not his opponents) should have been the one to be recommended by the Corinthians. Paul continues: *ouden gar hysterēsa tōn hyperlian apostolōn, ei kai ouden eimi. 12. ta men sēmeia tou apostolou kateirgasthē en hymin . . . . 13. ti gar estin ho hēssōthēte hyper tas loipas ekklēsias, ei mē hoti autos egō ou katenarkēsa hymōn?* The structure of 2 Cor. 12:11ff. is the same as that discussed above (11:1ff.): (*a*) the description as a "fool's speech" (11:1/12:11a): (*b*) "I think that I am not in the least inferior to these superlative apostles" (11:5/12:11b); (*c*) the proof (11:6/12:12); and (*d*) his renunciation of support (11:7ff./12:13).

This correspondence between 2 Cor. 11:1ff. and 12:11ff. easily leads to the conclusion that the superlative apostles described with the same words in both texts are identical. Since (*c*) and (*d*) clearly deal with points that the *opponents* had introduced against Paul, it is clear when one takes Paul's dialectic manner of speaking into account that he is describing *the opponents who had come into the Corinthian community from outside* as the "superlative apostles."[98]

Thus when Paul ironically speaks of his opponents as "superlative apostles," one reason for this is that they had in fact described themselves as apostles.

With this, we come to the question of the theological and historical evaluation of the anti-Paulinists on the basis of their claiming the apostolic title: the *historical* question is closely bound up with the problem of the origin of the title "apostle" as such. Above (pp. 50f.) it was shown that the Jerusalem church (under the leadership of James) had formulated a so-called "narrow" concept of apostleship. Alongside this there is supposed to have been a "broad" concept of apostleship (reflected in *Did.* 11.4), which was native to the region of Syria. The lack of sources prohibits us from describing it any more precisely. This information forbids us to render a certain judgment on the issue of whether or not the term "apostles of Christ" points to Jerusalem. Of course we must immediately add that a Jerusalem origin is made unlikely only if decisive counterarguments can be brought forth (cf. further below, pp. 94ff.).

A *theological* characterization of the opponents on the basis of their claiming the apostolic title is thus inadvisable because of disputed question of the origin of the title itself.

4.2.6.3 THE FINANCIAL SUPPORT OF THE ANTI-PAULINISTS[99]

In immediate connection with the passages just discussed (11:5f.; 12:11f.) Paul deals—as indicated above—in each case with the same issue: his renunciation of support (cf. 11:7–9 with 12:13). This observation indicates that the anti-Paulinists had directed an attack against the apostle on the basis of his renunciation of support from the community, for Paul can only respond with irony and sarcasm. It thus appears that the opponents had in the same breath attacked him concerning the collection. They apparently argued that, sure, the apostle had refused to be supported by the church, but at the same time he had taken advantage of them with a clever trick (2 Cor. 12:6; there follows a reference to the sending of Titus, who was involved in taking the collection).

If Paul was thus attacked in 2 Corinthians too on account of his renunciation of support by the congregation, then it is clear at the same time that his opponents themselves in fact were supported by the church. This follows from 2 Cor. 11:20, where Paul polemically speaks of the fact that the Corinthians bear it willingly when someone devours them (*katesthiei*).

The following historical-theological observations can now be made concerning the charge that Paul had renounced his (rightful claim to) support by the congregation: The attack very probably is related to a critique against the apostleship of Paul, and all the more so, since the opponents claimed to be apostles themselves. And that then means that the attack discussed here may be identical with the anti-Pauline argument at the basis of 1 Corinthians 9, namely, that Paul was not an apostle, since, among other reasons, he did not allow himself to be supported by the church. (For further historical-theological evaluation of the debate, cf. the discussion above on pp. 68f.) Here it is only to be emphasized that if the anti-Paulinists of 1 and 2 Corinthians are the same group, the point discussed here would cast light on those missionaries whose profile we have previously been able only to sketch, those missionaries whose arrival in Corinth would have led to the formation of the Cephas party. In this case, the supposition already advanced above would have to be emphatically affirmed, namely, that those missionaries described themselves as apostles (see above, pp. 72f., 79f., 86ff.).

4.2.6.4 THE ANTI-PAULINISTS AS PNEUMATICS

It was said above that the Corinthians and the external opponents agreed in their critique of Paul with regard to his lack of spiritual powers. Here we only want to ask whether this external critique can be classified historically and theologically with regard to the origin of anti-Paulinism.

We have already pointed out that the line of argument which lies behind 1 Corinthians 9 has points of contact with the missionary tradition found in the Gospels (see above, p. 69), which authorized those who preach the gospel to receive their support from the church. The arguments of the anti-Paulinists also manifest agreements with the Gospel missionary tradition on the question of miracles (see above, p. 85). Cf. Luke 10:8f.:[100] *kai eis hēn an polin eiserchēsthe therapeuete tous en autē astheneis.* In addition, Paul's response to the theme presented by the opponents, "visions and revelations of the Lord," indicates a distant point of contact with Q; cf. Matt. 11:25–27/Luke 10:21f. with regard to the revelation motif.[101, 102]

We have thus succeeded in setting two elements[103] of the (external) opponents' understanding and practice of spiritual powers in their context in the history of early Christian tradition. Since this element has the same point of origin in the history of traditions as the opponents' other *topoi*, what we discover here with regard to the opponents' view of spiritual powers confirms[104] what we have previously argued with regard to the historical setting of the anti-Paulinism of 2 Corinthians.

4.2.6.5 THE GOSPEL OF THE OPPONENTS

According to Paul, the opponents preached a different Jesus than he had preached to the Corinthians. The Corinthians received from this preaching a spirit different from that which they had received through the preaching of the apostle and accepted a gospel that was not that of Paul (11:4).

Much scholarly energy has been spent puzzling over this text. Thus according to W. Schmithals, "if one notes that with the mention of the *allos Iēsous* and the *heteron euangelion* Paul refers to two central and at the same time concrete doctrinal elements of the false teaching which he is opposing, then the preaching of the *heteron pneuma*, mentioned at the same time, cannot have been much less significant and specific."[105] This view, however, overlooks the polemical character of our passage. In the first place, it expresses how *Paul* regarded the preaching of the opponents, not so much what the anti-Paulinists themselves advocated. It is therefore not possible to speak here of "elements of doctrine," and all the less, since it is not clear from our verses how the gospel preached by the opponents deviated from that preached by Paul.

By rejecting one attempt at reconstructing the gospel of the anti-Paulinists, we have not yet said everything relevant with regard to the content of the opponents' preaching. One possibility for making progress on this point would be the analysis of passages outside 2 Corinthians that have the same polemic found in 2 Cor. 11:4.

It has always been noticed that a close parallel to 2 Cor. 11:4 is found in Gal. 1:6–9.[106] In both texts Paul polemically distinguishes his own preaching from that of his opponents. In 2 Corinthians he delineates the triad "Jesus, Spirit, gospel" as the points of difference, while in Galatians he speaks of the "gospel" alone. The difference between his and his opponents' preaching is indicated by Paul by the addition of *heteron* (2 Corinthians) or *allo* (2 Corinthians; Galatians) to their respective terms.

Since Paul in both cases is formulating his terminology in the heat of polemics, in my opinion the fact that Paul names "Jesus,

Spirit, gospel" in 2 Corinthians and only "gospel" in Galatians must not be overinterpreted, especially since in Paul "gospel" includes christological and pneumatological aspects.[107] It can thus hardly be considered accidental that in 2 Cor. 11:4 "gospel" stands as the final term of the triad. In reality, it is a summary of the whole triad.

In any case, it would be incorrect to say that in 2 Cor. 11:4 Paul "defines the difference to the opponents more precisely and radically than in the passage from Galatians. The difference appears most of all in the Christology. *Allos Iēsous* does not merely refer to the extreme possible consequences of a suspected contrast; it means a real difference."[108] If the matter were in fact as Georgi understands it, it would still be a puzzle why Paul does not express the difference between himself and his opponents still more precisely.

If then Paul uses similar phraseology in his attack on his opponents in 2 Corinthians and Galatians, this can be explained on the one hand by the similarity in the positions of his opponents and on the other hand by Paul's own polemical style.[109]

An isolated consideration of Gal. 1:6ff. in comparison with 2 Cor. 11:4 thus permits no certain conclusions with regard to the position of the opponents in 2 Cor. 11:4. Consequently, a more precise historical-theological classification of the opponents' gospel on the basis of 2 Cor. 11:4 is not possible,[110] although of course the demonstrable similarity between 2 Cor. 11:4 and Gal. 1:6ff. is to be kept in mind.

4.2.6.6. THE MISSIONARY TERRITORY OF THE OPPONENTS[111]

In 2 Cor. 10:15 Paul speaks in a manner that clearly alludes to the fact that his opponents boast in the work of others. Of course he does not dare to compare himself with them, with those who commend themselves (v. 12a). They measure themselves by one another, and compare themselves with one another, and are thus without understanding (v. 12b).[112] But Paul himself, contrariwise, will not boast beyond limits (*eis ta ametra*), but according to the measure of the limit (*kanōn*) which the Lord had apportioned to him,[113] to extend even to Corinth with his preaching of the gospel (v. 13). He plans to preach the gospel in lands beyond Corinth but not in territory that does not belong to him (as his opponents do).

Paul's delineation reflects an incursion of opponents from outside into the Corinthian church. We have already seen above that they had brought their opposition to Paul with them to Corinth (pp. 85f.). Although hostility to Paul is not found directly in the above passage (2 Cor. 10:12–16), on further investigation it may be presupposed as certain, so that one may speak of the anti-Pauline act of invasion of a Pauline congregation.

Can we now classify the anti-Pauline position in historical-theological terms on the basis of 2 Cor. 10:12–16?

An affirmative answer can be derived from the following observations: In 2 Cor. 10:13 Paul speaks of a limit (kanōn) given him by the Lord. This "'canon' is the missionizing of the entire gentile world,"[114] including Corinth. It is indeed quite possible that in the above-mentioned text Paul is thinking of the agreement that he had made with the leaders of the Jerusalem church and that had granted the Gentile mission to him and Barnabas. If so, he is holding up to the Corinthians the fact that the opponents had not kept their part of the Jerusalem agreement.[115]

This interpretative *possibility* then becomes more likely when we compare 2 Cor. 10:13 with 1 Corinthians 9, where it is not only possible but practically necessary to see a reference to the Jerusalem agreement.

If for purposes of argument we presuppose as correct that 2 Corinthians 10 alludes to the Jerusalem agreement, then Paul addresses two arguments against the invaders at Corinth: (a) his kanōn, which corresponds to the Jerusalem agreement, and (b) the existence of the Corinthian church; cf. 10:14: *ou gar hōs mē ephiknoumenoi eis hymas . . . achri gar kai hymōn ephthasamen en tō euangeliō tou Christou* ("For it is of course not the case that we [in fact] did not reach you, . . . but we have really come all the way to you with the gospel of Christ"). With this statement Paul wants to express: "Since I am the one who . . . founded your church, I have been certified by God."[116]

The same two points appear in 1 Corinthians 9: (a) a reference to the Jerusalem agreement (v. 5) and (b) certification of the Pauline apostleship by the church (v. 3). Although the respective references to the Jerusalem agreement have different functions in each case, this only makes the use of these two arguments as a defense against his opponents all the more noteworthy. They not only make it likely that there was a connection between the external opposition to Paul in 1 and 2 Corinthians but, beyond that, make its Jerusalem origin all the more probable.

4.2.7 The Anti-Paulinists of 1 and 2 Corinthians and Their Jerusalem Origin

The differences between the anti-Paulinism in 1 Corinthians and that of 2 Corinthians have already been noted several times in the above discussion (see pp. 79f., 85f.) and need not be repeated. We are concerned here to give a summary statement with regard to the advocates of this anti-Pauline polemic and to delineate their different relations to the Corinthian church at the times when 1 and 2 Corinthians were written.

At the time of the writing of 1 Corinthians, the anti-Paulinists had left the city but had found a responsive group which became the Cephas party. These were not yet a threat to the unity of the whole church. But between 1 and 2 Corinthians, there was a fresh incursion of anti-Paulinists into the church whose work was met with great success and who, in combination with the internal criticism of Paul which had grown in the meantime, seriously threatened the unity of the Corinthian church.

What, then, is the relation of the external anti-Paulinists of 1 Corinthians to those of 2 Corinthians?

There are the following points of agreement between the anti-Paulinists of both letters:

1. The opponents of both letters challenge the apostleship of Paul: in 1 Corinthians on the basis of his refusal of support by the congregation and on chronological and material grounds (the lack of contacts with Jerusalem), and in 2 Corinthians because of the lack of the signs of an apostle, among other grounds.

2. The opponents of both letters claim and exercise the right of support by the congregation.

3. In each case they call themselves apostles.

4. The views of both groups have points of contact with the tradition of the missionary discourse of the Gospels.

It must thus be considered certain that the external anti-Paulinism of both letters had the same historical context, which other evidence suggests as well: the position of the anti-Paulinists had a close connection to the Jerusalem Conference (see above, pp. 70, 93f.).

The thesis advocated above, that the opposition to Paul had a Jewish-Christian, Jerusalem origin, is usually questioned, with new evidence, especially since the work of W. Lütgert.[117] The contention is that the anti-Paulinists could not have had anything to do with Jerusalem, because Paul is not here opposing "the primary demands of the Judaists, circumcision and legalism."[118]

There are several reasons of a history-of-religions and historical nature why this argument is not persuasive. We will deal with the question first from a historical perspective and will discuss (a) the question of circumcision and then (b) the issue of "legalism."

a. The Jerusalem church did not have a consistent position with regard to the issue of observance of the law by Gentile Christians. We know for a fact that there were two factions in Jerusalem that maintained mutually exclusive views on this question: the one group insisted on the circumcision of Gentile Christians, the other did not. The majority probably had not come to a firm decision. At the time of the Jerusalem Conference, the "pillars" had spoken out against the faction that insisted on circumcision, although the "pillars" themselves did not all have the same theological views. Thus Cephas had certainly advocated a liberal attitude with regard to Gentile Christians (see Gal. 2:11ff.) and must thus already have been inclined toward a Gentile mission (which did not demand circumcision). And it is precisely from Gal. 2:11ff. that a more conservative position must be inferred for James—also toward the Gentile mission which did not demand circumcision. Still, at the time of the Jerusalem Conference he had endorsed such a mission. We know nothing at all about the views of John.

From these considerations it is thus perfectly clear that the absence of circumcision as a point of dispute is no argument against the origin of the external Corinthian anti-Paulinists from Jerusalem. Nor is it appropriate to infer from the fact that Paul had worked out an agreement with the part of the Jerusalem church that endorsed the law-free Gentile mission that later opposition could not develop from this same group but only from the "false brethren" who were advocates in Jerusalem of the necessity of circumcising Gentile converts. This is so, in the first place, because the boundaries between these Jerusalem groups were fluid and also because situations could arise in the Pauline churches that called forth the opposition of the Jerusalem groups. And finally we should note that in the second century the Jewish Christians portrayed in Justin, *Dial.* 47, have different views on the issue of the circumcision of Gentile Christians, even though they are united in their criticizing Paul (see below, p. 153, with n. 29).

b. The lack of "legalism" as an issue in the debate with the Corinthian opponents is also no argument against their Jerusalem origin, for the question of law observance—except for the issue of circumcision—was not discussed at the Jerusalem Conference, so far as we can discern from Galatians. Its lack can thus not be introduced as evidence against the thesis advocated above. Besides, "legalistic" demands could be evidence for the existence of the advocacy of Jerusalem views in Pauline churches only if these churches could have had no laws otherwise and only if such laws could have been introduced by agitators from Jerusalem. But this could not have been the case, if for no other reason than that ethical instruction of *Jewish* origin was already a constituent part of Paul's preaching which had founded the church.[119]

From the point of view of *the history of religions* the following response may be made to Vielhauer's opinion expressed above: The discussion being carried on here has a parallel in the question in the Jewish community of how the relation of Jews to Gentiles should be construed, that is, Gentiles who wanted to unite with Jewish synagogues. In this discussion a distinction was made between two different types of membership,[120] that of proselytes and that of "God-fearers." Proselytes were circumcised but not God-fearers. Under the presupposition that the Jerusalem Christians construed the Gentiles who were uniting with the churches as proselytes, they would have to be circumcised, but not if they were construed to be God-fearers. Since it cannot be excluded that the Jerusalem church thought of the Gentile converts as God-fearers, considerations from the history of religions also do not support Vielhauer's objection to the "Judaist hypothesis" (*Judaistenthese*).

The best hypothesis therefore remains: the external anti-Paulinists of 1 and 2 Corinthians were Jerusalem Jewish Christians who had been present at the Jerusalem conference and who afterward attacked Paul in his own Corinthian church.[121]

4.3 GALATIANS[122]

We will first look for clear reflections of anti-Paulinism and in conjunction with this—in accord with the method described above (pp. 31f.)—will then inquire after the relation of this anti-Paulinism to the theology of the opponents. Third, we will attempt to determine whether the anti-Paulinism is Jewish-Christian and then, fourth, will examine how it may be understood historically.

4.3.1 Anti-Paulinism in Galatia

Galatians 1:6ff. refers to an anti-Pauline agitation in Galatia. A certain group of persons (tines) had proclaimed a gospel to the Galatians that was exactly opposite to that of Paul. The Galatians believe(d) this preaching, which Paul can only consider an act of apostasy (v. 6). To be sure, Paul does not explicitly say that the opponents had attacked him directly. But that can still be inferred with certainty from the content of their gospel (see below) and from the fact that the Galatian churches were Pauline churches founded by him personally. If outsider preachers had achieved some influence here, it could not have happened without their making a critique of Paul.

A further anti-Pauline element can be inferred from the content of the opponents' preaching: the opposition had attempted to introduce the practice of circumcision into the Galatian churches (6:12) as well as other legal prescriptions mentioned in 4:10, namely, the observance of days, months, and years.[123] The demand of circumcision was strictly contrary to the apostle's practice of accepting Gentile Christians into the churches without circumcision and thus was anti-Pauline. The same is true of the other legal prescriptions,[124] for they were not a part of the Pauline tradition that he delivered to his churches.

In addition, the opposition had probably disputed Paul's apostleship.[125] This inference seems likely from the combination of Gal. 1:1 and 1:12. The primary emphasis of Galatians is the claim of Paul to be an apostle. Paul is an apostle, not from human beings or by human beings, but through Jesus Christ and God, who raised him (i.e., Jesus) from the dead. That is, Paul's apostleship has an eschatological origin.

In v. 12 Paul comes back to the declaration with which he had begun. *That* there is some connection between both passages is clear from the fact that the same antithesis, "humanity/God," present in v. 1 is taken up again in v. 12; cf. *oude gar egō para anthrōpou parelabon auto* 3. *alla di' apokalypseōs Iēsou Christou.* In vv. 15f. Paul provides the content for the "revelation of Jesus Christ": it is identical with the sending of Paul to the Gentiles and is grounded christologically. The revelation of Jesus Christ is, for Paul, his call to be an apostle (to the Gentiles).[126]

The emphatic declaration of (the independence of) the Pauline apostleship can, in my opinion, best be understood if its validity had been challenged from the opponents' side.

Finally, an additional element in the attack on Paul consisted in presenting Paul as dependent on the Jerusalem personages. This inference is made probable by Paul's extensive treatment of his relation to the Jerusalem church and the repeated emphasis on his independence (1:17; 2:2).[127] As everyone knows, the theme of the independence of Paul's message already comes to expression in the prescript (1:1). In this respect, the claim that Paul was dependent on Jerusalem was an auxiliary component of the disputation concerning the legitimacy of Paul's apostleship which immediately follows.

Now we should immediately note that the attacks spoken of here are subject to two possible interpretations: (1) The opponents brought up Paul's dependence on Jerusalem as an *accusation.* The meaning would then be that Paul's preaching is unworthy of belief, because he is dependent on Jerusalem.[128] (2) The opponents make an explicit point of Paul's dependence on Jerusalem. The significance of the point would then be that Paul has deviated from the Jerusalem authorities in an irresponsible manner and usurps independent authority against them.[129]

A decision with regard to the question here delineated can be made only after a discussion of the analyses indicated above.

Two additional passages that are sometimes used for the reconstruction of the anti-Pauline objections to Paul (Gal. 1:10; 5:11) do
not reflect anti-Paulinism but are to be credited to the account of
the polemicist Paul himself (see Luedemann, *Paul, Apostle to the
Gentiles*, 50–53).

4.3.2 Anti-Paulinism and the Theology of the Opponents

In this section, the second and third questions introduced above
(p. 97) will be discussed.

There is no doubt that the opponents of Paul are *Christian
preachers.*[129a] In addition, the details characterizing the opponents' preaching mentioned above (demand for circumcision,[130]
observance of days, etc.) show that they were Jewish Christians,
if one operates with the definition of Jewish Christianity given
above, pp. 29f.

Lütgert[131] has wanted to modify this old thesis in that he
believes he can recognize a second opposing front in Galatia,
which was libertine (on the basis of 5:1, 3, 13; 6:3) and which was
addressed by Paul in 6:1 ("you who are spiritual [*pneumatikoi*]").
But this argument cannot be maintained. The words just mentioned are obviously addressed to the whole congregation,[132] and
the passages introduced to support the idea of a second (libertine) front cannot bear the weight placed on them by Lütgert,
since they merely represent the standard Pauline teaching (cf.
5:21) given[133] at the founding[134] of the congregation.

4.3.3 Historical Evaluation of the Jewish-Christian
Anti-Paulinism of the Opponents

In Gal. 1:15ff. Paul defends himself against the charge of his
gospel being dependent on Jerusalem. He shows the falsity of
the alleged dependence first by a biographical-chronological
argument: immediately after his call he did not go to Jerusalem
to those who were apostles before him (v. 17). When he did go to
Jerusalem three years later, it was only for the purpose of getting
acquainted with Peter. And he stayed only two weeks. He did
not visit Jerusalem again until fourteen years later—and in
response to a revelation (2:1f.).

Then Paul contradicts the alleged dependency on Jerusalem

by a report of the events that transpired at the conference and by his portrayal of the incident at Antioch at which he openly resisted one of the pillars. In Jerusalem he was acknowledged as an equal partner, and the three pillars perceived the grace which rested on Paul's missionary work.

It is thus to be noted that Paul does not speak of an explicit acknowledgment of his apostleship by the Jerusalem leaders, which would have silenced one of the anti-Pauline attacks— perhaps the most important one—of his Galatian opponents; (cf. also p. 98, above).

Of course it is also noteworthy that Paul emphasized that the pillars had not supported the demand that was made by some that Titus must be circumcised, for this was also a major issue in the debate in Galatia.

Finally, it should not escape notice that despite the agreement Paul had worked out with the pillars, he speaks of them ironically. This not undisputed assertion is based on the following: in his report of the conference Paul four times speaks of those who are held in high regard (cf. v. 2: *tois dokousin*; v. 6a: *tōn dokountōn einai ti*; v. 6c: *hoi dokountes*; v. 9: *hoi dokountes styloi einai*). This expression is used predominately in Greek literature in an ironical[135] but also a factual sense,[136] so that the external data are ambiguous. We should note in addition that in Paul (apart from Galatians 2), of the fourteen occurrences of *dokein* about half suggest appearance rather than reality.[137] The decision in favor of the ironical meaning of this expression in Galatians 2 is finally given by the context itself, v. 6: "And from those who were reputed to be something (what they are[138] makes no difference to me, God shows no partiality [literally: "does not regard the face of a person"])."

With this final clause Paul relativizes all the distinguishing marks of human authorities, including those in Jerusalem "who were reputed to be something." At the same time, this throws some light on the interpretation of the expression "those who were reputed to be something" in Galatians 2, that is, it has in every instance a dialectical-ironical sense. On the one hand, the group thus described stands in high regard. On the other hand, to the extent that they claim to be more than they are in reality, they too must subject themselves to the critical principle expressed in the final clause of v. 6.[139]

The three observations made above suggest the hypothesis that the Galatian controversy was a continuation of the Jerusalem dispute. The opponents of Paul are identical with the so-called false brethren who were not able to execute their demand[140] at the Jerusalem Conference that Titus be circumcised and who obviously had not participated in the agreement that was worked out there. This is the reason they interfered in the Gentile Christian churches of Galatia, advocating here as already in Jerusalem that Gentile Christians should be circumcised, and obviously brought the collection to a standstill there.[141] They polemicized against Paul while appealing to the Jerusalem leaders for authority and emphatically asserted that Paul had never been acknowledged by them as an apostle of equal rank with themselves. They here touched on a tender spot, for Paul had obviously interpreted the Jerusalem agreement in this sense and understood it as he sets it forth in Galatians, although on this point he could not dispute the truth of the opponents' argument.

It is, however, not completely clear whether or not the opponents had backing in Jerusalem. What is clear is that Paul wants to put precisely this issue in doubt by his argument, in that he points out that the conduct of his opponents is not in accord with the agreement worked out in Jerusalem. Since Paul himself, however, interprets the Jerusalem agreement one-sidedly, and in Galatians subjects the Torah itself to a critique that would certainly have met with opposition in Jerusalem (not to mention that it did not correspond to the spirit of the agreement), in view of this *new situation* we must hesitate with regard to an answer to the question of whether the Galatian opponents had support in Jerusalem. This means that an answer to this question can be given only on the basis of general considerations that take account of the different developments in the Pauline churches, in Paul himself, and also in Jerusalem.[142]

The above representation of the historical origin of the anti-Paulinists in Galatia is sometimes called into question by referring to Gal. 5:3 and 6:13. Thus in conclusion these two texts need to be examined:

Gal. 6:13: *oude gar hoi peritemnomenoi autoi nomon phylassousin, alla thelousin hymas peritemnesthai, hina en tē hymetera sarki kauchēsōntai.* The present participle *peritemnomenoi* had already seemed troublesome in ancient times and led to changes in the text.[143] Literally, it is translated "those who are being circumcised," so that—considered in isolation—it refers to people who are having themselves circumcised at the present (=Gentiles). From this, E. Hirsch concluded that the anti-Paulinits in Galatia were Judaistic Gentile Christians.[144] He supposed this would throw light on Paul's statement in 6:13: that "Gentiles who had themselves circumcised could not keep the law like born Jews is self-evident. For to the keeping of the law there belongs . . . a competence and practice acquired through education from one's youth on."[145]

There are several reasons, however, why this iterative present can hardly bear the weight of this argument. The following speak against it:

a. The context suggests that v. 12 and v. 13 have the same subject (cf. *euprosōpēsai en sarki* of v. 12 with *en tē hymetera sarki kauchēsōntai* of v. 13).[146]

b. The expression *anagkazousin hymas peritemnesthai* (v. 12) refers to born Jews as the subject of the sentence.[147] They correspond to v. 13: *thelousin hymas peritemnesthai*. The iterative present *hoi peritemnomenoi* intends merely to express the fact that the opponents advocate the requirement of circumcision.[148] For "Paul is not concerned here with the presence of circumcised persons—like himself—in the church; he is concerned instead with those who now demand circumcision for Gentile Christians. Thus the present tense of the participle is demanded by the argumentative situation."[149]

c. And finally, one must also reject Hirsch's other argument that Paul's claim that the opponents themselves did not keep the law was determined by the fact that they were former Gentiles. Paul's claim is, rather, determined by his general view that *no one* can fulfill the law.[150] It is only a small step from this theological view to the polemic of Gal. 6:13.

The insight that Paul considers the fulfillment of the law to be an impossibility on theological grounds also gives us the key to an appropriate interpretation of Gal. 5:3: *martyromai de palin panti anthrōpō peritemnomenō hoti opheiletēs estin holon ton nomon poiēsai*. Paul here sharpens the argument to assert that everyone who has himself circumcised must keep the whole law. Such an act (circumcision) thus means an apostasy from grace (v. 4). Paul is formulating his argument here in view of the demand presently being made that the Galatians be circumcised, as especially the preceding v. 2 shows: "If you receive circumcision, Christ will be of no advantage to you."

To be sure, Schmithals writes with reference to Gal. 5:3:

"This [i.e., the necessity that the one who allows himself to be circumcised must keep the whole law] the Galatians had apparently not been able to gather from the message proclaimed by the false teachers. No wonder, since Paul finds that those who were circumcised *themselves nomon ou phylassousin* (Gal. 6:13), and this obviously means a renunciation of the law in principle. But then these false teachers can hardly have been Judaizers."[151]

Against such an opinion it must be objected that in 5:3 Paul is formulating his argument polemically, just as in 6:13: law and Christ are mutually exclusive—and whoever falls away from the grace given in Christ must keep the whole law, which is a theological impossibility.

Summary: Gal. 5:3 and 6:13 cannot be introduced as proof against the understanding of the anti-Pauline Jewish-Christian opposition in Galatia presented above. With this we come to a reconstruction of the anti-Paulinism in Philippians.

4.4 PHILIPPIANS

4.4.1 The Significance of Literary Criticism and Chronology for the Subject

Philippians is the most difficult of all the genuine Pauline letters to locate chronologically and geographically. This is why we have delayed treatment of it until now. The following three locations are generally proposed as its place of writing: Ephesus, Rome, and Caesarea.[152] The question of the place of composition and the date of writing are interrelated. It would take us too far afield to go into these questions here, so the reader is referred to the appropriate introductory works.

But Philippians also poses a riddle for the interpreter with regard to its literary integrity, which has led to its being divided into two or three letters or to a defense of its unity.[153]

To be sure, both the chronological-geographical problem and the question of the literary unity of the letter are of limited significance for the issue of anti-Paulinism that we are pursuing in this work. The reconstruction of the anti-Pauline views can be achieved independently of the two issues just mentioned. But these two points do gain in importance when we later attempt to correlate the anti-Paulinism of Philippians with that of the other Pauline letters, whose time and place of writing we know (cf. below, pp. 108f.).

In the following we will proceed through Philippians with the question of possible reflections of anti-Paulinism in mind and will treat these in accord with the procedural steps already discussed (see above, p. 32).

4.4.2 Philippians 1

Paul reports to the Philippians the fact that his imprisonment had led to the progress of the gospel. This progress is then described in two clauses introduced by *hōste* (vv. 13f.):

1. It has become known throughout the whole praetorium and to all the rest that Paul's bonds are "in Christ." That is, there have already been one or more occasions that gave Paul the opportunity to act as an advocate for his own cause, and "by talking of himself, he comes to the gospel."[154] This was in the service of the gospel, because it had had positive results for the missionary enterprise (v. 12).

2. For the majority of the Christians in Paul's locale, Paul's imprisonment had served as an occasion to proclaim the gospel all the more confidently (v. 14).

Paul then continues in v. 15: "Some indeed preach Christ from envy and rivalry (*phthonos kai eris*), but others from good will (*eudokia*). v. 16: The latter do it out of love, knowing that I am put here for the defense of the gospel (*eis apologian tou euangeliou keimai*); v. 17: the former proclaim Christ out of partisanship (*eritheia*), not sincerely but thinking to afflict me in my imprisonment (*thlipsin egeirein tois desmois mou*), v. 18: . . . in pretense (*prophasei*)."

This small section is, regarded formally, a brief excursus-like insertion,[155] which is only loosely attached to *hoi pleiones* and basically distinguishes two groups of preachers, depending on how they relate themselves to Paul's imprisonment. That is, both groups are obviously found in the same location where Paul is imprisoned.[156] The activity of the group described negatively is characterized by Paul as follows: they "preach Christ from envy and rivalry," "out of partisanship, not sincerely but thinking to afflict me in my imprisonment, . . . in pretense."

Now, parts of the description of their activity in vv. 15, 17, and 18 certainly originate from Paul's own polemical style[157] and thus provide no information on the views of his opponents or on the question of whether or not they had attacked the apostle. Thus all that remains as a possible reflection of anti-Paulinism is the following clause from 1:17b: *oiomenoi thlipsin egeirein tois desmois mou.*

The preceding statement shows that a group of Christian preachers had attacked Paul.[158] Their attacks must have had something to do with Paul's imprisonment, *in the first place* because Paul speaks explicitly of bonds (*desmoi*), and *in the second place* this sentence stands in direct contrast to the other group described by Paul positively, who preach Christ with goodwill (*eudokia*) and from love (*agapē*), *eidotes hoti eis apologian tou euangeliou keimai* (cf. v. 7, where *apologia tou euangeliou* is likewise related to his situation of being in prison).

Paul's imprisonment had thus caused considerable excitement in the church visited by Paul at the time of the writing of Philippians and had evoked the two reactions described above, one of which, the minority reaction, had been very critical of Paul.[159] A more precise description of the anti-Pauline position[160] is not possible.[161]

Even if we cannot say anything more precisely about the Philippian anti-Paulinism related to his imprisonment beyond the bare fact of its existence, the possibility still remains that we can locate it theologically and historically. Of course we must immediately add that vv. 17f. hardly deal with the same kind of preachers we find among the opponents in Galatia. If they had been such people, Paul could hardly have concluded the brief excursus of vv. 15–17 with the summary statement of v. 18 in which he expressed himself with regard to them as he does:[162] "But what does it matter? Only that in every way, whether in pretense or in truth, Christ is proclaimed; and in that I rejoice."[163]

4.4.3 Philippians 3

In 3:2 Paul uses sharp words to combat a group who must have been known to the Philippian church and who obviously had contact with it. The warning "Look out for those who mutilate the flesh! It is we who are the true circumcision" (vv. 2c–3a) makes it certain that this group had insisted that the Philippians obey the command of circumcision or—hardly possible—that they had only boasted in the fact of their circumcision. Both items, interference in a Pauline church while at the same time insisting on the religious significance of circumcision, make the conclusion unavoidable that this group had polemicized against the apostle. In addition, both items make it clear that the opponents could not have been non-Christian Jews but must have been Jewish Christians.[164]

A third characteristic of the anti-Paulinists is clearly discernible: in vv. 4f. Paul emphasizes its "fleshly" character. This allows the inference that the opponents had boasted to the Philippians about their Jewish origin, although the details of such boasting must remain unclear.

Many scholars believe they find in vv. 12ff. and v. 18 further[165] evidence for the views of the opposition reflected in vv. 2ff. In the following we will deal with these passages one at a time.

Vv. 12ff.: In the view of an imposing number of scholars, Paul here takes up the catchword *teleios* from the anti-Pauline opponents. They are supposed to have been advocates of a "perfectionist enthusiasm,"[166] to have boasted of their possession of the Spirit, and to have considered circumcision as the singular sign of perfection.[167]

There are considerable difficulties in this view.

1. *Teleios* is not an un-Pauline word. Apart from this passage, it appears in 1 Cor. 2:6; 13:10; 14:20; Rom. 12:2 (Col. 1:28; 4:12). The reference in 1 Cor. 2:6 in particular shows that the word was a standard element in Pauline school tradition. There is thus no reason to infer an external origin for it.

2. Paul is here speaking to the congregation, as especially the address "brothers" (vv. 13 and 17) shows.[168] The church does not appear actually to be threatened by the heresy, however. All that can therefore be inferred is that it is referring to some circumstance in the congregation not known to us. M. Dibelius rightly argued in his time: "In order to give the words [i.e., in vv. 12ff.] their particular application to a situation unknown to us, it is not advisable to interpret *heterōs* as referring to the 'errorists' and *tō autō* as referring to the doctrine of grace."[169] The view that *teleios* is a catchword taken over from the vocabulary of the

opponents is thus a second-degree hypothesis, to say the least, for (a) it presupposes that members of the congregation used the term and (b) that they took it over from the opponents. The first is no more than a possibility, and the second is all the more unlikely, since *teleios* was an element in Paul's own theological language.

With this we have adequately indicated that *teleios* cannot be used to reconstruct the anti-Pauline theology in Philippi and, accordingly, that vv. 12ff. hardly contain the views of Paul's opponents.

In my opinion, the same negative conclusion is to be drawn with regard to the whole attempt to find the views of Paul's opponents reflected in vv. 18ff.

> Vv. *18ff.*: Schmithals comments on this passage as follows: "Gnostic theology as it is expressed in the rejection of the cross and libertinism belong together. Especially instructive is the formulation *hē doxa en tē aischynē autōn*. It is in fact a sign of gnostic honor, i.e. of pneumatic self-consciousness, to demonstrate the shamefulness of the flesh through immoral conduct."[170]

First, such a view does not take sufficiently into account the polemical character of these verses (cf. only 1 Cor. 15:32 and Rom. 16:18).[171] Besides that, *polloi* (beginning of v. 18) sounds very general. Since Paul had often (*pollakis*) spoken of their ruin, the statement deals with that group of the lost who are to be distinguished from the saved (cf. the similar contrasting of *apollymenoi—sōzomenoi* in 1 Cor. 3:18; 2 Cor. 2:15; 4:3). In the second place, we should therefore maintain the conclusion that a new unit begins in v. 17, which makes questionable a supposed reference back to possible descriptions of the opposition in vv. 2ff.[172] Verses 18ff. thus do not belong with the anti-Pauline position reflected in vv. 2ff., nor do they in themselves describe an opposing position.

In summary, neither vv. 12ff. nor vv. 18ff. offer any sort of evidence for the views of the opponents.

4.4.3.1 HISTORICAL-THEOLOGICAL EVALUATION
OF THE ANTI-PAULINISM BEHIND PHILIPPIANS 3

In the course of our affirmative decision with regard to the question of anti-Paulinism in Philippians 3, we have above (p. 106) been able to establish its Jewish-Christian character, for its propagators advocated circumcision and in any case were not libertines. In addition, they were most likely born Jews (see above, p. 106). In the following, we will inquire whether it is possible to locate this group more precisely in its historical-theological context. Since we are unable to say anything about the history of the anti-Paulinism in Philippians 3 because of this passage's fragmentary character, it can only be a matter of correlating the results attained above with what we have learned from the other Pauline letters.

We may first notice that there are similarities to the *Galatian anti-Paulinists*: the opponents in both Galatia and Philippi advocate circumcision. In both letters in reaction to the anti-Paulinists, the apostle emphasizes to the church his blameless observance of the law (Phil. 3:4f./Gal. 1:13; cf. already 1 Cor. 15:8). In both letters Paul contrasts his Christian existence with his former life in Judaism (Phil. 3:8/Gal. 1:15ff.).

There are additional similarities between Philippians 3 and 2 Corinthians 10—13.[173] Thus, apart from 2 Cor. 11:13 the substantive ergatēs[174] appears as a description of the opponents only in Phil. 3:12.[175] Here as there, Paul is speaking apologetically: in Phil. 3:4ff. as in 2 Cor. 11:22 he enumerates his own Jewish points of superiority; cf. *peritomē oktaēmeros, ek genous Israēl, phylēs Beniamin* (Philippians) with *Hebraioi eisin? kagō. Israēlitai eisin? kagō* (2 Corinthians). To be sure, the same kind of defense in Philippians/2 Corinthians, like the similarity between Philippians 3 and Galatians, is not compelling proof of the identity of opponents, but their historical connection becomes the more probable when one also takes into account their anti-Paulinism and their admitted Palestinian origin. (An additional reason for seeing a historical connection between the groups is, finally, the fact that the anti-Paulinists of Philippi are found in the immediate geographical vicinity of the Corinthian opponents.)

The probability thus suggests itself that the anti-Pauline opponents in Philippians 3 should also be considered Jewish Christians in Jerusalem[175a] who, at a time that cannot be determined from Philippians 3, visited the Philippian church and polemicized against the apostle to the Gentiles. Additional inferences are not possible on the basis of Philippians 3. But once the historical connection between the anti-Paulinists of 2 Corinthians 10—13 and Philippians 3 is granted, then additional light falls on the opponents of 2 Corinthians from the demand for circumcision by the Philippian opponents. As previously stated, the primary objection against the "Judaist hypothesis" with regard to the Corinthian opponents consisted in the lack of any reference there to the demand for circumcision. This objection is mitigated by the above discussion. The circumcision theme in Philippians 3 is an additional argument against this objection, for it shows that it could nonetheless be brought into play by the same or a closely related group in another place (Philippi).

4.5 ROMANS

Paul's letter to the Romans was regarded by F. C. Baur as a document of the Pauline struggle against an anti-Pauline Jewish Christianity which was also present in Rome (see above, p. 12f.). Apart from a few exceptions, this view is no longer advocated in contemporary scholarship, and correctly so.[176] There appears to be a general consensus that any hypothesis regarding the occasion for the writing of Romans which presupposes that Paul has knowledge of the Roman church and makes this presupposition a factor in interpreting the letter has little chance of verification. "Against all these attempts at explanation which attempt to sniff out the existence of this or that group or even opponents of Paul on the basis of parties mentioned in the letter with whom Paul is supposedly in a dialogical or polemical conversation, the methodological objection is to be raised that this dialogical manner of speaking is nothing else than a stylistic means used by the apostle frequently elsewhere, a style derived from the Hellenistic Cynic-Stoic 'diatribe.'"[177,178]

In the light of G. Bornkamm's view just cited, one could be inclined to doubt the possibility in general of reconstructing anti-Pauline attacks from Romans. For if the objections (or false inferences) in Romans[179] "almost never allow us to infer views equally possible to those expressed in the text, or real views which could be entertained at all,"[180] pursuing the hypothesis of anti-Paulinism in Romans seems to be excluded in advance.

But there is certainly at least one passage in Romans for which such a judgment is invalid and which meets the criteria set forth above for the recognition of anti-Pauline statements: Rom. 3:8.[181]

Because of the particular manner in which we are posing the question, in the following we do not need to carry through a detailed exegesis of Rom. 3:1–8 in order to see v. 8 in its context.[182] Here we need only to maintain that we have a statement, formally in the style of an objection in a diatribe,[183] a statement directed against Paul, which he quotes: *phasin tines hēmas legein hoti poiēsōmen ta kaka, hina elthē ta agatha*. The apostle can only describe such a view as *blasphēmia*[184] and indignantly throw it back at those who said it (cf. the end of v. 8: "Their condemnation is just").

On the presupposition that the quotation in v. 8 is located in the proper context with regard to its subject matter, the anti-Pauline reproach had been sparked by Paul's doctrine of justification by faith alone, the negative counterpart of which was the invalidation of the law as a means of salvation. For since in Paul's view the righteousness of God convicts everyone as being under the power of sin, the question arose for Paul's opponents whether Paul's theology did not mislead people directly to libertinism. They thus attributed to Paul their conclusion: that he taught that people should do evil in order that good, that is, salvation in Christ, might come. The opponents could thus only be people who saw in Paul's doctrine of the law a fatal error, and then a self-contradiction if Paul also advocated the keeping of the (moral aspects of the) law. They are thus with great probability to be regarded as Jews[185] loyal to the law, who had taken note of Paul's doctrine and practice. We can also consider them to be Jewish *Christians*, for, first, we know for *certain* of hostility to Paul from Jewish Christians in Jerusalem, Antioch, and Galatia, and then the line of argument of Romans is closely related to that of Galatians, which had been formulated in response to Jewish-Christian actions and arguments. Thus the declarations in Galatians apparently provoke allegations such as those which become visible in Rom. 3:8. *That* the refutation of such objections was a central concern of Paul's is seen in Rom. 6:1, 15, where Paul, using the diatribe style as his manner of argument, rejects similar inferences as that in the quotation in Rom. 3:8.

If now, because of the reasons presented above (p. 110) the hypothesis is not demonstrable that Paul intended in Rom. 3:8 to repulse the attacks of Jewish Christians in *Rome*,[186] nevertheless the anti-Pauline quotation can be located in its historical-theological context:[187] it originates from the Jewish-Christian, anti-Pauline struggle from the period between the conference visit to Jerusalem and the visit to deliver the collection and throws additional light on this struggle.

5

ANTI-PAULINISM IN JERUSALEM
AND IN THE PAULINE CHURCHES

It is now time to summarize the results obtained in the previous chapter and then to attempt a synthesis of the results of chapters 3 and 4.

5.1 SUMMARY OF THE RESULTS OF CHAPTER 4

One firm conclusion of the preceding chapter consists in the fact that the (external) anti-Paulinists reflected in both the Corinthian correspondence and the letter to the Galatians can be understood only against the background of the Jerusalem Conference and the disputed issues that derive from it.[1] Since the fragmentary reports of Philippians and Romans can readily be fitted into this hypothetical framework, we can assert: all the visible data with reference to the (external)[2] anti-Paulinists are related to the conference.

A chronological-geographical argument provides support for this thesis: the anti-Pauline attacks took place during a relatively short period of time and within a limited area.

The material item that permits us to see a connection between the anti-Pauline attacks and the conference is Paul's claim to *apostleship* which he had hoped to establish at the Jerusalem Conference but which either was attacked by his opponents or the agreement worked out at Jerusalem had not been kept by them.

The opponents in Galatia and Corinth are not be assigned to the same faction within the Jerusalem church. At the same time, the Philippian anti-Paulinists show that the boundaries between both groups could be fluid.[3] The Galatian opponents are to be assigned to the "false brethren" who were present at the conference, while the preachers who had come to Corinth had more likely occupied a middle position at the conference and considered Peter to be one of their leaders.

The question of whether the anti-Paulinists of Galatians and 1 and 2 Corinthians were missionaries to the Gentiles is, in my opinion, to be answered negatively. With regard to the Galatian opponents, such an assumption is a priori unlikely. It seems here, rather, to be exclusively a matter of a countermission among the Pauline churches of Galatia, which had as its only purpose correcting the unsatisfactory preaching of Paul. One could at first be inclined to consider the Corinthian anti-Paulinists (also) to be Gentile missionaries, because of the lack of the demand for circumcision. But in reality there is not one clear indication[4] for such a hypothesis, while on the other hand the points of contact with the traditional requirements for missionaries found in the missionary discourses in the Synoptic Gospels rather suggest a Jewish mission. Their belonging to the group of missionaries *eis tēn peritomēn* (Gal. 2:9) points in this same direction. The fact that they appeared in Corinth and that they had letters of recommendation is of course no evidence that the missionaries were themselves Gentiles but only a means of opening communication with other Gentile Christian congregations.[5]

> At the same time, we need to keep in mind that repeated contact with Gentile Christian churches was from their side an important factor in their later Gentile *mission*.

We are not well informed on the theology of the opponents, due to our lack of primary sources.[6] Whatever the precise contours of their theologies were, they received their forms through the anti-Pauline movement's bitter resistance to Paul and his claim to apostolic authority. Apostolic authority meant for Paul himself two things. On the one hand it authorized him to carry on his Gentile mission, and on the other it put him on the same plane as the Jerusalem apostles. The Galatian opponents challenged both items, the Corinthian anti-Paulinists only the latter.[7]

5.2 INTEGRATION OF THE RESULTS OF CHAPTERS 3 AND 4

In the preceding we have left open the question of whether or not the Galatian and Corinthian opponents were backed by the Jerusalem mother church in their struggle against Paul. It is now all the more urgent to answer this question, since a compromise formula was attained at the conference which had made an agreement possible, thus keeping the possibility open that Paul's opponents were in fact false brethren or false apostles who had no support at all from the Jerusalem church.[8] At the same time, the problem, dealt with above only incidentally, still awaits a solution, namely, why the Corinthian opponents who apparently belonged to the mediating party at the Jerusalem Conference still joined in the later polemical attacks against Paul.

One of the most important results of chapter 3, above, was that a change in the leadership of the Jerusalem church had taken place between the conference visit and the visit to deliver the collection. The result was not only that James the Lord's brother attained a leading position in the Jerusalem church but also that the "false brethren" of the Jerusalem church attained a position of greater influence, although—reversing the situation that had obtained at the time of the conference—the more liberal Jewish Christians of course continued as members of the Jerusalem church. Paul, who was a disputed figure in Jerusalem circles anyway (see above, chapter 2) fell more and more into the twilight zone, so that in the following period anti-Paulinism emerged victorious and the collection no longer acceptable. Theologically, the anti-Pauline resistance in Jerusalem precipitated out into the declaration that Paul's preaching and practice were causing the Jews of the Diaspora to give up their identity as Jews.

The results of chapter 3 suggest the conclusion that the Galatian opponents, despite their obvious failure to observe the Jerusalem agreement, were able to count on at least the neutrality of Jerusalem[9] until the Jerusalem leaders would decide to sever their connection with the Pauline churches.

As shown above, the Galatian anti-Paulinists were in agreement with the Jerusalem concordat in their denial of Paul's apostleship. Paul's claim to apostleship, as understood by himself in the sense of equality with the Jerusalem apostles, they could consider to be only presumption, since for them the church was bound to Jerusalem and the other missionary centers could be understood only as branches of the mother church.[10]

On this point the Jerusalem leaders (at the time of the conference *and* at the time of the visit with the collection), the Galatian opponents, and the Corinthian anti-Paulinists all agree. The debates in Corinth were thus not so much struggles over the issue of whether Gentile Christians should be circumcised—in this regard the Corinthian opponents were liberal in comparison to the Galatian opponents (see above)—but over the authority of Paul in relation to that of the Jerusalem leaders. What we have, then, is a struggle over primacy: "both the primacy of certain persons and primacy of place."[11] Obviously Cephas and his followers had not taken seriously enough the Pauline claim to equality as an apostle made during the conference, or else Paul had not attributed enough importance to the emphasis on theological differences. But in Pauline territory the net weight of the fact that Paul had founded the Gentile churches himself was clear to them, as was the correlative claim that Paul was apostle to the Gentiles. Thus it was decided after a hesitant beginning (visible in 1 Corinthians) to send a corrective mission into Paul's territory.

We may conclude Part I with the summary comment that since the Corinthian and Galatian crisis at the beginning of the fifties, both the liberal and conservative wings of Jerusalem Jewish Christianity had shared an anti-Pauline attitude.[12] It was necessarily the case that Paul's claim to apostleship would be the spark that kindled this attitude, and, regarded theologically, this claim was the bone of contention between a nomistically oriented Christianity and the christologically based religion of Paul.

PART II
ANTI-PAULINISM
IN THE POST-PAULINE PERIOD

6

ANTI-PAULINISM
OF THE *DESPOSYNOI*

The expression *desposynoi*[1] is here used, as is generally the case, as a term for the relatives of Jesus, to the extent that they can be perceived in the sources available to us from the period 70–120 C.E.[2] For such reports, we are indebted to Hegesippus and Julius Africanus, although the term itself is used only by the latter.

6.1 THE TRADITION REWORKED
BY HEGESIPPUS

We will here deal not with Hegesippus himself but only with the tradition which he reworked. For the basis for the division that is here presupposed between tradition and redaction, cf. the discussion of Hegesippus below in chapter 10.

6.1.1 Simeon

Hegesippus reports the following event: (After the death of James) "Simeon, the son of Clopas, an uncle of the Lord,[3] was named bishop. All the others had suggested him as the second bishop, because he was the Lord's cousin" (Eusebius, *Hist. Ecc.*. 4.22.4).[4]

The idea that James was the first and Simeon was the second "bishop" of Jerusalem certainly goes back to Hegesippus, who was concerned to establish the continuity of the officeholders of the Jerusalem church (see below, p. 165). Even though as a consequence of this interest he projects the monarchial episcopate back to the earliest time, this does not necessarily mean that the report that James was followed by Simeon[5] was created out of thin air, for the list of Jerusalem bishops (Eusebius, *Hist. Ecc.* 4.5.3),[6] which is independent of the fragment of tradition preserved in Hegesippus, in any case names Simeon as the successor of James.[7]

A further element in the tradition is found in the report that

119

Simeon was a kinsman of Jesus and it was on this basis that he was selected to be James's successor. It is true enough that Hegesippus is our only source of this information, but still its redactional origin is unlikely, since at the time of Hegesippus there was no dynastic principle at work in the selection of bishops.[8] The conclusion is therefore unavoidable that we are here dealing with tradition that can only be named historical and thus that the decisive factor in Simeon's choice was his familial relationship with Jesus.[9]

Hegesippus provides the following report of Simeon's death. "Some of these (that is to say the heretics) accused Simon the son of Clopas of being descended from David and a Christian and thus he suffered martyrdom, being a hundred and twenty years old, when Trajan was emperor and Atticus was Consular" (Eusebius, *Hist. Ecc.* 3.32.3).[10]

The reports are in part legendary (the high age of Simeon: 120 years) and tendentious (charges made by heretics,[11] descendants of David[12]). The historical kernel of the tradition is the fact of Simeon's martyrdom. It came to Hegesippus either as an isolated element of tradition or within the framework of a martyrology. In any case, it serves to document that fact that Simeon had been a well-known figure in Palestinian Christianity. If he cannot be relegated to the realm of legend,[13] then the observations made above in regard to the possibility of a dynastic principle operative in his being chosen gain additional weight. In addition, they fit well into the Jewish sense of family.[14]

6.1.2 The Grandsons of Judas

Hegesippus reports the following incident:

> "Now there still survived of the family of the Lord grandsons of Judas, who was said to have been his brother according to the flesh, and they were delated as being of the family of David. These the officer brought to Domitian Caesar, for, like Herod, he was afraid of the coming of the Christ. He asked them if they were of the house of David and they admitted it. Then he asked them how much property they had, or how much money they controlled, and they said that all they possessed was nine thousand denarii between them, the half belonging to each, and they stated that they did not possess this in money but that it was the valuation of only thirty-nine plethra of ground on which they paid

taxes and lived on it by their own work."[15] They then showed him their hands, adducing as testimony of their labour the hardness of their bodies, and the tough skin which had been embossed on their hands from their incessant work. They were asked concerning the Christ and his kingdom, its nature, origin, and time of appearance, and explained that it was neither of the world nor earthly, but heavenly and angelic, and it would be at the end of the world, when he would come in glory to judge the living and the dead and to reward every man according to his deeds. At this Domitian did not condemn them at all, but despised them as simple folk, released them, and decreed an end to the persecution against the church. But when they were released they were the leaders of the churches, both for their testimony and their relation to the Lord, and remained alive in the peace which ensued until Trajan. (Eusebius, *Hist. Ecc.* 3.20.1–6).[16]

Which elements of the above text may be regarded as historical? In the following we will attempt an answer to this question by separating the features that are certainly redactional from the statement of the story itself.[17]

In my opinion, the claim to Davidic descent for the grandsons of Judas can only be considered to be redactional. At the time that the story was composed (the beginning of the second century),[18] Davidic sonship was already an element of christological doctrine,[19] and "in the whole of the Gospel materials there is no piece of tradition on the theme 'Son of David' that could be traced back to Jesus himself with any degree of certainty."[20] Thus the statement that Jesus' relatives were denounced before Domitian as descendants of David must be considered as unhistorical.[21]

At the same time, the confession of faith that Judas' grandsons are supposed to have made before Domitian is even less reliable historically: the kingdom of God will come at the end of the world, when Christ will appear in his glory to judge the living and the dead and to reward each according to his works. This theology is too Christian-in-general to serve for the reconstruction of the theology of Judas' grandsons in particular.

So also, the statement that the Domitian persecution was stopped immediately after the release of the Lord's relatives is certainly redactional. In addition, it is located, like the confession of faith of the *desposynoi*, in that section in which Eusebius is summarizing the Hegesippus text (cf. above, n. 15).

121

On the other hand, the fact of the interrogation of Judas' grandsons by the Romans, and the further description of their occupation, namely, that they were (poor) farmers[22] who paid taxes, appear to derive from historical tradition. Suetonius, *The Lives of the Caesars* 8.12.2, reports that Domitian[23] collected taxes from the Jews, using severe violence:

> Besides other taxes, that on the Jews was levied with utmost rigour, and those were persecuted who without publicly acknowledging that faith yet lived as Jews, as well as those who concealed their origin and did not pay the tribute levied upon their people.[24]

Thus the above story may have originated on the basis of some experience of interrogation during the process of collecting taxes.[25] This also, of course, involved the Jewish-Christian grandsons of Judas, who were Palestinian farmers and earned their own living with their hands.

And finally, it is probable that the conclusion of the story rests on historical tradition. It reads in Greek: *tous de apolythentas hēgēsasthai tōn ekklēsiōn, hōs an dē martyras homou kai apo genous ontas tou kyriou.* This conclusion has a parallel in Eusebius, *Hist. Ecc.* 3.32.6: *Erchontai oun kai proēgountai pasēs ekklēsias hōs martyres kai apo genous tou kyriou.*

The version cited last probably stands nearer to the original text of Hegesippus, because it is presented explicitly as a *quotation*, while the first passage is a Eusebian paraphrase (see above, n. 15). The better version must therefore be used in the following considerations on the historical value of the tradition.

The historical core of the tradition consists of two elements: (a) the grandsons of Judas have a leading role within the church, (b) which is based on their witness before the Roman authorities and on their kinship to the Lord.

Concerning (a): In the Christian vocabulary of the second century, the verb *proēgeomai* describes a *concrete* position of leadership. It is used this way in the table of household duties in *1 Clem.* 21.6[26] for the presiding officials and in *Herm. Vis.* 2.2.6 and 3.9.7 of the leaders of the church (*proēgoumenoi tēs ekklēsias*).[27] Thus when it is said of Judas' grandsons that they are leaders of each (and every)[28] church, this can be meant only in the sense of a leading position in the church as a whole,[29,30] analogous to that claimed by James the brother of the Lord a few decades earlier.

Concerning (b): This claim to a position of leadership is based on their role as witnesses and on their kinship to the Lord. One can only ask which of these two qualifications was decisive in their being acknowledged to have positions of leadership. Since we already know of one case in which it was kinship to the Lord that was the decisive (and only) basis for being chosen for a respected position of leadership in Palestinian Christianity (the choice of Simeon as James's successor), it is easy to suppose that this was also the case here and that this relationship was the basis of their choice, independently of the fact that they came near to martyrdom. The fact of their interrogation by the Roman authorities was then an additional confirmation[31] of their position of leadership established on other grounds.

6.2 THE TRADITION REWORKED BY JULIUS AFRICANUS

Julius Africanus, in an excerpt in Eusebius *Hist. Eoo.* 1.7.14, reports the following incident. The relatives of the Lord (*desposynoi*), "when they went out from the Jewish villages of Nazareth and Cochaba to other parts of the world, explained the aforementioned genealogy also[32] from the Book of the Days, as faithfully as possible" (trans. by M. Eugene Boring from the German).

In order to separate tradition from redaction, we must first deal with the question of why Africanus reports the incident that deals with the *desposynoi*: In the letter to Aristides[33] partially preserved in Eusebius, *Hist. Ecc.* 1.7, Africanus is concerned to harmonize the contradictory genealogies of the evangelists. His solution: the list of ancestors in Matthew describes Jesus' forefathers *kata physin*; that in Luke, Jesus' forefathers *kata nomon*.[34] All the same, both genealogies prove the Davidic sonship of Jesus. This truth,[35] affirmed by both Matthew and Luke, is confirmed by the Lord's relatives. Africanus has the documented information[36] from them that, despite Herod's attempt to burn all the genealogical records of the Jews, Jesus' family and a few others had been able to save their records. And these records would now be able to clarify the genealogical tables contained in the Gospels.

This should make clear why it is that Africanus brings up the subject of the Lord's relatives in a commentary on the genealogies of Matthew and Luke. The documented fact that some families, including Jesus', had been able to save their genealogical records is supposed to show that a precise genealogical chart was available for Jesus.[37] At the same time, confirmation is provided that Jesus was a descendant of David.

In the following we will attempt to establish the (historical) tradition present in Africanus's report. We will proceed in such a manner that at first the form and extent of the tradition that came to Africanus is presented. Then we will deal specifically with the historical value of this tradition.

Africanus introduces his narrative with the following words: "This report [i.e., concerning the genealogies of Jesus] is by no means incapable of proof, nor is it simply composed from thin air. For the physical relatives of the Saviour (*tou sōtēros hoi kata sarka syngeneis*), whether in order to display their own illustrious origin, or simply to state the facts, but in any case adhering strictly to the truth, have also transmitted the following accounts (Eusebius, *Hist. Ecc.* 1.7.11).

One might be tempted to assume that in what follows, Africanus is quoting a source written by the Lord's relatives themselves. So, for example, R. Knopf holds that Africanus paraphrases or quotes verbatim from the Book of the Days named later (1.7.14). In this book was supposedly recounted "how the Herodian dynasty ascended to power, that Herod had burned the archives with the family registers of the Jews, and finally that in spite of all this Jesus' relatives had been able to hand on the genealogy of the Lord in the book."[38] But two objections are to be raised against that.

(*a*). Africanus is not at all quoting but is speaking himself. Otherwise, a passage such as 1.7.14 cannot really be understood. It says, in paraphrase: "To those who saved their family records there belonged the aforementioned *desposynoi*." Such a sentence is inconceivable in a source deriving from the *desposynoi* themselves. But it is readily explainable, if Africanus is himself composing.

(*b*). The Book of the Days never existed. The expression rather designates the Old Testament books of Chronicles[39] (Hebrew *dibre hayammaim*), which will have helped the *desposynoi* with their genealogy.

For these two reasons one must forsake the theory of the use of a source here and instead only presuppose that Africanus himself composed the story in Eusebius, *Hist. Ecc.* 1.7.11–15, on the basis of traditions.

With this we come to the question of the preservation of (historical) traditions in this section. Our methodological procedure is the same as above (p. 120f.), namely, that we first remove the unhistorical features from the text in order to reveal the (historical) traditional elements.

The following legendary details may be peeled off: the story of the burning of the archives by Herod (1.7.13) is found only here in the Jewish-Christian literature[40] and does not generate trust. It is easy to suspect that it goes back to Africanus himself, who uses it as a foil for the statement about the trustworthiness of the Synoptic genealogies.[41]

Further, it is extremely doubtful that laypersons—as the text presupposes—maintained genealogical registers.[42] Thus this feature of the anecdote probably also goes back to Africanus's zeal to verify the trustworthiness of the evangelists' genealogies by the Lord's relatives. Similarly, whether Jesus' family made use of the books of Chronicles[43] is also uncertain. This element in the story could likewise derive from Africanus. Of course, in both cases we do not get beyond general possibilities.

Thus the following tradition remains as the probable historical element of the traditional material used by Africanus: the association of Jesus' family with Nazareth and Cochaba. In favor of the historicity of the Nazareth tradition, we need only say here that nothing is more natural than that Jesus' relatives should have continued to live in their hometown. But the question immediately rises concerning the relation of Cochaba[44] to Nazareth. The confusion appears to be all the greater, since there existed a Cochaba east of the Jordan, which was inhabited by Jewish Christians (Epiphanius, *Heresies* 29.7.7; 30.2.7f.). Can this refer to the same Cochaba? Harnack objects:

> One can hardly think of Epiphanius's Cochaba, which is located east of the Jordan, . . . since Africanus names Nazareth and the other village in the same breath as the homeland of Jesus' rela-

tives, who, after all, were Galileans. It must then be considered simply a coincidence that the hometown of Jesus' family and a location east of the Jordan, later inhabited by numerous Christians, sound almost alike.[45]

Harnack's explanation does not satisfy. Although the name Cochaba was not an uncommon place-name in Palestine,[46] still it seems very "coincidental" that relatives of Jesus and Jewish Christians would have been located at two different places with the same name.[47]

One additional text is now to be added to the texts from Epiphanius named above, a passage that will (finally) confirm the trustworthiness of the aforementioned data on Cochaba: Eusebius, Onomasticon, par. 172.1ff. in Klostermann's edition: Chōba (Gen. 14:15) [hē estin en aristera Damaskou]. estin de kai Chōba kōmē en tois autois meresin, en hē eisin Hebraiōn hoi eis Christon pisteusantes, Ebiōnaioi kaloumenoi. This establishes that "Ebionites"[48] lived in Cochaba in the second and third centuries. Since these, along with the relatives of Jesus, are to be understood as Jewish Christians in the sense defined above, and since they probably honored James as a revered leader of the past, one can hardly consider it accidental that their respective cities bear almost the same names. It is much more likely that they all lived in the same village, in Cochaba.

Geographically, the village is probably to be located in Batanaea, as indicated by Epiphanius, Heresies 29.7.7 and 30.2.8. This same area would also be indicated by Eusebius's note in the Onomasticon, although it apparently stands in contradiction to it.

In the Onomasticon, Eusebius writes that a village Choba, in which "Ebionites" lived, is to be located in the area of (en tois autois meresin) the biblical Choba (cf. above, p. 125).[49] Since biblical Choba was to be sought "left" of Damascus, the same must be true—so one must infer—with regard to the Choba of the Ebionites. But that must mean that since in the Old Testament "left" means "north,"[50] the biblical Choba was located north of Damascus.

However, if Eusebius is describing the location of the Cochaba of the Ebionites in conjunction with that of the biblical Cochaba, then we would have a dilemma, for Batanaea is not situated north of Damascus.[51] But against this is immediately to be objected that it is not clear how Eusebius understood "left." Perhaps he did not associate it with any point of the compass[52] but understood it generally as meaning "near" to something.[53] In this case, one could reconcile Epiphanius's location with that of Eusebius, if one takes into account the imprecise usage of the latter. It should also be mentioned that Eusebius may have adopted the Egyptian usage, in which "left" means "south."[54] In this case, Epiphanius's location would fit that of Eusebius perfectly, for Batanaea lies about forty miles south of Damascus.

To be sure, the geographical problem discussed here can be settled only with more or less probability.[55] But it is worthy of more than passing notice that the identification of the Cochaba of Africanus, Epiphanius, and Eusebius achieved here primarily by literary methods does not evoke any counterarguments on geographical grounds.[56] On the contrary, Epiphanius and Eusebius may even point to the same geographical location for Cochaba.

With this we come to the question of how the tradition preserved by Africanus fits in and how the place-names Nazareth and Cochaba are to be related to each other. It is in fact remarkable that Africanus names Nazareth and Cochaba in the same breath, although according to the view suggested here they were separated by two hundred kilometers.

In my opinion, the problem can be solved only when one resolves, contrary to Harnack's approach, to renounce a historicizing exegesis and instead to work purely on literary grounds. Then the following state of affairs emerges: Africanus knows a tradition,[57] according to which the relatives of Jesus went forth into Palestine (a) from Nazareth and (b) from Cochaba. That by no means indicates that they proceeded from both places at the same time. The dates of these two events could have been completely different. (Africanus is not writing about this until the beginning of the third century.)[58] Since it is clear that Cochaba is located in Batanaea, and thus in the immediate vicinity of the east Jordan territory, the residence of Jesus' relatives in Cochaba can have taken place only after their residence in Nazareth. This means that they must have gone there[59] from Nazareth as a result of the Jewish War.[60]

6.3 THE ANTI-PAULINISM
OF THE *DESPOSYNOI*

After this extended preliminary discussion, we come finally to the question of the anti-Paulinism of the relatives of the Lord.

The result of the above discussion is that in the second century Ebionites and the Lord's relatives dwelled together in the same location in Transjordan. To be sure, it is more likely that only a part of the *desposynoi* lived together in one location rather than the whole clan. It is thus probable that the tradition used by Hegesippus comes at least in part from Cochaba. An explicit rejection of Paul by the Ebionites is reported by Irenaeus, *Heresies* 1.26.2.[61] It is very probable that they had lived in Cochaba already before the composition of Irenaeus's work. The *desposynoi* (as a result of the Jewish War) had fled from Nazareth to Cochaba. The hypothesis is thus permitted that the *desposynoi* brought their hostility to Paul with them to Cochaba and did not only later take it over from the "Ebionites." Rather, the name "Ebionites" probably includes the relatives of Jesus.

The above reflections on the anti-Paulinism of the *desposynoi*, because of the questionable situation with regard to the sources, do not of course prove anything. They do attempt, however, to explain the remarkable fact that relatives of Jesus and "Ebionites" had the same residence in Transjordan during the second century.

These reflections in this chapter thus lead us finally to the existence of a Jewish Christianity on Palestinian soil and in Transjordan after the first Jewish War and prior to the second, a Jewish Christianity that has dynastic traits and is anti-Pauline. Whether this anti-Paulinism was traditional, that is, taken over from James and directed against the historical Paul, or—in my opinion more likely—whether there was a real debate with contemporary Pauline tradition and pictures of Paul, is an issue that can no longer be definitively decided. In any case, there can hardly be any doubt concerning the fact of an anti-Pauline attitude of the *desposynoi*, and it is clear that even if it were only a matter of anti-Paulinism at the level of an inherited tradition, this could immediately become a sword in the hand of those who might need to resist Pauline disciples or expositors.

7

THE ANTI-PAULINISM
OF THE ELKESAITES

On procedure: It is not the task of the following discussion to present a detailed description of the various groups of the Elkesaites and their theology. That would require an analysis of the whole corpus, which is not possible here.[1] The relevant texts will instead be discussed, with the question in mind presented above on p. 32. The following problems with regard to the Elkesaite texts will incidentally be clarified:

a. Do the texts contain an anti-Pauline element?

b. How is it anchored in the system of thought as a whole? (Is it a secondary accretion or an original element?)

c. Are the Elkesaites to be regarded as Jewish Christians?

d. How may the Elkesaites be categorized in terms of chronology and geography?

7.1 ORIGEN'S EXPOSITION OF PSALM 82
(IN EUSEBIUS, *HIST. ECC.* 6.38)
AS A WITNESS TO THE ANTI-PAULINISM
OF THE ELKESAITES

The anti-Paulinism of the Elkesaites is documented by no less a figure than Origen. In *Hist. Ecc.* 6.38, Eusebius cites from an exegesis of Psalm 82 that Origen had delivered in Caesarea:

> There has come just now a certain man who prides himself on being able to champion a godless and very impious opinion, of the Helkesaites, as it is called, which has lately come into opposition with the churches. I shall lay before you the mischievous teachings of that opinion, that you may not be carried away by it. It rejects some things from every Scripture; again, it has made use of texts from every part of the Old Testament and the Gospels; it rejects the Apostle entirely (*ton apostolon teleon athetei*). And it says that to deny is a matter of indifference, and that the discreet man will on occasions of necessity deny with his mouth, but not in his heart. And they produce a certain book of which they say that

it has fallen from heaven, and that he who has heard it and believes will receive forgiveness of his sins—a forgiveness other than that which Christ Jesus has bestowed.[2]

If one deletes the first and last sentences of this report as typical heresiological polemic,[3] what remains is a good summary (see below for reasons) of the information about the Elkesaites available to us from other sources. More precisely, we must immediately add to what has just been said that the excerpt from Origen is our only unambiguous source for an anti-Pauline attitude among the Elkesaites.[4] If this should belong to a later stage in the development of the sect, as is sometimes affirmed in the literature,[5] then the Elkesaites would be of only limited significance for the theme pursued here. Or was anti-Paulinism directly linked to the beginning of the sect after all?

On the basis of the evidence presented above, it would be a fatal mistake to claim that only the later Elkesaites had been anti-Pauline. For of course the date when anti-Paulinism is documented among the Elkesaites need not coincide with the time of its actual emergence. On the other side, of course, whoever affirms a connection between anti-Paulinism and the beginning of the sect must be able to substantiate this assumption. For it would be easily imaginable that later Elkesaites had adopted anti-Paulinism from other groups such as the Ebionites.

The following criteria for the resolution of this problem are here suggested: In the event that Elkesaitism had been purely Jewish in its beginnings, it would be probable that an anti-Pauline attitude was only later acquired,[6] as the group developed closer ties with the Ebionites. Only if Elkesaitism had originally been a Jewish Christian sect is there the possibility that it had been anti-Pauline from the beginning. But since there was certainly a Jewish Christianity untouched by Paul (see above, pp. 29f.), even if there were proof of the Jewish-Christian origin of the Elkesaites, this would still not prove its anti-Pauline attitude but only open up this possibility.

7.2 THE BASIC ELEMENTS OF ELKESAITE DOCTRINE: JEWISH OR JEWISH-CHRISTIAN?

In the following we will reconstruct, in conjunction with the report from Origen and on the basis of the other sources at our disposal, the basic elements of Elkesaite doctrine: Origen tells of a book that fell from heaven, in which there was a new announcement of the forgiveness of sins. Quotations from it are found in Hippolytus and Epiphanius. We will devote ourselves primarily to the report in Hippolytus, because it is sometimes used to support the hypothesis that the basic elements of the Elkesaite system are not recognizable, since they are so covered over by the editing process. Thus for us the decisive question will be whether Hippolytus, in his portrayal of the Elkesaite advance on Rome and of the Elkesaite views, quotes extensively from the Book of Elkesai or whether he primarily describes the life style and teaching of the Elkesaite Alcibiades. In the latter case, inferences with regard to the Book of Elkesai and thus the basic elements of the Elkesaite system would be uncertain, since its contents would be known to us only through the editorial work of Alcibiades.[7] In the first case, we would have direct access to the preaching of the prophet Elkesai.

The issue can be settled only by a literary-critical analysis of the relevant chapters.[8,9]

7.2.1 Structure and Train of Thought of Hippolytus, Ref. 9.8–12

Ref. 9.8 (p. 251.9—252.4) reports the coming of Alcibiades, who was originally from Apamea, to Rome. He brought a book with him, claiming that a certain righteous man, Elkesai, had received this from the people of Seræ,[10] a town in Parthia, and that he had given it to a man called Sobiaï:

> And the contents of this volume, he alleged, had been revealed by an angel whose height was 24 schœnoi, which make 96 miles, and whose breadth was 4 schœnoi, and from shoulder to shoulder 6 schœnoi; and the tracks of his feet extend to the length of three and a half schœnoi, which are equal to 14 miles, while the breadth is one schœnos, and a half, and the height half a schœnos. And he alleges that also there is a female with him, whose measurement, he says, is according to the standards already mentioned. And he asserts that the male (angel) is Son of God, but that the female is called Holy Spirit. (9.8 = 251.14–20)[11]

He continues with a report of the contents of the book as follows:

> ... "that there was preached unto men a new remission of sins in the third year of Trajan's reign." And Elchasai determines the

nature of baptism, and even this I shall explain. He alleges, *as to* those who have been involved in every description of lasciviousness, and filthiness, and *in* acts of wickedness, if only any *of them* be a believer, that he determines that such a one, on being converted, and obeying the book, and believing *its contents,* should by baptism receive remission of sins. (9.8 = 251.22–252.4)[12]

At this point a redactional seam becomes visible. In the following section Hippolytus compares the shady practices of Alcibiades with those of Callistus, whose tricks had formed the point of departure for Alcibiades' own machinations. After this he continues his own summary:

> But since we have commenced, we shall not be silent as regards the opinions of this *man*. And, in the first place, we shall expose his life, and we shall prove that his supposed discipline is a mere pretence. And next, I shall adduce the principal heads of his assertions, in order that the reader, looking fixedly on the treatises of this (Elchasai), may be made aware what and what sort is the heresy which has been audaciously attempted by this man. (9.8 = 252.12–17)

This comment by Hippolytus on how his report concerning the heresy is to be utilized is of great significance for the separation of tradition (the Book of Elkesai) and redaction (Alcibiades' life and teaching). According to Hippolytus, in his report so far he had only placed Alcibiades' life in the proper light and had shown that his asceticism was only pretended. To which part of his report is the heresy fighter referring with this remark? Obviously, to the redactional passage which concerns the relationship of Alcibiades to Callistus (p. 252.4–12). Here, Hippolytus had in fact described Alcibiades as the kind of person who was only lying in wait to capture the sheep who had been scattered by Callistus with the seductive message of the Book of Elkesai, that is, as a fraud who in fact was not sincere about the value of asceticism. Otherwise, Alcibiades would not have stepped forth into the public view with such a lax understanding of morality. (For Hippolytus, Alcibiades is the shadow image of Callistus.)

If this thus provides a satisfactory explanation for p. 252.4–12 on the basis of the summary statement of Hippolytus cited above, this is by no means the case for the previously discussed section, p. 251.9—252.4, for here Alcibiades' life is only incidentally mentioned. Rather, Hippolytus appears there to cite only in an anticipatory manner from the Book of Elkesai which Alcibiades had brought with him to Rome.[13] Otherwise there is no explanation for the comment that in the third year of Trajan a new forgiveness of sins had been proclaimed to humanity. And in any case, such a presupposition offers the best basis for understanding the description of the Son of God and the Holy Spirit, which obviously belongs to the book's introductory vision. (For further evidence for the view that Hippolytus is already quoting from the Book of Elkesai[14] at the beginning of this report, see below, p. 134.)

With this, we return to the outline of Hippolytus's report of Elkesai:

In 9.8 (p. 252.12ff.), Hippolytus had announced that he would present the main points of Alcibiades' doctrine. He carries out this intention in the following:

Ref. 9.9 (p. 252.19ff.) reports the fact that he (Alcibiades) lived according to the law and demands that believers be circumcised. In regard to Christology, he accepts the view that *ton Christon . . . anthrōpon koinōs pasi gegonenai* ("Christ was born a man in the same way as common to all") (p. 252.20f.), which appears to point to nothing else than an adoptionist Christology. But one is then surprised to find the following: *touton de ou nyn prōtōs ek parthenou gegennēsthai, alla kai proteron. kai authis pollakis gennēthenta kai gennōmenon pephēnenai kai phyesthai, allassonta geneseis kai metensōmatoumenon* ("Christ was not for the first time on earth when born of a virgin, but that both previously and that frequently again He had been born and would be born. Christ would thus appear and exist among us from time to time, undergoing alterations of birth, and having his soul transferred from body to body") (p. 252.21–24). According to Hippolytus, this is borrowed from Pythagoras.

Following this (p. 252.25ff.), the church father reports that they (*sic*) call themselves superior Gnostics (*prognōstikoi*), occupy themselves with mathematical and astrological things, and resort to incantations for those who have been bitten by dogs.[15] The key word "Pythagoras", to whom both Alcibiades (p. 252.24) and Roman Elkesaites (p. 252.19ff.) are traced back, is an external point of contact which binds together both sections (p. 252.19ff. and p. 252.25ff.).

Hippolytus concludes the section begun with 9.8 (p. 252.25) with the words:

> Having then sufficiently explained their principles, and the causes of their presumptuous attempts, I shall pass on to give an account of their writings. (9.9; p. 252.6–9)

In section 9.15—17.1 (p. 253.10—255.11), the church father cites extensively. *Ref.* 9.10 begins with an excerpt on the significance of the second baptism:

> If, therefore, (my) children, one shall have intercourse with any sort of animal whatsoever, or a male, or a sister, or a daughter, or hath committed adultery, or been guilty of fornication, and is desirous of obtaining remission of sins, from the moment that he harkens to this book let him be baptized a second time in *the* name of the Great and Most High God, and in *the* name of His Son, the Mighty King. And *by baptism* let him be purified and cleansed, and let him adjure for himself those seven witnesses that have been described in this book—the heaven, and the water, and the holy spirits, and the angels of prayer, and the oil, and the salt, and the earth. (p. 253.11–19)

After some polemical remarks, Hippolytus continues with his citation (9.10):

> Again I say, O adulterers and adulteresses, and false prophets, if you are desirous of being converted, that your sins may be forgiven you, as soon as ever you hearken unto this book, and be baptized a second time along with your garments, shall peace be yours, and your portion with the just. (p. 253.23–26)[16]

The two examples quoted show that Hippolytus in fact did carry out his intention and quoted from writings, or a writing, of the Elkesaites, in the course of which he also cites verbatim several additional passages.[16a] It is noticeable that from 9.10 on he again speaks of *one* person and obviously is quoting his sayings. That can mean nothing else than that Alcibiades and/or Elkesaites who had settled in Rome appealed to sayings of a prophet as support for their preaching. Since at the beginning of his report (9.8) Hippolytus speaks of the fact that Alcibiades had brought a book with him to Rome, there can be only one conclusion: sayings of this book composed of "I sayings" are quoted from 9.10 on.

This hypothesis can be supported by two arguments:

1. The citations in 9.8 correspond to the citations in Epi-

phanius, *Pan.* 19.4.1 and 30.17.6f., where admittedly it is the Book of Elkesai that lies behind the quotations.[17]

2. The content of 9.8 is taken up again in 9.10f. In 9.8 Hippolytus appears to have already quoted from the Book of Elkesai or to have paraphrased it (see above, p. 134).

Summary of the literary-critical analysis of Hippolytus, *Ref.* 9.8–12: It is not possible to separate the preaching of Alcibiades from that of Elkesai. The section in which Hippolytus lets Alcibiades speak is extremely terse and general. It is by no means adequate to permit an analysis of a redactional tendency of the Elkesaite from Apamea. Rather, it is easy to see traditional Elkesaite views expressed in each of the two individual points that Hippolytus introduces as doctrines of Alcibiades (circumcision and reincarnations of Christ).[18] The basic features of the content of the book are to be reconstructed from the fragments[19] preserved in Hippolytus and Epiphanius,[20] which means that the basic outline of the Elkesaite system becomes visible in Hippolytus's report.

7.2.2 The Jewish-Christian Basic Elements of the Elkesaite System

If there is any validity to the literary-critical analysis of Hippolytus's report given above, then it is of the highest significance for the question of whether the basic elements of the Elkesaite system are Jewish or Jewish-Christian. For now, the conclusion seems unavoidable that Christian elements had been present in Elkesaite theology from the very beginning.

1. The vision of the Son of God and of the Holy Spirit points to a Christian provenance.

2. So also does the baptismal formula "in the name of the Son, the great King."

3. And the doctrine of forgiveness of sins has no parallel in the functions and effects attributed to the Jewish ritual baths.[21]

4. "Elkesaite baptism is applied in the same manner as Christian baptism. Its restriction to gross sinners does not give it the general significance of an initiatory act but does presuppose such an understanding, namely, that of Christian baptism."[22]

5. The expectation of the imminent end[23] is reminiscent of Christian models, as is that of

6. The virgin birth.

135

The advocates of the purely Jewish origin of Elkesaitism have an element of truth in their view, namely, that unquestioned doctrines such as circumcision and daily ritual baths, which are to be distinguished from baptism, can only be traced back to Jewish influence. Still, they must have been mediated through a kind of Christianity that perceived no clash between the Christian elements named above and these Jewish elements. Thus regarded historically, Elkesai belonged to Jewish Christianity.[24, 25] The same conclusion is also required by the following parallels that the Elkesaites have with Jewish Christianity.

1. The Book of Elkesai directs that prayer should always be made in the direction of Jerusalem[26] (Epiphanius, *Pan.* 19.3.5[27]).[28] To be sure, the Jews of the second century also follow this custom,[29] but Irenaeus, *Heresies* 1.26.2, documents for us that this was also the practice of the Ebionites.[30]

2. The observance of the Sabbath (for the Elkesaites, cf. Hippolytus, *Ref.* 9.11) is documented as a Jewish-Christian practice by Eusebius, *Hist. Ecc.* 3.27.5.[31]

3. Reincarnations of Christ (Hippolytus, *Ref.* 9.9) are documented in Epiphanius, *Pan.* 30.12.5, as an item of Ebionite doctrine.

4. Another parallel between Elkesaites and Ebionites consists in their common hostility to sacrifice (cf. Epiphanius, *Pan.* 19.3.6 [Elkesaites] and Ps-Clem. *Recg.* 1.37). (On the Ebionite character of this and other passages from the Pseudo-Clementines, see below, pp. 182, 190, and often.)

The Jewish-Christian origin of Elkesaitism being thus firmly established,[32] we may in this same connection point out that the sect is to be considered a characteristic development of Jewish Christianity. The figure of the prophet thus appears to have increasingly gained center stage in the development of the religion, so that Elkesaitism could not improperly be described as a "pre-Manichean Manicheism."[33]

In the preceding discussion, we indicated that the question of whether an anti-Pauline element should be considered to belong to the primary ingredients of Elkesaite doctrine would depend upon, among other things, whether the basis of Elkesaitism was Jewish or Jewish-Christian. After the proof just presented of the Jewish-Christian presupposition of Elkesaite preaching, the possibility now exists that an anti-Pauline element belonged to the earliest phase of the Elkesaites.[34] Before we address the question of the degree of probability that this possibility might have, we will first take a brief look at the chronological and geographical location of the beginnings of the Elkesaite movement.

7.3 THE CHRONOLOGICAL AND GEOGRAPHICAL LOCATION OF ELKESAI

Our sources permit us to locate the date of Elkesai's appearance exactly. Two witnesses, who confirm each other, stand against those judgments[35] which would like to mislocate the beginning of the sect as late as the third century.

1. Hippolytus, *Ref.* 9.8, mentions that Elkesai appeared in the third year of Trajan (=100 C.E.).[36] (Cf. Epiphanius, *Pan.* 19.1.4, who locates the time of Elkesai's appearance generally in the time of Trajan).

2. The revelatory book contains an unfulfilled prediction of the apocalyptic end,[37] which was supposed to take place "when three years of the reign of the emperor Trajan are again completed from the time that he subjected the Parthians to his own sway" (Hippolytus, *Ref.* 9.11). The subjection of the Parthians occurred around the year 115 C.E.,[38] and the catastrophic end announced for 117 C.E. did not materialize. We are thus justified in taking the year 117 C.E. as the *terminus ad quem* of the preaching of Elkesai. He would then have been active in the years 100 to 117 C.E.

The place[39] of Elkesai's activity is to be inferred from the datum that the prophet received his revelatory book "from Seræ, a town of Parthia" (Hippolytus, *Ref.* 9.8). The name "Seræ" provides no geographical information and is only an indication of the book's mysterious origin.[40] All the same, the further indication "in Parthia", the prophecy concerning the Roman war, and the fact that the book was composed in Greek[41] point to the area of the Syrian-Parthian boundary in the upper course of the Euphrates as the region where Elkesai was active.[42] The fact that the Elkesaite Alcibiades lived in Apamea of Syria also fits in well with this.

7.4 ON THE QUESTION OF ANTI-PAULINISM AT THE ROOTS OF THE ELKESAITE MOVEMENT: ITS IMPORTANCE

We have suggested above that an anti-Pauline attitude possibly belonged to the Elkesaite movement already at its beginning. This possibility has become a bit more probable now that the newly opened Cologne Mani codex[43] appears to presuppose an anti-Pauline attitude of Mani's Elkesaite mother congregation.[44]

> Cf. CMC 80.6–18: Now when I destroyed and put to nought their words and mysteries, demonstrating to them that they had not received these things which they pursue from the commandments of the Savior, some of them were amazed at me, but others got cross and angrily said: "Does he not want to go to the Greeks?"[45]

Presupposing that a historically dependable tradition lies behind this,[46] it is possible to assume that the Baptists in this passage implicitly reject Paul as a Greek.[47] Such an assumption can appeal to the datum that the Paul of the Ebionites in Epiphanius is likewise described as a "Greek."[48] And it appears that Mani's departure from the Elkesaite congregation went hand in hand with a turn toward the disciples of Marcion or to Bardesanes,[49] both of whom used the Pauline letters and neither of whom had anything in common with Judaism or Jewish Christianity. In this case, the expression "He is going to the Greeks"[50] appears all the more appropriate as an anti-Pauline expression.[51]

If these explanations are valid, we have attained an additional item of evidence for an anti-Pauline Elkesaite group.[52] It is to be located in southern Babylonia, and since the beginning of the third century its theology is characterized by an anti-Pauline attitude.

Such a result is of significance for the question raised above as to whether anti-Paulinism was a traditional constituent element in Elkesaite doctrine. Since we now possess two independent witnesses for anti-Pauline Elkesaites from the beginning of the third century, widely separated from each other geographically, this result strengthens the hypothesis that anti-Paulinism had been a traditional constituent element of Elkesaite doctrine. The opposite hypothesis, that at the same period two Elkesaite communities had taken over an anti-Pauline attitude independently of each other, is quite improbable.

If Elkesaitism was thus probably anti-Pauline from the very beginning, we may conclude this section by raising the question of the role of anti-Paulinism in the Elkesaite system. There are no indications in the reports of the church fathers of an actual contemporary debate with Paul ('s disciples), so that here the same thing is to be said as in the case of the *desposynoi*: anti-Paulinism belongs (*a*) to those items of doctrine taken over from Jewish Christianity which (*b*) at any time could become sharp weapons against Paul ('s disciples). The last-named possibility appears to have become an actuality in Mani's mother congregation, as Mani withdrew from the Elkesaite congregation and turned toward the Pauline disciples.

8

ANTI-PAULINISM IN JAMES

The following discussion presupposes the "inauthenticity" of James.[1] In accord with our theme, the key question here will be whether there is any passage that polemicizes against Paul.[2] Since this artificial letter is certainly to be dated after 70 C.E., the following kinds of polemic against Paul are possible: (a) polemic against a picture of Paul spread abroad by his followers, either orally or by written documents, (b) polemic against slogans associated with Paul in the oral tradition, and (c) polemic against passages in Pauline letters. The initial step in the following analysis consists of a rigorous *source criticism*. (In case the hypothesis of anti-Paulinism can be verified, the next questions would concern the possible Jewish-Christian character of this anti-Paulinism, the extent to which it is anchored in the theology of James, and its history.) The problem of the theological relationship that obtains between James and Paul, though often dealt with in this connection, is not debated here on methodological grounds (cf. the discussion below under 8.2), since a decision concerning the theological proximity of James to Paul is independent of the question of whether James *intended* to attack Paul.

8.1 ANTI-PAULINE EXPRESSIONS IN JAMES

In this section we will deal with those passages in James which possibly refer to Paul in any of the three ways sketched above.

8.1.1 James 1:2–4 and Romans 5:3–5*

James 1:2–4: *Pasan charan hēgēsasthe, adelphoi mou, hotan* PEIRASMOIS *peripesēte poikilois,* GINŌSKONTES HOTI (I)
to **dokimion** *hymōn tēs pisteōs* **katergazetai hypomonēn. hē de hypomonē** *ergon teleion echetō* (II),
hina ēte teleioi kai holoklēroi, en mēdeni leipomenoi (III).

---

*In the following comparison, exact agreements are in bold face and related phraseology in small caps.

140

Rom. 5:3–5: *kauchōmetha en tais* THLIPSESIN. *EIDOTES HOTI* (I)
he thlipsis **hypomonēn katergazetai, hē de hypomonē dokimēn,** *hē
de* **dokimē** *elpida* (II).
hē de elpis ou kataischunei (III).

The following could be evidence of the literary dependence of
James on Romans: (a) identical vocabulary (in boldface above)[3]
and (b) parallel structure: both texts consist of three units:

(I) The authors begin with the situation of the addressees, who
are in some sort of distress or temptation. In this situation they
should rejoice or boast, for (II) this distress or faith leads to
patience, which in turn leads to hope or a complete work. (III)
The third member forms the climax of the series, in which the
authors point to the unfrustrated goal to which hope finally
comes, or else that the addressees will be complete and whole.

If we assume that the thesis advocated by A. E. Barnett[4] and
others is correct, that the passage from James cited above is
literarily dependent on Rom. 5:3ff., then James would have
destroyed the artfully constructed second part of Paul's chain of
thought in that he would have taken the *dokimē* from the chain
and, connecting it with *pistis*, have placed it at the emphatic
beginning point of the sentence. This would not have happened
without theological intention, since what for Paul first emerges
as the fruit of *thlipsis* stands in James—as an achievement—
already at the beginning.

On the other hand, the agreements pointed out above can just
as well be explained by a common Christian tradition[5] on which
Paul and the author of James were both dependent,[6] all the more
so since in 1 Peter 1:6 a chain of thought parallel to James 1:2ff.
and Rom. 5:3ff. appears.[7]

A dependence of James on Paul's letters is thus not to be
established on the basis of this passage. Therefore James 1:2ff.
also provides no information concerning a possible anti-Paulinism in James.

8.1.2 James 2:10 and Galatians 5:3 (3:10)

James 2:10: *hostis gar holon ton nomon tērēsē, ptaisē de en heni,
gegonen pantōn enochos.*
Gal. 5:3: *martyromai de palin panti anthrōpō peritemnomenō hoti
opheiletēs estin holon ton nomon poiēsai.*
Compare Gal. 3:10: *epikataratos pas hos ouk emmenei pasin tois
gegrammenois en tō bibliō tou nomou tou poēsai auta.*

The verbal agreements between James 2:10 and Gal. 5:3 (3:10) are slight (only *holos ho nomos*). But in terms of content, the passages are practically identical.

The different function of the statements is to be noted. Paul's statements are formulated in order to exclude the way of the law as an option for his congregations: not only can no one fulfill the law, no one should fulfill it (see above, p. 102). On the other hand, the author of James writes his sentence in order to challenge his congregation to keep the law. Verse 10 thus stands in the unit vv. 8–11, which deals with keeping the law. The key word *prosōpolēmptein* (v. 9) binds that unit to the preceding context.

The chain of thought in vv. 8–11 may thus be sketched as follows:

V. 8: The addressees do well when they keep the royal law in accord with the command, "You shall love your neighbor as yourself."

V. 9: However, when they show partiality to certain people (such as the rich of 2:1ff), then they are convicted by the law as transgressors.

V. 10: Whoever keeps the whole law but transgresses in only one matter (as in the example named) has become guilty of transgressing all (the commandments of the law).

Verse 11 illustrates v. 10 (the trangression of only one commandment) and links back to the key work "transgressor" in v. 9: for the one who said "Do not commit adultery" also said "Do not kill." But if you do not commit adultery but kill, you have become a transgressor of the law.

We will return below to the idea of fulfilling the whole law[8] in terms of its content. Here we need to ask only whether James is alluding to a Pauline passage such as Gal. 5:3 or Gal. 3:10. The following reasons speak in favor of such a possibility:

a. The expression "do/observe the whole law" occurs only here in the New Testament.

b. The rigorist content of Gal. 5:3 (3:10) is too isolated in the New Testament[9] and in Judaism[10] not to indicate a literary dependence between the texts cited above. If, as is probable, we thus have here an allusion in James to Galatians or to oral Pauline tradition, the anti-Pauline thrust of this passage is more than clear: against Paul, the author emphasizes the necessity of fulfilling the whole law.

8.1.3 James 2:14–26

This section[11] contains the following points of contact between James and the Pauline letters:

James 2:21: *Abraam ho patēr hēmōn ouk ex ergōn edikaiōthē (aneneg-kas Isaak ton hyion autou epi to thysiastērion)?*
Rom. 4:2: *ei gar Abraam ex ergōn edikaiōthē, echei kauchēma (all' ou pros theon).*

The verbal agreements between the two texts[12] clearly indicate a literary connection between them, whether it is that James know the letter to the Romans itself or a tradition corresponding to Rom. 4:2. This conclusion is also demanded by the fact that prior to Paul no one had ever advocated that Abraham was not justified by works.[13] In this passage James is thus combating a Pauline thesis.[14]

James 2:23: *(kai eplērōthē hē graphē hē legousa:) episteusen de Abraam tō theō, kai elogisthē autō eis dikaiosynēn.*
Rom. 4:3: *(ti gar hē graphē legei?) episteusen de Abraam tō theō kai elogisthē autō eis dikaiosynēn.*

A literary connection between the two texts is suggested by the observation that they agree verbatim with each other but agree in deviating from the LXX (Gen. 15:6) in two otherwise insignificant points: in the spelling of *Abraam* rather than *Abram* and in the addition of *de* after *episteusen.* This means that the author of James had accepted the example of Abraham but uses it *against* Paul as proof for his view that faith is made complete by works (vv. 22b, 24).

James 2:24: *(horate hote) ex ergōn dikaioutai anthrōpos kai ouk ek pisteōs monon.*
Gal. 2:16: *ou dikaioutai anthrōpos ex ergōn nomou ean mē dia pisteōs Iēsou Christou.*
Rom. 3:28: *logizometha gar dikaiousthai pistei anthrōpon chōris ergōn nomou.*

As in the texts discussed above, the verbatim agreements point to a literary connection. The hypothesis that James is dependent on Paul is further supported by the fact that the polar opposition of faith and works is not documented prior to Paul.[15] It is interesting that the *monon* of James 2:24 does not appear in Rom. 3:28. Since the *pistei* of Rom. 3:28 must, however, be understood in an exclusive sense,[16] *monon* is thoroughly appropriate and cannot be used as an argument against a dependence of James on Paul.

In addition, James 2:24 has only *ex ergōn* instead of *ex ergōn nomou*. This datum can by no means call our hypothesis into question but rather indicates that the author of James no longer perceived the function that the concept of law exercised in Pauline theology and "therefore saw no difference between 'works' and 'works of the law.'"[17] In James 2:24 the author of James is thus attacking the Pauline doctrine of justification.

If it is thus established that in the passages discussed above James consciously presents a polemic against Paul, we must now deal with the question of the reason for this attack, a question we have not found necessary to deal with so far. A successful answer to it will perhaps throw light on the theological and historical locus of James and on the other problem that has been left open, whether James knows Pauline letters or is responding on the basis of oral tradition.

Here we must make it very clear that James never really touches Paul's own position. The apostle to the Gentiles knows of no faith that is not at the same time obedience (cf. Rom. 1:5) and that is not active in deeds of love (cf. Gal. 5:6).[18] James's portrayal of the "Pauline" understanding of faith, to the extent that it can be related to the historical Paul, is a caricature.

But what about the possibility that James does not have the historical Paul in view anyway but some group of Paul's followers? Is his description of Paulinism in James 2 then perhaps no caricature after all? In the following, we will address this question and will deal with the issue of the Pauline counterpart of James 2:

a. Did James know Pauline letters or oral Pauline tradition?

b. Who are the bearers of this Pauline tradition (whether oral or written)?

On *a*: In favor of the hypothesis that James knew only oral tradition,[19] one might point out that, apart from the sloganlike statements quoted above in which Pauline doctrine is concentrated, there are no other passages from the Pauline letters reflected in James. But on the other hand, it is to be doubted whether James would have had occasion to allude to other Pauline statements or to enter into debate with them, since his document consists mostly of (sapiential[20]) parenesis. Because of the extensive agreement in vocabulary, I thus consider it more probable that the author of James made use of written sources (Pauline letters).

On b: In recent scholarship on James it has become common to regard the bearers of the Pauline tradition attacked in James 2 as hyper-Paulinists who had misunderstood the Pauline theological antithesis "faith/works of the law."[21] Against this hypothesis is the fact that no text known to us illustrating the gnostic[22] use of Paul corresponds to the position presupposed in James 2.[23] Further, in the deutero-Pauline literature, which theoretically must also be considered when enumerating Paul's opponents, the term "works" is adopted in a positive sense,[24] so that a supposed attack of James against Paul's followers would be even less likely than against Paul himself. (In this case, James would be laboring under an even greater misunderstanding than if he were attacking Paul himself.) It is therefore better to suppose that James is here combating passages from Paul's own letters. He was probably acquainted with Romans and Galatians, or at least passages from them.

All of this raises the question of whether the conclusion that James has misunderstood Paul does not exclude the possibility that the author of James was really attacking Paul. More than eighty years ago, H. J. Holtzmann addressed the counterargument that calls into question the above hypothesis:

> This would mean "that every instance of a polemic that has a distorted view of its opponents' views and thus is directed against a false target would at the same time be proof for any lack of polemical intention against the real target. On this basis it could thus easily be shown that it is impossible that the decrees of the Council of Trent concerning faith and justification could have been directed against the corresponding articles of the Augsburg Confession, since the Catholic understanding of *fides* has a different content than the Protestant."[25]

An important parallel to the misdirected polemic in James is given by the apostle to the Gentiles himself in Rom. 3:8 (6:1) (cf. above, pp. 110f.). Already during Paul's lifetime Paul's Jewish-Christian opponents caricatured his doctrine of justification by claiming that it provoked an immoral life. Similarly, James caricatures the key sentences from Galatians and Romans in such wise that the Pauline concept of faith purportedly does not result in works, that is, ethical conduct.[26]

In the discussion below we will further pursue the issue of whether this interesting parallel in anti-Pauline polemic does not help to determine more closely the provenance of the author of James.

8.2 ON THE RELATION OF
THE THEOLOGY OF JAMES TO ANTI-PAULINISM

The theology of James does *not* correspond to the definition of "Jewish-Christian" worked out above (pp. 29f.). The author never even hints that the so-called ceremonial law[27] is still valid. For him, only the moral law is of significance. He calls it "the perfect law of liberty" (1:25) or the "royal law" (2:8),[28] which is still binding in its totality (2:10). James's doctrine of the law is accompanied by the deep confidence that the believer can accomplish the works that are demanded by the law, so that he or she will be justified in the final judgment (2:12). James is thus a witness for a "nomistic positivism,"[29] the content of which is influenced by the Hellenistic Judaism of the Diaspora.[30]

In James, *pistis* ("faith") is essentially subordinated to the law.[31] In individual cases, *pistis* can refer either to faith in God (2:19 = considering it to be true that God exists) or to faith in Christ (2:1). It is interesting that James 1:6 challenges the reader to pray for wisdom en *pistei*, a wisdom referred to in 3:13:

> Who is wise and understanding among you? By his good life let him show his works in the meekness of wisdom.

This means that *pistis* is bound to works[32] via the concept of wisdom, which comes "from above" (3:15, 17). *Pistis* is accordingly not, as in Paul, primarily understood in relation to Christology. It "does not really become real apart from obedience to

146

the law,"[33] without at the same time being corrupted in a legalistic fashion. In James, the indicative of the saving event and the
imperative coincide.[34] So what is, then, the connection between
the theology of James and anti-Paulinism?

Some help in answering this question is provided by 1 Clement, which on the one hand is in the theological vicinity of
James with regard to its soteriology[35] but on the other hand uses
Paul and the Pauline letters. While we undertake to clarify the
manner of, and reason for, the use of Paul in 1 Clement, we also
hope to shed some light on the relation of the theology of James
to anti-Paulinism

We will not here discuss all the passages in 1 Clement that
reflect the Pauline letters[36] but only 1 Clement 32f.:

> 1 Clem. 32.4: And therefore we who by his will have been called
> in Christ Jesus, are not made righteous by ourselves, or by our
> wisdom or understanding or piety or the deeds which we have
> wrought in holiness of heart, but through faith, by which Almighty
> God has justified all men from the beginning of the world; to him
> be glory for ever and ever. Amen.

The passage was probably formulated in dependence on the
Pauline terminology of justification, although, in addition to
other differences from Paul,[37] the concept of faith is not here
formulated christologically, as in Paul, but theologically. That 1
Clement is formulating these statements in dependence on Paul
is also seen in the immediately following sentences:

> 1 Clem. 33.1: What shall we do, then, brethren? Shall we be
> slothful in well-doing and cease from love? May the master for-
> bid that this should happen, at least to us, but let us be zealous to
> accomplish every good deed with energy and readiness.

The transition from 1 Clem. 32.4 to 1 Clem. 33.1 is strongly
reminiscent of that from Rom. 5:21 to Rom. 6:1, where a fictitious
objector introduces a false inference from Paul's declaration
about justification and is immediately corrected by him. So also
here: after justification by faith is established in 1 Clem. 32.4, the
author of 1 Clement raises the artificial question of whether
Christians can then cease from doing good and immediately
rejects such a suggestion with vigor.

It is thus very likely that 1 Clement 32f. presupposes Paul's letter to the Romans[38] and intends to give his own presentation a Pauline tinge. But one must immediately add that there is an obvious artificiality about this (cf. the letter as a whole) that is really attained only at the expense of a distortion of Paul, although it cannot be said that 1 Clement's theology stands in complete contrast to Paul's.[39]

Something similar is to be said with regard to James: its anti-Paulinism is tacked on,[40] and its picture of Paul is distorted. It "does not, in fact, represent the principal opposition to Paul."[41]

1 Clement and James are thus not witnesses to a Paulinism or an anti-Paulinism in the theological sense but rather documents of an un-Pauline[42] Christianity.[43]

8.3 ON THE HISTORY OF ANTI-PAULINISM IN JAMES

The arguments just presented have consequences for the history of anti-Paulinism in James. For if James is not essentially anti-Pauline, then there must be some reason why he can include passages that are in fundamental opposition to his own theology. The same is true for 1 Clement: if his writing is not really Pauline, then we must be able to discover the reason for his artificial Paulinism.

In my opinion, the following hypothesis suggests itself: 1 Clement and James each have a Pauline and an anti-Pauline tinge, because they possessed a positive or a negative picture of Paul which was already established in their communities. Anti-Paulinism was thus a part of the tradition that had already come to the author of James[44] before he began his composition, and he gave eloquent expression to it in James 2. Perhaps it is also seen in the attribution[45] of the writing to James,[46] for in the fifties of the first century he had become the rival of the apostle to the Gentiles and had been acknowledged in anti-Pauline Jewish-Christian circles as an authority already during his lifetime as well as afterward.

If the above hypothesis is correct, then we may see in James an offshoot of an anti-Pauline Jewish Christianity,[47] whose author, himself a Christian teacher (James 3:1), is no longer to be considered a Jewish Christian. But the attack on Paul makes certain his origin in or familiarity with Jewish Christianity. The observation that the author of James, just like the Jewish-Christian contemporaries of the apostle, misunderstood the Pauline doctrine of justification and thus attacked it confirms the conclusion reached above. To this extent, James casts a refracted light on the theology and history of Jewish Christianity.

8.4 TIME AND PLACE OF
THE COMPOSITION OF JAMES

In conclusion we may note with regard to the chronological and geographical provenance of James that the best date for this artificial letter is the beginning of the second century, especially because of the parallels to contemporary writings (1 Clement, Hermas). Geographically, it is probably to be located in the East,[48] where the figure of James carried weight. But, to be sure, in each case we remain in the realm of conjecture.

9

THE ANTI-PAULINISM OF JUSTIN'S
JEWISH CHRISTIANS (*DIAL.* 46–47)[1]

In this chapter we will depart from the method we announced
and explained at the beginning of this study (above, p. 31),
namely, of dealing only with those texts which contain an explicit polemic against Paul. The justification for this step will be
seen (it is hoped) in what follows. The peculiar nature of the text
to be dealt with (*Dial.* 46–47) calls for this deviation from the
method pursued in the other chapters. In this instance, we will
first delineate the Jewish-Christian character of the Christians
described by Justin. Only after this will we address the question
of whether these Christians advocated an anti-Paulinism.

9.1 THE JEWISH-CHRISTIAN CHARACTER
OF BOTH TYPES OF CHRISTIANS IN *DIAL.* 46–47,
AND THEIR PROVENANCE

During his dialogue with Trypho the Jew, Justin speaks of a type
of Christianity that is characterized by the following praxis:

Dial. 46:2: *to sabbatizein, to peritemnesthai, ta emmēna phy-
lassein, to baptizesthai hapsamenon tinos hon apegoreutai hypo
Mouseos ē en synousia genomenon.* ("The keeping of the sabbath, circumcision, observation of months, and ritual ablutions
if one has touched anything [prohibited by Moses] or after sexual
intercourse"). *Dial.* 47.2: *peritemnesthai, sabbatizein* ("To be circumcised, to keep the sabbath"). This praxis can be described as
ennomos politeia (47.4, literally, "conduct according to the law"
or "the legal community"), which may be freely translated "the
Jewish way of life."[2]

The features pointed out by Justin indicate that the Christians
he is referring to are Jewish Christians (but cf. our definition
above, pp. 29f.).[3] In addition, we may describe them predominantly as Jews in the ethnic sense. To be sure, Justin presup-

poses that a Gentile Christian could become a Jewish Christian,[4] or even a Jew.[5] But still, those are special cases, exceptions that prove the rule, for in *Dial.* 46f.[6] Justin is dealing with the relation of Judaism to Christians who were born Jews.[7]

The Jewish Christians described by Justin have different attitudes with regard to Gentile Christians. They have differing opinions as to whether they should demand from Gentile Christians that observance of the law which they themselves practice. One groups breaks off fellowship with Gentile Christians who do not adopt the Jewish way of life (47.3). The other group advocates fellowship with them without any such demand (47.2).

What sort of fellowship does he have in mind?

In *Dial.* 47.2 Justin speaks of this fellowship as social contact and eating together (*koinōnein homilias ē hestias*) and in the same place can describe it as living together (*syzēn*).

The problem is primarily a theoretical one[8] and at the most became acute for traveling Christians[9] who sought lodging in Christian homes. Justin, who originally came from Palestine and had resided in Ephesus and Rome,[10] is himself one of the few who could answer such a question at all and who could bring some understanding of the features of Jewish Christianity into his response.[11] Other Gentile Christians lacked this, and they rejected the idea of having fellowship with Jewish Christians wholesale.[12]

Justin appears to have known Jewish Christians of both types personally, so that his report is especially valuable. Since the only controversial item between them seems to have been their attitude toward Gentile Christians, we may proceed on the basis that they did not belong to different congregations, but rather both types would be found together in the same congregation.[13] A parallel is found in the Jewish-Christian church of Jerusalem prior to 70 C.E., which constituted one congregation despite its differing attitudes toward Gentile Christianity.

Unfortunately Justin does not provide any information concerning the geographical location of Jewish Christianity. One thinks either of Asia Minor or—more likely—Palestine. Justin had lived in each area for considerable periods.

9.2 ANTI-PAULINISM OF
JUSTIN'S JEWISH CHRISTIANS?

In order to make anti-Paulinism among Justin's Jewish Christians probable, two lines of evidence are necessary. Two items call for explanation:

a. Why do the characteristics present in his report allow one to infer that there was hostility to Paul?

b. Why does Justin not refer to the hostility to Paul inherent in these characteristics, especially since he is personally acquainted with Jewish Christianity?

Concerning a: In the first half of the second century Paul was no unknown figure in the Christianity of both East and West.[14] Although it is true that one cannot presuppose the use of his letters and/or an acquaintance with his person in every Gentile Christian congregation, both were surely known in the major centers of Christianity such as Antioch (Ignatius!), Asia Minor, Greece, and of course Rome.[15]

One type of Jewish Christians known to Justin had insisted on rigorist demands from the Gentile Christians and, whenever these were not met, had withdrawn fellowship from them. This presupposes that Jewish Christians were informed concerning Gentile Christians, including their respect for the apostle to the Gentiles. A refusal to fellowship with Gentile Christians was therefore in many cases *necessarily* bound with a rejection of Paul.[16]

Concerning b: The question of whether Justin knew and used letters of Paul is to be answered in the affirmative.[17] Some scholars have taken Justin's failure explicitly to mention Paul along with other evidence to argue for an anti-Paulinism in Justin himself[18]—no doubt incorrectly, for Justin raises no objections against Paul at all.[19] Andreas Lindemann has recently given a different explanation for this state of affairs, as follows:

> That he [i.e., Justin] . . . does not mention Paul is the result of his theological principle: the truth of Christianity is proven from the Old Testament. In addition to this, only the words of Jesus are of significance, as they are preserved in the *apomnēmoneumata tōn apostolōn*, that is, the Gospels.[20]

But against this the question immediately presents itself, Why, then, does Justin use Pauline letters?[21]

In my opinion, the above data are to be interpreted as follows: Justin stands between two fronts.[22] On the one hand, he is attacking Marcion and over against him developes his own characteristic doctrine of the law in order to secure the continuity between Old Testament and New Testament revelation. On the other hand, Justin found himself in a dialogue with Judaism,[23] however monologically this may have been carried out. The embarrassing element in this situation consisted in the fact that the Christian heretic Marcion, whom Justin had explicitly opposed in an earlier work,[24] had emblazoned Paul on his own banner, and, on the other hand, this same Paul was taboo to the Jews. To have mentioned the apostle to the Gentiles explicitly would thus have brought Justin too close[25] to Marcion[26] and have made the dialogue with the Jews more difficult.[27]

The observations just made have, of course, consequences for the evaluation of *Dial.* 46f. For if Justin had intentionally avoided mentioning Paul for the reasons just given, it is clear that he could not discuss the rejection of Paul by the Jewish Christians. It is thus improper to infer from Justin's failure to introduce the topic of Jewish Christianity's rejection of Paul that the Jewish Christianity he knows did not in fact reject Paul. In any case Justin could not have reported their anti-Paulinism.[28]

If plausible answers are thus given to questions *a* and *b*, then it is probable that at least one[29] of the two groups of Jewish Christians named in *Dial.* 47 had rejected Paul.

9.3 ON THE HISTORY OF THE ANTI-PAULINISM OF JUSTIN'S JEWISH CHRISTIANS

There are two possibilities for determining the age of the anti-Paulinism of the rigorist Jewish Christians.

a. This anti-Paulinism originated spontaneously as the reaction to the encounter with Gentile Christians and their authority, Paul. In this case, at the earliest it comes from the beginning of the second century.

b. This anti-Paulinism was already a traditional constituent element of the views of Justin's Jewish Christians and flamed up again upon encountering the "lawless" Gentile Christians.

This question cannot be answered on the basis of an isolated analysis of *Dial.* 46f. We will here leave it open and will return to it in chapter 13, where it will be our task to provide an integrative summary of the individual results of our investigation.

10

THE ANTI-PAULINISM OF HEGESIPPUS[1]

Hegesippus was a younger contemporary of Justin.[2] He came from an eastern province. This may be deduced from his trip,[3] which brought him via Corinth to Rome, and from his knowledge of Palestinian church history. The fragments of his work *Hypomnemata* ("Memories"), with two exceptions, are preserved in the *Ecclesiastical History* of Eusebius. The following analysis will therefore have to deal primarily with them. The characteristic manner in which Eusebius quotes his sources thus makes the distinction between tradition and redaction of the utmost importance.

But before we turn to this task, let us first discuss that fragment from Hegesippus which is preserved not in Eusebius but in Stephanus Cobarus and which—because of its supposedly explicit attack on Paul—has, in the eyes of many scholars, stamped Hegesippus as an anti-Paulinist (see above, chapter 1). Although Stephanus Gobarus wrote two centuries after Eusebius, such a procedure is required by the method we are using throughout this study. In the process, we will anticipate section 10.2 and use one passage from Eusebius in advance, a passage that is free from the suspicion of having redactional tendencies.

10.1 THE QUOTATION FROM STEPHANUS GOBARUS

The passage reads:

> *ta hētoimasmena tois dikaiois agatha* (I)
> *oute ophthalmos eiden oute ous ēkousen* (II)
> *oute epi kardian anthrōpou anebē* (III).

> "The good things prepared for the righteous (I)
> eye has not seen nor ear has heard (II)
> nor have they entered into the human heart" (III).

(Gobarus continues:) Hegesippus, an ancient writer who belonged to the apostolic age, says in the fifth book of his memories, on what basis I do not know: "This is said in a twisted manner,

155

and those who use this saying are liars, since the Holy Scriptures and the Lord say 'Blessed are your eyes, which see, and your ears, which hear'".[4]

According to the report of Photius, Gobarus constructed his work as a series of juxtapositions of contradictory opinions.[5] This means two things: (a) The contrast between the two quoted sayings derives from the redactor Gobarus. Although in the *Hypomnemata* he had read a critique based on Matt. 13:16 of another saying similar to 1 Cor. 2:9, it is (b) not certain whether Gobarus quotes the text of Hegesippus accurately.

Gobarus, who considers Hegesippus to be an author of the apostolic age,[6] construes the polemic to be directed against Paul and thus comments that he does not know why Hegesippus rejects the text cited above and its application.[7] Stephanus obviously has 1 Cor. 2:9 in mind, where a quite similar saying is found:

ha ophthalmos ouk eiden kai ous ouk ēkousen (I)
kai epi kardian anthrōpou ouk anebē (II)
ha hētoimasen ho theos tois agapōsin auton (III).

"What no eye has seen, nor ear heard, (I)
nor the heart of man conceived, (II)
what God has prepared for those who love him" (III).

The only difference, apart from trivial details, between 1 Cor. 2:9 and the saying criticized by Hegesippus consists in the fact that stich III of Paul's text is stich I of Hegesippus's text and that in Hegesippus *tois dikaiois* stands in the place of *tois agapōsin auton*.

The following possibilities present themselves as answers to the question whether Hegesippus in fact, as Gobarus thinks, is attacking Paul:

1. Hegesippus did not have Paul in view but Jewish apocalypticists who had made use of the text.[8]

2. He did not have Paul in view but Christian circles who had cited the saying as from Jesus or the Old Testament.[9]

3. He could not here be attacking Paul, since he did not know Paul('s letters).

4. He was acquainted with Paul. However, he does not have him in view here but rather Gnostics who are making use of the saying cited above.

5. He does not have Paul in view but rather later disciples of Paul who use 1 Cor. 2:9.

6. Hegesippus has Paul *and* his later disciples in view.

Possibility 3 is excluded, since Hegesippus would have become acquainted with Paul's letters at the latest in Corinth.[10] By the same token, possibility 1 is to be excluded, since the *Christian* context in Hegesippus is clear from the quotation of Matt. 13:16 (or a similar saying). Thus the remaining possibilities 2, 4, 5, and 6 must be examined.

The following three items of evidence seem to speak in favor of possibility 2:

(a) According to Eusebius, Hegesippus had entered into debates with the apocryphal literature (*Hist. Ecc.* 4.22.9—they were written by the heretics of his time). (b) Hegesippus appeals to the Lord and the Scriptures in order to refute the saying. (c) There are close parallels between the text attacked by Hegesippus and Jewish apocalyptic texts[11] which were used by Christians.[12] It is to be remembered that the saying we are discussing appears in both early catholic and gnostic texts.[13] But at the same time, it should be noted that most gnostic and Jewish apocalyptic texts do not contain all three stichs.[14] For this reason, possibilities 2 and 4 are improbable. On the other hand, proper consideration must be given to the fact that the saying attacked by Hegesippus, 1 Cor. 2:9, and *1 Clem.* 34.8 agree in their stichometry and that *1 Clem.* 34.8[15] in all probability is copied from 1 Cor. 2:9.[16]

Is Hegesippus referring to 1 Cor. 2:9? The different order of the stichs appears to stand against an affirmative answer to this question. But this can readily be explained by the redactional work of Gobarus[17] (or Hegesippus), who could have improved the sentence construction[18] by rearranging the lines.[19] I thus consider it probable, for the reasons given above, that Hegesippus is attacking 1 Cor. 2:9 and its use by contemporary disciples of Paul.[20] Its use (in abbreviated form) is clear in contemporary gnostic documents (see above, n. 13), and Hegesippus's catalogue of heresies (see below) documents the fact that he opposed the Gnostics in general.

The results obtained here can be made more precise with the help of *1 Clement*. According to Eusebius, Hegesippus knew this letter and obviously found nothing in it to which he objected (cf. *Hist. Ecc.* 4.22.1).[21] Now *1 Clem.* 24.8 explicitly cites the saying in

1 Cor. 2:9 criticized by Hegesippus and contains a positive picture of Paul (1 Clement 5). I thus consider the possibility to be excluded that Hegesippus criticizes Clement's *acceptance* of Paul as such. He must have in mind a gnostic interpretation of Paul. That is, *it is primarily this interpretation which he attacks and in the course of his critique includes 1 Cor. 2:9 in his attack.*[22]

But also the second part of the fragment of Hegesippus preserved in Gobarus, in which Hegesippus gives his reason for his rejection of 1 Cor. 2:9 and its use, indirectly confirms the hypothesis of Hegesippus's anti-Paulinism,[23] namely, in that Hegesippus here plays off the knowledge of the earthly Jesus against the Pauline revelation.[24] For Hegesippus, the criteria are the "divine Scriptures" and "the Lord," against which (Paul and) the bearers of this revelatory saying had transgressed. These two criteria appear in the fragment preserved by Eusebius described more precisely as "Law," "Prophets," and "Lord" (*Hist. Ecc.* 4.22.3). This triad is probably to be identified with the above dyad.

It is noticeable that Hegesippus does not refer to the apostles (including Paul) as bearers of the tradition. Two things are to be inferred from this: (a) On the issue of the canon, Hegesippus advocates a standpoint older than that of the churches he visits,[25] for whom in the second half of the second century the apostles already belonged to the canon. (b) Hegesippus is (for this reason) not an advocate of (early-) catholic Christianity.[26] But this lets an important general argument against a possible anti-Paulinism in Hegesippus slip away, for if he came from a non-catholic[27] Christianity, then of course it is not necessary that he operated with the same norms as the Roman church and the churches in its sphere of influence.[28]

The lack of the apostles in Hegesippus's canon is all the more amazing in that Eusebius presents him as one who deals with the concepts and subject matter of apostolic succession and tradition. Or is it precisely that which goes back to Eusebius's own redaction? This question is so urgent that it must be dealt with before the reconstruction of Hegesippus's theology.

10.2 APOSTLES IN HEGESIPPUS'S WRITINGS?[29]

Eusebius's *Ecclesiastical History* is directed by his intention[30] to chronicle the apostolic succession from the time of Jesus into his own time (cf. the beginning of Book 1, the end of Book 7, and the beginning of Book 8). Eusebius emphasizes that he has hardly any predecessors in this task (1.1.5) and lifts up the fact that he used sources and the writings of other authors with this question in mind:

> We have therefore collected from their scattered memoirs all that we think will be useful for the present subject, and have brought together the utterances of the ancient writers themselves that are appropriate to it, culling, as it were, the flowers of intellectual fields. We shall endeavour to give them unity by historical treatment, rejoicing to rescue the successions, if not of all, at least of the most distinguished of the apostles of our Saviour throughout those churches of which the fame is still remembered. (1.1.4)[31]

These programmatic statements mean, in reference to Hegesippus, that because of the dogmatic principle enunciated above and because of the lack of other sources Eusebius had to construe him as the guarantor for apostolic succession in the Jerusalem mother church.[32] This gives us a handle for getting hold of Eusebius's redactional tendencies. Can it be applied to the fragments of Hegesippus, and does it provide assistance in the establishment of the authentic materials from Hegesippus?

As a point of entry into the task of answering this question, we may use a passage from the *Ecclesiastical History* that is to be understood as a doublet from the work of Hegesippus: Eusebius, *Hist. Ecc.* 3.11:

> After the martyrdom of James and the capture of Jerusalem which immediately followed, the story goes (*logos katechei*) that those of the Apostles and of the disciples of the Lord who were still alive came together from every place with those who were, humanly speaking, of the family of the Lord, for many of them were then still alive, and they all took counsel together as to whom they ought to adjudge worthy to succeed James, and all unanimously decided that Simeon the son of Clopas, whom the scripture of the Gospel also mentions, was worthy of the throne of the diocese there. He was, so it is said, a cousin of the Saviour, for Hegesippus relates that Clopas was the brother of Joseph.

Eusebius refers to *logos katechei*[33] ("the story goes") as the source for his report. An indication of the possible origin of his tradition is given by the church father at the end of the quoted text itself. After he has reported as the content of the (old) Logos that Simeon the son of Clopas was the successor of James, he adds:

"For Hegesippus relates that Clopas was the brother of Joseph." This raises the question of whether Hegesippus is the source that underlies all of 3.11. We are able to answer this question, since Eusebius in another passage gives a report that is very similar to the one above and that he explicitly introduces as a quotation from Hegesippus. It is thus advisable to compare[34] this report (B) with 3.11 above (A):

Eusebius, *Hist. Ecc.* 4.22.4–5 (=B)

> The same writer [Hegesippus 22.1] also describes the beginning of the heresies of his time as follows: "After James the Just had suffered martyrdom for the same reason as the Lord (*hōs kai ho kyrios epi tō autō logō*), Symeon, his cousin, the son of Clopas was appointed bishop, whom they all proposed because he was another cousin of the Lord. For this cause they called the church virgin, for it had not yet been corrupted by vain messages, but Thebouthis, because he had not been made bishop, begins its corruption by the seven heresies, to which he belonged, among the people."

Both texts speak of a choice of Symeon as the successor of James, after the latter's death. Report A registers in addition the conquest of Jerusalem, while Report B contains no reference to it. On the other hand, B describes the death of James in more detail, in that he relates it to the death of the Lord, in fact describing it as having resulted from the same cause as that which led to Jesus' death (*hōs kai ho kyrios epi tō autō logō*).[35]

The participants in the selection of Symeon are described differently in A and B. In A they are the apostles and disciples of the Lord who were still alive at that time and the Lord's family. In B the circle of participants is described only as "all."

In both cases, the choice is unanimous.

In B, the basis for the choice of Symeon obviously consists in the fact that he was a relative (cousin) of Jesus. In A, this datum is only appended at the end, and in contrast to B it remains unclear whether there is a causal connection.

> The information about Thebouthis that B gives in conjunction with this report of Symeon's selection has no parallel in A and need not occupy us further here (but cf. below, pp. 164f.).

Everything considered, the report in B appears to have the priority over against A. The following considerations speak in favor of this: (a) its introduction as a citation from Hegesippus's

Hypomnemata, (b) the significance that the role of physical relationship to Jesus plays in this report, and (c) the role that the Lord's disciples and apostles play in A. Here we need to remember the Eusebian intention of portraying apostolic succession described above, which makes suspect the focus on apostles in A corresponding to Eusebius's own interest (especially since it does not appear at all in B). The suspicion of Eusebian redaction was also already present because of the fact, already noted, that the Gobarus fragment knows nothing of apostles as authorities.

With this, we come to another text from Hegesippus handed on by Eusebius, a text that mentions the apostles. Does this reference also finally go back to the hand of the redactor?

Hist. Ecc. 2.23.4: *diadechetai tēn ekklēsian meta tōn apostolōn ho adelphos tou kyriou Iakōbos* ("The charge of the Church passed to James the brother of the Lord, together with the Apostles"). This statement introduces an extensive quotation from the work of Hegesippus which has as its content the martyrdom of James. The citation closes with the words: *kai euthys Ouespasianos poliorkei autous* ("and at once Vespasian began to besiege them") (*Hist. Ecc.* 2.23.18).

Before we come to the question of the relation of tradition and redaction in *Hist. Ecc.* 2.23.4, we will first assemble the remaining passages from Eusebius's church history that report the inauguration of James, in each case distinguishing tradition and redaction:

> *Hist. Ecc.* 2.1.2: . . . James, to whom the men of old had given the surname of Just for his excellence of virtue, is narrated (*historousin*) to have been the first elected to the throne of the bishopric of the Church in Jerusalem.
>
> *Hist. Ecc.* 3.5.2: . . . James, who was the first after the ascension of our Saviour to be appointed to the throne of the bishopric in Jerusalem.

Both passages belong together. In *Hist. Ecc.* 2.1.2 Eusebius refers explicitly to tradition as his source. He might be referring to Clement of Alexandria (*Hist. Ecc.* 2.1.3), Hegesippus, or the Jerusalem list of bishops (*Hist. Ecc.* 4.5), all of which consider James to have been the first bishop of Jerusalem. In *Hist. Ecc.* 3.5.2 Eusebius appears to refer back to *Hist. Ecc.* 2.1.2. The almost identical vocabulary speaks in favor of this, as do the chronological data: both passages speak of receiving the bish-

op's throne after the ascension of Jesus (cf. *Hist. Ecc.* 2, introduction 2 ("what followed his ascension") as specifying the "at
the same time" of 2.1.2; for 3.5.2, see the above text).

Hist. Ecc. 2.1.2f. (and thus also *Hist. Ecc.* 3.5.2) therefore goes
back to tradition, and all the more so since Eusebius in an earlier
work, the *Chronicle*, which provides the basis for the *Ecclesiastical History*, already has the information that enables him to
report that James was the first bishop of Jerusalem—with a
characteristic addition:
Chronicle, par. 175.24–26 (Helm):

> Ecclesia Hierosolymarum primus episcopus *ab apostolis* ordi-
> natur Iacobus frater Domini.

This datum is a further argument for the hypothesis that the idea
that James had been made the first bishop of Jerusalem by the
apostles derives from Eusebian redactional work.

This becomes even more clear from the following two passages from the *Ecclesiastical History*:

> a. *Hist. Ecc.* 2.23.1: [The Jews] turned against James, the brother of
> the Lord, to whom the throne of the bishopric in Jerusalem had
> been allotted by the Apostles (*pros tōn Apostolōn*).
> b. *Hist. Ecc.* 7.19: Now the throne of James, who was the first to
> receive from the Saviour and the apostles the episcopate of the
> church at Jerusalem . . . has been preserved to this day.

Concerning *a*: The passage 23.1–2 is a summary in which
Eusebius makes use of the reports of Acts,[36] Josephus,[37] Hegesippus,[38] and Clement of Alexandria.[39]

Concerning *b*: Par. 19 is likewise heavily flavored with redactional traits. James's episcopal throne was hardly known before
the fourth century.[40] The report that, besides the apostles, the
Lord had also participated in the conferral of the bishop's office
on James is probably a selection from Eusebius's reading or his
independent combination.[41] In any case, in this passage Eusebius is himself composing, not reproducing a tradition.

In summary, it is clear that all passages in the *Ecclesiastical
History* (and in the *Chronicle*) which speak of James, the first
bishop of Jerusalem, and which manifest redactional influence,
indicated that the apostles participated in selecting him for this
office. But in those passages where Eusebius is reproducing

162

tradition concerning James's episcopacy, the apostles do not come within his purview (exception: *Hist. Ecc.* 2.1.3, on which see below, pp. 163f.).

We now turn once again to the passage in Hegesippus that is transmitted in Eusebius's *Hist. Ecc.* 2.23.4: *diadechetai tēn ekklēsian meta tōn apostolōn ho adelphos tou kyriou Iakōbos.* The following reasons support the view that the present text has not been transmitted correctly.

a. The sentence is syntactically rough. The verb stands at the beginning in the singular and leads one to expect only one subject. All the same, the logical subject is expanded by *meta tōn apostolōn.*[42]

b. The statement that James with the apostles[43] took over the church has a puzzling content, especially since it is not said which church is intended. As the sentence now stands, it can refer only to a local church. There are thus grounds in both the syntax and the content for supposing that the text contains redactional additions and modifications. (We may also plausibly suspect redactional activity here since the sentence in question introduces a quotation.) This hypothesis is further supported by the following evidence:

1. The apostles are participants in all other redactionally influenced passages in the *Ecclesiastical History* that speak of James's inauguration into office.

2. Eusebius had found the same thesis in Clement of Alexandria, which he mentions immediately preceding the quotation from Hegesippus in 2.23.3. This author had helped Eusebius legitimize his correction advocating his orthodox claims, for he had already cited him to this effect (*Hist. Ecc.* 2.1.3):

> Peter and James and John after the Ascension of the Saviour did not struggle for glory, . . . but chose James the Just as bishop of Jerusalem.[44]

3. As we know from *Hist. Ecc.* 4.22 (=B), in Hegesippus the apostles play no role in the choice of James's successor Symeon, while in Eusebius's paraphrase of this passage (*Hist. Ecc.* 3.11 = A) it is exactly the opposite.

It has thus become probable for several different reasons that *meta tōn apostolōn* in Eusebius's *Hist. Ecc.* 2.23.4 goes back to

Eusebian interpolation and that "apostolic succession" has no place in Hegesippus's own picture of early Christian history. This section has thereby provided an essential preliminary insight for the question to be pursued in the next section regarding the theology of Hegesippus.

10.3 ON HEGESIPPUS'S THEOLOGY

At the beginning a word of caution is advisable. From Hegesippus we have only about five pages from five books, part of which is in poor textual condition. This makes the task uncommonly difficult and gives reason to be very cautious, which in turn leads to the insight that we will be able to grasp only *aspects* of Hegesippus's theology, principally the ecclesiological aspect.

10.3.1 Ecclesiology

Hegesippus speaks of the Jerusalem church "as though it were simply the church as such."[45] James takes it over and is then succeeded by his cousin Symeon. To be sure, Hegesippus is aware of the existence of other churches, for, after all, his trip takes him to Rome via Corinth, and in these churches he could have been convinced of the orthodox teaching.[46] Still and all, that cannot obscure the fact that the Jerusalem church continued to have a special significance for the whole of Christianity.

This can be further illustrated from Hegesippus's explanations of the advent of heresies. According to Hegesippus, the church (of Jerusalem) remained a virgin[47] only during the lifetime of James (*Hist. Ecc.* 4.22.5). This report conflicts with another in *Hist. Ecc.* 3.32.7–8:

> Besides this the same writer [*Hegesippus*, 32.2], explaining the events of these times [i.e., until the reign of Trajan, during which Symeon suffered martyrdom], adds that *until then the church remained a pure and uncorrupted virgin*, for those who attempted to corrupt the healthful rule of the Saviour's preaching, if they existed at all, lurked in obscure darkness. But when the sacred band of the Apostles and the generation of those to whom it had been vouchsafed to hear with their own ears the divine wisdom had reached the several ends of their lives, then the federation of godless error took its beginning through the deceit of false teachers who, seeing that none of the Apostles still remained, barefacedly tried against the preaching of the truth the counter-proclamation of "knowledge falsely so-called."

The passage just cited is an additional example of Eusebian redactional work. The evidence of this is: (a) 32.7f. is formally not a quotation but a paraphrase;[48] and (b) the mention of the apostles reflects Eusebian redaction.

It thus remains the case that Hegesippus dates the advent of heresy differently from Eusebius, although the latter (incorrectly) introduces Hegesippus as support for his own view. According to Hegesippus, the virginal purity of the church was brought to an end by Thebouthis, who defiled the church by his unsuccessful attempt to become James's successor.

That the advent of heresy is bound up with the succession of leadership after James again throws a characteristic light on the special place of the Jerusalem church in Hegesippus's thinking. Does this not suggest that for him the defiling of the Jerusalem church had paradigmatic significance for the other churches?

> Additional illumination on Hegesippus's ecclesiology can be derived from his understanding of the nature of heresy. Hegesippus preserves a list of Christian heresies (Hist. Ecc. 4.22.5), which originated from the seven heresies among the people (ibid.). Thebouthis also belonged to those groups. The number seven was certainly intended to brand the heresies with a kind of negative ideal of demonic perfection,[49] especially the Christian heretics who had grown out of the Jewish heresies. But if Christian heresy is only a branch of Jewish heresy, then on the positive side Christian orthodoxy is only a derivative of Jewish orthodoxy, that is, in Hegesippus's view the church is only the fulfillment of Judaism.[50]

The significance of the Jerusalem church extended historically into the second century. So it is that Hegesippus reported of the Davidites' hearing before Domitian and their triumphal return (Hist. Ecc. 3.32.6[51]), and the Lord's kinsman Symeon, the successor of James, maintained leadership within the Jerusalem church until the time of Trajan (Hist. Ecc. 3.32.4).

For Hegesippus's own time, the question of the significance of the Jerusalem church is much more difficult to answer, especially since it appears not to be the case that Jesus' family continued to maintain its leadership there. But on the basis of the results achieved so far, three statements can still be made concerning Hegesippus's ecclesiology:

a. The orthodoxy of the universal church was assured not, by lists of episcopal succession of the church centers founded by apostles, as in Eusebius, but by the continuity of officeholders on the bishop's chair in Jerusalem in the earliest times.[52]

b. Hegesippus's trip through the West bespeaks the awareness of the universality of the church.

c. The congregation from which Hegesippus comes claims to be the heir of the older Jerusalem church. Otherwise, the extremely extensive and positive role it plays cannot be properly understood.[53]

10.3.2 Hegesippus: A Jewish Christian?

It has just been explained that Hegesippus manifests a special interest in the history of the Jerusalem church and its leaders. His work thus contains, among other things, an extensive report of the martyrdom of James, which, because of the Jewish description of the Lord's brother,[54] could suggest the hypothesis that Hegesippus was acquainted with Jewish tradition and thus was perhaps a Jewish Christian. But against such an inference is to be objected that this would document the Jewish-Christian origin of the *tradition* used by Hegesippus but not necessarily that the redactor Hegesippus was a Jewish Christian.

Information that might possibly lead us farther is given by Eusebius, *Hist. Ecc.* 4.22.8:

> And he [Hegesippus] makes extracts from the Gospel according to the Hebrews, and from the Syriac and particularly from the Hebrew language, showing that he had been converted from among the Hebrews, and he mentions points as coming from the unwritten tradition of the Jews.[55]

The specification that Hegesippus provided information from the Jewish oral tradition is too concrete to be unreliable. An additional valuable item is the report that Hegesippus cited some words from the Syriac (=Aramaic) Gospel. This data misled Eusebius to the false conclusion that Hegesippus had converted from Judaism to Christianity.[56]

> The passage cited above cannot be adduced as evidence that Hegesippus had a good knowledge of Aramaic, for Eusebius only speaks of Hegesippus's citing "some" words in the Aramaic language. Besides, Hegesippus used the LXX.[57] His mother tongue was most likely Greek.[58]

Also Eusebius's report that Hegesippus quoted from the *Gospel of the Hebrews* is probably reliable, since Eusebius was acquainted with it.[59] It was written in Greek and, prior to Hegesippus, already known to Papias. "The title characterizes the book as the Gospel of Greek-speaking Jewish-Christian circles."[60] Its content fits well the extant fragments of Hegesippus and their transfiguration of James, for the *Gospel of the Hebrews* obviously concluded with the first appearance of the risen Lord to the Lord's brother.[61]

Now the question is: Do the reflections on Eusebius, *Hist. Ecc.* 4.22.8 make any contribution to the issue of whether or not Hegesippus was a Jewish Christian?

The answer here corresponds to that given to the question of whether the Jewish description of James proves Hegesippus's Jewish Christianity. That is, the tradition used by Hegesippus certainly has a Jewish-Christian character—especially the *Gospel of the Hebrews*, the title of which must have originated to describe as its readers the Hebrews as a people.[62] But this does not necessarily mean that Hegesippus belonged to Jewish Christianity.

Thus our consideration of this point must end with the insight that the issue of whether Hegesippus was a Jewish Christian or not probably cannot be decided on the basis of our present sources. It has only been established that (*a*) he belonged to a noncatholic stream of Christianity that was characterized by the three features discussed above (pp. 165f.), (*b*) he repeatedly used traditions probably of Jewish-Christian origin, and (*c*) he had a canon already antiquated in his time, which consisted of the Law, the Prophets, and the Words of the Lord.

In conclusion, we may only mention the following reflection on the history of Hegesippus's church, to which we will return in the summary below (pp. 197f.). Even if the question of whether Hegesippus belonged to a contemporary stream of Jewish Christianity cannot be definitively answered, still the three features of his theology discussed above are best to be explained by the hypothesis that the church to which he belonged had been Jewish-Christian in an earlier phase.

10.4 THEOLOGY AND ANTI-PAULINISM: ITS HISTORY

Anti-Paulinism is no constitutive element of Hegesippus's theology. So far as we can see, he engages in polemic against only one

Pauline verse, which obviously was being used by the Gnostics against whom he was struggling. The extant fragments of Hegesippus unfortunately do not suffice for drawing any further conclusions on the issue of Hegesippus's anti-Paulinism. We do not know, for example, whether Hegesippus merely criticized Paul (because he was being claimed by the Gnostics) or fundamentally rejected him.[63]

Additional understanding on this issue will be forthcoming only if we should succeed in relating more closely the extant fragments of Hegesippus to texts in the history of the tradition that contain a clear anti-Paulinism. From this it would be possible to draw inferences concerning anti-Paulinism as a constituent element of the traditions used by Hegesippus and his own stance toward them. Also, additional light would then be cast on the question posed at the conclusion of the last section concerning the history of Hegesippus's church.

These considerations, which at first glance might strike one as simply curious and puzzling, may in fact undergo a shift in actual practice. Hence one might perhaps expect from the next chapter a further contribution to the question of Hegesippus's anti-Paulinism.

11
ANTI-PAULINISM IN THE PSEUDO-CLEMENTINES[1]

The term "Pseudo-Clementines" refers to several documents that treat the life of Clement of Rome and have Clement himself as (pseudonymous) author. The following texts are extant: (a) the Greek *Homilies* (=H),[2] (b) the (originally Greek) *Recognitions* in the Latin translation of Rufinus (=R),[3] and (c) the Syriac Clementines,[4] which contain part of the Greek *Recognitions* 1—4, 1.4) and the *Homilies* (10—14).[5]

From the point of view of literary criticism (source analysis), there is a general consensus today that the *Homilies* and the *Recognitions* are based on a basic source (*Grundschrift* =G).[6] To be sure, it is disputed whether H and R independently make use of G[7] or whether R used H as well.[8] (That H used R is today hardly considered to be a possibility by contemporary scholars —but cf. the new attempt by J. Rius-Camps [see below, p. 297 n. 10a].)

In previous research, the question of anti-Paulinism in the Pseudo-Clementines has been most closely bound up with the literary-critical problems just mentioned. To be sure, hardly anyone ascribes anti-Paulinism to G.[9] But one stream of investigation distills anti-Pauline sources from G, while another stream considers anti-Pauline passages to be mainly interpolations in H.[10]

Since the foundational works of B. Rehm and G. Strecker, it is astounding that hardly anyone has published an independent literary-critical source analysis of the Pseudo-Clementines.[10a] Rather, work on these texts seems to have stagnated, a state of affairs that is not altered by the fact that Strecker's theory has been adopted with approval in several contributions to the discussion.[11] In my opinion, however, the literary-critical problem of the Pseudo-Clementines still remains unsolved: Strecker's pioneering attempt is burdened with the difficulty that he reconstructs a source used by a document that itself must be recon-

169

structed as a source of our existing documents.[12] Statistical analyses of the vocabulary have shown, however, that the passages of the *Homilies* considered by Strecker to be an element of the *Kerygmata Petrou* have no peculiar linguistic features,[13] and Strecker himself emphasizes that no definite stylistic features of the *Kerygmata Petrou* are identifiable.[14] But does not this mean that the *Kerygmata Petrou* has lost its claim to the designation "source"?

> It is to be emphasized that, according to Strecker, a key position in the reconstruction of the *Kerygmata Petrou* is to be ascribed to the *Epistula Petri* (=Ep Petr.) and the *Contestatio* (=Cont.). Without these, he too would consider the possibility of a reconstruction to be excluded. But J. Wehnert has shown that the linguistic usage of the *EpPetr./Cont.* manifests no significant agreement with the other texts claimed by Strecker for the *Kerygmata Petrou*. In addition, Wehnert has correctly pointed to the use of introductory writings in ancient novels. "An outstanding . . . parallel example is provided by the *tōn hyper Thoulēn apistōn logoi kd'* of Antonius Diogenes, in which in like manner two letters (namely, in H, *EpPetr.* and *EpClem.*) are placed in deliberate incongruence at the beginning or end of the novel. These letters have . . . the sole purpose of making credible to the reader the reliability of the (fictitious) report."[15] *EpPetr./Cont.* cannot thus without further ado be used as the key for the reconstruction of a source document.

Strecker correctly points out that the impossibility of isolating the so-called Ebionite interpolations on stylistic grounds—and, we might add, on the basis of vocabulary statistics—speaks against Rehms's attempt. An additional objection to Rehms's attempt is the late dating of the anti-Paulinism of the Pseudo-Clementines which is bound up with it, or also the evidence of anti-Pauline literature in the second century, however much this may be opposed by E. Schwartz and A. von Harnack on ideological grounds.[16]

In the following a new effort at the investigation of the Pseudo-Clementines is attempted, which promises to do the most justice to the state of our sources discussed above. We will undertake to analyze the anti-Pauline passages primarily in terms of the discipline of the history of traditions, in order to have a broader basis for sorting out their historical and theological elements than would be the case if one simply adopts the theories of Rehm or Strecker.

11.1 PS.-CLEM. *RECG.* 1.33–71

In the following, R 1.33–71 will be investigated, primarily from the point of view of the history of traditions. In order to have the broadest possible basis in the sources, we will begin with an analysis of texts that, from the point of view of the history of traditions, have some connection with those chapters (R 1.33–71) or parts thereof.[17] Only after this will we proceed to a source-critical analysis and, finally, will attempt to sort out the traditions discovered in the process.

11.1.1 The Martyrdom of James in Hegesippus and in the *Second Apocalypse of James* from Nag Hammadi[18] (Synoptic Comparison)

Preliminary comment: Verbatim agreements are underlined. The form of the materials in Hegesippus is used as a guide for the following comparison, which means that lines 61.13f. and 62.7 of the *Second Apocalypse of James* do not stand in their original location. For analysis and interpretation, see immediately below. The framework within the narrative of the *Second Apocalypse of James* is ignored.

Hegesippus (in Eusebius, *Hist. Ecc.* 2.23.8–18)	**Second Apocalypse of James** (from the Nag Hammadi Codex V.44.11—63.2)
1. 8–11: First Speech of James (=the Just: 12.15f., 18)	45.27(?)—end: Speech of James (the Just: 44.13f., 18; 59.22 and often) on the fifth step
in the temple	of the temple (45.24)
on the question: "Who is the gate of Jesus?" (8)	on, among other things, "the gate" (55.6ff.)
Success of the speech(9f.)	Failure of the speech (61.3f.; 45.11.f)
Tumult among the people (10)	Tumult among the people 61.1ff.; cf. 45:3ff.
II. 12–14a: On the same question (12)	61.7f.:
a second speech (13) of James	a second speech of James
from the pinnacle (12)	from the pinnacle (61.20ff.)
of the temple	of the temple

Success of the speech among the people (14a)	(cf. 45.11f.; 61.3f.)
III. 15b–15 <u>Decision</u> by the <u>Pharisees</u> and scribes to <u>put the just one to death:</u>	61.12–19: <u>Decision</u> by the priests to <u>put the just one to death:</u>
"Let us go up and throw him down that they may not be afraid and believe in him." (14b)	"Let us kill this man, that he may be taken out of our midst, for he will in no way be useful to us." (61.16–19)
"Oh, the just one has also <u>erred</u>." (15)	"You have <u>erred</u>!" (62.7)
IV. 16–18: <u>Murder of James</u>	61.25—63.33: <u>Murder of James</u>
<u>Cast down from the pinnacle</u> (16)	<u>Cast down from the pinnacle</u> (61.25f.)
<u>"Let us stone the just one,</u>	<u>"Come, let us stone the just one!"</u> (61.13f.)
James" (16)	
<u>The Stoning</u>	<u>The Stoning</u>
<u>James's prayer</u> of intercession (16)	<u>Gnostic prayer</u> of James (62.16— 63.29)
Death blow from the fuller (18)	—

The synoptic arrangement of the text above can leave no doubt that there is a literary relationship[19] between the two passages.[20] The following evidence indicates that the present text of the *Second Apocalypse of James* is the later text: the series "premeditation to kill, call for the stoning of James, throwing him down from the pinnacle, stoning" in the *Second Apocalypse of James* is secondary to that of Hegesippus for reasons that can easily be observed by examination of the synopsis above. Likewise, the priority of Hegesippus's report is seen from the different positioning of the cry, "Oh, the Just has also erred!" (Hegesippus)/ "You have erred" (62.7).[21] Finally, the (first) speech of James in the *Second Apocalypse of James* is already gnosticized (=an indication of an earlier text's having been reworked or of further development of an original text) but still has some connection with the Hegesippus account, as is evidenced by the common "gate" symbolism.[22] Two other details are probably related to this gnostic reworking:

a: The statement that James had no success (note on the opposite side how in the Hegesippus form of the story the success of James is an organic part of the account which motivates the attack of the opponents), *b.* The gnostic deathbed prayer at the end, which has no integral connection with what has preceded.

On the other hand, it remains of course an open question as to whether there are individual elements of the *Second Apocalypse of James* that preserve older material.

11.1.2 A History of the Tradition of the Martyrdom of James[23]

Before we present additional comparisons of the text in Hegesippus with similar passages, it is advisable to reconstruct the tradition history of the account of the martyrdom of James.[24]

There are two reports of the martyrdom of James: the account of Josephus (*Ant.* 20.199ff.), according to which James and some others were put to death by stoning; and the Christian tradition, which is found in its purest form in Clement of Alexandria. In a fragment of the *Hypotyposes* preserved in Eusebius, *Hist. Ecc.* 2.1.5, we find: James *ho dikaios, ho kata tou pterygiou blētheis kai hypo gnapheōs xulō plēgeis eis thanaton* ("the Just, who was thrown down from the pinnacle of the temple, and beaten to death with a fuller's club"). The versions are mutually exclusive. To be sure, the procedure for stoning prescribes that the condemned be thrown down from a height that must be twice that of a human being.[25] But this "high place" cannot be the pinnacle of the temple.

Nevertheless, both versions are combined in the account from Hegesippus found in Eusebius[26] and—as we can now say on the basis of the above comparison—in the *Second Apocalypse of James*. The occasion for this was probably given by the account in Josephus, which was highly valued in Christian circles. In addition, it is probably the case that details from the account of the martyrdom of Stephen worked themselves into the story at this stage of the tradition.[27] Thus the intercessory prayer (cf. Acts 7:60 with part IV of the synopsis above) and the Son of man motif (cf. Acts 7:56 with Eusebius, *Hist. Ecc.* 2.23.13) derive from the Lukan account.

Before we come to a comparison of the account of James's martyrdom in Hegesippus with that in R 1.33–71, we may present in summary form what can be established as the earliest form of Hegesippus's account and how this tradition was developed further.

The original version in Hegesippus[28] dealt with a public discussion between James and the representatives of Judaism on the issue of whether or not Jesus was the promised Christ. The setting was the temple in Jerusalem, and James was regarded as an authoritative figure. When his speech made a great impression on the people, he was thrown down from the pinnacle of the temple. The deathblow was then given by a fuller.[29]

At a second level of tradition, visible in the interpolated version of Hegesippus found in Eusebius and in the *Second Apocalypse of James*, the account of being cast down from the pinnacle of the temple appears to have been enriched by being combined with the version in which James was then stoned to death.

Finally, in a third layer of tradition visible in the *Second Apocalypse of James*, a gnostic reworking of the account of James's martyrdom becomes visible. This stands at the end of a gnostic revelatory discourse, in which details of the report have been changed (James's preaching experienced *no* success) or replaced by the gnostic editor (the intercessory prayer becomes a gnostic prayer). This history of the tradition of the account of James's martyrdom has now established a basis on which the account preserved in R 1.33–71 may be related to the history of this tradition.

11.1.3 Hegesippus's Report on the Martyrdom of James and Ps.-Clem. *Recg.* 1.66–70

Previous research has often pointed out a connection between the two accounts.[30] There have, of course, been different hypothesis about the nature and direction of their literary relationship. Is Hegesippus indebted to R 1, or vice versa?[31] Do both texts go back to a common source?[32] Since finally G. Strecker[33] and in his wake S. K. Brown[34] have advocated the view that the data are not sufficient to support any of the above hypotheses, the first item of business will be to place both texts side by side in a synoptic comparison in order to clarify the question of whether any kind of genetic relationship at all exists. Only after this has been done is the nature of the literary dependence to be clarified, if the question is still applicable.

One additional preliminary remark with regard to method is still necessary: generally, the account in Hegesippus is compared with the narrative in R 1.33–71 as a whole. But at the present stage of our investigation we must confine ourselves to comparing only those parts of that account which—standing in some narrative unity—have some possible correspondence to the account in Hegesippus. Only after a literary connection has been established and the direction and nature of the dependence have been clarified, can the question be raised as to what relation the whole narrative in R 1.33–71 stands to the report in Hegesippus.

We now come to the synoptic comparison:

Hegesippus (in Eusebius, *Hist. Ecc.* 2.23.8–18	**Recognitions** 1.66–70
1. 8–11: First speech of James (=the Just: 12.15f., 18) in the temple	66f.: James (=the Bishop [of Bishops]: 66.2, 5; [68.2] 70.3) wants to dispute with the leaders of the people in the temple (cf. 68.2)
on the question, "Who is the gate of Jesus?" (8)	
Success of the speech (9f.); tumult among the people (10)	—
—	Speech of Gamaliel (67)
II. 12–14a: On the same question from the Pharisees and scribes: "Who is the gate of Jesus?" (12),	68f.: On the question of Caiaphas: "Is Jesus the true Christ?" (68.2)
a second speech (13) of James (13) from the pinnacle of the temple (12)	a speech (68.3—69.7) of James from the highest point of the temple (66.3; 70.8)
Messianic confession (Jesus is the Son of man: 13)	Messianic confession (Jesus is the Christ: 69.3)
Parousia (on the clouds of heaven: 13)	Doubled parousia (in lowliness and in glory: 69.4)
Success of the speech among the people (14a) (and its leaders: cf. 10)	Success of the speech among the people and its leaders (69.8):
"Hosanna to the Son of David!"	desire to be baptized

III. —	70.1–7 Tumult at the appearance
	of the "enemy" (70.1ff.)
	in the temple
14b–15: Decision of the	Demand of the enemy
Pharisees and scribes	
to kill James	to kill James and his companions:
"Let us climb up and throw	Why don't we grab them and
him down!" (14b)	tear them in pieces?" (70.5)
IV. 16–18: Murder of James	70.8: Attempted murder of James
Throwing him down	Throwing him down
from the pinnacle	from the highest pint
of the temple (16)	of the temple
⌈ Stoning (16)	—
⎢ James's prayer ⎤ interpolation	
⌊ of intercession (16) ⌋	—
Deathblow from the fuller (18)	Remains lying as one dead

This synoptic comparison reveals striking similarities in structure and content. (Exact parallels are underlined.) Point IV has a remarkable parallel in that in each case a single individual is actually responsible for the death of James. The supplementary comment in R, that James was (only) apparently dead, is a clear indication of redactional work. But it is required, since the Lord's brother must be preserved for further activities in the narrative (cf. R 1.72.1). Is there thus a direct literary dependence between R and the report in Hegesippus?

The following evidence stands against this hypothesis:

In I, the questions at most correspond in terms of their content. The questioners are not identical. The key word "the gate of Jesus" does not appear in R.

In II, R, in contrast to Hegesippus, presents the scriptural proof of Jesus' messiahship in full.

In IV, according to R the enemy pushes James from the highest point of the temple, while according to Hegesippus the Pharisees and scribes push the Lord's brother from the pinnacle of the temple.

Summary: *That* a literary connection is present is clear enough. It is probably not direct but of such a nature that both reports have further developed a common tradition, the core of which consisted in James's being thrown from the pinnacle/highest point of the temple after having delivered a christo-

176

logically oriented speech which met with success among the people. (For further analysis of the relation of R to the archetype, see below, pp. 183–85.)

11.1.4 A Stemma of the Reports of the Martyrdom of James

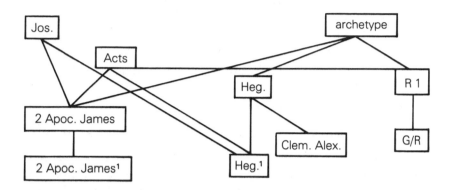

NOTE: 2 Apoc. James = Source (*Grundschrift*) of the *Second Apocalypse of James*
2 Apoc. James¹ = gnostic reworking of this *Grundschrift*
Heg = the interpolated version of Hegesippus in Eusebius
R1 = the tradition preserved in R 1.66–71.

If it is now clear that R 1.66–71 and Hegesippus's report of the martyrdom of James are dependent on a common archetype, it must next be asked whether, on the basis of a source-critical analysis of R 1.66ff. and R 1.33ff., the common tradition underlying them both can be more precisely determined, which would at the same time perhaps bring us nearer to the archetype lying behind both R 1 and Hegesippus.

11.1.5 On the Literary Criticism of Ps.-Clem. *Recg.* 1.33–71

11.1.5.1 Ps.-CLEM. RECG. 1.33–65

We will deal first with R 1.33–65 and may appropriately begin with an analysis of the structure of this section.[35]

I. An outline of redemptive history from Abraham to the

establishment of the church (33–43). (a) Old Testament section: 33–38; (b) New Testament section: 39–43.

II. (Seven years after the resurrection of Jesus:) Decision of the disciples to move up to Jerusalem in order to discuss Jesus with the Jews (44, 53).

III. The Jewish sects (54).

IV. The twelve apostles have a discussion with the representatives of the sects (55–65).

Concerning I: This section is easily seen to stand apart from the rest. In a manner reminiscent of Stephen's speech in Acts 7, it offers an outline of redemptive history.[36] Its peculiarity consists of two features: (a) the doctrine of the (true) Prophet, who appeared to Abraham (33.1) and Moses (34.4), the latter of whom predicted the advent of the true Prophet (in Jesus) (36.2 [Deut. 18:15]); (b) the doctrine of the law, which is closely related to the Christology described in (a): the prophet Jesus came, as prophesied by Moses in the Old Testament, in order finally to make the sacrificial system null and void through baptism (39.1–3). Since it could not be stamped out anyway, Moses had permitted sacrifice to the Jews as a concession,[37] of course only to God alone, in order to reduce by half the defect they had received by their long association with the Egyptians. The other half was to be corrected by the (true) Prophet.[38,39]

Concerning II: This section, together with III, is already a transition to the public discussion with the Jewish sects reported in IV. The redactional character of this section is, on the one hand, seen from the fact that the text gives the impression that the twelve apostles are carrying on a mission outside Jerusalem (cf. also 44.1: "Iacobo interrogante quae a nobis per loca singula gesta sint." "Each one of us, at the request of James, stated briefly, in the hearing of the people, what we had done in every place"), but, on the other hand, it is presupposed that the apostles have constant contact with the Jerusalem priests, who finally pester them into conducting a public disputation about Jesus (43.1). The figure of James as the first bishop of Jerusalem appears quite unexpectedly and has nothing to do with the dispute that is beginning between the twelve apostles and the Jews.

III: This section is an insertion, its character as a list indicating that it certainly goes back to tradition.[40] It is required for the discussion that follows in the next section.

IV: The content of this section revolves around themes that have already been opened up in section I: abolition of sacrifice through baptism (36f., 39 = 55, 64); polemic against the temple (37f., 41 = 64); the promise of the Prophet by Moses (36, 43 = 57); paralleling of the miracles of Moses and Jesus (40f. = 57ff.); the call of the Gentiles after the unbelief of the Jews (42 = 64). It was probably composed on the basis of the content of I, for IV artificially connects the sects named in III with the twelve apostles, who from case to case refute the objections of the representatives of the Jewish sects. But since twelve apostles give speeches, and the tradition in chap. 54 knows of only five heresies (Sadducees, Samaritans, scribes, Pharisees, disciples of John the Baptist), the narrative does not proceed without tensions. It is partially smoothed out by the fact that the sons of Zebedee, James and John, give only one speech between them (57.2–5), that James the son of Alphaeus (59.4–6) and Barnabas (60.5–70) do not speak directly against any Jewish heresy, and that the pontifex (55.2–3) and Caiaphas (twice, 61.1–2; 62.1–2) appear as advocates of Jewish heresies. The content of the speeches of the representatives of the Jewish heresies does not bring the reader beyond what has already been learned in chap. 54. The five heresies appear in chaps. 55—65 in the same order as in chap. 54, and the speeches of the twelve apostles are in each case completed with the same concluding formula: "haec et his similia prosecutus siluit" or the like (cf. 55.4; 56.3; 57.5; 58.3; 59.3; 59.6; 60.4; 61.3; 62.3; 63.1). It should probably be clear that section IV is *en toto* redactional.[41,42] As support for this statement, we may point to the figures of Gamaliel (65.2) and Caiaphas (61.1; 62.1), which are redactional anticipations of 66.2–71. Chapter 66:1 is a transition to the new unit and portrays the return of the twelve apostles to James.

11.1.5.2 Ps.-Clem. Recg. 1.66–71

Chapter 66:2 begins a new unit: "*Iacobus . . . ascendit ad templum.*" Since section IV is redactional, it now becomes clear that the beginning of IV, the report of the ascent of the twelve apostles to the temple (55.1: "ascendimus ad templum"), is modeled on 66.2 ("Iacobus . . . ascendit ad templum").

Chapter 66.2–71 is easily separable from its context and is a self-contained unit understandable in and of itself. The section portrays the ascent of James to the temple, his discussion with the representatives of Judaism, his success, and in conclusion his finally being thrown down from the highest step of the temple.

In the preceding we have set forth the hypothesis that R 1.66f. goes back to a firmly structured tradition. Now the question is whether there are parallel texts to it, and what relation this tradition has to the section R 1.33–54.

11.1.5.3 ON THE RELATIONSHIP OF PS.-CLEM. RECG. 1.66.2–71 (=A) TO 1.33–54 (=B)

It has always been noticed that A contains the same theme as B: cf. the abolition of sacrifice by baptism (69.4f. = 36f., 39, 55, 64), rejection of the Old Testament kings (69.2f. = 38), the relation of the prophets to the law (69.1 = 59), the first advent of Jesus (69.4 = 49.2), the second advent of Jesus (69.4 = 49.2). The suggestion that A and B have a genetic relation thus has some basis. Before we pursue this further, we must first take a look at the so-called *Anabathmoi Jakobou*, which is sometimes connected to R 1.33–71.

Excursus: The *Anabathmoi Jakobou* (=AJ) and Ps.-Clem. *Recg.* 1.33–71

Epiphanius reports in *Pan.* 30.16.6–9 as follows: "They tell also of other Acts of Apostles, in which much that is godless is to be found, which they use to arm themselves against the truth. They also fabricate certain ascensions and speeches, namely, in the *Anabathmoi Jakobou*, as though he [James] had spoken against the temple and sacrifice, or against the fire and sacrificial altar, and much else full of empty prattle (they attribute to him). In the same way they say libelous things with lying, evil, and misleading words of their false apostle Paul, by saying that he was, to be sure, a native of Tarsus, which he himself acknowledges and does not deny, but they claim that he is from a Greek family. As the occasion for this claim, they use the passage in which Paul correctly says, 'I am from Tarsus, a citizen of no insignificant city' (Acts 21:39). They thus claim that he was a Greek, a child of a Greek mother and a Greek father. After he had gone up to Jerusalem and remained there a long time, he wanted to marry the daughter of the (high?) priest. This is why he became a proselyte and had himself circumcised. But when he did not get the girl, he became angry and wrote against circumcision, as well as against the law and the Sabbath."[43]

According to G. Strecker there is such a close relation between the

AJ and R 1.33–71 that the suggestion is near at hand that AJ II should be described as the source for R 1.33–71.[44] The parallels may not be overlooked. They consists of (a) James's critique of the sacrificial system,[45] (b) the fact that the place of the critique, the temple, is the same in each case, and (c) the fact that both AJ and R 1.70f. are anti-Pauline, since in conjunction with a speech by James they speak of Paul in a hostile manner. But of course the discrepancies between AJ and R 1.33–71 are considerable: (1) In the AJ, Paul appears as a critic of the law but in R 1.70f. as its defender. (2) R 1.66ff. has literary contacts with the reports of the martyrdom of James but obviously not the AJ. The agreements and discrepancies are thus, in my opinion, explained best on the hypothesis that the AJ is dependent on the firmly fixed tradition lying behind both the AJ and R 1.33–71. In the AJ the report of the martyrdom of James, which had already somewhat faded in R 1.70ff. (James was not really dead),[46] disappears completely, and the polemic against Paul is modified, in which case it is significant that it too (as in R 1) is constructed on the basis of Acts. This means that the AJ is not important for the literary prehistory of the traditions used in R 1 with which we are concerned in this chapter, although it is important for the question of the anti-Paulinism of R 1 itself, to be discussed later.

With this we return to the conjecture mentioned above, that R 1.33ff. (B) and R 1.66ff. (A) belong together genetically. Since the speech of Peter (and the other apostles) in 1.33ff. and the speech of James in 1.66ff. have the character of doublets, I consider it plausible that the redactor has extracted material from the tradition that he has used, which becomes visible especially in 1.66ff., and has placed it in the mouth of Peter (and the other apostles). (It should be noted that from R 1.15ff. on, Peter is the principal narrator or the main speaker, who is hardly interrupted except by Clement's questions). If this is correct, then also in 1.33ff. we have traditional material from the speech of James, which with all due caution may be used for the chronological and theological evaluation of the firmly structured tradition behind R 1.66ff. In the following we call this the R 1 source. (It corresponds to Strecker's "AJ source" [see, above, n. 44].

11.1.6 Concerning the Dating of the Source
Used in Ps.-Clem. *Recg.* 1

The fixed points for the dating of our text are the use[47] of Matthew,[48] Luke,[49] and Acts,[50] which places the *terminus a quo* at

181

the end of the first century. A more specific chronological indication, which is at the same time a pointer toward the geographical location of the source, is given by two passages (1.37 [Syr.]; 39.3), which allude to a tradition that knows of a preservation of the Jerusalem church from the Jewish War.[51] In addition, it presupposes the edict of Hadrian.[52] The source was thus composed after 135 c.e. The *terminus ad quem* is provided by the AJ named by Epiphanius or, if the author of the basic source (=G) is regarded as the redactor of R 1.33–71, the time in which he composed his work, that is, sometime in the third century.

The fact that the tradition of a prewar flight of the Jerusalem church was probably handed on only by Aristo of Pella[53] suggests Pella east of the Jordan as the place where the R 1 source was composed.[54]

11.1.7 The Theology and Jewish Christianity of the Source Used by Ps.-Clem. *Recg.* 1

The source has universalistic features[55] and advocates the Gentile (and Jewish) mission. In the Hellenistic city of Pella, its bearers found a rich field of activity for this mission. Its Christology affirmed the preexistence of Jesus ("Christus aeternus": 43.1; 44.2; 63.1),[56] in accord with Aristo of Pella, who, true to the Christian standpoint of the second century, developed the theme of Christ as the mediator of creation.[57] The doctrine of the law contained in the source also has features that correspond to the typical understanding of second-century Christianity.[58] For the time of the author of R 1 source, the Decalogue is especially binding (1.35.2 [a paraphrase of Exodus 20]). On the other hand, circumcision[59] and purification rites[60] seem no longer to be practiced. To be sure, both are mentioned in 1.33.5, but here both are only decorative elements in the historical narrative[61] and in any case do not have the weight given to the Decalogue in 1.35.2.[62]

There is no parallel in the catholic literature to the idea that the gospel was to be preached to the Gentiles only after the end of the Jewish War (64.2).[63] In addition, a peculiarity of this source is the special veneration of James as the one who was on the point of achieving the conversion of the whole Jewish community of Jerusalem. Finally, within the traditions about the preservation of the original Jerusalem church, the special claim of the tradents of our source comes to expression: that they stand in a special relationship to this primitive community or are even its successor. Thus a speech is placed in James's mouth that obviously reflects the theological views of the community of the R 1 source.

A static perspective on history will simply have to establish the presence of these characteristics and let it go at that, and will correctly deny the predicate "Jewish Christian" to the R 1 source.[64] In contrast, a truly historical view of the matter will immediately add that the critique of the law of a church which claims to be the successor of the original Jerusalem church is best understood as the reworking[65] of the tradition in the light of the catastrophe that happened to Judaism in 70 C.E. This war, with its desecration of the temple, let to the radical view that it could only be the visible expression of the wrath of God against his people. It revealed not only that elements of the Mosaic law had been given for only a limited period of time but, above all, the necessity of preaching the gospel to the Gentiles. This is one of the responses that an originally Jewish-Christian group made to the war. A historicizing interpretation, which attributes a speech such as 1.33ff.[66] to the historical James, misdirects our view from the interesting development within an originally Jewish-Christian community which becomes visible behind the R 1 source.[67]

11.1.8 Anti-Paulinism in the Source Used by Ps.-Clem. Recg. 1

The tradition history of the martyrdom of James presented above has as its result that the source used in R 1.33ff. goes back to the same archetype as the (original) report of Hegesippus. The literary-critical analysis of the R 1 source shows that the redaction of the archetype which it manifests has made extensive use of Acts. Indeed, one can say that as a result of this redaction the R 1 source has been made virtually into a competitor with Acts. It is different from the various apocryphal Acts current in the Great Church, which devote themselves to providing information about those figures not dealt with in the Lukan Acts of the Apostles, in that it intentionally sets out to correct a section of Luke's Acts with its own version of the story.

At the same time, it is "clearly the document of a particular Christian group that wants to be able to recognize its own dogmas, teaching, and perspectives in the portrayal of the past."[68] Like the author of Luke-Acts, but different from the authors of the apocryphal Acts, its author is also "concerned to provide his church with the history which gives it its distinctive identity."[69]

The summary of the work of the author of the R 1 source can be expressed in one sentence: Paul bears the blame for the fact that James was not successful in converting the whole Jewish community in Jerusalem to the Christian side,[70] that is, that he was not able to bring them to a (cultically) critical understanding of the Scriptures with respect to the cult and to the confession of Jesus as the Messiah. This statement is all the more amazing, since Paul is subjected to a strict Judaism[71] and James basically advocates a universalism free from the law, except that he still affirms the moral law.[72] The confusion could not be greater. The author turns the report of (the pre-Christian) Paul's presence in Acts 7:58 against the apostle to the Gentiles and does this on the basis of an approach that is almost Pauline. (The second part of Acts is ignored.[73]) In terms of content, the anti-Paulinism of our source only confirms what was said above concerning the theological perspective of its author: the source is critical of the law.

Formally, however, anti-Paulinism in this document—despite its internal tensions—is still prominent and must be explored further. For assistance at this point we may bring in the anti-Paulinism of the AJ source discussed above. Here Paul clearly appears as an antinomian and is the exact opposite of the zealot for the law of the R 1 source. On the other hand, in the content of the speech attributed to James a similarity between the AJ and the R 1 source was established: both have an anticultic perspective. It is clear, now, that both are directed toward the apostle to the Gentiles, although he is described differently in each case. It is also curious that in each case the anti-Paulinism seems to be patched on, for in neither document is there any organic connection to the speech of James. In the AJ, after the speech of James the rejection of Paul is grounded *afresh* on the fact that he is a Greek, while in the R 1 source it is the pre-Christian figure of Paul that is attacked in order to discredit the apostle to the Gentiles.[74] Both forms of polemic can thus best be described as popular anti-Paulinism which does not operate on the plane of a genuine debate but on the level of pure polemics.

It will hardly be possible for us to decide which form of anti-

Paulinism—that of the AJ or that of the R 1 source—is original.[75] The criteria for making such a decision are simply inadequate. Nonetheless, we may assume that the anti-Paulinism of both sources must have had a longer prehistory in their communities. This is demanded for the R 1 source, because otherwise the unrelated juxtaposition of universalism and criticism of Paul cannot be explained.[76]

From a source-critical point of view we may say in conclusion with regard to the R 1 source that the older anti-Paulinism was precipitated out in a later literary deposit at the time when the source that contained the report of the martyrdom of James received an anti-Pauline redaction along with a polemical use of Luke's Acts of the Apostles. This throws some light on the question addressed at the end of chapter 10, above, of whether the material concerning James's martyrdom used by Hegesippus already contained anti-Paulinism as an element of its tradition. The answer is negative. This anti-Pauline element first entered the report of James's martyrdom at the level of the R 1 source.[77] An attempt to find a direct anti-Paulinism in the material used by Hegesippus will therefore be unsuccessful.[78]

11.2 THE HOMILIES[79]

In the following we will first analyze those passages in the Pseudo-Clementine *Homilies* which unambiguously attack Paul.[80] After that, we will attempt to locate the relevant passages more precisely in the history of the tradition, in order at the conclusion of our work to set them into their proper historical and theological context. A supplementary discussion of their relation to the R 1 source will then be presented.

11.2.1 Exegesis of the Individual Anti-Pauline Passages in the Ps.-Clem. *Hom.*[81]

11.2.1.1 HOM. 18.13–19[82]

The discussion begins with a skirmish between Simon and Peter on the question of whether a vision is more reliable than personal association with a person or thing. Simon begins the attack with the following statements to Peter:

> You claim that you have learned the teaching of your master exactly, because you have directly seen and heard him, but that it is impossible for another to learn the same thing by means of a dream or vision. (13.1)

The contrast "personal association"—"vision/dream" stands like a title over the whole discussion and is clearly related to the conclusion of the debate reported in chap. 19, a conclusion that removes all doubt as to who is really being attacked. Before we turn to that resolution of the debate, we will briefly sketch the train of thought in 14ff.

Peter responds in chap. 14: whoever puts his faith in a vision does not know in whom he believes. The object of faith could, for example, be an evil daimon or a deceitful spirit. From this the general conclusion is drawn:

> Whoever trusts an apparition, vision, or dream finds himself in uncertainty. (14.3)

The opposite is true in the case of the true prophet, to whom unlimited trust can be given: *ho prophētēs, hoti prophētēs estin plērophorēsas prōton, peri tōn enargōs hypo autou legomenōn asphalōs pisteuetai kai alēthēs ōn proepignōstheis kai, hōs ho manthanōn thelei, exetastheis kai anakritheis apokrinetai* (14.3, par. 237.2ff. Rehm) ("The prophet, because he is a prophet, having first given certain information with regard to what is objectively said by him, is believed with confidence; and being known beforehand to be a true prophet, and being examined and questioned as the disciple wishes, he replies" [trans. from *ANF*, 8.322]. That is, the prophet can be trusted because of the words he has spoken during his personal association with the disciples,[83] and in addition, he gives reliable answers to questions put to him. In the case of Simon, the historical evidence is lacking that would be the basis for the ongoing presence of a prophet. He does not know, of course, whom he can ask for confirmation of his visions.

Chap. 15: Simon objects that only a righteous person can receive a dream from God.

Chap. 16: To this Peter responds with two lines of argument:

1. No human being can see God, the Son, or an angel, Whenever one supposes that he has had such a vision, that is the work of a demon.

2. The Scripture shows that the godless, too, have received dreams sent from God. Thus one cannot infer from such dreams that the one who receives them is truly pious. With this as a point of contact, Peter begins immediately to describe the truly pious person:

> For to a truly pious person, the truth discloses itself in its natural and pure meaning, not worked up through dreams, but conferred to the good through insight. (17:5)

In this connection the nature of revelation as a gift of grace is explained by Peter by means of Matt. 16:13ff.: not visions or dreams, but God had led him to this confession. This revelation comes from *within*, in that the hand of God awakes the knowledge already *spermatikōs* present in the human recipient (par. 239.13ff.; cf. already par. 239.4ff.).[84] Apprehensions through dreams and visions come from *outside* (*exōthen*, cf. par. 239.26, 16) and are not a sign of revelation (par. 239.16ff.) but of wrath. And finally the chief argument against Simon: Jesus spoke to Peter, as to a friend, *stoma kata stoma* (mouth to mouth), *en eidei* (a matter of physical seeing), not in riddles, appearances, and dreams as to an enemy (*hos pros echthron*, par. 239.23f.). Besides that, he instructed his disciples for a whole year.[85] How can these then believe that he had also appeared to Simon (par. 239.28—240.2)? With this, no doubt the high point is reached, and the reader is ready for the solution of the riddle of who, then, is meant by the figure of Simon, and all the more so since in the sentence *pōs de soi kai pisteusomen auto kan hoti ōphthē soi?* ("And how then shall we believe that he also appeared to you?"[par. 240.1ff.]) there is a clear allusion to 1 Cor. 15:8. The next allusion to a Pauline letter follows immediately:

> But if you were seen and taught by Him, and became His apostle for a single hour, proclaim His utterances, interpret His sayings, love His apostles, contend not with me who companied with Him. For in direct opposition to me, who am a firm rock, the foundation of the Church, you now stand. (Par. 240.3–6; trans. from *ANF*).

Paul is then called upon to subject himself to the apostles. When he declares Peter to be guilty (*kategnōsmenos*, cf. Gal. 2:11), he reproaches God, who revealed Christ to Peter (par. 240.9ff.). Peter's concluding appeal summarizes his case once again: *mathe prōton par' hēmōn, ha hēmeis par ekeinou amathomen. kai mathētēs alētheias gegonōs genou hēmin synergos* ("Learn first from us what we have learned from that one, and become our co-worker as a disciple of the truth" [par. 240.12–14]).

After this depiction of the train of thought of 18.13ff., there can be no doubt that polemic against Paul is present and that the author had the apostle to the Gentiles in view from the very beginning.[86]

The critique of Paul can be summarized as follows: Paul lacks legitimization, since he was not instructed by the historical Jesus; his claim that Jesus had appeared to him, in view of the lack of confirming legitimization, is worthless. Paul is not an equal partner to the apostles. He could be their co-worker only if he were willing to be instructed by them. His vision made him not into a friend of Jesus but into his enemy.

The results of the above analysis provide the basis for tracing out additional elements of "anti-Paulinism" in the Pseudo-Clementine *Homilies*.

11.2.1.2 EPISTULA PETRI/CONTESTATIO

The *Epistula Petri*, a letter to James, bishop of the holy church, represents itself as the accompanying letter for a document sent at the same time (the *Kerygmata Petrou*), while the *Contestatio* is the certification of the letter's recipients. In the letter, Peter asks for compliance with certain prescribed rules. The reasons for this action are as follows:

> For some from among the Gentiles have rejected my legal preaching, attaching themselves to certain lawless and trifling preaching of the man who is my enemy. (2.3)

There can be no doubt that this passage is related to the anti-Pauline section 18.13–19 of the Ps.-Clem. *Hom.* For there Peter charges Simon=Paul with resisting his kerygma (*to di' emou kērygma eloidoreis*, par. 240.7f.) and implicitly says that Jesus stands against Simon=Paul as an enemy (par. 239.23f.). If the anti-Pauline character of the *EpPetr./Cont.* is thus established, then other accusations from the same document may be considered anti-Pauline, such as the statement that some (=disciples of Paul) had attempted even during Peter's lifetime

to pervert my words by various interpretations, as though I taught
the abolition of the law, as though I myself were of such a mind,
but did not freely proclaim it [the law]. (*EpPetr.* 2.4, trans. from
ANF)

And further:

But these people . . . professing to know my mind, undertake to
explain my words, which they have heard from me, more intelli-
gently than I who spoke them, telling their catechumens that this
is my meaning, which indeed I never thought of. But if, while I am
still alive, they dare thus to misrepresent me, how much more will
those who shall come after me dare to do so! (*EpPetr.* 2.6f., trans.
from *ANF*)
Cont. 5.2: If we turn the books over to anyone, and when they are
falsified by the most impudent men and are disfigured by their
interpretations—as you have no doubt heard that some have
already done this—then it will happen that also those who ear-
nestly seek the truth will constantly be led into error.

These three passages are all anti-Pauline in that they attribute to
Paul('s disciples) a perversion of the Petrine position: Paul or his
disciples represent Peter as having fundamentally abolished the
law, although he openly proclaims the opposite. (The comment
in *Cont.* 5.2 to the effect that the opponents falsify the books of
Peter, the *Kerygmata Petrou*, goes back to the literary fiction of a
transmission of these books.)

G. Strecker has correctly recognized an anti-Pauline polemic
in the above passages and thinks that, especially in the passages
from the *EpPetr.*, "there is an allusion to the Pauline portrayal of
the events in Antioch (Gal. 2:11ff) and that Paul and his disciples
had falsely represented the encounter at Antioch."[87] But in what
is this false portrayal supposed to have consisted? Its tenor (in
Gal. 2:11ff.) is, after all, precisely *not* that Peter was teaching a
fundamental abrogation of the law but that he was a hypocrite.[88]
We should then not see the anti-Pauline charge as primarily a
matter of a false portrayal of the events at Antioch as such.
Rather, *EpPetr./Cont.* appear to think of what is, in their view, a
misleading description of the antinomistic *presupposition* of
Peter, to which Gal. 2:15 refers: *hēmeis . . . eidotes . . . hoti ou
dikaioutai anthrōpos ex ergōn nomou . . . kai hēmeis eis Christon
Iēsoun episteusamen.* It is supposed to be misleading for pre-

cisely this reason: Peter, like Jesus, had taught the eternal validity of the law (*EpPetr.* 2.5).

11.2.1.3 *Hom.* 2.17.3–4

Simon appeared as the seventh pair of a series of syzygies and preceded Peter as the first to go to the Gentiles. Peter, who followed him, was like light to the darkness, knowledge to ignorance, healing to sickness. In view of the theme "mission to the Gentiles" being pursued in *EpPetr.* 2.3, in the context of an anti-Pauline statement, the possibility is easily suggested that also an anti-Pauline element should be recognized in the above text.[89] It is interesting that, despite the polemic against Simon/Paul, some credit for the Gentile mission is not denied him. It was through him, so to speak, that Peter's approach to the Gentiles was first motivated.

A more precise description of the relation of Paul's preaching to that of Peter is found in 2.17.4:

> First a gospel from a deceiver must come, and after the destruction of the Holy Place, a true gospel must be sent out secretly, in order to correct the heresies that are to come.[90]

The false gospel is without doubt to be understood as the Pauline gospel, and the true gospel is certainly that of Peter. This passage has a clear point of contact to the *EpPetr.* in that it speaks, exactly as does the letter, of a *secret* propagation of the Petrine gospel. By the date it assigns to this propagation, it incidentally casts an interesting light on the historical-theological location of the bearer of the anti-Paulinism of the above passage. On the one hand, with a radicality that can only bring Marcion to mind, it deems the whole Christian period prior to 70 C.E. to have been corrupted—of course, by Paul. On the other hand, it relates its own preaching, in a positive sense, to the fall of Jerusalem. The last point allows us to see the anticultic attitude of the bearer of the critique of Paul.[91] Thus in 2.17.4, critique of Paul and critique of the cult are interrelated.

11.2.1.4 *Hom.* 11.35.3–6 (Ps.-Clem. Recg. 4.34–35)

There are here no allusions to Acts or the letters of Paul, so one cannot infer an anti-Paulinism from this passage.[92] But there are noticeable allusions to the sections identified above as anti-

Pauline: thus *astrapē ex ouranou* is reminiscent of 18.14.5 (*ponēros astrapsas, meinas hoson thelei, aposbennytai*); Simon is described as one who sows *planēn* (par. 172.1)—2.17.3 identifies this with *agnoia*. And finally, the discussion of James may contain an indirect anti-Paulinism: No one should be accepted—this is the view attributed to Peter—who has not previously submitted his kerygma to James, called the brother of my Lord, to whom the leadership of the church of the Hebrews in Jerusalem has been entrusted. This passage reminds one of the *EpPetr.*, in which Peter speaks of the fact that an enemy has falsified his (Peter's) kerygma, while James helps spread it abroad.[93] To be sure, the above passage, taken by itself, does not suggest any particular anti-Pauline element. But taken in connection with the other sections, it does appear to have traces of an anti-Pauline attitude.

This concludes the exegesis of those passages from the Ps.-Clem. *Hom.* which contain anti-Pauline elements. May they be located more precisely in the history of the tradition?

11.2.2 A More Precise Determination of the History of the Tradition of the Anti-Pauline Sections of the Ps.-Clem. *Hom.*

There are obvious connections with the Elkesaite tradition in particular. Cf. the following points:

1. Enumeration of the elements and their use as legal witnesses.[94] Cf. Hippolytus, *Ref.* 9.10 (par. 253.17ff. Wendland): *ton ouranon kai to hydōr kai ta pneumata ta hagia kai tous angelous tēs proseuchēs kai to elaion kai to halas kai tēn gēn* ("the heaven, and the water, and the holy spirits, and the angels of prayer, and the oil, and the salt, and the earth",[95] cf. *Cont.* 2.1 (=4.1: "I call to witness *ouranon, gēn, hydōr*, through which everything holds together [these I call as witnesses], and the air [*aera*] which permeates everything, without which I cannot breathe, that I will always be obedient to the one who transmits these books to me"). After this oath, the novice is to share bread and salt with the transmitter of the books. "From the words and expressions by which here the summoning of cosmic elements is described it is clearly visible that the author was aware of practices of the Elkesaites (or of Ebionites influenced by Elkesaites)."[96]

2. Both reject Paul.

3. Both distinguish the feminine and masculine principles.[97]

4. Both demand circumcision (cf. *Cont.* 1.1).

In my opinion, these agreements are sufficient to justify the conclusion that the anti-Pauline sections of the Ps.-Clem. *Hom.* have a literary-traditional connection to Elkesaite traditions.[98] There are also lines of connection with the R1 source with which our section has the following in common:

1. Anti-Paulinism[99]

2. Hostility to the cult.

3. The destruction of Jerusalem as the beginning of the Gentile mission. (To be sure, this is not explicitly said in 2.17.4, but the context of 2.17.3–4 suggests such an inference; see above, pp. 189f.).

4. The high esteem they have for James.

The fragmentary character of the anti-Pauline texts in the Ps.-Clem. *Hom.* does not permit a more precise determination of the manner of literary-traditional relationship to the Elkesaite traditions and the R 1 source. But it can probably be accepted that the bearers of the anti-Pauline traditions of the Ps.-Clem. *Hom.* worked in the same milieu as the Elkesaites and the community of the R 1 source. Chronologically, these tradents will probably have to be placed in the second century. The places that come into consideration as provenance are Syria or—more likely—the Transjordan.

11.2.3 Theology

The following undertakes a delineation of the basic theological views of the anti-Pauline sections of the Ps.-Clem. *Hom.* without dealing with the important question of the form of *EpPetr./Cont.* I am aware of the lack involved in this but at the present state of research do not know how it can be helped. The spectrum of opinions on the determination of the form of *EpPetr./Cont.* ranges from the supposition that they reflect real events[100] to the hypothesis that both documents are pure fiction[101] and are completely useless for establishing the views of a community.

The theology of this section deserves the title "Jewish-Christian." *Contestatio* 1.1 documents the practice of circumcision, and the legal kerygma that Peter preaches (*EpPetr.*) is identical with the law of God "which was promulgated through Moses and has been confirmed by our Lord to last forever" (*EpPetr.* 2.5).

The attitude toward the Gentiles is not consistent. On the one hand, the books of Peter may only be transmitted "to one of the circumcised who has become a believer" (*Cont.* 1.1), that is, Gentiles are excluded. On the other hand, other passages, such as 2.17.3f., document the fact that the Gentile mission—even if not until after the fall of Jerusalem—is commended. The same is already implied in *EpPetr.*; cf. 1.2 and especially 3.1: the books should be transmitted "neither to a fellow member of the Jewish people nor to a foreigner (Gentile) before they [i.e., the persons concerned] are checked."

Strecker and others have explained this tension from the literary character of the *EpPetr./Cont.*[102] But one can just as well see in this tension a phenomenon which necessarily must exist in a Jewish-Christian community that, on the one hand, has decided in favor of a Gentile mission but, on the other hand, of course has maintained the demand of circumcision for born Jews. (The manner in which the law of Moses is to be observed by newly converted Gentiles may thus have remained vague.) The passages discussed above then correspond to a Jewish Christianity that has gone only halfway toward the community of the R 1 source. Like this latter community, it works the catastrophe of the destruction of Jerusalem into its thinking by rejecting the cultic law. But in contrast to the R 1 source, the commandment of circumcision remains at least partially in force.[103]

11.2.4 Theology and Anti-Paulinism

If one compares the content and claim of the "legal preaching" of Peter, no contradiction appears between the anti-Paulinism and the theology of that section. In fact, of all the texts we have analyzed thus far, those above came the closest, in terms of their content, to the critique of the Jewish-Christian contemporaries of the apostle to the Gentiles, for they take objection both to Paul's claim to apostolic authority and to his preaching of freedom from the law among the Gentiles.

In addition, we have to take into consideration the difference between the time of Paul's historical opponents and the situation of the tradents of our texts in their own day. They are already looking back on the destruction of Jerusalem and understand it—as did the community of the R 1 source—as a challenge to the Gentile mission. That is, in contrast to the historical opponents of Paul, they are primarily missionaries to the Gentiles.

The result of our investigation, that Paul is almost involuntarily acknowledged as the one who must be credited with beginning the Gentile mission, in my opinion points to a long pre-history of the rejection of Paul in this group. This acknowledgement, together with the dating of the Gentile mission after the war, thus appears to be best regarded as a coming to grips with the past, since in the second century the historical foundations of the community were rethought from the point of view of Jewish Christianity. Within the context of this new consciousness, anti-Paulinism did not simply fall from heaven, and, since contemporary Paulinists are excluded as possible targets of his polemic, anti-Paulinism must have been an already traditional feature of the theology of this community. In other words, anti-Paulinism has a long prehistory in this community.[104]

12

THE ANTI-PAULINISM OF IRENAEUS'S JEWISH CHRISTIANS (*HERESIES* 1.26.2)[1]

Irenaeus has no firsthand knowledge of those Jewish Christians whom he calls Ebionites. From *Heresies* 1.23 on, he is reproducing a source.[2] The statements he makes in other passages,[3] in which Ebionites, Valentinians, and Marcionites are all measured with the same yardstick,[4] are a clear indication of his lack of direct knowledge of the Ebionites.

If we now turn to the content of the report in the source, we find that it ascribes to the Ebionites the following characteristic doctrinal features:

1. Monotheism.
2. Adoptionistic Christology.[5]
3. Use of Matthew alone.[6]
4. Rejection of Paul.
5. A characteristic use[7] of the prophetic scriptures.
6. Keeping of the law, including circumcision.
7. Praying in the direction of Jerusalem.

Since it is here a matter of a report of heresy and not a matter of primary sources[8] or even of a report based on direct knowledge, it would serve no purpose to attempt to categorize the Ebionites of Irenaeus, *Heresies* 1.26.2, chronologically (beyond their *terminus ad quem*), geographically, historically, or theologically. Nor can it be presupposed that the report gives a historical description of a definite group. Rather, it summarizes in stereotypical fashion, under the heading "Ebionites," a number of Jewish-Christian communities that are characterized by the list od doctrinal peculiarities.[9,10,11] The name "Ebionites" is probably the self-designation[12] of one of these groups. Irenaeus or his source uses it without further comment—probably because he/it knew nothing more detailed to say about them.[13] It is derived from the Hebrew word *'bywnym*. With this self-designation this group of Jewish Christians adopted for their own use a Jewish honorific title.[14] It cannot be proven that we may take the further step and affirm that they took the designation "the poor" from the earliest Jerusalem church,[15] since there is not a single certain indication for the view that the early Jerusalem church used this phrase as a self-designation in a religious sense.[16,17]

The reference in Irenaeus—as said at the beginning (above, p. 32)—forms the outer limit of our investigation, for in him for the first time anti-Pauline Jewish Christianity is declared to be heretical. By way of conclusion, we can describe the irony inherent in the process which unfolds in the course of a century and a half with the words of W. Bauer:

> Thus, if one may be allowed to speak rather pointedly, the apostle Paul was the only heresiarch known to the apostolic age—the only one who was so considered in that period, at least from one particular perspective. It could be said that the Jewish Christians in their opposition to Paul introduced the notion of "heresy" into the Christian consciousness. The arrow quickly flew back to the archer.[18]

13

SUMMARY

13.1 SUMMARY OF THE RESULTS OF PART II

Part II has introduced us to a surprising number of texts and traditions that document an anti-Paulinism in their bearers. A necessary result of the fact that some of the extant witnesses exist only in fragmentary form is that some conclusions can be stated only with degrees of probability. Still, in view of the whole—even if this or that witness of anti-Paulinism should be excluded—there can be no doubt concerning the relatively large number of anti-Pauline texts and traditions.

The texts and traditions (or their bearers) that document this extend over a period of about a hundred years (80—180 C.E.) and belong geographically to the Syrian-Palestinian area.[1] They have primarily Paul himself—and not disciples of Paul—in view,[2] whether this is because their anti-Paulinism was already a constitutent part of the tradition of their community (*Desposynoi*, Elkesaites, James) and/or because Paul himself was attacked afresh on the basis that Paul had been traditionally rejected in their community (James, R 1 source, Ps.-Clem. *Hom.*).[3] Both items, the polemic against the historical Paul or his letters and the fact that in most cases anti-Paulinism had had a prehistory, that is, it was already conventional to it bearers, give rise to the question of whether or not the anti-Paulinism of the different groups had a common root or—to continue the same metaphor—were branches from the same stock (cf. further below, p. 198).

This anti-Paulinism was in different ways related to the theology of its bearers or not integrated into this theology at all. We have observed Jewish-Christian and Gentile Christian anti-Paulinists. The existence of Gentile Christian anti-Pauline communities (James, Hegesippus, R 1 source), however, can be explained only in terms of their internal development. They probably gave up their Jewish manner of life as the result of theo-

197

logical and political influences and as a result became Gentile Christian churches. Thus their anti-Paulinism derives from their Jewish-Christian past. To this extent, the results of Part II form an adequate basis for this thesis: *Also in the period after 70 C.E. anti-Paulinism was originally limited to Jewish-Christian communities.*

The texts that we have studied and the groups that transmitted them are a long way from possessing a unified theology. The Elkesaites and the tradents of James stand at the two poles of the texts/traditions with which we have dealt. The former group developed on a Jewish-Christian foundation, emphasizing more and more the role of the prophet Elkesai, until it became a *new religion*. The latter group became closer and closer in its understanding of the law to the average catholic understanding of second-century Christianity. This latter group fits the tradents of the R 1 source, in which the original Jewish-Christian foundation is even clearer than in James.[4] The observations made in this section on the theology of the anti-Pauline texts/traditions thus show that Jewish Christianity possessed an amazing *capacity for development.*[5]

13.2 INTEGRATION OF THE RESULTS OF PARTS I AND II

We presented above as the results of Part I that an anti-Pauline attitude had been shared by both the liberal and the conservative Jewish Christians of Jerusalem since the beginning of the fifth decade C.E. One of the results of Part II is that the anti-Pauline attitude of the different communities of this later period all point back to a common root. We could thus formulate the integrated results of Parts I and II as follows: the phenomenon of apparently unrelated elements of anti-Paulinism in the texts and traditions studied in Part II is best explained by the hypothesis that it is the offshoot of the chronologically earlier anti-Paulinism of the Jerusalem church. The communities that stand behind these traditions and texts only continued after the Jewish War to propagate what the Jerusalem mother church had actively propagated. The anti-Pauline attacks are genetically related by their common roots and are not to be regarded as isolated phenomena.

At the end of Part I, we said that the opposition of the Jerusalem church was necessarily ignited by the apostleship of Paul to the Gentiles. One can no longer say this with regard to the anti-Paulinists after 70 C.E. There are two reasons for this: (a) Their anti-Paulinism was already traditional, an item of doctrine, and, except for the traditions of the Ps.-Clem. *Hom.*, manifests no real debate with Paul. (b) Some anti-Pauline communities carried on an active Gentile mission themselves: to the extent that these Gentile converts then had to start keeping the law, an indirect light is hereby cast on the theological rightness of Paul's Gentile mission advocating freedom from the law. But to the extent that a "law-free" gospel was preached to the Gentiles from the anti-Pauline side, the work of the apostle to the Gentiles received, in an ironical way, a late vindication.

APPENDIX: THE SUCCESSORS OF EARLIEST JERUSALEM CHRISTIANITY: AN ANALYSIS OF THE PELLA TRADITION*

1. INTRODUCTION AND THE POSING OF THE PROBLEM

Not many hypotheses with regard to the early history of Christianity have met with such general agreement as the supposition that the Jerusalem community fled to Pella[1] before the beginning of the Jewish War.[2] Of the few scholars who have doubted the historicity of that flight,[3] only S. G. F. Brandon[4] has attempted a full refutation of the above view. Not only have his arguments exercised no influence on the general opinion, they have recently been independently attacked in essays by S. Sowers,[5] M. Simon,[6] J. J. Gunther,[7] and B. C. Gray.[8] In view of such a majority, has the Pella problem been finally resolved in favor of the historicity of the Pella flight? I would say definitely not and add at the same time that the Pella discussion suffers from a methodological weakness. This is illustrated by the subtitle of the essay by M. Simon: "Legend or Truth?" Most scholars have approached the Pella problem with the alternative: the Pella flight is either historical or unhistorical. This issue, which remains important in the exegesis of the relevant texts, sometimes inhibits scholars from posing questions that must be dealt with before a decision on the alternative mentioned above is made, questions that are more readily answered. As in research on the historical Jesus, where literary criticism, form criticism, and redaction criticism are done first (a methodological procedure that has led to unanticipated insights into the self-under-

*This Appendix is based on a presentation given before the Habilitationskommission of the Theological Faculty of the University of Göttingen on June 11, 1977. An English version of the lecture appeared in the E. P. Sanders, ed., *Jewish and Christian Self-Definition*, vol. 1, *The Shaping of Christianity in the Second and Third Centuries* (London/Philadelphia, 1980), 161–73, 245–54. The present form is a new translation of the German Appendix, which was an exapnsion of the English article (with permission of SCM Press, London).

standing of the earliest Christian communities), so an analysis of the relevant texts, using the same methods mentioned above, should be carried out *before* the historical question is faced.

In addition, the limits of such an investigation of the Pella tradition should be taken into consideration. Those who have doubted the historicity of a flight to Pella have sometimes overestimated the significance of such a conclusion. In the case of Brandon, for example, the denial of a flight to Pella is closely bound up with his additional hypothesis that the Jerusalem Christians made common cause with the Zealots. This means that, for him, disputing the flight to Pella provides support for his view of the revolutionary role of the Jerusalem Christians during the revolt against Rome. On the other side, J. Munck would like to show that (heretical) Jewish Christianity after 70 C.E. had no connection with the prewar Jerusalem church.[9] Disputing the historicity of the Pella flight is used by him to sever any historical connection between the two. Munck and Brandon proceed on the basis of the same presupposition: the unhistoricity of the Pella flight excludes any historical connection between the early Jerusalem church and post-70 C.E. Jewish Christianity. It is important for the hypotheses advocated by both scholars that the Jerusalem church perished during the Jewish War. Otherwise, Brandon would have to modify his principal thesis and Munck would be confronted with serious objections against his hypothesis that (heretical) Jewish Christianity did not come into being until the postapostolic age after 70 C.E.

Thus, though it is otherwise well founded, both Brandon and Munck have overdone their criticism of the Pella tradition and thereby overlooked the fact that the inferences they draw from this criticism represent only two among various other possibilities. Disputing the historicity of the flight to Pella does not automatically mean that the Jerusalem Christians had made common cause with the Zealots or that they remained in Jerusalem during the war or that they perished in the course of the revolt. Judgments such as Munck's and Brandon's presuppose some additional investigations (which have not yet been done), for example, an analysis of the attitude of the Jerusalem church toward the Jewish authorities or a study of the relation of the theological teaching of the Jerusalem church before 70 C.E. to that of the (heretical) Jewish Christians after 70 C.E.

In the following investigation, we must then attempt to avoid two things: (a) a historicizing exegesis that has in view only the alternative "historical or unhistorical?" and (b) an exegesis that proceeds too quickly from the results of an analysis of the Pella tradition to general theories about Jewish Christianity before and after 70 C.E. If, as argued below, the extant Pella texts do not permit the conclusion that a flight of the Jerusalem Christians to Pella occurred, then that means (contra Brandon and Munck) neither that no Christian left Jerusalem at that time[10] nor that Jerusalem Christianity perished during the war, in which case there would be no historical connecting link between prewar and postwar Jewish Christianity.

Such a method as the one just described requires the following steps.

1. First, a literary analysis of those texts which explicitly describe the flight of the Jerusalem church to Pella should be made (§2). In this section, an attempt should also be made to distinguish tradition and redaction. As soon as we have obtained a firm knowledge of the oldest elements of the Pella tradition, we can proceed to the question of whether other texts can supply us with additional information concerning the Pella tradition. Here it is a matter of texts that could not be dealt with at first because their relation to the Pella tradition was only implicit and so not beyond all doubt.

2. We may then ask which texts come into consideration as indirect witnesses for the Pella tradition (§3). Do they enlarge our knowledge of it? After this literary inventory and analysis of the Pella texts undertaken in steps 1 and 2, we ask as step 3 whether there were competing versions of the story of what happened to the Jerusalem church during the Jewish War (§4). Only after this step do we (in the form of an excursus under §4) deal with the question of the conditions and possibilities of a flight from Jerusalem to Pella before and during the Jewish War.

After we show in steps 1-3 that the Pella tradition is confronted with overwhelming literary difficulties and problems involving its content which exclude its dependability as a historical report of the fate of the Jerusalem church, we will proceed to step 4, the final step, in which we shall show its true historical value (which, in any case, provides an additional argument against its historicity in the above sense as a report of a prewar event). This section bears the title: "The Successors of Earliest Jerusalem Christianity" (§5). It is intended to show that the Pella tradition had its origin in the Jewish-Christian community of Pella, which with this tradition established the claim to be the true successor of the Jerusalem church.

2. LITERARY ANALYSIS OF THE EXPLICIT PELLA TEXTS

The oldest extant text that explicitly refers to the church leaving Jerusalem for Pella prior to the Jewish War is found in Eusebius, *Hist. Ecc.* 3.5.3.[11]

> The people of the church in Jerusalem were commanded by an *oracle* given by revelation before the war to those in the city who were worthy of it *to depart* and dwell *in one of the cities of Perea* which they called *Pella.*

Epiphanius of Salamis mentions the exodus to Pella three times:[12]

> *Pan.* 29.7.7: This heresy of the Nazoraeans exists in Beroea in the neighbourhood of Coele Syria and the Decapolis in the region of Pella and in Basanitis in the so-called Kokaba, Chochabe in Hebrew. For from there it took its beginnings after the exodus from Jerusalem when all the disciples went to live in Pella because Christ had told them to leave Jerusalem and to go away since it would undergo a siege. Because of this advice they lived in Perea, after having moved to that place, as I said. There the Nazoraean heresy had its beginning.
>
> *Pan.* 30.2.7: After all those who believed in Christ had generally come to live in Perea, in a city called Pella of the Decapolis of which it is written in the Gospel and which is situated in the neighborhood of the region of Batanaea and Basanitis, Ebion's preaching originated here after they had moved to this place and had lived there.
>
> *Treatise on Weights and Measures* 15:[13] When the city [i.e., Jerusalem] was about to be taken by the Romans, it was revealed in advance to all the disciples by an angel of God that they should remove from the city, as it was going to be completely destroyed. They sojourned as emigrants in Pella . . . in Transjordania. And this city is said to be of the Decapolis (But after the destruction of Jerusalem, when they had returned . . . , they wrought great signs).

After citing the extant texts that describe the Pella flight, the question must be posed: Is there a literary relationship among these four texts?[14] In my opinion, it is possible to give a clear answer to this question. The numerous identical or similar words and phrases[15] suggest the following conclusion: In all three passages Epiphanius is dependent on Eusebius, *Hist. Ecc.* 3.5.3![16]

Before we turn to those texts which are sometimes introduced as implicit witnesses to the Pella tradition, we must attempt to separate tradition and redaction in the texts from Eusebius cited above and to ascertain the origin of the tradition. We thus ask:

a. Is *Hist. Ecc.* 3.5.3 from Eusebius himself or does it derive from the use of a source? (In the latter case:)

b. What elements of *Hist. Ecc.* 3.5.3 come from this source?

c. Where does the source itself come from?

Concerning *a*: The most important reason for believing that *Hist. Ecc.* 3.5.3 did not originate from Eusebius himself is that he never mentions a flight from Pella in any of his other works, though he had many other opportunities to work in a reference to it.[17]

Concerning *b*: In the context of *Hist. Ecc.* 3.5.3, Eusebius explains that the wrath of God came upon the Jews as punishment for their crime against Jesus, Stephen, James the son of Zebedee, and James the Just. This type of explanation of the destruction of Jerusalem was stock in trade of early Christian literature.[18] For this reason it cannot with sufficient certainty be assigned to Eusebius's Pella source but most likely comes from Eusebius's own pen.

What, then, was the extent and content of the source used by Eusebius? In my opinion, this source combined the miraculous deliverance of the Jerusalem Christians with the destruction of Jerusalem without precisely dating their flight. The source spoke further of a settling down of the Jerusalem Christians in Pella. Evaluated in terms of form criticism, Eusebius's source contained the building blocks for the founding legend of the Pella community, a legend that originated after the Jewish War.[19] It should be pointed out in any case that the source[20] presupposes no return of the Pella Christians to Jerusalem.[21]

Concerning *c*: We have already (above, n. 17) rejected the suggestion that *Epiphanius* owes his knowledge of the Pella tradition to Hegesippus. Since *Eusebius*, however, is often dependent on Hegesippus for his information about Palestinian

Christianity, we must first examine the view that Eusebius is indebted to Hegesippus for the Pella tradition:

In his work *Hypomnemata*,[22] Hegesippus describes in detail the martyrdom of James the Lord's brother (Eusebius, *Hist. Ecc.* 2.23.4ff.), the siege of Jerusalem by Vespasian (Eusebius, *Hist. Ecc.* 23.18), and the choice of Symeon as James's successor to the bishop's seat in Jerusalem (Eusebius, *Hist. Ecc.* 2.22.4). Will Hegesippus not also have described a flight of the Jerusalem church to Pella and its return to Jerusalem, where the selection of Symeon would have taken place? Although I agree with the view that according to Hegesippus the selection took place in Jerusalem,[23] nonetheless there are weighty objections against the view discussed above that Eusebius received his Pella report from Hegesippus:

1. The kernel of the Pella tradition presupposes Pella as the place of emigration, not as a temporary refuge.

2. Eusebius often indicates that his reports concerning the Jerusalem church are quotations from Hegesippus. This is not the case with the Pella report.[24] Those who advocate the view that the Pella report is taken from the work of Hegesippus must explain this exception.

3. In those parts where Eusebius copies extensive passages out of Hegesippus, Pella is not mentioned, although a reference to Pella would be expected.[25]

4. The extant fragments of Hegesippus's work are self-consistent in that they emphasize that after the rebuttal of the first heretic, Thebouthis, the succession of James was well settled by the selection of Symeon.[26] The Pella tradition is dispensable and for this reason should not be read into the extant fragments.[27]

In sum, Hegesippus's *Hypomnemata* were in all probability not Eusebius's source for the report of the flight to Pella.

Where, then, could Eusebius's source for the Pella tradition have come from? A. von Harnack[28] and A. Schlatter[29] suggested Aristo of Pella as Eusebius's informant. Aristo's *Dialogue Between Jason and Papiscus*[30] comes from the middle of the second century and was used by Eusebius for his report of the Bar Kochba war; cf. *Hist. Ecc.* 4.6.3:

Hadrian then commanded that by a legal decree and ordinances the whole nation should be absolutely prevented from entering from thenceforth even the district round Jerusalem, so that not even from a distance could it see its ancestral home. Aristo of Pella tells the story.

Since Aristo described the second Jewish War, it seems entirely reasonable to assume that he also recounted something about the (first) Jewish War and in this connection also knew something about the flight to Pella to report, and all the more so since his own home was Pella. We may thus be permitted carefully to develop Harnack's suggestion further.

3. AN ANALYSIS OF TEXTS REGARDED AS IMPLICIT WITNESSES OF THE PELLA TRADITION

1. *Mark 16:7*: W. Marxsen uses the Pella tradition as the basis for his own interpretation of Mark, which he regards as having been composed between 66 and 70 C.E. In Mark 16:7 *proagei hymas eis tēn Galilaian. ekei auton opsesthe* ("He is going before you to Galilee; there you will see him"), the evangelist is urging the Christians to leave Jerusalem and move to Galilee, in order there to experience the parousia.[31]

However, Marxsen has a serious problem to overcome. Since Pella does not belong to Galilee,[32] he is forced to assume that the church which left Jerusalem in the direction of Galilee finally ended up in Pella, a development of which the author of Mark had not yet learned.[33] Such an interpretation, which erects one hypothesis on another, can hardly encourage anyone to regard Mark 16:7 as implicitly referring to the Pella flight. Marxsen's interpretation of the Pella tradition is a fourth-rate hypothesis; for neither Galilee as the original place where the parousia was expected, nor the shift of the original direction of the flight somewhat to the east, nor Pella as the new place where the parousia was expected, nor the writing of Mark during the Jewish War can be made plausible. Mark 16:7 is thus to be excluded as an implicit reference to the Pella tradition.

2. *Mark 13*: Most scholars agree that Mark 13 makes use of older traditions.[34] Our only task will be to examine the hypothesis of some scholars who, after reconstructing the tradition used in Mark 13 relate it to the prophecy reported in Eusebius, *Hist. Ecc.* 3.5.3.

In the view of C. H. Dodd[35] and H. J. Schoeps[36] the tradition begins in Mark 13:14 and is to be identified with the oracle discussed above.[37] This suggestion is to be rejected on the following grounds:

a. Mark 13:14ff. speaks only in general about a flight (without a definite goal),[38] unless one is willing to accept Schoeps's identification of the "hill country" (Mark 13:14) with the hill country east of the Jordan (including Pella).[39]

b. Mark 13:14ff. presupposes another chronology of the flight than that of the prophecy preserved in Eusebius. The latter was given before the war, while Mark 13:14ff. calls for the departure from Jerusalem when the "desolating sacrilege" comes in sight, that is, in the midst of the war itself (if Mark 13:14ff. refers to the war at all). Thus neither can Mark 13:14ff. be understood as an indirect reference to the Pella tradition.

3. *Luke 21:* In his second apocalyptic speech, the author of the Third Gospel has, in distinction from Mark 13:14a, the following statement (Luke 21:20): *Hotan de idēte kykloumenēn hypo stratopedōn Ierousalēm, tote gnōte hoti ēngiken hē erēmōsis autēs* ("But when you see Jerusalem surrounded by armies, then know that its desolation has come near"). The following sentence (Luke 21:21a) then agrees verbatim with Mark 13:14b: *tote hoi en tō Ioudaia pheugetōsan eis ta orē.* Only a historicizing exegesis is in the position to see in this Lukan passage an indirect reference to the Pella tradition.[40] An appropriate exegesis, however, must begin with the generally accepted presupposition that Luke 21:20f. presupposes Mark 13:14.[41] Luke interprets his Markan source in the light of the destruction of Jerusalem[42] (cf. Luke 19:41ff.), that is he historicizes his source by applying the "desolating sacrilege" to the destruction of Jerusalem.[43] Luke wants to point out that the siege of Jerusalem is the beginning of the city's destruction.[44] Thus there is no way that Luke 21:20 can be considered to be an indirect witness to the Pella tradition.

After this survey and discussion of those New Testament texts which are sometimes regarded as (indirect) evidence for the Pella tradition,[45] we must state our conclusion in summary: the Pella tradition is reflected in no New Testament text, not even indirectly. Thus far we have found only a single text to document this tradition, a text that probably comes from the Christian community at Pella.

Do we possess other texts outside the New Testament that may be said to refer to the Pella tradition? Or does a source exist that also comes from the neighborhood of Pella? With this question in mind, we turn again to the Pseudo-Clementine *Recognitions*.

R 1.37.2 (Syriac): *hoi autō (i.e., tō prophētō) pisteuontes theou sophia eis ischyron tēs chōras topon eis sōtērian synēgmenoi, tērēthein dia ton polemon, hos tois apistousi dia tēn dichonoian eis olethron epeleusetai* (retranslated into Greek by W. Frankenberg) ("Those who believed in him [i.e., the prophet] by the wisdom of God having been gathered for salvation into a strong place of the country, to be kept through the war, which will bring the unbelievers to destruction because of their disagreement" [literal trans. of the Greek into English by M. Eugene Boring]).

R 1.39.3: "omnis qui credens prophetae huic . . . ab excidio belli quod incredulae genti inminet ac loco ipsi, servaretur inlaesus, non credentes vero extorres loco et regno fiant, ut vel inviti intellegant et oboediant voluntati dei" ("Everyone who, believing in this prophet who had been foretold by Moses, is baptized in his name, shall be kept unhurt from the destruction of war which impends over the unbelieving nation, and the place itself; but those who do not believe shall be made exiles from their place and kingdom, that even against their will they may understand and obey the will of God" [trans. from *ANF*]).

Both texts agree in declaring that those who believe in the true prophet Jesus would be saved from the impending war in a safe place, while the war will bring destruction on the unbelievers. When we compare these statements with the authentic elements of the Pella traditions established above, we arrive at the following results:

a. Both traditions distinguish dualistically between those saved and those destroyed.

b. The source to which both passages from R belong[46] derives from a Christian community in or near Pella.[47] If Eusebius in fact owes his information about the Pella flight to Aristo of Pella, it is all the more likely that a source from the vicinity of Pella, when describing the deliverance of those who believed on the true prophet before the war in "a safe place", is thinking of Pella as the safe place. We may therefore probably regard the two passages from the Pseudo-Clementines as additional Pella texts. These passages increase the number of our Pella sources, even as they confirm what we have said above with regard to the provenance of the origin of the Pella tradition.

How should our investigation proceed from this point? Are we now ready to pose the historical question, namely, whether or not the Pella tradition is of historical value for the reconstruction of what really happened during the Jewish War? Before we come to this important question, we need to investigate whether there existed different or even competing versions of the fate of the Jerusalem church before and after the Jewish War. This question must be posed first, in order to place the Pella tradition in the context of early Christian views of the Jerusalem church before and after the Jewish War. If one keeps the exclusiveness of the Pella tradition in view (it presupposes no return of the emigrants to Jerusalem), then it is a priori likely that other traditions concerning Jerusalem Christianity came into being. If this hypothesis can be made probable, that would doubtless have some importance for the proper evaluation of the Pella tradition.

1. COMPETING TRADITIONS CONCERNING THE DESTINY OF THE JERUSALEM CHURCH DURING AND AFTER THE JEWISH WAR

Our discussion of Hegesippus above has already pointed out two important items: Hegesippus saw Symeon as the second bishop of Jerusalem (Eusebius, *Hist. Ecc.* 4.22.4) and thought that the Jerusalem church continued to exist in Jerusalem (immediately) after the Jewish War, with James its first bishop[48] having become in a sense the founder of the whole church.[49] Hegesippus's view thus conflicts with the Pella tradition, which knows of no continuity of the earliest church in Jerusalem but sees the Jerusalem tradition continued in Pella.

An understanding of the continuity of the Jerusalem church similar to that of Hegesippus is the base for the list of fifteen Jewish-Christian bishops up to 135 C.E.[50] which is found in Eusebius, *Hist. Ecc.* 4.5.[51] This list too—independently of its origin[52]—excludes a permanent emigration of the whole Jerusalem church and stands in conflict with the Pella tradition.

Finally, we may refer to one other text that illustrates the continuing existence of the Jerusalem church after the war:

Epiphanius, *Treatise on Weights and Measures* 14: [Hadrian found] the temple of God trodden down and the whole city devastated except for a few houses and a small church of God, in the upper room to which the disciples had gone after the ascension of the Savior from the Mount of Olives. For there it had been built, namely in that part of Zion which had escaped destruction."

This text shows how it was possible to combine the destruction of Jerusalem with the idea that the Christian building (and thus also the Christian community) survived the destruction. An exodus was thus dispensable.

On the other hand, Epiphanius himself is an example of how one could combine the exodus tradition with the idea of the continuing existence of the church in Jerusalem. As indicated above, Epiphanius knew the Pella tradition from his reading of Eusebius's *Ecclesiastical History*. How would he fit this tradition together with the other one? Here the reader is referred to the text from Epiphanius's *Treatise on Weights and Measures* 15 cited above, where he states that the disciples of the apostles[53] returned to Jerusalem from Pella *after* the destruction of the city. For Epiphanius that means that the (true) successors of the original Jerusalem church also after 70 C.E. are to be sought in Jerusalem. Obviously Epiphanius had reasons for this statement. He knew from firsthand experience (see, below pp. 212f.) the claim of Christians—inhabitants of Pella and other places in the Transjordan—to be the heirs of the original Jerusalem church. Thus the idea of a return of those Christians who had gone to Pella back to Jerusalem is due to his concern to reject these claims.

The insights achieved in this section have their historical value in that they help us to evaluate the variants of the story of the continuing existence of the Jerusalem church in Jerusalem. In addition, the conflicting claim of the Pella church is illuminated, as is its context in early Christianity.

The other question, whether the Pella tradition is of historical value for the question of what happened to the Jerusalem church during the war, must, however, be answered negatively for the following reasons:

1. Evidence of a flight to Pella is scarce and limited to the region of Pella.

2. The sources are relatively late.

3. There is conflict with other evidence.

The following excursus can only confirm the conclusions we have drawn from the literary data. This excursus deals with the question of whether it was possible anyway for a group to leave Jerusalem shortly before or during the Jewish War.

Excursus: The Conditions Under Which a Flight from Jerusalem to Pella Would Have Been Possible Just before or during the Jewish War

Since S. G. F. Brandon has written in detail on this issue (see above, n. 4), we may limit ourselves to some brief remarks. There is no doubt that shortly before the war some[54] Jews left Jerusalem[55] in order to seek refuge in foreign provinces.[56] of course, leaving Jerusalem anytime after 67 c.e. must have been very difficult,[57] and for a large group entirely impossible.[58] Therefore our task will be to investigate whether it would have been historically possible for the Jerusalem church to flee to Pella *before* 66 c.e.

The following evidence is opposed to this possibility:

1. Pella was a Gentile city.[59] Is it likely that the Jerusalem church would have looked for[60] and found shelter in such a city?[61]

2. According to Josephus, *War* 2.450, Pella had been sacked by Jews in retaliation for a pogrom of Jews in Caesarea.[62] If Pella had thus been made uninhabitable, then it is hardly imaginable how the refugees could have found shelter here. If they had arrived before the retaliatory strike, they would, as deserters, hardly have been able to escape the wrath of their fellow countrymen.[63] If Pella had been only attacked but not destroyed, or destroyed only in part,[64] it is still equally unlikely that the refugees could have found refuge here; for, after having their lives threatened by Jews, the Gentile residents would hardly be inclined to allow Jewish Christians to emigrate to Pella.[65]

The evidence just adduced as to whether a Jewish group would have been able to flee from Jerusalem to Pella shortly before 66 c.e. without great difficulties confirms the results of our literary work: the Pella tradition has no value at all for the question of the fate of the Jerusalem church during the Jewish War.

It is nevertheless of great historical value in that it reflects the claims of a Christian community in or around Pella in the second century. In order properly to appreciate this claim and fit it in with our other knowledge, we must attempt in a concluding section to relate this claim to analogous claims from other Christian groups of that time and compare them with that of the Pella community. If such an attempt succeeds, it will provide an additional argument against the historicity of the Pella tradition (in the other sense of "historicity").

5. THE SUCCESSORS OF
EARLIEST JERUSALEM CHRISTIANITY

The death of the first Christian generation, especially the death of the apostles, created a problem[66] for early Christianity. Who, and which Christian community, could claim to be the legitimate successor of the apostles? In the realm of Paul's influence, for example, this vacuum of authority which originated at the death of the apostle led to the composition of the Pastorals, in which by the use of Paul's name conflicting gnosticizing teachings were attacked.[67] Speaking more generally, the whole corpus of pseudonymous writings in the New Testament attempts, by the use of the names of the apostles or by indirect claims to apostolic authorship,[68] to bridge the gap between apostolic times and their own.[69] This kind of concern to derive the contemporary form of Christianity from the apostolic form appears to have been held in common by almost all Christian groups from 70 C.E. until the end of the second century.[70]

Without going into details, we may here point out that the phenomenon we are describing was also widespread in heretical-gnostic circles.[71] Basilides referred to Glaukias, the interpreter of Peter (Clement of Alexandria, *Stromata* 7.106.4), and Valentinus is supposed to have been instructed by Theodas, a pupil of Paul (ibid.), and Ptolemy in Rome claimed already in the fourth decade of the second century[72] to possess apostolic tradition which he had received through "*diadoche*" (Epiphanius, *Pan.* 33.7.9).[73]

In my opinion, the Pella tradition owes its existence to this phenomenon, the claim to apostolicity understood in the broadest sense.[74] Among the Pella Christians, this claim was concretized in the claim that they were the successors of the *Jerusalem* church. It is now generally acknowledged that the Jerusalem church, so influential during the time of Paul, never regained its unique status after the Jewish War.[75] When the Pella church[76] raised the claim to be the (legitimate) successor of the Jerusalem mother church, it held up a view of the significance of Jerusalem Christianity that other Gentile Christian churches could hardly have shared. It is for this reason that I think the Pella tradition can only come from an (originally) Jewish-Christian[77] church which still in the middle of the second century placed value on tracing its existence to a kind of Christianity which in the west was already suspect at least from the middle of the second century (Justin, *Dial.* 47).

An analogous case to the claim to that postulated by us for the Pella community is found in Epiphanius, *Pan.* 30.17.2, where the so-called Ebionites explicitly identify themselves with the "poor" of Acts 4:32, 35,[78] and who did not live far from Pella.[79] Epiphanius reports

> They themselves are obviously proud of themselves, saying that they are poor because they sold their belongings in the time of the apostles and laid the money at the feet of the apostles and because they looked for poverty and the abolition of worldly goods. (Trans. from Klijn and Reinink, 185).

How did other Christians react to such claims? We have already pointed out that Hegesippus, Jerusalem Christianity as reflected in the lists of bishops, and Epiphanius sought to refute such a claim by saying that Jerusalem Christianity had never left Jerusalem or had left it only temporarily.

Which of these two parties, regarded historically, stands closer to the story as it really happened?

In claiming that the exodus to Pella cannot be verified historically, I do not wish to rehabilitate the view of the church fathers that the Jewish Christianity beyond the Jordan was heretical and the true successors of the earliest church are to be found in Jerusalem. Our work has not at all been concerned with the question of the historical continuity[80] between the Pella Christians and the Jerusalem mother church or with the fate of the latter during the Jewish War. These questions doubtless deserve further study.[81] Nonetheless, the Pella tradition cannot be used as a historical connecting link between the Jerusalem church and the Christians of Pella. Instead, it gives us some interesting insights concerning the claim[82] of a Jewish-Christian community in Pella in the second century to be the legitimate successor of the Jerusalem mother church.*

*J. Verheyden, in a recent comprehensive analysis of the research, also contests the historicity of the flight; see *De vlucht van de christenen naar Pella, Onderzoek van het getuigenis van Eusebius en Epiphanius* (Brussels, 1988).

NOTES

CHAPTER 1: A SURVEY OF THE RESEARCH ON JEWISH CHRISTIANITY AS A MEANS OF FORMULATING THE PROBLEM

1. Klijn, "Study," 419. Cf. also Hoennicke's history of research in *Judenchristentum*, 1–19, which begins with Baur. The history of research on the Pseudo-Clementines in Strecker, *Judenchristentum*, 1–34, likewise begins with Baur. Cf. also the surveys of Ropes, *Age*, 289–324; and Koch, *Investigation*, 5–107 (a history of the study of Epiphanius, *Pan.* 30). Much is also to be learned with regard to our topic from Mattill, "Luke"; it is regrettable that this Vanderbilt dissertation has not been published. On the other hand, it is surprising that for his material on the nineteenth century Haenchen's history of research in his *Acts* 14–50, is somewhat dependent on McGiffert, "The Historical Criticism of Acts in Germany," in Jackson and Lake, *Beg.* I.2, pp. 363–95, because various resources (mostly derived from Hilgenfeld, *ZWTh* [sic] "simply were not available" (29 n. 2). (TRANSLATOR'S NOTE: This term is not in the 1971 English translation, which was made from an earlier edition.] Thus the history of research cannot be considered the most successful part of Haenchen's commentary, since it exhibits great lacunae and ignorance of British and American work. For example, Haenchen (*Acts*, 50–51) represents *The Beginnings of Christianity* as an "Anglo-Saxon" (instead of American) product—as does G. Klein in *ZKG* 68 (1957): 362 n. 2. Cadbury was born in America (on his life and career, cf. A. N. Wilder in *NTS* 21 [1975]:313–17, and K. Lake and F. J. Foakes-Jackson taught primarily in the United States. In this regard, cf. the instructive essay by K. Lake, "The Problem of Christian Origins," in *HThR* 15 (1922):97–114. In addition, Haenchen devotes only two lines to J. B. Lightfoot: "The only followers that F. C. Baur found in England, where the great scholar J. B. Lightfoot opposed the Tübingen theories, . . . were Samuel Davidson and W. R. Cassels" (*Acts*, 22). No comment is necessary on this description of English-language scholarship, since once again the information is drawn only from secondary sources.

In passing, we may also note the instructive summary of the positions argued by the scholars of the (older) Tübingen school in Mackay,

School. (The obvious critique of the church which hovers in the background is of course to be kept in mind as one reads.) In addition, cf. the deeply insightful observations on Baur found in Bartsch, "Frühkatholizismus", 103–31, 481–502, and passim.

2. *TZTh* (1831):61–206, reprinted in Baur, *Untersuchungen*, 1–146. The page numbers in the following refer to the edition of 1831. With the portrayal of Baur given above, compare my remarks in Luedemann, "Antipaulinismus," 437–38, which in part agrees verbatim.

3. "They called themselves *tous Kēpha* because Peter enjoyed the primacy among the Jewish apostles, and *tous Christou* because they claimed direct contact with Christ as the primary indication of their authentic apostolic authority" (Baur, "Christuspartei," 84).

4. The Apollos group belongs to the Paul party: Baur, "Christuspartei," 77.

5. The opponents denied apostolic rank to Paul, "because, unlike them—or, rather, unlike the apostles who formed the leadership of their party—he had not seen the Lord nor lived in direct contact with him" (Baur, "Christuspartei," 86).

6. Baur, "Christuspartei," 107.

7. Baur, "Christuspartei," 107–8.

8. In Galatia "they sought different ways to oppose the apostle in accordance with the difference in the situation" (Baur, "Christuspartei," 108).

9. Baur, "Christuspartei," 109.

10. Baur, "Christuspartei," 114.

11. Baur, "Christuspartei," 116.

12. Contrary to Dilthey, "Ferdinand Christian Baur" (1865), in idem *Gesammelte Schriften*, 4:417, it was not Baur's discovery that Simon Magus stands for the apostle Paul in many passages of the Pseudo-Clementines but Neander's (see below, n. 24).

13. It is important to be aware that already in 1831 Baur implicitly regarded Jewish Christianity and anti-Paulinism as identical, and from 1845 on explicitly did so. On the truth and error in such an assumption, see below, n. 55.

14. Not in *1 Clement* 5! In this regard Baur writes, "He knew only in general that Peter had died a martyr but appears not to have known where or how" ("Christuspartei," 151). A contemporary perspective on the problem is found in Cullmann, *Peter*, 70–152.

15. Baur, "Christuspartei," 153ff., correctly notes that the reliability of the Dionysius report is dependent on the historicity of the tradition of a second Roman imprisonment of Peter.

16. Baur, "Christuspartei," 164.

17. "One can also observe clearly, from the whole tendency and

composition of the letter, from the prejudices and errors which he combats, from the particular features of the doctrines that Paul sets forth as the constitutive elements of Christianity, that the apostle considers it his major responsibility to resist wherever possible the predominant influence of Judaism which in part had already obtained access to the church and in part threatened to develop even further" (Baur, "Christuspartei," 164–65).

18. Baur, "Christuspartei," 164.

19. Baur, "Christuspartei," 169ff.

20. We do not need to pursue all the details of Baur's argument here. In the 1831 essay he sees the *immediate* basis for affirming that Peter spent more time in Rome and died there in the identification of a statue inscribed "Semo Sancus" as one erected in honor of Simon Magus, who therefore, he assumes, must have been in Rome. Then Peter too must have been in Rome, since he was always on the track of Simon (cf. Baur, "Christuspartei," 176ff.). Baur later changed his mind with regard to the development of the Peter/Simon Magus legend. He then advocated the view that *1 Clement* already harmonizes an antithesis between Peter and Paul and does not go back to the claim of Petrine Christians who argued that their hero, like Simon Magus, must have been in Rome. With regard to the details, cf. Luedemann, *Untersuchungen*, 11–12.

21. Cf. Neander, *History*, 348–53; and Fraedrich, *Baur*, 151. Cf. also Uhlhorn, "Kirchengeschichte," in JDTh 3 (1858), 283–302 (Baur's counterarguments are in his *Die Tübinger Schule und ihre Stellung*; on the Uhlhorn-Baur controversy, cf. Harris, *Tübingen*, 78–88.

22. Cullmann fails to note this in *Peter* 74, although he gives an interesting history of the research on the issue of Peter's residence in Rome (ibid., 71–77).

We may briefly note here that in an 1836 essay (Baur, "Zweck"), Baur sought to demonstrate that the tradition of Peter's residence and death in Rome was unhistorical (on Dionysius, pp. 172ff.; on Gaius, pp. 166ff.), as well as to strengthen his case for the Jewish-Christian character of the Roman church. Baur proceeds on the basis that the Pseudo-Clementine *Homilies* are a Roman writing and strives to find parallels between them and the views that he presupposes to be in the Roman church. He thus takes Romans 13 to be combating a type of two-aeons doctrine as it is manifest in the Pseudo-Clementines (*Hom.* 15.7; cf. Epiphanius, *Pan.* 30.16; Baur, "Zweck," 131ff.), and the prohibition against eating meat (Romans 14) has a counterpart in the Pseudo-Clementines (*Hom.* 12.6; cf. Epiphanius, *Pan.* 30.15; Baur, "Zweck," 128–29). In this essay Baur is aware of the chronological distance between Paul's letter to the Romans and the Pseudo-Clementines (Baur, "Zweck," 132: "We . . . therefore must not attempt to make the comparison between the Roman Christians and the later Ebionites too extensive"). In this essay he also draws a distinction between the earliest Jewish Christians and the Ebionites. He nonetheless regards them as closely related: "The Roman Jewish Christians, like the Jewish Christians of earliest Christianity generally, [had] practically everywhere more or less Ebionite characteristics" (Baur, "Zweck," 128; cf. also 129, 138.)

23. Baur, Kirchengeschichte, 395.

24. Cf. Uhlhorn, Homilien, 10–12; and Neander, Entwickelung, 361–421 (Beilage: "Über die pseudoclementinischen Homilien, ein Beytrag zur Geschichte der Ebioniten").

25. Gieseler, "Nazaräer."

26. Credner, "Essäer." For additional research on the Pseudo-Clementines prior to Baur, cf. Uhlhorn, Homilien, 1–10; and Credner, Beiträge, 364–74.

27. E.g., on the question of which literary relationship exists between the reports in the church fathers and the Pseudo-Clementines.

28. For research on the Essenes done during the nineteenth century, cf. Wagner, "Essener" (on the connection between the Essenes and the Ebionites, see pp. 186–89 and 231–33; important contemporary studies of this issue are Braun, Qumran, 211–28: "Die Ebionites und die Pseudoklementinen", which gives additional literature, and Fitzmyer, "Qumran Scrolls").

29. We do not need to go into detail here, and can simply refer the reader to Schliemann, Clementinen, who presents a history of research on pp. 17–48. He himself distinguishes two groups of Jewish Christians, namely, Nazareans and Ebionites (pp. 445ff.; cf. similarly Credner, Beiträge, 269ff.; Gieseler, "Nazaräer," passim; and Lutterbeck, Lehrbegriffe, 109ff.). The Ebionites were heretical and must themselves be divided into two groups, "popular" and "gnostic" Ebionites (pp. 481ff.). The Nazareans were the tolerant Jewish Christians and identical with one of the two parties in Justin, Dial. 47. Ebionites and Nazareans existed only since the founding of Aelia Capitolina (pp. 406ff.). The Jewish Christians had to decide whether to become members of the new Gentile Christian church of Aelia Capitolina, or to tolerate it (i.e., to become Nazareans), or to split off into a new group (i.e., to become Ebionites). Strecker, Judenchristentum, discusses Schliemann's work along with that of Baur and Schwegler under the rubric "The Tübingen School" (p. 4). This is misleading, since Schliemann wants to oppose Baur's use of the Pseudo-Clementines and, as a

pupil of Neander, is himself of course not a member of the Tübingen school. Cf. further Baur's own sharp critique of Schliemann's work in ThJb (T), 3(1844), 536–85.

30. Cf. Fraedrich, *Baur*, 66–67.

31. Baur thus, in agreement with Neander, regarded the views expressed in the Ps.-Clem. *Hom.* "as the further development and elaboration of the doctrines and ideas already present in the sect of the Ebionites" (Baur, *Gnosis*, 403).

32. Cf. Fraedrich, *Baur*, 67–68.

33. On this, cf. Neander, *Entwickelung*, 362.

34. "In the propagation of their fundamental principles, the pseudo-apostles of this party appealed primarily to his [i.e., James's] and Peter's authority, though it is hardly conceivable that it was with the approval of the Jewish apostles themselves, who could hardly have acknowledged alleged emissaries of this sort" (Baur, "Christuspartei," 114; cf. 83: "Peter himself had nothing to do with this party in Corinth which bore his name, as can already be inferred from the fact that Peter himself had not been to Corinth, but it is just as clearly the case that itinerant pseudo-apostles who appealed to Peter's name had in fact visited Corinth").

35. Appropriately pointed out by Uhlhorn, "Kirchengeschichte," 296.

36. Baur, *Consilio*, does not yet discuss the possibility that Acts 7 is not an accurate report.

37. Cf. Fraedrich, *Baur*, 75.

38. Cf. Dilthey's summary with regard to the problem, "Baur," 417: "But in the midst of these discoveries, how far Baur still is from drawing the conclusions that seem to us today to follow unavoidably from his statements! When the Jewish-Christian apostles in Corinth appealed to the Palestinian apostles, that still meant to him that they were misrepresenting them. 1 Peter was still regarded by him as authentic, and Acts' story of Simon Magus as historical. As Zeller, who heard his 1833 lectures on Acts, reports, he as yet had no doubts concerning either the authenticity or the historical purpose of this document, the thoroughly tendentious character of which, along with its setting in the midst of a very late stage of the struggles between Paulinism and Jewish Christianity, is the most certain result of later critical study."

39. Baur, *Pastoralbriefe*.

40. Baur, *Pastoralbriefe*, iii–iv.

41. Baur's primary evidence: (a) the heretics of the Pastorals are Marcionites (*Pastoralbriefe*, 8–39) and thus 1 Tim. 6:20 is an allusion to Marcion's major work (ibid., 26–27); (b) the ecclesiastical-hierarchical

tendency points to a later time, and indeed to Rome (ibid., 78–89); and (c) various features such as the prohibition against women teaching in the church (1 Tim. 2:11) and the existence of an organized group of widows as part of the church structure in the Pastorals (1 Tim. 5:3ff., 9, 11, 16) belong to the post-Pauline period (Pastoralbriefe, 40–42, 48–49).

42. Baur points in particular to the concept of "good works" (Pastoralbriefe, 58 n. *).

43. Baur, Pastoralbriefe, 58.

44. Baur, Paul.

45. Baur, Paul, 1:5.

46. Baur, Paul, 1:110–17.

47. Baur, Paul, 1:116–45.

48. Baur, Paul, 1:195–215.

49. Cf. Baur's reference in Paul, 1:6, n. 1.

50. On this, cf. Schneckenburger, Zweck; and Baur's discussion of this work in Jahrbücher für wissenschaftliche Kritik 15 (1841), cols. 369–75, 377–81. On Schneckenburger, Zweck, cf. Mattill, "Luke," 20–46; and idem, "Purpose." Nevertheless, Schneckenburger held fast to the view that a companion of Paul was the author, and Mattill follows him in this.

51. Baur, Paul, 1.5–6.

52. Cf. Baur, Paul, 2:207–08; und further in idem, Christenthum, 122–23.

53. On this, cf. Pfleiderer, Development 234: "This legend belongs to that category of convenient fables which ignorance customarily spreads. . . . The truth is that Baur's view grew out of the most arduous and fundamental studies of the biblical and patristic texts, that it was a result of precise, detailed investigation which slowly, step by step and without arbitrariness forced its conclusions on the critical scholar and had nothing, absolutely nothing, to do with Hegelian philosophy." Cf. Pfleiderer's further comments in Entstehung, where in chap. 1 (esp. pp. 11ff.) Baur's scholarly significance is indicated, as well as the words of Weizsäcker cited by Pfleiderer in Entwicklung, 2:7f. In addition, an excellent introduction to the work of Baur is given in Holtzmann, "Baur." On the present issue, cf. also Kümmel, Testament, 127ff.; Bruce, "History," 42; Morgan, "Classics," 4; idem, "Baur," 202–3; and Berger, Exegese, 27–48.

54. Of many possible examples, cf. Longenecker, Christology, 5: "It was Ferdinand Christian Baur who, on a theory of antithetical relations between Petrine and Pauline Christianity, first clearly treated Jewish Christianity as an entity"; Hoennicke, Judenchristentum, 2; and Ellis, Prophecy, 87. This reproach against Baur originated in his own generation. He defends himself against it in Baur, Lehrbuch, vi: A

critic claims that I "merely construct the history according to the pre-conceived perspective of a speculative system, imposing on it a scheme constructed in advance, into which all the details must fit." Baur's answer: "Only the most crude empiricism could suppose that things simply present themselves for observation, that the objects of historical study can be perceived just as they lie before us" (ibid., vii). Cf. also the Foreword to Baur, *Church History*, iv–v: "My standpiont is in one word the purely historical one: namely, that the one thing to be aimed at is to place before ourselves the materials given in the history as they are objectively, and not otherwise, as far as that is possible." On the residuum of truth contained in the reproaches discussed here, cf. what is said above in the text. On the question of the dependence of Baur on Hegel's philosophy, Hodgson, *The Formation of Historical Theology*, 1–8 (on which see K. Penzel in *JR* 48 [1968]: 310–23). It may be noted incidentally that Wellhausen's critique functioned by the same means and denounced him as a Hegelian; cf. Perlitt, *Vatke und Wellhausen*, esp. 153–243.

55. As one of several examples that could be cited, cf. Eckert's mis-judgment concerning Baur, *Verkündigung*, 4 n. 3: "Baur published his new conception of the history of earliest Christianity in his essay 'Die Christuspartei.'" Eckert's statement shows that Baur himself can be unknown to such scholars whose own conclusions are not all that different from his.

56. An important question in this regard was that of miracle. Baur excluded miracle a priori from consideration as a category for his historical work, since it was a violation of natural law. In this connec-tion, cf. Lipsius, "Baur," 237ff. Thus one can say that Baur used the principle of analogy which Troeltsch was later to undergird theoreti-cally Cf. Troeltsch, "Über die historische und dogmatische Methode in der Theologie," in idem, *Gesammelte Schriften, vol. 2: Zur religiösen Lage, Religionsphilosophie und Ethik* [Tübingen, ²1922], 729–53).

The comments of Zeller, "Schule," deserve to be cited here: "The obligation to exercise this historical fairness toward both sides with regard to Christianity and the Christian church, in order to attain a picture of its origin and development which is as true as possible, which corresponds to the real facts and that which was historically possible and probable—this is the task which the 'Tübingen school' assigned to itself. . . . Its ultimate goal [is] pure historical knowledge . . ., and, however wide the opinions may range regarding its particular results, no one can fail to acknowledge that its fundamental principles are only the same as those which have dominated all the nontheo-logical German historiographical disciplines since Niebuhr and Ranke" (p. 172). Lightfoot, *Essays* 25, refers to the "skepticism" of Baur and Niebuhr but without recognizing that critique of the tradition (methodological skepticism) is the indispensable presupposition of historical criticism. On this point, cf. Fueter, *Geschichte*, 461ff. (on the philological-historical method). On the relationship of Baur to Niebuhr, cf. Scholder, "Baur," 437ff.; and Geiger, *Spekulation*, 175.

57. On Schwegler, who is almost unknown to contemporary scholarship, see Zeller "Schwegler," and Baur's letter to Hilgenfeld of 17 January 1857, in Pölcher, *Hilgenfeld*, pt. 4, 180f. Cf. further Harris, *Tübingen*, 78–88; and now E. Bammel, "Albert Schwegler über Jesus und das Urchristentum," in *ZKG* 91 (1980): 1–10. Schwegler is remembered by Krüger, *Dogma*, 27: "Schwegler belongs to the few German theological historians who are not dominated by set theological or philosophical categories." Cf. further Holtzmann, "Baur," 183ff.; and recently Bartsch, "Frühkatholizismus," 138–44, 503–6.

58. Schwegler, *Zeitalter*.

59. Schwegler, *Zeitalter*, 1:179ff.

60. Schliemann, *Clementinen*, 459ff.

61. Schwegler, *Zeitalter*, 1:196.

62. Schwegler, *Zeitalter*, 1:23f.

63. Schwegler, *Zeitalter*, 1:187.

64. Schwegler, *Zeitalter*, 1:197ff.

65. Schwegler, *Zeitalter*, vol. 1, names additional witnesses: Eusebius (p. 203), Cerinthus and Carpocrates (p. 204), James, and 2 Peter (p. 209).

66. Schwegler, *Zeitalter*, 1:216ff.

67. "When the apostle John resettled in Ephesus, the Johannine period of the church in Asia Minor began, i.e., the period dominated by the Jewish, apocalyptic Christianity which can be seen as represented by the Apocalypse" (Schwegler, *Zeitalter*, 1:259).

68. "The sharpest and most glaring example of this type in the Johannine period is represented by Montanism" (Schwegler, *Zeitalter*, 1:259.

69. Schwegler, *Zeitalter*, 2:1–244. Schwegler presents no line of development for the history of the church in Asia Minor. To be sure, he did attribute a Pauline character to the following documents from Asia Minor: Colossians, Ephesians, Hebrews, John (ibid., 2:270ff.).

70. Christianity in Asia Minor developed in a manner analogous to that in Rome. They both represent "the gradual development from Ebionism to Catholicism. Like the Roman church, [the church in Asia Minor] began with the sharpest antagonism between the Jewish (i.e., Ebionite) and the Christian (i.e., Pauline) principles. In this regard the letter to the Romans corresponds to the letter to the Galatians. Just so, it ends with the establishment of the standpoint of catholicity: the letters

of Ignatius have as their counterpart the Gospel of John" (Schwegler, *Zeitalter*, 2:245f.).

71. Schwegler, *Zeitalter*, 1:33. "It is precisely the postapostolic age which proved to be . . . a series of developmental stages by which Ebionism, by solicitously working its way into Paulinism and permeating it, became catholicism.

72. Cf. on the following also Pfleiderer, *Development*, 233–35.

73. Georgii, *Charakter*. This essay was published before the appearance of Schwegler, *Zeitalter*, and is directed against Schwegler, *Montanismus*. Since in *Zeitalter*, Schwegler only repeats what Georgii criticized, it appears to be justifiable to discuss Georgii's critique in the above context. On Georgii's critique, cf. Schwegler, *Zeitalter*, 1:20ff.; and idem, "Charakter."

74. Planck, "Judenthum"; idem, "Princip."

75. Köstlin, "Geschichte."

76. One example may suffice: In the opinion of Lange, *Geschichte*, Baur persisted in confusing the second century with the first (p. 57) and thus reversed the actual order of (a) sound doctrine and then (b) heresy (p. 58). The Tübingen criticism was regarded as a negative stance over against the miraculous character of early Christianity (similarly Beckh, "Schule"). Whoever today raises similar objections against Baur—even if not so candidly—might well note in what company one places oneself.

77. In the following the contributions of J. B. Lightfoot will also be discussed, although Lightfoot already presupposes the work of Ritschl (cf. Lightfoot, *Galatians*, 295 n.1). This is the result of the fact that in the Anglo-Saxon world Lightfoot is understood as *the* critic of Baur (as indeed he was). Lightfoot's works are not here discussed in connection with Ritschl's because, unlike Ritschl, he was not interested in the theme "the *origin* of the catholic church." We will not discuss Lightfoot *after* Ritschl (as we do, e.g., with Hort), because he worked independently of Ritschl.

78. Schliemann, *Clementinen*; and Lechler, *Times*. The first edition of Lechler's book (1851) was crowned with an award from the Teyler Theological Society. The competition for the award required that the author refute Baur's critical results, with the best refutation receiving the prize; the text of this requirement is reprinted in Lechler, *Zeitalter*, iii–iv. It begins with a statement that needs no commentary: "It is well known that the so-called Tübingen school attempts to base its hostility to Christianity on its assumption that there was an absolute difference between the doctrine and orientation of the apostle Paul and the other apostles" (ibid.). Cf. further Schaff, *History* (on Schaff, cf. Penzel, "Church History"; Lightfoot, *Galatians*; and idem, *Essays*.

79. Lightfoot, *Galatians*, 124–26; and Lechler, *Times*, 1:193ff.

80. Lightfoot, *Galatians*, has an interesting discussion of the question of whether Paul's opponents could have been, among other things, personal disciples of Jesus. Even so, he succeeds in neutralizing the theological danger inherent in such a possibility: "There are some faint indications that such was the case; and remembering that there was a Judas among the twelve, we cannot set aside this supposition as impossible" (p. 372).

81. Lechler, *Times*, contains no explicit source criticism and presupposes the Pastorals to be authentic without mentioning the problem.

82. Schliemann, *Clementinen*, 380; Lechler, *Times*, 2:237ff.; Schaff, *History*, 1:744; and Lightfoot, *Galatians*, 369ff.

83. Cf. Lightfoot, *Galatians*, 164 (cf. p. 370); and Schaff, *History*, 1:744: "Its doctrine of justification is no protest against that of Paul, but prior to it, and presents the subject from a less developed, yet imminently practical aspect, and against the error of a barren monotheism rather than Pharisaical legalism, which Paul had in view."

84. Lechler, *Times*, 2:239, discusses as one possibility among others that James really disputes a point of Pauline doctrine. He continues: "On the other hand, there can be no justification for sharpening this into an opposition which indicates a real break between the two (ibid.).

85. For the text, see below, pp. 166 68.

86. Cf. below, p. 293 n. 13.

87. Cf. Lightfoot, *Galatians*, 334 n. 1; Schliemann, *Clementinen*, 428ff.; and Lechler, *Times* 2:279ff.

88. Lange, *Geschichte*, 39ff.; Lechler, *Times*, 2:268ff. n. 2, 288; and Lightfoot, *Galatians*, 352f.

89. Schaff, *History*, 2:436.

90. Lightfoot, *Galatians*, 352f.

91. Cf. Lightfoot, *Galatians*, 370f., on the Ebionite representation of James.

92. On both scholars, cf. above, p. 3.

93. Cf. Schliemann, *Clementinen*, 29ff., 493ff.; and Lightfoot *Galatians*, 318ff. Lechler, *Times*, 2:280ff., argues against Schliemann's distinguishing Ebionites and Nazareans.

94. "In the past century the English were in the habit of deriving the subject of their research from themes of German historiography, producing those solutions based on 'judicial' examination of documents and on simple common sense that the Germans have always found difficult to reach" (Momigliano, *Studies*, 229). This generalization seems also to apply to the writing of church history represented by the present and following examples.

95. Unfortunately it is too often forgotten that, quite apart from the

question of the validity of Baur's thesis, the critical impulse that Baur mediated to research was of the greatest significance. Ellis, *Prophecy*, 80–115, does not deal with this aspect and—supported by the authority of Lightfoot—points out Baur's "error." It is almost with a note of relief that Ellis comments in regard to English scholarship: Lightfoot's work "largely accounts for the failure of Baur's Tübingen school even to gain a sizeable following among English-speaking scholars, as E. Haenchen . . . has rightly noted. It remains instructive today, especially for a generation that 'knew not Joseph' and is attracted to the view of a more recent Bauer on *Orthodoxy and Heresy in Earliest Christianity*" (Ellis, *Prophecy*, 89f. n. 28). No comment is necessary.

96. This theological approach is comprised of the following elements: (1) Lightfoot had great confidence in the traditional authorship of the New Testament documents and in the historical reliability of Acts. It then becomes clear that—unlike the mature Baur (see above, pp. 5f.)—more historical value is attributed to canonical documents than to other sources. (2) Lightfoot was not willing to renounce the supernatural category of "miracle" for the description of early Christianity. In this regard he had no response to the noteworthy part 1 of Cassels, *Religion*, 1:1–124, however superior he may have been to the (at that time) anonymous author in regard to knowledge of the texts. Cf. Lightfoot, *Essays*, passim, and the, in my opinion, quite correct evaluation of the Lightfoot–Cassels controversy by Conybeare, *History*, 154–57, esp. 157: "In critical outlook Lightfoot held no superiority, though he was a better scholar and, within the narrow circle of his premises, a more careful and accurate worker." Cf. further Pfleiderer, *Development*, 396–99, who calls Lightfoot's answers to Cassels "extraordinarily weak" (p. 397). In my opinion, an inadequate appraisal of the above controversy is made by Ropes, *Age*, 313; Chadwick, *Church*, 71; and Gasque, *History*, 114–17.

97. Cf. esp. Lightfoot, *Dissertations*. In addition, Lightfoot's works on the apostolic fathers are also of great value. Cf. in this regard Neill, *Interpretation*, 40ff.; and Kümmel, *Testament*, 544 n. 223.

98. It should be noticed that Lightfoot also, at least in part, unfortunately shared that judgment which was later spread abroad by Sir William Ramsay and today by W. W. Gasque, namely, that German scholarship is skeptical and speculative. Cf. Lightfoot, *Essays*, 24: "It would be difficult, I think, to find among English scholars any parallel to the mass of absurdities which several intelligent and very learned German critics have conspired to heap upon two simple names in the Philippian Epistle, Euodia and Syntyche."

99. The differences between the first and second editions are described by O. Ritschl, *Leben*, 151–66, 284–94. In the Foreword to the

second edition A. Ritschl wrote that he considered some of the first results of the work of the Tübingen school to be subject to criticism. But he continued: "But I had not yet reached that level of opposition to these results which called for a fundamental and comprehensive critique" (A. Ritschl, *Entstehung*, 2d ed., v). The following discussion is restricted entirely to the second edition. For further discussion of this book, cf. Bartsch, "*Frühkatholizismus*," 144–55, 506–11.

100. We should emphasize at the beginning that for Ritschl "Jewish Christianity" was not identical with Judaizing Christian groups. Groups such as Ritschl's Nazareans, who were tolerant with regard to Gentile Christians, belonged to the Jewish wing of Christianity but not to the exclusive Judaizing Christianity of the Ebionites.

101. Ritschl, *Entstehung*, 104.

102. Ritschl, *Entstehung*, 106 (printed in bold type).

103. Ritschl, *Entstehung*, 107.

104. Thus Ritschl (*Entstehung*, 107) affirms that many Jewish elements are also found in Paul.

105. Even later, Ritschl continued to consider 1 Peter and James "as documents of the pre-Pauline understanding of Christianity" (*Lehre*, 2:317).

106. Ritschl, *Entstehung*, 147: "When the Judaizing Christians in Galatia, and probably elsewhere as well, pursued their plans against the freedom of the Gentile Christians purportedly under the authority of the original apostles, they were making a false use of their names, whether intentionally or as a misunderstanding of Jewish practices which both sides had already rejected."

107. Ritschl, *Entstehung*, 151.

108. Ritschl, *Entstehung*, 143.

109. Ritschl, *Entstehung*, 152.

110. Ritschl, *Entstehung*, 152f.

111. Ritschl, *Entstehung*, 171.

112. Ritschl, *Entstehung*, 159–71, on Hebrews.

113. Ritschl, *Entstehung*, could even give the immediate occasion for the writing of Hebrews: Pharisaic Christians began to leave the Christian (Nazarean) community (pp. 159, 170).

114. The author of Hebrews "was able to develop the Christian insight of the original apostles in such a manner that the uselessness of sacrificial worship, and the impossibility of combining it with the Christian confession, became clear" (Ritschl, *Entstehung*, 169). In this regard, Hebrews thus represents "a later level of development of the Christian insight of the apostles" (ibid., printed in bold type by Ritschl). This further development of the insight of the original apostles was thus in part occasioned by the secession of the Pharisaic Christians (see

previous note). For a critique, cf. Hilgenfeld, *Einleitung*, 359, 379ff.; and H. Holtzmann in *JPTh* 2 (1876):258ff.

115. Slingerland, *Testaments*, 8–18, presents a history of the research on the *T. 12 Patr.* during the nineteenth century; pp. 9ff. deal with Ritschl.

116. Ritschl, *Entstehung*, 171ff. Ritschl notes on p. 177 that *T. Benj.* 11 refers to Paul positively.

117. Cf. Ritschl, *Entstehung*, 205f.

118. Ritschl, *Entstehung*, 207. Since Epiphanius and Ps.-Clem. *Hom.* contain the Ebionite tradition which holds marriage in high regard, Ritschl considers this to have been a development within the group: "The older custom of the Ebionites corresponded much more closely to the strict practice of the Essenes" (ibid.).

119. Ritschl, *Entstehung*, 208f.

120. Ritschl, *Entstehung*, 206.

121. Ritschl, *Entstehung*, 204. Ritschl understands Elkesai not as a historical person but as the name of a book (ibid., 245) and thinks it impossible to give a precise date for the beginning of the Elkesaite movement. It probably began about the end of the second century (ibid., 246f.). On Elkesai, cf. also below, pp. 129–39.

122. Ritschl, *Entstehung*, 234ff.

123. Even Ritschl held to the view that the stance toward heresy here taken was the same as that adopted by the original apostles themselves (*Entstehung*, 257). It is illuminating to see how Ritschl explains the exclusion of Jewish Christianity (=the Christianity of the original apostles) by the Gentile church: "To be sure, the strict Judaizing Christians' constant pushiness and agitation with regard to the Gentile Christians must bear the major part of the blame for this result [i.e., the exclusion of Jewish Christianity]; but it would have happened anyway" (ibid.).

124. Cf. the section "Gentile Christianity to the Middle of the Second Century" (Ritschl, *Entstehung*, 271–311).

125. Ritschl, *Entstehung*, 266.

126. Cf. his cautious comments: "Neither is the polemic against Paul so clear as Schwegler and Baur indicate" (Ritschl, *Entstehung*, 267). "It may well be, however, that the personal views of Hegesippus bear the stamp of Judaizing Christianity much more clearly than we are able to perceive" (ibid., 268).

126a. Ritschl names *Ap. Const.* 2.39; Tertullian, *Praescr.* 36; Irenaeus, *Heresies*, 2.35.4; Diogn. 11 (Ritschl, *Entstehung*, 268 n. 3). For a critique, see below, p. 294, n. 26.

127. Ritschl, *Entstehung*, 268.

128. Cf. the extraordinarily instructive and important comments of Holtzmann in this regard, "Baur," 234f.

129. It is at the same time curious and annoying that Harris, *Tübingen* —who otherwise has superior documentation—attempts to dismiss the Tübingen school by appealing to the reliability of Acts and the authority of F. F. Bruce. On Harris, *Tübingen*, cf. the excellent discussion by R. Morgan, in *HeyJ* 17 (1976):357–61.

130. Cf. Kümmel, *Introduction*, 179.

131. Hirsch, *Geschichte*, 5:557.

132. The distinctions that Ritschl attempted to make in this connection between Nazareans and Ebionites (for his predecessors in this, cf. above, n. 29) stand on weak historical footing. See below, pp. 16 and 20.

133. I do not wish to deal here with the systematic bases for Ritschl's delineation of Gentile Christianity, which is just as distant from Pauline Christianity as was Schwegler's "Ebionite Christianity." Cf. Wagner, *Ursprüngen*, 276ff., who rightly saw in Ritschl's understanding of Gentile Christianity an attack on the contemporary catholic church. On the systematic bases for Ritschl's historical work, cf. further Hefner, "Baur." An important conclusion of Hefner's work is that Ritschl was concerned to represent the development from Gentile Christianity into the catholic church as the culminating point in the departure from the heritage of Jesus.

134. Hirsch, *Geschichte*, 5:557.

135. Ritschl, *Entstehung*, 20ff.

136. With reference to the writing of church history, Ritschl's (antithetical) dependence on Baur is rightly documented by Andresen, *Kirchen*. In the realm of systematic theology, Slenczka, *Geschichtlichkeit*, 184–87 ("The Evolutionary Idea"), well points out how Baur's evolutionary ideas reemerge in Ritschl disguised as the historical process of revelation, under the rubric of the kingdom of God manifest in the realization of the ethical ideal.

137. We will deal with the following works: Sorley, *Christians*; Harnack, *Dogma*; Purves, *Christianity*; Ropes, *Age*; McGiffert, *History*, and Hort, *Christianity*. Some brief comments on Hoennicke, *Judenchristentum*, are also included because of the promising title. He equates Jewish Christianity and Judaizing Christianity, and believes that after Paul's struggle against his opponents (=Judaizers) was over, there was no longer any danger of a "Jewish perversion of the gospel" (p. 348). On the other hand, Hoennicke uses the term "Jewish Christianity" for the acceptance of the gospel among the Jewish people, thus also in reference to people such as Paul and Barnabas. Thus, Hoennicke's inconsistent terminology breeds confusion. His thesis, that Paul

was able to silence his opponents, is hardly correct. On Hoennicke's work, cf. also Holtzmann, "Literature," 397f., who thought that Jewish Christianity was thereby only "relatively rehabilitated" (ibid., 397). In another place (Holtzmann, *Lehrbuch*, vol. 1), he justifiably complains that the Pseudo-Clementine literature "is conspicuously absent" from Hoennicke's work (ibid., 468 n. 1). Cf. on Hoennicke's work also Bauer, "Neues Testament," 459ff.

138. Harnack, *Dogma*, 1:287–89 n. 1.

139. Harnack, *Dogma*, 1:289. The first edition (1886, German pp. 216f.) has only insignificant differences. It does not yet contain the quotation from the Pseudo-Clementines (which in fact is found in Ps.-Clem. *Hom.* 11.16.3).

140. Harnack, *Dogma*, 1:301; cf. also Nitzsch, *Grundriss*, 42, and above, p. 227, n. 132.

141. Hort, *Christianity*, 180, 200f.

142. "Thus the Jewish Christianity of the Mother Church finally eventuated in the heretical Ebionism of the second and following centuries" (McGiffert, *History*, 567).

143. Sorley, *Christians*, 74–84.

144. And this was the case precisely because he rightly refused to divide Nazareans and Ebionites into two different groups. See Harnack, *Dogma*, 1:301.

145. Sorley, *Christians*, 174–84.

146. McGiffert, *History*, 557.

147 Hort, *Christianity*, 66f.

148. Hort, *Christianity*, 81–83; and Sorley, *Christians*, 40–44.

149. Ropes, *Age*, 236; Purves, *Christianity*, 5f.; and Hort, *Christianity*, which presupposes Lukan authorship without discussion.

150. Sorley, *Christians*, 24; Hort, *Christianity*, 147ff.; and Purves, *Christianity*, 133ff. On the other side, McGiffert, *History*, 579ff.; and Ropes, *James*, 43–52.

151. Purves, *Christianity*, 126.

152. Hort, *Christianity*, 165.

153. McGiffert, *History*, 584.

154. Hort, *Christianity*, 165.

155. Ropes, *Age*, 95.

156. Harnack, *Dogma*, 1:295 n. 2 (on p. 296).

157. Ropes, *Age*, 96: toward the end of the second century.

158. "It is a glorification of Peter, in which Paul is perhaps not attacked, but only ignored" (Ropes, *Age*, 96). Cf. also Hort, *Notes*, 120–32.

159. For a history of this research, see Strecker, *Judenchristentum*,

1–34. Of course, Hort, *Notes*, continues to be an important contribution to the study of the Pseudo-Clementines.

160. Hort, *Christianity*, 201ff.; and idem, *Notes*, 85f; similarly Harnack, *Dogma*, 1:311f.

161. Ropes, *Age* 321f. Cf. idem, *Romans*, 364: "The Judaizing propaganda seems to have died down after the Galatian episode, checked by the prompt and effective counter of Paul."

162. Harnack, *Dogma*, 1:290.

163. It should be noted here that there was no lack of critical voices raised against individual works among the group discussed above, although no scholar of the caliber of Hilgenfeld devoted a full monograph to the theme. The following critical treatments may be mentioned: on Hort, *Christianity*, cf. Lüdemann in ThJber 14 (1895), 172: "The author wants to use the term 'Jewish Christianity' to apply strictly to the Pharisaic Jewish Christianity which held fast to the Mosaic law but nonetheless believed that he had proven that 'the Tübingen thesis of a Jewish-Christian leaven in numerous early Christian documents' was based on an error—a superfluous proof, when the term is so understood as above. Obviously, with this shadow boxing the author only indicates that he belongs to a whole army of such brave warriors. The Tübingen school is treated as though it were already extinct. But foreigners apparently do not recognize that in Germany it is not considered to have been refuted in a critical, scholarly manner, but to have been eliminated, or to be in the process of elimination in an essentially easier manner, namely, through administrative channels. As recommended 'Books for Students' we find Ritschl, Lechler, Ewald, etc., and, with some disclaimers, even Weizsäcker. But about Baur, Hilgenfeld, Holsten, Hausrath, Lipsius, and others 'the English student' may not read or even hear anything at all." On Harnack's understanding of Jewish Christianity, cf. Lüdemann in ThJber 6 (1887), 115f.

164. On Hilgenfeld and his work, cf. Pölcher, *Hilgenfeld* (both the dissertation as a whole and the part published).

165. So far as I know, Hilgenfeld's last work was "Der Clemens-Roman" in ZWTh 49 (1906):66–133. His earliest work was *Die clementinischen Recognitionen und Homilien* (Jena, 1848).

166. Hilgenfeld, *Urchristenthum* (1855), 56ff.

167. Hilgenfeld, *Urchristenthum* (1855), 67.

168. Hilgenfeld, "Darstellung," passim.

169. Cf. Hilgenfeld, "Urchristenthum" (1886), 427–31.

170. Hilgenfeld, *Judenthum*, 43ff.; idem, "Hegesippus," 203–6; and idem, "Noch einmal Hegesippus," 320f. He had previously expressed a different view in *Urchristenthum* (1855), 88.

171. Hilgenfeld, *Judenthum*, 45.

172. Hilgenfeld, *Judenthum*, 46.

173. Hilgenfeld, *Judenthum*, 117.

174. Hilgenfeld, *Judenthum*, 117.

175. Hilgenfeld, *Judenthum*, 117.

176. The earliest extant texts that refer to a historical person "Ebion" are Hippolytus, *Ref.* 7.35; and Tertullian, *De carne* 14; *De virginibus velandis* 6; and *Praescr.* 35. Cf. Hilgenfeld, *Ketzergeschichte*, 422f.; and idem, *Judenthum*, 101.

177. Hilgenfeld, *Urchristenthum* (1855), 885. The critique of Baur is to be noted here.

178. Hilgenfeld, *Recognitionen* (see above, n. 165); cf. Strecker, *Judenchristentum*, 5f.; and Pölcher, *Hilgenfeld*, pt. 2, 68–71.

179. Koch, *Investigation*, appropriately comments with regard to the purported fragment from "Ebion": "Actually, a study of these fragments shows an interest in the monotheletic controversy, as Hilgenfeld admits. They can hardly be introduced, then, as evidence for earliest Ebionitism" (p. 31).

180. This had already been rejected by Gieseler, "Nazaräer," 299ff.; Credner, *Beiträge*, 365; and Lutterbeck, *Lehrbegriffe*, 71ff.

181. Cf. the objections already raised by Uhlhorn in the article "Ebioniten" in *RE*[3], 2.125–28, esp. 126. On the other side is to be found, of course, Zahn, *Geschichte*, 2:642–723, esp. 648ff., 668ff., 721ff.; and most recently Simon, "Migration," 47ff.

182. Cf. Knopf, *Zeitalter*, 1–30; Dobschütz, *Apostolic Age*, 23ff., 81ff. (on both, cf. Hilgenfeld, "Ernst von Dobschütz," 260–304, 517–59); Weiss, *Earliest Christianity*, 2:707ff.; and Weizsäcker, *Apostolic Age*, 2:1–58.

183. I here omit from consideration the extensive discussion of the Pseudo-Clementines from the point of view of source analysis (Waitz, Rehm, Schwartz, Strecker) and those primarily from the history-of-religions perspective (Thomas, Cullmann).

184. Cf. the Bibliography, and esp. H.-J. Schoeps, *Ja—Nein und trotzdem* (Mainz, 1974), 216ff. (a survey of his own works on Jewish Christianity).

185. Schoeps, *Theologie*, 7.

186. Schoeps, *Theologie*, 7f.

187. Schoeps, *Theologie*, 45–61.

188. Schoeps, *Theologie*, 381–456.

189. Justin, *Dial.* 47; Irenaeus, *Heresies* 26; and Epiphanius, *Pan.* 29f.

190. Schoeps, *Theologie*, 262ff.

191. Cf. Schoeps, *Theologie*, 71–116.

192. Cf. Schoeps, *Theologie*, 117–218.

193. Cf. Schoeps, *Theologie*, 305ff.

194. For such an understanding, cf. Goppelt, *Times*, 165ff.; and Cullmann, "Ebioniten", cols. 237f.

195. Schoeps, *Theologie*, 305–15; and idem, *Urgemeinde*, 61–67.

196. Schoeps, *Theologie*, 325–34.

197. Schoeps, *Theologie*, 247–55, 315–20.

198. Eusebius., *Hist. Ecc.* 4.6.17: "It is to be noted that Symmachus was an Ebionite. . . . And memoirs too of Symmachus are still extant, in which, by his opposition to the Gospel according to Matthew, he seems to hold the above-mentioned heresy."

199. Schoeps, *Theologie*, 350–65; and idem, *Zeit*, 82–89.

200. Schoeps, *Theologie*, 33.

201. Schoeps, *Theologie*, 366–80.

202. It is also to be noted, however, that Schoeps believes that he can use the Pseudo-Clementines as sources for the reconstruction of Jewish Christianity without making any critical decisions in terms of source analysis (cf. Schoeps, *Theologie*, 457–79). In a discussion of Strecker's *Judenchristentum* (Schoeps, *Studien*, 91–97), he himself expresses fundamental reservations regarding the possibility of reconstructing the *Kerygmata Petrou*, although he continues to assume Ebionite elements in the Pseudo-Clementines (less than one third).

203. Cf. Schmidtke, *Fragmente*, 230 n. 2.

204. Strecker, *Judenchristentum*, 117–36; cf. idem, "Eine Evangelienharmonie bei Justin und Pseudoklemens?" and the literature there given.

205. Cf. the annihilating critique by Barthélemy, "Qui est Symmaque?" (=in idem, *Etudes d'histoire du texte de l'Ancien Testament*, OBO 21 [Fribourg/Göttingen, 1978], 307–21).

206. Criticisms of Schoeps's works have been ignited primarily by his treatment of the pre-70 c.e. period. Cf. Kümmel, "Theologie," 192f.; idem, "Urchristentum," *ThR* NF 22 (1954). 140ff.; Bornkamm, "Schoeps," 196–204; and Schneemelcher, "Problem," 237f.

207. Cf. Schoeps's analysis of James (*Theologie*, 343–49): James was not Ebionite, but Jewish-Christian, and thus (!) belongs to the catholic church.

208. For Munck's works, see the bibliography.

209. Cf. Harnack, *Dogma*, 1:287ff. Harnack could admit without embarrassment that the Jewish Christians (for his definition, see above, pp. 15f.) were in the majority in Palestine until the middle of the second century and that they were the descendants of the original Jerusalem church.

210. Munck, *Paul*, 87–134.

211. Munck, *Paul*, 135–67. Oddly enough, Schmithals (*Paul and James*, passim; and idem, *Gnosticism in Corinth*, passim, advocates a similar view, although differences in detail between Munck and Schmithals cannot of course be denied (cf. Munck's critique of Schmithals's *Gnosticism in Corinth* in "The New Testament and Gnosticism"). In any case, Schmithals' view of the non-Jewish constituency of Paul's opponents fits the view of a harmonious relationship between Paul and James. Both Schmithals and Munck understand real Judaistic Christianity to be a phenomenon of the period after 70 C.E., although Schmithals, *Paul and James*, 114 n. 35, does not advocate the view that the Jerusalem church perished during the Jewish War.

212. Cf. Munck, "Primitive Jewish Christianity," 90f.; similarly Keck, "Saints," an essay that has not received enough attention and to which we shall return below.

213. See above, pp. 216f., n. 22.

214. Munck, "Jewish Christianity", 103f.; and idem, "Primitive Jewish Christianity", 89f.

215. Cf. *Paul, Apostle to the Gentiles*, 110–11 n. 2.

216. Cf. also the acknowledgement by Schmithals, *Paul and James*, 13ff. Brown, "James," has followed in Munck's wake (on this, cf. below, p. 183).

217. Munck, *Paul*, 76–77.

218. Daniélou, *Theology*. The page numbers given in the text refer to this principal work of Daniélou's. A survey of his works on Jewish Christianity is found in *RSR* 60 (1972): 11–18. The significance of Daniélou's work for the history of theology is evaluated by Grillmeier in "Hellenisierung," 540–47.

219. "Between the NT and the advent of Hellenistic theology as expressed by the Apologists, there was an intermediate period the contours [*physionomie*] of which are little known" (Daniélou, *Theology*, 17).

220. Cf. A. Orbe in *RSR* 47 (1959): 544–59; H. Doerrie in *Erasmus* 15 (1963): 713ff.; and Murray, "Studies," 414–26.

221. The NT itself extends into the second century (2 Peter!).

222. The NT has been influenced by the Hellenistic spirit because the Palestinian Christianity of the first century was Hellenized.

223. Compare the justified criticism by Murray, "Studies," 419f.

224. "What is the Judaeo-Christianity, if not merely an aspect of the Great Church? And if it is only an aspect, how can its 'theology' be summed up in abstraction from the New Testament canon?" (Murray, "Studies," 420).

225. Cf. Bibliography.

226. Simon, *Israel*, 249.

227. Simon, *Israel*, 243.

228. Cf. Simon and Benoît, *Judaïsme*, 268 (cf. also p. 104, where Simon speaks of a "rigorous observance of the Jewish law").

229. Simon, *Israel*, 265f., 390ff.

230. So Bauer, *Orthodoxy*, 87.

231. Simon, *Israel*, 481 n. 107; cf. idem, *Judaïsme*, 259.

232. Simon, *Problèmes*, 6f.

233. Simon, *Israel*, 247f.

234. Simon, *Israel*, 261f.

235. Simon, *Israel*, 265ff.

236. Simon, *Israel*, 414ff.

237. Simon, *Stephen*, 113f.

238. Cf. already Simon, *Israel*, 246f.; idem, *Stephen*, 91ff.; and idem, "Migration," 47ff.

239. Simon's works are not once referred to in Klijn and Reinink, *Evidence*.

240. Daniélou's approach to the problem has been adopted by, among others, Bagatti, *Church*; Manns, *Essais sur le Judéo-Christianisme*; and Mancini, *Archaeological Discoveries Relative to the Judaeo-Christians*. On the archaeological critique, cf. Meyers and Strange, *Archeology*, 100 and passim.

241. Klijn, "Study," 426.

242. Cf. Simon, "Réflexions", 66ff., for a critique of Longenecker, *Christology*. Surprisingly, Murray gives Longenecker's work a positive review in "Christianity," 450.

243. Quispel, "Discussion." Since Quispel uses the expression "Jewish Christian" in this essay as a synonym for "Judaic," we are justified in discussing Quispel together with Daniélou.

244. Harnack *tends* in this direction (despite the quotation above, pp. 15–16).

245. This would include most of the works mentioned above under 1.3 and 1.4.

246. Cf. now similarly Strecker, "Gnosis," 263, who in addition points "to the maintaining of unity with the Jewish nation and religion" by the Jewish Christians.

247. Here belong, e.g., the pre-Matthean and pre-Johannine churches as well as the opponents of Ignatius. On this latter, cf. P. J. Donahue, "Jewish Christianity in the Letters of Ignatius of Antioch," *VigChr* 32 (1978): 81–93; and C. K. Barrett, "Jews and Judaizers in the Epistles of Ignatius," and the bibliography give there. I am grateful to U. Luz for helpful questions on this point.

248. The remark in 2 Peter 3:15f. (which betrays uncertainty with regard to Paul) is no more anti-Pauline than the reinterpretation of 1 Thessalonians in 2 Thessalonians (cf. Lindemann, *Paulus*, 42ff., 91ff.).

249. It is absolutely necessary to distinguish an attack on Paul from either simply ignoring him or failure to take him into consideration. To have neglected this distinction throughout (an extreme case: pp. 84f.) is a severe methodological failure of Müller, *Theologiegeschichte*. In addition, whoever shares Müller's correct view that one "must reckon with the possibility of a continuing opposition to Paul through the decades" (ibid., 84) cannot exclude from consideration the so-called nomistic Jewish Christians (on Müller, ibid., 11).

250. Strangely enough, neither Lindemann, *Paulus*, nor Dassmann, *Stachel*, deals with the picture of Paul held by the anti-Pauline contemporaries of the apostle.

251. It is self-evident that in the above survey it was impossible to include all the recent contributions to the study of (ancient) Jewish Christianity. But cf. Schille, *Judenchristentum*; Malina, "Jewish Christianity: A Select Bibliography"; idem, "Jewish Christianity and Christian Judaism"; Riegel, "Jewish Christianity: Definitions and Methodology" (on Malina's and Riegel's essays, cf. the [justified] criticism of Strecker, "Gnosis," 262, with n. 5). It is also understandable that works such as Pieper, *Kirche*, or Schlatter, *Geschichte*, have been left out of consideration, for—with all the intuitition of their authors—they present only uncritical paraphrases of the biblical text.

CHAPTER 2. THE OLDEST RECOGNIZABLE CASES OF ANTI-PAULINISM

1. The material in this chapter may be compared with Luedemann, "Antipaulinismus," 442ff., with which parts of the following agree verbatim.

2. Cf. Luedemann, *Paul, Apostle to the Gentiles*, 69–77, on the conference and the Antioch incident. The exposition there is summarized here and of course accented differently because of the different issue in question here. I will also take advantage of the opportunity to deal with important literature with which I either was not yet acquainted at the time of the previously mentioned work or did not then discuss because I was there primarily oriented to the issue of chronology.

3. It was demanded by Jewish Christians, not by Jews who were "officially commissioned to investigate the attitude of the Christian church" (Schmithals, *Paul and James*, 107). Against such theses, see

Pfleiderer, "Studien," 80f., and (against Schmithals) Georgi, *Geschichte*, 16 n. 19.

4. Cf. Lietzmann, *An die Galater*, ad loc.; and Georgi, *Geschichte*, 15; cf. already Pfleiderer, "Studien," 82f., 246. Differently Suhl, *Paulus*, 65f., whose proposal is based on an understanding of the occasion for Paul's second trip to Jerusalem which is, in my opinion, incorrect (cf. Luedemann, *Paul, Apostle to the Gentiles*, 127 n. 116, and 123f. n. 102). Cf. now the correct view in Eckert, "Kollekte," 67f. Borse, "Paulus," takes up again the old view that Paul brought a collection to the conference at Jerusalem (p. 52). His painstaking work, however, continues to perpetuate the error of attempting to harmonize Acts and Paul's letters.

5. Pfleiderer, "Studien," 249.

6. Cf. even Ritschl, *Entstehung*, 150f.: "It appears that even the original apostles let themselves be dominated for a while by the strict Jewish Christians, since Paul hints that he had to struggle to deflect the demand that Titus be circumcised."

7. Hilgenfeld, "Urchristenthum" (1858), 79.

8. Cf. correctly Pfleiderer, "Studien," 88.

9. On the concept *koinōnia* in Gal. 2:9, cf. Hainz, "Gemeinschaft," who argues that this concept "was of great ecclesiological significance" for Paul and the Jerusalem leadership (p. 42); Hainz presents a comprehensive survey of the secondary literature. The contemporary hermeneutical relevance of such a conclusion for confessional differences which Hainz emphasizes is, in my opinion, doubtful, however, since each side understood this "fellowship" differently, as we may learn from the subsequent events. (On this, cf. esp. Brown, *Community*, 209, and n. 71.) On *koinōnia* in Paul in general, cf. Panikulam, *Koinonia*, and Hainz, *Koinōnia*.

10. Smith, "Problems," correctly points out the meaning the collection had for the agreement that had been reached and well describes the attitude of the Jerusalem leadership to Paul: "The Jerusalem group may have been of two minds about Paul's work: On the one hand, it was inadequate, since his converts did not keep the Law, and even dangerous, since it might lead Jews to transgression; on the other hand it was better than nothing, since it did preach Christ, and it created centers in which further work by their own representatives could easily be started. In the event of such a balancing of considerations, a generous gesture on the part of Paul may have been enough to turn the balance, temporarily, at least, to the side of approval" (p. 122). In addition, cf. Hurd, *Origin*, 263f.; and already Wrede, *Paul*, 70f.

11. Cf. Georgi, *Geschichte*, 21; and Betz, *Galatians*, ad loc.

12. According to Smith, "Problems" (and similarly Weiss, *Earliest*

Christianity 1:268; and Holmberg, *Paul*, 29f., who gives bibliography), "it is most probable that Paul is not here talking about the division of the mission field at all, but about his previous subject, the authority of the gospel" (pp. 123f.), for "Paul's purpose . . . was not to report a division of the mission field but to insist on the approval of his gospel by the Jerusalem group" (ibid., 125). There is in fact a distinction to be made between Paul's intention and the arrangements achieved by the conference. The question is whether in Galatians 2 Paul transmits *traditions* from the conference. And for reasons of syntax, language, and content, of this there can be no doubt (cf. Luedemann, *Paul, Apostle to the Gentiles*, 69ff.).

13. "Thus the agreement made by the apostles for unity was at the same time an agreement to a separation between the two churches, the one loyal to the law and the other free from it" (Pfleiderer, "Studien," 96; cf. also Wrede, *Paul*, 43).

14. Schmithals, *Paul and James*, 44f., is completely right in affirming that any other interpretation of Gal. 2:9 must be forced. Cf. also Brown, *Community*, 207; and Eckert, "Kollekte," 71.

15. Georgi, *Geschichte*, is representative of many who object to the above proposal. In Gal. 2:9 "there is no thought of a separation into Gentile and Jewish peoples as the objects of missionary work. That could hardly be harmonized with the actual historical situation" (p. 21). But the question is, rather, whether an interpretation based on the language and grammar does not lead to the insight that the formula seeks to *cancel the validity of* an actual historical situation.

16. The correctness of the statement made above is not changed in the least by the fact that an acknowledgment of Paul's apostleship is repeatedly read into Gal. 2:7ff. (cf. most recently Holmberg, *Paul*, 54, although only "privately"). Cf. now Betz, *Galatians*, ad loc.

17. Cf. Luedemann, *Paul, Apostle to the Gentiles*, 76f. Contra Oepke, *Galater*, 81: "The claim that Paul does not use this expression [i.e., *apostolē*] for himself because his apostleship was not fully accepted in Jerusalem could only derive from being hyperconcerned about the subject and from lack of sensitivity to the nuances of the language."

18. Betz, *Galatians*, from his correct observation that Paul had not been acknowledged as an apostle in Jerusalem, incorrectly infers that at the time of the Jerusalem Conference Paul had not (yet) claimed to be an apostle (cf. pp. 98f., n. 394f.).

19. We may also surmise that Paul avoided raising other questions in Jerusalem on which he had an understanding different from that of the Jerusalem leadership (e.g., his understanding of the Christ as the end of the law). On this problem, cf. Hengel, "Mission," 52.

20. Cf. Pfleiderer, *Primitive Christianity*, 1:118f.: "Thus Paul had attained his immediate object—the recognition of the freedom of his Gentile converts from the Jewish law; to make demands of a more far-reaching kind, to contest the obligation of the law for Christians in general, including Jewish Christians, would only have frustrated his immediate aim, and he had no reason for attempting it. . . . But it must be admitted that this understanding was only arrived at by evading the question of principle regarding the relation of the Christian faith and the Christian church to the Jewish law."

21. For bibliography, cf. Betz, *Galatians*, ad loc. Overbeck, *Auffassung*, is still important for the interpretation of this passage, because those interested in apologetics, ancient and modern, can see a mirror image of themselves reflected in his work throughout.

22. From the context it is clear that these Jews belong to the Christian community in Antioch. Contra Richardson, *Israel*, 93–95.

23. The verb *phobein* here has the meaning of a theologically grounded fear. Peter permitted himself to be controlled by the authority of James. To be sure, Suhl, *Paulus*, writes: "There is no evidence that by the mere arrival of people from James there suddenly existed some threat from the direction of the unbelieving Jews in Antioch" (p. 72). However, Suhl (a) falsely presupposes that the "circumcision group" were the unbelieving Jews (cf. the following note) and (b) unnecessarily regards the thing that was feared to be threats of physical violence from the Antiochene Jewish community.

24. The circumcision group are members of the Christian community in Jerusalem (cf. Luedemann, *Paul, Apostle to the Gentiles*, 123f. n. 102).

25. Vv. 15ff. shift back to Paul's current composition of the letter and are no longer a part of the report of his speech at Antioch.

26. Ward, "James," 176, following Munck's lead, even manages on the basis of Gal. 2:11ff. to establish an untroubled friendly relationship between Paul and James. Peter in fact was afraid, not of the Christians who had been sent by James, but of the Jews. But why was he not afraid of them until the people from James arrived?

27. Contra Lietzmann, *An die Galater*, ad loc.: Gal. 2:11ff. only means that some people who were associated with James refused to join the Gentile Christians, Jewish Christians, and Peter in a common meal. But then the reaction of Peter and Barnabas becomes incomprehensible.

28. Cf. Bill. IV/1:374–78; Moore, *Judaism*, 2:75f.; Acts 10:28; John 18:28; *Jub.* 22:16; Tob. 1:10f. Cf. the comprehensive work of Stern, *Greek and Latin Authors* 2:39ff.

29. Schmithals, *Paul and James*, 63–78. Dietzfelbinger, *Irrlehre*,

passim, well shows against Schmithals that the attitude of the Jerusalem group was not nearly so conditioned by tactics as Schmithals represents it to have been.

30. Suhl, *Paulus*, 51–64.

31. Schmithals, *Paul and James* p. 60, points out "that Paul utters no word of criticism against either James' messengers or James himself" and would like to use that as an indication of the friendly relationship which existed between Paul and James. In my opinion, sound methodology does not permit that, since James is also included in the attack against Peter. Both belong to the "pillars." Goguel, "Apôtre," 472, thinks that "those from James" had not necessarily been *sent* by him. But the fear of the "circumcision group" which suddenly fell on Peter speaks against this (cf. above, n. 26). Another variety of harmonization is found in Howard, *Paul*, 42: Paul did not attack James publicly "without first having faced him personally in order to see if Peter's reaction to the envoys was warranted . . . . Secondly, it may be that Paul suspected that Peter's reaction to the envoys was due to a misunderstanding of what James meant." No comment is necessary.

32. In my opinion, the incident occurred before the conference (see Luedemann, *Paul, Apostle to the Gentiles*, 75f., 291), but this need not be discussed here, where we are concerned with the anti-Pauline nature of the phenomenon itself, and since, in any case, the two events were not very far separated from each other.

3. ANTI-PAULINISM IN JERUSALEM AND JAMES THE LORD'S BROTHER

1. For the following, cf. the appropriate chapters in the relevant histories of early Christianity in the Bibliography. Cf. esp. Goguel, *Birth*, 106–48; Longenecker, *Paul*, 271–88; and W. D. Davies, in *PCB*, 760a–70c (870–81). Gaechter's collected essays, *Petrus*, are not dealt with here (as also in chap. 2 above) since their author, though well read, intentionally practices psychological exegesis (cf. p. 9) and presupposes the authenticity of James and 1 Peter as well as handling Acts as though it were always a historically accurate account.

2. Cf. Schille, "Anfänge"; idem, *Judenchristentum*; and idem, *Osterglaube*. Schille's works emphasize the significance of Galilee as the oldest center of the Christian mission (as does Schmithals, *Paul and James*, 33f. n. 69). Arguments against the view that the earliest resurrection appearances occurred in Galilee are found in Burkitt, *Beginnings*, 76–97; and Weiss, *Earliest Christianity*, 1:11ff.; arguments to the contrary, in Jackson and Lake, *Beg.* 1.5, pp. 7–16. Cf. further the survey

in Kasting, *Anfänge*, 85f. n. 24. I consider it certain that the first appearances occurred in Galilee. No one yet has been able to explain how the Galilean appearances could possibly have happened after those in Jerusalem (cf. Vögtle, in Lohse and Vögtle, "Geschichte," 26).

3. Cf. Mark 14:27f., 50; John 16:32; John 21. On the historicity of the flight of the disciples, cf. Grässer, *Problem* 21ff. Counterarguments in Klein, "Verleugnung," 69 and often.

4. This conclusion is independent of the question of whether or not Mark ended with 16:8. For even if Mark never contained an appearance story, the first appearance to Peter is already reflected in 16:7. This of course presupposes that 16:7 does *not* refer to the parousia (cf. Pesch, *Markusevangelium*, vol 2, ad loc.), and further, that the verse did not originate with the redactor (cf. ibid., ad loc.).

5. "John 21:1–17 (19b) and Luke 5:4–11 are two variations of one basic story in which Peter played a leading role, a story that told of an amazing catch of fish by Peter and that somehow became a special revelation of the risen Lord" (Kasting, *Anfänge*, 51).

6. This is conceivable only against the background of a first appearance to Peter (my response to Kattenbusch, "Vorzugsstellung," 322 and passim). Kattenbusch's essay is nevertheless in many points a corrective to Holl, "Kirchenbegriff," who, for the reasons given in the preceding text, knows too much about the theology of the Jerusalem church. And that the order of the names indicates a *ranking* is shown by Hengel, "Maria," 248ff.

7. For the evidence, cf. Klein, "Verleugnung," 76, who also gives bibliography.

7a. Usually *two* christophanies are seen to be reflected in 1 Cor. 15:5 (cf., e.g., Kasting, *Anfänge*, 89). It is not impossible, however, that the text indicates only *one* (cf. below, in n. 55). The delineation given above can be reconciled with either understanding, although in my opinion the former is to be preferred.

8. Weizsäcker, *Apostolic Age*, 1:1–6; Kasting, *Anfänge*, 86–89 (bib.): "Peter, the First Missionary"; and Kraft, *Entstehung*, 209–11.

9. Cf. the survey in Trilling, "Zur Entstehung des Zwölferkreises, 201–22 (bib.).

10. Cf. Holl, "Kirchenbegriff," 47 n. 1. Against Jerusalem as the location: Schille, "Anfänge," 198 n. 134. Cf. the surveys in Kremer, *Zeugnis*, 71ff. (bib.); and Grass, *Ostergeschehen*, 99ff. (bib.).

11. On the appearance to the women, cf. Hengel, "Maria."

12. Cf. Schmithals, *Office of Apostle*, 81f.

13. On the Hellenists, cf. Hengel, "Between Jesus and Paul", 14; and idem, *Acts and Earliest Christianity*, 71–80.

14. Cf. Luedemann, *Untersuchungen*, 39–42.

15. Cf. Luedemann, *Untersuchungen*, 121 n. 17.

16. Cf. Conzelmann, *Apostelgeschichte*, ad loc.

17. Cf. Hengel, "Between Jesus and Paul", 19; and Koester, *Introduction*, 2:90. Hengel supposes that Acts 6:13f., despite its redactional echoes of Mark 14:38, reflects tradition ("Between Jesus and Paul", 21–25). In my opinion, in particular the motif of *changing* the law (ibid., 23) can reflect the historical facts. Cf. Luedemann, *Early Christianity*, 81–85.

18. It should be noted that their critique was an inner-Jewish phenomenon (cf. esp. Simon, *Stephen*, 46ff., 78ff.) and is to be qualitatively distinguished from Paul's critique of the law (cf. my forthcoming volume on the theology of Paul).

19. Cf. Schürer, *Geschichte*, 3:144ff.; and J. A. Goldstein, *1 Maccabees*, AB 41 (New York, 1976), 547.

20. Cf. Maier and Schubert, *Qumran*, 36ff.; and Murphy-O'Connor, "Essenes." If, as Murphy-O'Connor thinks, these Essenes were returnees from Babylon who (for cultic reasons) had turned their backs on Jerusalem, then there would be another parallel to the exodus of the Hellenists from Jerusalem: the original moving *to* Jerusalem.

21. A further analogy may be provided by the counsel given in *1 Clem.* 54:1 that it would be better for all concerned if the (leadership of the) dissidents in Corinth would simply leave the city. This Christian example, like the Jewish examples, by no means was understood as leaving the religion itself.

22. Whether the Hellenists were bearers of an enthusiastic baptismal tradition, as we find, e.g., in Gal. 3:28 (cf. Luedemann, *Paul, Apostle to the Gentiles*, 66f.), is of course not certain. Hengel, *Acts and Early Christianity*, 78, rightly (because of Acts 21:9; Eusebius, *Hist. Ecc.* 3.31, 39) regards the emphasis on the Spirit and the gift of prophecy as of a piece with an "archaic, enthusiastic feature typical of the 'Hellenists'." But that, of course, is still not antinomianism. We must, rather, suppose that it was in the course of the mission itself that the Hellenists' critique of the law, which was somewhat groping and tentative at first, became a fundamental abrogation of the law: "'mission' and 'Hellenization' must necessarily have become one and the same thing" (Betz, *Galatians*, 191b).

23. Paul did not persecute the Christians in Jerusalem. Such a thesis (vehemently advocated most recently by Hengel, "Between Jesus and Paul," 2:143 n. 80; and idem, *Acts and Earliest Christianity*, 74) cannot appeal to Acts 7:58 (cf. Luedemann, *Paul, Apostle to the Gentiles*, 41 n. 89).

24. Cf. esp. Koch, "Jakobusfrage."

25. The translation "Other than the apostles I saw none except

James, the Lord's brother" (so Trudinger, "Note," 201) is erroneous and reads Acts 9:26f. into Galatians 1 (cf. ibid., 202). Cf. Howard's critique of Trudinger in *NovTest* 19 (1977): 63ff., which is not exactly on target, since Trudinger is not primarily concerned to dispute James's apostleship but to point out that Paul had seen other apostles besides Peter. Howard correctly points out, however, that "the ambiguity that does remain lies within the force of *ei mē*, not *heteron*" (ibid., 64).

26. An exact parallel is found in 1 Cor. 1:14, but Koch, "Jakobusfrage," 208, incorrectly minimizes its significance.

27. Even if Gal. 1:19 ultimately remains ambiguous with regard to our question, it is made clear that the apostolic title belongs to James in 1 Cor. 15:7 (correctly Roloff, *Apostolat*, 64 n. 82; idem, art. "Apostel" in *TRE*, 3:433). But cf. Holl, "Kirchenbegriff," 49: James "had in it [i.e., the Jerusalem church] not only the position of an ordinary or even highly respected church member but was counted among the apostles. . . . And also 1 Cor. 9:5 *hoi loipoi apostoloi kai hoi adelphoi tou kuriou kai Kēphas* presupposes the same." Cf. the same argument in Jackson and Lake, *Beg*, I.5, p. 55; Wilckens, "Ursprung," 67f.; and Bruce, *Men*, 89f. Differently Schmithals, *Office of Apostle*, 78f.; and Klein, *Apostel*, 46 n. 190.

28. The importance of the context for this question is rightly emphasized by Roloff, "Apostel," 64 n. 82.

29. Differently, e.g., Klein, *Apostel*, who asks: If James had been an apostle, "is it conceivable that Paul would have referred to the brother of the Lord in an incidental supplementary remark?" (p. 46 n. 190). I think the answer must be yes, since for Paul it was a matter of the independence of his own apostleship. It was in his interest to play down his contact with James.

30. Von Campenhausen, *Ecclesiastical Authority*, 19 (and similarly Berger, *Auferstehung*, 623), vainly contests the view that Paul's visit must *also* have had the purpose of getting acquainted with the leader of the church. Stauffer, "Petrus," 365f., despite some exaggerated subtleties, seems to me to be nearer the historical truth.

31. Luedemann, *Paul, Apostle to the Gentiles*, 69ff.

32. Stuhlmacher, *Evangelium*, lists the different subjects that could have been discussed.

33. Haenchen, "Petrus-Probleme," 56.

34. Cf. Holsten, *Evangelium*, 11, who already correctly saw this.

35. Hengel, "Mission," thinks Herod "Agrippa I . . . was allied less with the Pharisees than with the Sadducean nobility" (p. 30 n. 53), and it was for this reason that he had James the son of Zebedee executed. But Hengel's statement is incorrect. Cf. Schürer, *Geschichte*, 1:549–64 (new English ed. 1:442–54), who rightly shows the pro-Pharisaic char-

acter of Agrippa's political stance. Agrippa had to adopt such a position in order to defend himself from the (justified) suspicion of the population, who looked to the Pharisees rather than to the Sadducees for leadership, that he didn't really understand the Jewish people. As an example, cf. the report in Josephus, *Ant.* 19.332–34: Simon was *exakribazein dokōn ta nomima* (332), and Pharisaic, to be sure. On this passage, cf. Le Moine, *Sadducéens*, 395 n. 4; pp. 394ff. should be consulted on the whole issue discussed here; cf. also the apt comments by Smith, *Jesus*, 29, 173; Reicke, *New Testament Era*; and Kraft, *Entstehung*, 281f.

36. On the martyrdom of James in Acts 12, cf. the comments of Cullmann, "Courants," which only indicates, however, that the immediate reason for the execution of the Zebedee brothers cannot be determined on the basis of our available sources. (Cullmann believes that James had Zealot tendencies.) On Acts 12, cf. in addition Suhl, *Paulus*, 316–21 (bib.), who attempts to show—in my opinion, without success—that "Luke knew of the death of John which also occurred in the Acts 12 incident but intentionally does not report it" (ibid., 318). Cf. now Luedemann, *Early Christianity*, 139–46.

37. Cf. Luedemann, *Paul, Apostle to the Gentiles*, chap. 3.

38. Cf. Conzelmann, *Apostelgeschichte*, ad loc.

39. Schürer, *Geschichte*, 1:553ff. (new English ed., 1:445ff.).

40. The classical proof in Schwartz, "Tod." Cf. now Pesch, *Markusevangelium*, 2:159f. The early dating of the Jerusalem Conference, which Schwartz and others relate to this view, cannot, however, be maintained (see Luedemann, *Paul, Apostle to the Gentiles*, 193 n. 105).

41. Brandon, *Jesus*, 196ff., speculates that the "other place" (Acts 12:17) was Alexandria.

42. Weizsäcker, *Apostolic Age*, 1:184.

43. Kraft, *Entstehung*, considers this to be one of the offices established by the historical Jesus (!) (cf. pp. 220f., 275). In my view, the texts simply provide no support for such a hypothesis.

44. Contra Suhl, *Paulus*, 320. Why should Peter not have temporarily returned to Jerusalem, if Paul himself—twice!—returned to Jerusalem?

45. So Wilckens, art. "*styloi*" in *TDNT*, 7:735.

46. Cf. Lietzmann, *An die Galater*, ad loc.

46a. Cf. Luedemann, *Paul, Apostle to the Gentiles*, 69, and 120 n. 78 (contra Conzelmann, *History*, 40–41).

47. Harnack, "Verklärungsgeschichte", 63.

48. Harnack, "Verklärungsgeschichte", 63.

49. Harnack, "Verklärungsgeschichte", 63.

50. Harnack's conclusion has been widely accepted: cf. Kümmel,

Kirchenbegriff, 3; Schmithals, *Office of Apostle*, 72–74; Klein, *Apostel*, 39; and Kasting, *Anfänge*, 59. Differing conclusions are argued in Stuhlmacher, *Evangelium*, 267ff.; Schmahl, *Zwölf*, 20–24; and Hahn, "Apostolat", 56f. n. 16. Unfortunately Alsup, *Appearance*, 56, does not pose the question of the stratification of vv. 3–7.

51. This formula perhaps derives from Paul (cf. 1 Cor. 8:4 as a parallel; see Murphy-O'Connor, "Tradition," 583f. [bib.]; and Schille, *Osterglaube*, 17 [bib.]).

52. On the disparate character of vv. 3–5, cf. Wilckens, "Ursprung," 73f.

53. Its traditional character is indicated by the non-Pauline ideas and vocabulary. Cf. Jeremias, *The Eucharistic Words of Jesus*, 101–3; and Schmahl, *Zwölf*, 21. The argument presented above is independent of the question of the origin of the traditional unit 1 Cor. 15:3–5 itself; for a discussion of this issue, see Schmahl, *Zwölf*, 21 (bib.).

54. Cf. Harnack, "Verklärungsgeschichte," 68ff.

55. So Strecker, "Evangelium," 200 (contra already Wilckens, "Ursprung," 63 n. 15). At the most, one can ponder whether *cita* "has been substituted by Paul for an original *kai*, in view of the additional appearances which he intended to report" (Seeberg, *Katechismus*, 57).

56. Jerome, *De Vir.Ill.* 2: ". . . euangelium quoque, quod appellatur Secundum Hebraeos et a me nuper in Graecum sermonem Latinumque translatum est, quo et Origenes (v. Adamantius) saepe utitur, post resurrectionem saluatoris refert: Dominus autem cum dedisset sindonem seruo sacerdotis, iuit ad Iacobum et apparuit ei; iurauerat enim Iacobus se non comesurum panem ab illa hora, qua biberat calicem Domini, donec uideret eum resurgentem a dormientibus; rursusque post paululum: Adferte, ait dominus, mensam et panem, statimque additur: Tulit panem et benedixit ac fregit et dedit Iacobo iusto et dixit ei: Frater mi, comede panem tuum, quia resurrexit filius hominis a dormientibus. ("The Gospel also, which is called the Gospel according to the Hebrews, and which I have recently translated into Greek and Latin and which also Origen often makes use of, after the account of the resurrection of the Savior says, 'But the Lord, after he had given his grave clothes to the servant of the priest, appeared to James (for James had sworn that he would not eat bread from that hour in which he drank the cup of the Lord until he should see him rising again from among those that sleep)' and again, a little later, it says '"Bring a table, and bread," said the Lord.' And immediately it is added, 'He brought and blessed, and brake, and gave to James the Just and said to him, "my brother eat thy bread, for the son of man is risen from among those that sleep"'" [English trans. from *NPNF*, 2d ser. 3:362].

57. If one follows Kümmel,*Kirchenbegriff*, 5, in regarding v. 5 as a free formulation of Paul himself, then one must presuppose that Paul creates a statement of his opponents out of thin air in order to defend himself against his opponents. But we know from other passages in 1 Corinthians (!) that Paul's apostleship was challenged in Corinth at the time he wrote 1 Corinthians. (9:1, on which see below, pp. 165ff.). Kümmel, ibid., writes the following in order to prove that *pasin* is a free composition of Paul: "On the one hand, Paul cannot include himself in this category (i.e., of the apostles), since his call only came later, but on the other hand it is precisely in this context that Paul claims the apostolic title for himself. We must then necessarily [?] infer that this can hardly be a formulation of the earliest church which contains the claim that with the appearance of the Resurrected One to the exclusive group of 'all the apostles' this meant the absolute cessation of the resurrection appearances, for against such a formula Paul would have had to explain why he had the right to be called an apostle on the basis of the later appearance and call which he nonetheless received" (ibid., 6). Paul would thus regard his having seen the risen Lord as the great exception! Against Kümmel, *Kirchenbegriff*, cf. in addition the correct arguments of Wilckens, "Ursprung," 70f. n. 32. On the traditional character of v. 7, cf. further Hahn, "Apostolat," 56f.; and Klein, *Apostel*, 40f., with n. 167. Murphy-O'Connor, "Tradition," has recently expressed the view that Paul added *pasin* in 1 Cor. 15:7 in order to show "that 'the apostles' could and should be extended (p. 589). But *pasin* is to be understood *exclusively!*"

58. Wilckens, "Ursprung," 70f.; and idem, *Resurrection*, 27.

59. If 1 Cor. 15:5 reflects only *one* christophany (see above, p. 239, n. 7a and p. 243, n. 55), it is still significantly characteristic that Cephas in particular is named.

60. It is therefore methodologically inadequate when Kümmel, *Kirchenbegriff*, 4, objects to the above reconstruction: "The two allegedly rival formulae in 15:5 and 15:7 [have] nothing like a polemical tone and give no indication that they are intended to be understood as mutually exclusive" (similarly: Kremer, *Zeugnis*, 83f.; Klein, *Apostel*, 40; and Schmithals, *Office of Apostle*, 74). But this does not take into account the manner in which both formulae have the same structure. It is certainly correct to say that the two formulae have no mutually exclusive character in their present location. The real issue, however, concerns the original historical setting of the two formulae. The above reconstruction thus rests on a series of exegetical-historical steps and cannot be disposed of so easily as attempted by Kümmel and others.

61. Differently Klein, *Apostel*, 40 n. 167: "the formulation of [1 Cor. 15:] [was] entirely spontaneous."

62. Understanding *epeita* in v. 7 in an associative sense (so Bammel, "Herkunft," 414; Winter, "Corinthians," passim; and Bartsch, "Argumentation," 264 n. 10) complicates the matter too much, in addition to the fact that it is difficult in view of Paul's use of *epeita* elsewhere (see Luedemann, *Paul, Apostle to the Gentiles*, 63).

63. Harnack, "Verklärungsgeschichte," 62–68.

64. Harnack was followed by, among others, Wagenmann, *Stellung*, 16; H. Rückert (oral communication from Hans Conzelmann); and Kemler, *Herrenbruder*, 32ff. (bib.). A similar view is advocated by Berger, *Auferstehung*, 217, although he disputes the rival character of the traditions that underlie 1 Cor. 15:5 and 7 but nonetheless understands them "in the sense of the validation of authorities of different groups from their respectively different aspects." Berger too understands 1 Cor. 15:5 and 7 to go back to originally separate traditions (idem, 471). In another passage Berger concedes that there is "a de facto" rivalry between 1 Cor. 15:5 and 7," but "there is no indication of a replacement of the authority of Peter in Jerusalem by that of James" (ibid., 623). In the light of the reasons given in the text above, this cannot be correct.

65. Harnack, ""Vorklärungsgeschichte," 67. He is followed by Winter, "Corinthians," 145 (who does not mention Harnack).

66. Cf. the foundational work of Klein, *Apostel*. Against Klein, however, the question of the availability of preliminary stages of this view is to be raised (cf. Grässer, "Acta-Forschung seit 1960" [bib.]).

67. Cf. Hengel, "Mission," 59: "In Gal. 1.17ff., 1 Cor. 9.5 and 15.7f., Paul presupposes that the *apostoloi* were a fixed, closed group which had its point of origin in Jerusalem or Palestine." Cf. Holl, "Kirchenbegriff," 51.

68. Contra Kümmel, *Kirchenbegriff*, 7.

69. Rom. 16:7 can only strengthen the case argued above for a group of apostles who considered Jerusalem their home church. *Episēmoi en tois apostolois* means, of course, that Andronicus and Junia(s) were well-known members of the apostolic group (cf. Jackson and Lake in *Beg.* I.5, pp. 55f.). Thus it is all the more significant that Paul here too (as in 1 Cor. 15:7f.) points up to the chronological gap which separates him and the two other apostles. Cf. further Roloff, "Apostel," 434.

70. Both cases probably deal with delegates of Pauline churches; cf. Ollrog, *Paulus*, 79f. To see in them, with reference to 2 Cor. 8:23, "agents from the Judean churches" (as do Holmberg, *Paul*, 47 [bib.], and Hurd, *IDBSup*, 650b) is misleading and to be rejected because of the connection between 2 Cor. 8:18f. and 8:23. We know nothing of a participation of the Judean churches in the *gathering* of the collection.

71. Roloff, "Apostel," 435f., sees here, in Paul's opponents in 2

Corinthians, in the missionary discourses in the Synoptics, and in the *Didache* a pneumatic-charismatic itinerant group of apostles native to Syria, which is to be distinguished from the Jerusalem apostleship constituted on the basis of the resurrection appearances. The difficulty in making such a distinction is due to the fact that in Paul *both* types are found. It should be pointed out that Roloff rightly refuses to place the Jerusalem apostleship based on resurrection appearances in a secondary position over against the itinerant apostles. In this case "the struggle Paul carried on in behalf of his own name and his role as an apostle [would be] an absolute historical riddle" (Lüdemann in ThJber 4 [1885], 106).

72. Cf. Bammel, "Herkunft," 417 n. 71: James "checkmates the previous leadership of the church by enlarging it."

73. Cf. von der Osten-Sacken, "Apologie," 256.

74. On this, see esp. Murphy-O'Connor, "Tradition," 583ff.

75. Lehmann, "Tag," 31: "The interpretation [of this text] as 'competitive' enumeration [is] clearly rejected," because Paul "understands the 'roster of witnesses' as a chronological enumeration of christophanies"; Güttgemanns, *Apostel*, 82 (bib.), presents the same argument.

76. Cf. also Radl, *Paulus*, 135f.

77. Cf. Radl, *Paulus*, 140–45.

78. Cf. Radl, *Paulus*, 159–62.

79. Contra Schmithals, *Paul and James*, 87, the presumption of a redactional origin is strengthened by the fact that Acts 15:4 in turn reflects Acts 14:27.

80. Schmithals, *Paul and James*, 89, of course, argues from the presupposition that vv. 17f. is material taken over from a source; on this, see the explanation above.

81. Seven times in the NT, twice in Luke, and five times in Acts.

82. Fifty-seven times in Acts. Of course the expression "the brethren" has the congregation as whole in view (cf. Overbeck, *Apostelgeschichte*, 380). V. 22, sometimes considered a counterargument (Conzelmann, *Apostelgeschichte*, ad loc.; Haenchen *Acts*, ad loc.; and Suhl, *Paulus*, 290), is not convincing, since v. 22 is tradition. Ancient and modern historicizing exegesis has seen "the brethren" as primarily "Mnason and those of this house" (Herzog, "Gefangennehmung," 211). Cf. Haenchen, *Acts*, ad loc.: Mnason and the Hellenistic Christians he had gathered around himself. Contra Schmithals, *Paul and James*, 87.

83. One hundred times; cf. Blass and Debrunner, *A Greek Grammar of the New Testament and Other Early Christian Literature*, § 423 (p. 218).

84. Cf. Radl, *Paulus*, 137f.: typically Lukan is the expression *hēme-*

ras pleious, as well as the verb *katerchesthai* with reference to Judea and the connection with the *ēlthon* which follows in v. 12. The introductory expression *de . . . tis* followed by the name of the person is found in the NT only in Luke (cf. Luke 10:38; 16:20; Acts 5:1; 8:9; 9:10, 36; 10:1; 18:24; 20:9; without the *de* in Luke 1:5; Acts 16:1, 14; 18:7; 19:24).

85. The evidence is given in Strecker, "Jerusalemreise."

86. Differently Suhl, *Paulus* (following Ramsay), 288ff.: "As is clear from Acts 23:32, Luke knew . . . that the trip of about 60 miles could not be made on one day. So he had to work in a stop at the house of Mnason en route to Jerusalem."

87. Cf. Josephus, *Ant.* 20.197ff. (see below, pp. 62f.), and the tradition reworked in the Pseudo-Clementines and by Hegesippus (see, e.g., below, pp. 160ff. and 183ff. and often).

88. In my opinion, it is not possible to consider the view advocated by Bornkamm (art. "*presbys ktl.*" in *TDNT*, 6:662f.) and many others to be historical, namely, that the leadership of the Jerusalem church represented in Acts 21, with a council of elders presided over by James, is a historical representation. Leadership by a council of elders is the church order that prevails in Luke's church and also appears in Acts 15 and 20 (Bornkamm, however, considers the last mentioned passages not to be historical, ibid., 663f.).

89. Schwartz's (*Chronologie*, 290) conjecture ad loc.: "Like many Jews zealous for the law" follows the ruts of a historicizing exegesis. It is accepted by, among others, Weiss, *Earliest Christianity*, 1:370; Munck, *Paul*, 242f.; and Nickle, *Collection*, 71f. It was advocated already by Baur, *Consilio*, 38, but then withdrawn in *Paul*, 1:230 n. 1. Contra: Holl, *Kirchenbegriff*, 66 n. 3; Smith, "Problems," 114; Schmithals, *Paul and James*, 73; and Stolle, *Zeuge*, 75f. n. 86.

90. Smith, "Reason," 265f. The other possibility is that Paul's letters are here Luke's source (cf. Lindemann, *Paulus*, 170). But Paul never expresses himself in his letters in the manner which v. 21 ascribes to him.

91. Cf. esp. Haenchen, *Acts*, 611 n.1.

92. Haenchen, *Acts* 611: "Luke seems to assume that for this Paul himself had to become a Nazirite until the time of their absolution." Acts 21:18–27 has nothing to do with James's own Nazirite lifestyle (on Black, *Scrolls*, 82).

93. This ceremony consisted in cutting the hair, presenting it as an offering, and then bringing an additional offering: cf. Num. 6:13ff.

94. "Seven" occurs elsewhere in Acts, cf. 20:6; 21:4; 28:14, which suggests the possibility of a redactional origin. In addition, one may ponder whether Luke owes the number "seven" in this passage to Num. 6:9 (Conzelmann, *Apostelgeschichte*, ad loc.).

95. Haenchen, *Acts*, 612.

96. Cf. Stolle, *Zeuge*, passim. Cf. Luedemann, *Early Christianity*, 221–25.

97. The name Mnason is found rather often in Greek inscriptions (cf. Bauer, *Lexicon*). Like Barnabas, Mnason came from Cyprus (Acts 21:16) and, after leaving Jerusalem for a while (cf. Acts 11:20), returned once again. Cf. Haenchen, *Acts*, 607.

98. There is no reason to follow Stolle, *Zeuge* (79f. n. 94) in relating the Nazirite tradition to the Jerusalem visit in Acts 18:22. This is unlikely for the following reasons: (1) The precise dating of "seven days" (Acts 21:27a) belongs to the Nazirite tradition and is the motivation for Paul's being in the temple. I can thus find no reason to see the "legal report" (vv. 27ff.) and the Nazirite tradition as competing with each other. (2) That Paul "is not accused in vv. 27ff. with accompanying the four Nazirites" (ibid., 78) is easily understood, for there was nothing reprehensible about this. On the contrary! Acts 21:29 does not say that Paul had taken Trophimus into the temple (ibid.) That was only alleged about Paul. (3) Paul had not been in Jerusalem between the conference visit and his last visit to Jerusalem in Acts 21 (see Luedemann, *Paul, Apostle to the Gentiles*, 37 n. 51). If on the basis of Galatians 2 we exclude the possibility that Paul could have participated in the Nazirite ceremony during the conference visit, then such an act must belong to the last visit to Jerusalem.

99. Cf. the evidence in n. 87, above, and Rom. 15:25f. There is the additional consideration that only a congregation faithful to the law could have continued to exist for so long in Jerusalem (cf. Hengel, "Mission," 56).

100. Did Paul find it necessary to take a considerable sum from the collection in order to pay the expenses of the Nazirites? So Weiss, *Early Christianity*, 1:371; Suhl, *Paulus*, 291f.; Holmberg, *Paul*, 43; and Duncan, *Ministry* (with arbitrary reasons).

101. Cf. Bornkamm, "Verhalten," 160f.; Georgi, *Geschichte*, 90; Suhl, *Paulus*, 291f.; and Holmberg, *Paul*, 42 n. 152.

102. The injustice of this charge is shown, e.g., by Weiss, *Early Christianity*, 1:45; and Schmithals, *Paul and James*, 89f.

103. The charge was thus justified and unjustified at the same time. "Paul suffered in Jerusalem for something which was not at all his own doing, namely, the total separation that was occurring between Christianity and Judaism. But hostile eyes always look more sharply at such historical situations. They were right: Paul's effect . . . was the destruction of Jewish customs and bringing the Law of Moses to an end" (Harnack, *Date of Acts*, 77 n. 1). Cf. further Goppelt, *Christentum*, 97; and already Baur, *Paul*, 1:198–200.

104. Not, however, the much-discussed "we source," since it is precisely parts of this source which do not have the "we" (see vv. 20ff.), while redactional sections do have it (see vv. 17f.).

105. Response to Overbeck, *Apostelgeschichte*, 374 n. *.

106. Cf. Luedemann, *Paul, Apostle to the Gentiles*, 80–98. Morton Smith, in a letter of 24 August 1980, states that the collection may also have suffered defeat at Corinth: "Notice that no Corinthians were with Paul on his final trip to Jerusalem, Acts 20:4. Had the Corinthians made a substantial contribution, they would most certainly have sent some representative to accompany it and attest its proper delivery (especially after all the trouble and embezzlement that had been made while the money was being raised)." But according to Rom. 15:25f., the Corinthian collection is already assured, and Paul was staying in Corinth at the time. On Acts 20:4, cf. Luedemann, *Paul, Apostle to the Gentiles*, 130 n. 148; and now the valuable discussion of Ollrog, *Paulus*, 52–58.

107. Cf. Käsemann, *Romans*, 407. Bornkamm, "Verhalten," 160, infers its "surrender" already from Rom. 15:31f. Precisely this possibility is what is to be examined here.

108. Klein, "Verleugnung," 320. Cf. von Campenhausen, *Ecclesiastical Authority*, 34.

109. Cf. Harnack, *Date of Acts*, 65–66; and Koester, *Introduction*, 2:143. Differently Jülicher, "Schranken," 13: "I need posit no other motive for that dangerous trip of the apostle than that he had committed himself to undertake it by numerous promises to the Gentile churches, provided they would collect a sizable offering."

110. Somewhat differently Knox, *Chapters*, 54: "He can hardly feel such great anxiety that the offering be simply accepted; what he wants is that is be accepted with full and cordial recognition of its significance." On p. 70 Knox calls the collection a "peace offering."

111. In general, it is remarkable that the obvious question of how the collection turned out is seldom raised: Kittel, "Stellung," 154ff. (and cf. his "Jakobusbrief"), although he considers 21:18ff. to be a part of the "we source" and thus historically unassailable, he nonetheless does not raise the question of what happened to the collection. Schmithals, *Paul and James*, 85–96, deals extensively only with the Nazirite vow, the historicity of which he affirms. Only Meyer, *Ursprung*, 3:477–80, clearly sees the problems and ascribes the reception of the offering, despite the fact that Paul's doctrine was an abomination to James, only to the mood of Christian reconciliation which prevailed—and to the size of the offering. Cf. now Koester, *Introduction*, 2:142f. (methodologically inadequate, despite his good questions). The fact that the collection is mostly ignored may simply be a result of the fact that Acts

does not mention it. As a rule, the report in Acts is only paraphrased: cf. Peake, "Paul," 31; Knox, *Paul*, 357–62; Duncan, *Ministry*, 51–55; and Strobel, "Aposteldekret," 95–98. An explanation such as Telfer's, *Office*, 13, however, is quite rare: Acts 21:18–24 "leaves us with the picture of a great man at the height of his power and success, a man whose talents are matched with the singular role which he believed himself divinely called to play" (concerning James).

112. Haenchen's statement that Luke "is silent . . . about the [collection's] delivery, which must have been mentioned in the itinerary" (*Acts*, 612), is too hasty, for whether or not the collection was successfully delivered is precisely the question.

113. Cf. correctly Knox, *Chapters*, 71. Differently Strecker, "Jerusalemreise," 75 n. 50 (=*Eschaton*, 140 n. 51), who holds the view that the collection motif "had no place in the pre-Lukan tradition of the stations of Paul's journeys."

114. Cf. Luedemann, *Paul, Apostle to the Gentiles*, 23f.

115. Morton Smith (in a letter of 24 August 1980) writes: "If the offering was officially accepted, *surely* Luke would have reported its acceptance. This I find persuasive. But between *nonacceptance* and *rejection* there are many other possibilities, and here one is indicated by the course of events: the Jerusalem authorities decided to delay the official presentation and acceptance until Paul, by demonstrating *his own* willingness to obey the laws (of which there is no doubt, 1 Cor. 9:20) could make himself acceptable to the many new, law-observant converts (so explicitly, Acts 21:20ff.). Paul therefore undertook to finance the Nazirites and himself through the purification ritual. Before (21:27) the purification was completed he was arrested, so neither it nor the official presentation of the offering was ever completed—at least by Paul. (The offering may have been handed over later by Paul's companions. Since Acts follows Paul, its omission of this would be understandable)." Smith here argues on the level of the Lukan narrative (just as, e.g., Bruce, *Men*, 105–110; and Borse, "Paulus," 62ff.). I have argued on the basis of the tradition used by Luke. (Luke was no eyewitness!) Certainly, the concluding suggestion made by Smith is an interesting historical possibility. Still, source analysis offers no help in testing it, and it is just as possible that Paul's companions left Jerusalem *with* the collection.

116. Likewise, Georgi, *Geschichte*, 89, thinks that there is "no reason to think of [Luke's] having suppressed an account of a demonstrative delivery and joyful acceptance [of the collection]." He infers a conclusion different from that given above: "Thus the collection . . . was apparently delivered and received in a backroom, in whispers" (ibid.). That is *petitio principii*. It proceeds from the uncritically accepted

presupposition that the Jerusalem church wanted to avoid a break with Paul at all costs. But that is precisely the issue.

117. The following scholars likewise affirm that the Jerusalem church rejected the Pauline collection: Dunn, *Unity*, 256f.; Mattill, "Purpose," 116 (Mattill, however, considers Luke to have been an eyewitness of the events and speculates: "Possibly the collection was so small it reflected lack of Gentile interest in the mother church, thus offending the Jewish Christians," ibid.); perhaps also Wuellner, "Jakobusbrief," 27, 57. Roloff considers the acceptance of the collection "hardly conceivable" and speaks of the "shattering of the work Paul had done in behalf of unity" (*Die Apostelgeschichte*, NTD 5, 17th ed. [Göttingen, 1981], 313). Cautious skepticism concerning the acceptance of the collection is expressed by Cullmann, "Dissensions," 89; idem, *Petrus*, 46 n. 36 [TRANSLATOR'S NOTE: This note is not in the English translation, made from the first edition]; and, Craig, *Beginning*, 260f. Keck, "Poor", 107, thinks Luke avoided the subject in Acts 21 because he knew that the collection "failed to do what Paul hoped it would." On the issue, cf. further Johnson, *Function*, 32–36, who, however, in my opinion, does not really give an explanation (despite pp. 219f.) of why Luke avoids the subject in Acts 21. (He himself considers an explanation like that of Keck, "Poor," 107, to be "speculative", p. 35). Keck, in the article "Armut, III," in *TRE*, 4:76–80, now considers it possible that the collection was not accepted at all.

118. "The conduct of the earliest congregation during Paul's arrest and imprisonment is more than puzzling" (Holl, "Kirchenbegriff," 66 n. 3); cf. in the same direction Pfleiderer, *Primitive Christianity*, 1:120; Goguel, "Apôtre," 500; and G. Johnston, in *PCB*, 631e (p. 725b).

119. Stauffer, "Kalifat," 205, describes this attitude as follows: James had "systematically indoctrinated the Jewish-Christian congregation in an anti-Pauline attitude." Such a statement can no longer be shrugged off (cf., e.g., Mussner, *Jakobusbrief*, 10 n. 2). Stauffer's delineation of Jacobite Christianity has unfortunately hardly found a hearing in recent scholarship (and cf. already Harnack, *Entstehung*, 24–28): thus according to Roloff, *Apostolat*, 63 n. 81, Stauffer's hypothesis of a Jacobite califate lacks "any basis in the NT [sic]."

120. Contra Müller, *Kirchengeschichte*. He first quite correctly observes with regard to the inner situation of the Jerusalem church at the time of Paul's last visit (p. 32): "That the church still persisted in the same hostility toward him [Paul] is indicated by their conduct revealed in the historical components of Acts 21." But then he declares with regard to James: "But his relationship to Paul is nevertheless not hostile; it is only the case that in his own life style he continued to embody the strict type of Torah-observant Christianity" (ibid; cf. similarly Car-

rington, *Church*, 1:190f.). These depictions reflect the pressure of dealing with Acts as a canonical book. But a judgment made on the basis of what was historically probable will have to presuppose that the leader of the Jerusalem church had the same attitude the church as whole had adopted.

121. These concluding sentences are taken in part from Luedemann, "Antipaulinismus," 448.

122. Cf. the circumspect discussions by Goguel, *Birth*, 124–32; and Brandon, *Fall*, 95–100. Cf. also Strobel, *Stunde*, 31–36. Complete collection of the extant texts on the martyrdom of James is found in Lipsius, *Apostelgeschichten*, 238–57. I am presupposing that the report in Hegesippus is secondary (see text above): contra Telfer, *Office*, 14; Burkitt, *Beginnings*, 57–65; Simon, *Stephen*, 71f., 99; and Black, *Scrolls*, 82. On the interrelationship of the Josephus and Acts texts, cf. further Munck, *Paul*, 113ff.

123. Schürer, *Geschichte*, 1:581f., however, considers the report in Josephus to be an interpolation (so also Zahn, *Introduction*, 142; idem, *Forschungen*, 6:301–05; and von Dobschütz, *Church*, 274). But this thesis has not been able to maintain itself. Cf. correctly Dibelius, *James*, 27f.; and P. Winter, in Schürer, *Geschichte*, vol 1 (new English ed., 1:428ff. [bib.]).

124. The description of Ananus in *Antiquities* stands in a strange contrast to that in *War* (4.319f.), where he is described as a new Pericles. On Ananus in Josephus, cf. S. J. Cohen, *Josephus in Galilee and Rome: His Vita and Development as a Historian* (Leiden, 1979), 150f. [bib.].

125. It is not said who the others were whom Ananus had arrested. Hengel, *Charismatic Leader*, 41, regards them as Jewish Christians. That is only one possibility, however. For the opposite point of view, see Goguel, *Birth*, 150.

126. *Paranomēsantes* (*Ant.* 20.200). The Pharisees, however, considered the charges to be unjustified, which should warn us against reading into this debate a separation of the Jerusalem church from Judaism (contra Klausner, *Paul*, 598f.).

127. Simon, *Israel*, expresses it nicely: "Thus, by an irony of fate, the brother of Jesus, the notorious opponent of the apostle to the Gentiles, seems to have perished in his place, the victim of a solidarity about which he, doubtless, had reservations" (p. 261).

128. The theological reason was *not* that the Jerusalem church had not participated in the sacrificial cultus (contra Lohmeyer, *Galiläa*, 63 n. 1; and idem, *Kultus*, 124); cf. correctly Simon, *Stephen*, 98f. Gaston, *Stone*, 98, thinks that the Markan conflict stories derive from the Jerusalem church and thus that the Jerusalem Christians had "from the

very beginning abstained from any cultic activity within the temple."
But I, with U. Luz, would prefer to locate "these conflict stories at . . .
not too great a distance from the Jewish heartland, in a setting in
Hellenistic Jewish Christianity" (Luz, "Die Jünger im Matthäusevan-
gelium," 167). The discussion in the text above also speaks against
Gaston's suggestion.

129. Cf. McGiffert, History, 560; and Goguel, Birth, 124–32 (Kümmel's argument to the contrary is not persuasive, ThR NF 18 [1950]: 6).
According to Brandon, "Death," 67, Ananus moved against James
because the latter "would surely have sympathized with the lower
priests in their cause against the Sadducean aristocracy, and he may
well have been regarded as their champion." This is pure speculation,
and all the more improbable if the identification of the peri tous
nomous akribeis as the Pharisees is correct.

130. With Smith, Jesus, 173. The report thus contains "a certain
sympathy of the Pharisees with James" (Windisch, "Urchristentum,"
293). Differently Weiss, Earliest Christianity 2:709f.: the event is adequately explained on the basis of the general rivalry between the
Pharisees and the Sadducees.

131. This does not mean, however, that a positive attitude toward
Paul can be attributed to the Pharisees of Jerusalem. The verse to
which Smith, Jesus, 29, appeals to support such a hypothesis (Acts 23:9)
is probably from Luke himself (cf. the parallel Acts 5:34ff., and Overbeck, Apostelgeschichte, 404f.) and fits in too well with the (redactional) positive portrayal of the Pharisees in Luke's two volumes to be
historical. (In addition to Acts 5:34ff., cf. Luke 13:31; Acts 26:5; on the
general issue, cf. Ziesler, "Luke and the Pharisees.") Besides, they
could hardly have been very tolerant of Paul, since he was a renegade
(contra Knox, Paul, 359). Smith, Jesus, 29, must account for the strange
contradiction that the Pharisees sanctioned the execution of James
Zebedee and then fifteen years later defended Paul, of all people, who
considered his earlier Judaism to be garbage (Phil. 3:8), and concerning
whose views and praxis the Jerusalem people were well informed
(Acts 21:21).

132. Contra Baumbach, "Konservatismus," 210: "The historian
should not seek the reason for the hostility of the Sadducees against the
Christian apostles, which Acts reports, in the Christians' resurrection
faith but in their rejection of the whole cultic law along with the
institution based on it, as can be seen from the incident of the stoning
of James the brother of the Lord . . . and also from Acts 21:28; for what is
attacked here is Paul's teaching 'against the people and the law and
this place [=the temple].'" Counterargument: There is no indication of
any criticism against the temple in Josephus's account. Acts 21:28

derives from Lukan redaction (see above, p. 55). Likewise unsatisfactory is Schnackenburg, "Urchristentum," 304, who discusses the death of James under the heading "The Separation from Judaism." Cf. already n. 126, above.

133. It should also be noted that even the high priest Ananus, who had James stoned, belonged to the moderate party (cf. Josephus, *War* 4.318–25). The portrayal given by Stuhlmacher, "Versöhnung," 31, thus rests on a serious historical error: "It was that Judaism which was fomenting rebellion against Rome which stoned James in 62 C.E. and forced his church, which refused to participate in the rebellion, to emigrate east of the Jordan."

134. Contra Schnackenburg, "Urchristentum," 307, who wants to exclude the Jerusalem Christians from armed struggle against the Romans on apologetic grounds. He writes: "All the parties in Jerusalem participated in the fight for freedom, even though some did it reluctantly (cf. the 'peace party'). . . . That the Jewish Christian community stood aside from this must have contributed not a little to their alienation from Judaism" (ibid.). Cf. similarly Goppelt, *Christentum*, 98. I can find no reason why what he says concerning the "peace party" should not also apply to the Christians. When their lives were in danger during the last phase of the war they had no alternative but to fight.

135. On the number of fatalities and survivors, cf. A. Büchler, *The Economic Conditions of Judaea After the Destruction of the Second Temple* (London, 1912), 3–29.

CHAPTER 4: ANTI-PAULINISM IN THE PAULINE CHURCHES

1. See Luedemann, *Paul, Apostle to the Gentiles*, 41 n. 83.

2. Cf. also Vielhauer's precautionary measures, *Geschichte*, 146: "The manner in which Paul polemicizes and defends himself makes a precise reconstruction of the situation difficult to grasp: he does not first present a systematic statement of the position of his opponents— which was of course already known to his readers—in order then to demolish it, but determines the course of his argument against them himself. It is thus not always clear whether he is quoting, exaggerating, or distorting their views." On this question, cf. further von Campenhausen, *Ecclesiastical Authority*, 32f. (the reversal of Paul's polemical response does not as such present us with a picture of the theology of the opponents); and Eckert, *Verkündigung*, 23: "Although the problem of Paul's 'reporting' is thoroughly familiar to exegetes, the implications

of this awareness for a proper exposition and evaluation of the views of his competition have for the most part not been adequately appreciated."

3. We are sorely in need of a discussion of the methodology of reconstructing the views of opponents reflected in various NT documents. Cf. now Berger, "Gegner," and the Introduction in Meeks and Francis, Conflict, 1–12. The method pursued in the present study is to be fundamentally distinguished from that used in most studies of the issue of opponents, e.g., in Schmithals, Gnosticism in Corinth; Georgi, Opponents; Güttgemanns, Apostel; Oostendorp, Jesus, Jewett, Terms; Winter, Pneumatiker; and Sandelin, Auseinandersetzung. These and similar works fail to make clear just who a particular opponent is supposed to be and thus, despite correct observations on individual points, proceed on the basis of methodologically inadequate presuppositions. Cf. further Luedemann, "Antipaulinismus," 441f., on the hermeneutical function of the reconstruction of the theology of the opponents; and Conzelmann, 1Kor², for an analysis of the details with regard to 1 Corinthians. In addition, cf. Wischmeyer, Weg, 59–69, on a theme that once dominated the discussion of Paul's opponents, "Gnosis in Korinth." On texts such as 1 Corinthians 1 2; 12:3; 15:12, which reflect no anti-Paulinism (cf. Luedemann, "Antipaulinismus," 449), see my forthcoming volume on the theology of Paul.

4. The contribution of Gunther, Opponents, calls for special comment. He wants to study the opponents against the background of Jewish sectarian teaching. With this purpose in mind, his chap. 1 (pp. 1–58) discusses the source documents for Jewish sectarianism. Chapters 2—8 (pp. 59–307) arrange the supposed statements of the opponents reflected in NT letters (beginning with Paul's letters, except 1 and 2 Thessalonians) under the following heads: chap. 2: Judaic Legalism (59–94); chap. 3: Asceticism (95–133); chap. 4: Sacerdotal Separatism (134–71); chap. 5: Angelology (172–208); chap. 6: Messianism and Penumatology (209–70); chap. 7: Apocalyptic, Mystic Gnosticism (271–97); and chap. 8: Apostolic Authority (298–307). The book concludes with a separate chap. 9 on 2 Cor. 6:14—7:1 (pp. 308–13; the author considers the passage to be either a fragment of the opponents' teaching or something very close to it), and chap. 10: Conclusions. One is constantly torn between irritation at the author's inadequate method and admiration for his industry. The (ancient) sources are dealt with in a thoroughly uncritical manner, and the many names of scholars who advocate a particular thesis are for the most part garnered from secondary sources. The author is directly acquainted only with the literature of the last thirty years. His interpretation of the Pauline letters is dependent on his own work, Paul: Messenger and Exile, which was

also written uncritically (cf. Luedemann, *Paul, Apostle to the Gentiles*, 37 n. 51). As a sample, cf. Gunther, *Opponents*, 317, where the author expatiates on Paul's "persistent loyalty to Pharisaism" (on the basis of Acts 23:6 and Phil. 3:5).

5. Contra Schmithals, *Gnosticism in Corinth*, 345: "Methodologically, it is absolutely necessary to use the whole of Paul's correspondence with Corinth in answering the question of the identity of Paul's opponents in Corinth. This methodological decision does not mean that the question of the identity of Paul's opponents has been decided in advance, but is the presupposition of any decision at all."

6. With Conzelmann, *First Corinthians*, 2ff., the unity of 1 Corinthians is here presupposed. Cf. Merklein, "Einheitlichkeit."

7. One example: According to Weiss, *Der erste Korintherbrief*, ad loc., the question "Am I not free?" was originally a marginal note which was later taken up into the text.

8. We may take the emphatic demonstrative pronoun *hautē* as referring to what follows, as in 1 Cor. 1:12; 7:29; 15:50 (Weiss, *Der erste Korintherbrief*, ad loc.; so also Conzelmann, *First Corinthians*, ad loc., who in addition refers to the position of the pronoun at the end of the sentence and the solemn form of the sentence itself [p. 152 n. 13]). Heinrici's explanation (*Der erste Brief an die Korinther*, ad loc.; so also Robertson and Plummer, *Corinthians*, ad loc.), that *hautē* refers to the preceding, has an element of truth in that Paul in vv. 2–3 already touches on what he will develop in vv. 4ff. (see above, pp. 66f.).

9. The term was obviously used by the Corinthian Christians (cf. 1 Cor. 6:12) and is here taken up by Paul in a polemical sense (see further in Conzelmann, *First Corinthians*, 159 n. 16).

10. Bauer, "Uxores," 101, thinks that *adelphēn gunaika periagein* means "to have a Christian wife." "In any case, with this verb (*periagein*) the meaning 'to have with one constantly' is to be preferred to the alternative possibility 'to travel around with.'" (Dungan, *Sayings*, 6 n. 1, follows this suggestion uncritically.) Against this is to be said: (a) In the context Paul is speaking of his mission(-ary travels). So the two alternatives given by Bauer are in this case identical, for if the missionaries constantly have their wives with them, then they obviously travel around with them! (b) Bauer has only given the possibility of another translation of *periagein* than the usual one and unfortunately does not discuss the parallels listed by Bauer, *Lexicon*, which speak in favor of the usual translation of *periagein* by "travel around with" (cf. esp. Diogenes Laertius 6.96–98: Crates the Cynic takes his wife, who also had a philosophical education, with him on his trips made in the service of philosophy).

11. In vv. 7–14, Paul's right to support from the churches is sup-

ported in the following variety of ways: (1) by an analogy taken from daily life (v. 7), (2) by the law (vv. 8f.), (3) by an *a maiore ad minus* argument, (4) by a reference to the practice of others, and (5) by a dominical saying (v. 14).

12. So, e.g., Lietzmann, *An die Korinther*, 1:ad loc. This explanation does not exclude the possibility that Paul intentionally did not go into further details on the matter of eating and drinking, in order to refer to chap. 8, where eating and drinking is a matter of freedom and the law, without regard to the source of the food and drink (cf. Barrett, *First Corinthians*, ad loc.).

13. To the contrary, Bauer, "Uxores," thinks that Paul in 1 Cor. 9:4 "is defending the right of the apostle, like that of Christians in general, to eat and drink but that he makes clear by his own example how one voluntarily (for the sake of one's own salvation and that of the brother) may renounce this right to food and drink" (p. 98). Vv. 7–26 would then be referred exclusively to v. 6, while vv. 4–5 would belong together with vv. 24–27 (ibid., 97). Such an interpretation does not do justice to the fact that the immediate context of vv. 4–5 is the dispute concerning Paul's apostleship. It is therefore probable that Paul's rhetorical questions are all related to this one disputed issue. Conzelmann, *First Corinthians*, 153 n. 15, rightly finds Bauer's interpretation too schematic, without of course establishing why it is that Paul is concerned in these verses with "simply a question of his freedom in general" (*First Corinthians*, 153 n. 15).

14. Cf. Pratscher, "Verzicht," 295 (bib.). That it was "the presence of agitation caused by his opponents which led him to make this choice" (ibid.) is incorrect, for Paul had of course already at the time of the founding of the church declined to accept such support: cf. Luedemann, *Paul, Apostle to the Gentiles*, 106; Hurd, *Origin*, 204; and Hock, *Context*, 47. Hock's additional assumption that Paul everywhere supported himself with his own hands (p. 26 and often) is, however, too one-sided. The data that we have concerning Paul's stay in Ephesus (Acts 19:9, cf. thereto Hock, *Context*, 32) and—indirectly—in Philippi (Phil. 4:15ff.) appear to point to the contrary view. If the Philippian church supported Paul several times while he was in Thessalonica (Phil. 4:16), sent him gifts to Corinth (2 Cor. 11:9), and helped him during his imprisonment (Phil. 4:10), then it probably supported him during his first missionary work in Philippi (cf. also Wischmeyer, *Weg*, 78f.).

15. Barrett, "Cephas," 3. The other possibility, that it refers to the brothers of Jesus and Cephas, Barrett rightly excludes.

16. So obviously also von der Osten-Sacken, "Apologie," 258; cf. already Klein, *Apostel*, 57.

17. According to Schmithals, *Gnosticism in Corinth*, 383, vv. 4–18 may not be reckoned as a defense of Paul's apostleship but only to the theme of freedom. To the contrary, the theme of "freedom" does not appear in vv. 4–18, but first in v. 19. Hock, *Context*, 60, 62, thinks 1 Corinthians 9 is a defense of Paul's work as a tentmaker. Yes, but only to the extent that his work is related to the real point disputed *theologically*, namely, Paul's apostolic office.

18. Conzelmann, *First Corinthians*, 152.

19. So, e.g., Lietzmann, *An die Korinther* 1, ad loc.; and Conzelmann, *First Corinthians*, ad loc., among others.

20. According to Dautzenberg, "Verzicht," 213, the occasion that gives rise to the arguments in 1 Cor. 9:4ff. "is more likely to be found in circles of the Corinthian church which accused Paul of selfishness and egotism in his missionary activity and leadership of the church and which perhaps also were scandalized at his weakness and features of his personality and lot." He thus argues that the interpretation given above in the text is already improbable, because already from v. 6 on the concept of apostle no longer plays a role (ibid., 213 n. 2). To the contrary, there is no trace of a defense against selfishness or the like in 1 Corinthians 9. The theme "apostleship" stands, in fact, as the heading over vv. 7ff., since *monos egō kai Barnabas* is correlated with the triad of v. 5 (the rest of the apostles, the brothers of the Lord, Cephas), and since in the following verses Paul expresses himself on the theme of apostles' *rights*.

21. Jeremias, "Chiasmus," 156 (=*Abba*, 289f.).

22. Already Barrett, *First Corinthians*, 16: "Paul had appealed to the Corinthians for voluntary limitation of their freedom and surrender of their rights. He immediately adds that he is not asking them for what he himself will not give. He has voluntarily surrendered his own apostolic rights."

23. Smith's commentary to an earlier version of the above text reads: "This analysis is not satisfactory. The primary question is *ouk eimi eleutheros?* not *ouk eimi apostolos?* The apostolicity, the vision of Jesus, the foundation of the church are all alleged as proofs *not* of themselves—ergo they were not *primarily* in question—but of Paul's freedom which was being denied. The argument of the opponents was evidently: 'Paul has not been wholly freed, he is still living in servitude to ascetic prohibitions. He dare not eat and drink (food offered to idols, or, on fast days), he dare not live with a woman, he dare not live without working, at the expense of his converts, as a true master would. All this shows he is not a true apostle of Jesus the liberator. Neither is Barnabas, who behaves like him. The other apostles and the brothers (plural, *not* James) of the Lord and Cephas do all these things and show

by their freedom, their true rank as emissaries of Jesus.'" The decisive presupposition of the above objection, namely, that there was a widespread libertine stream in early Christianity, I consider to be incorrect (cf. also Smith, *Clement*, 254–63. The evidence that he gives there for libertinism in the Pauline churches [1 Cor. 5:2; Rom. 3:8; Phil. 3:18f.] is not persuasive: see above, pp. 108f., 109f. On 1 Corinthians 5 and libertinism in Corinth, cf. the correct views of Hurd, *Origin*, 86–89, 278).

24. Differently Hock, *Context*, 64f., who in his learned book on the subject strives "to place the Corinthian controversy over Paul's tent-making as his apostolic means of support in the larger cultural context of discussions and debates regarding the appropriate means of support for a philosopher." Hock commits the same methodological error as the theological interpreters of Paul he opposes (see above, p. 255 n. 3). He does not first define who an opponent might in fact be, and he elaborates the cultural background on the basis of comprehensive parallel material, instead of first giving attention to the historical foreground, which would be required methodologically.

25. On the analysis of the missionary discourse, cf. Hahn, *Mission*, 41ff.; Georgi, *Opponents*, 165ff.; Schulz, *Q*, 404ff.; Hoffmann, *Studien*, 235ff.; and Laufen, *Doppelüberlieferungen*, 201ff., 491ff.

26. The Lukan form is more original than the Matthean (Matt. 10:11); cf. Dautzenberg, "Verzicht," 216; Schulz, *Q*, 406; Hoffmann, *Studien*, 272; and Laufen, *Doppelüberlieferungen*, 207–10, 449f. Matthew is more original, according to Dungan, *Sayings*, 56, 62 (with questionable evidence).

27. Dautzenberg, "Verzicht," 217, affirms the following with regard to the parallels between 1 Corinthians 9 and Q introduced above: "Paul argues in 9:7–13 with a series of analogies that derive from vocational and economic life; the unexpressed *tertium comparationis* is the right of the worker to be paid . . . or to a share of the products of the work. In addition, the pictures of work in the vineyard, of pasturing the flock (9:7), of plowing and threshing (9:10) are related to the same circle of motifs as the Q logion of the great harvest and few *ergatai* transmitted in the missionary discourse to the disciples (Luke 10:2/ Matt 9:37f.; cf. John 4:35 38). The saying about the *ergatēs* who is worthy of his hire is an aspect of this same pictorial complex, from which it is readily derived."

28. Cf. Schulz, *Q*, 404ff. (bib.), who of course, like many others, considers Luke 10:8b to be Lukan (ibid., 407 n. 25). Cf. to the contrary Laufen, *Doppelüberlieferungen*, 219f. Against Luke 10:8 as an element of Q, cf. Dungan, *Sayings*, 46f., 60.

29. Luz, "Logienquelle," gives a survey of recent Q scholarship.

Additional Q parallels in 1 Corinthians (esp. chaps. 1—3) are noted by Sandelin, *Auseinandersetzung*, 149–52. But the author has still not proven their *anti-Pauline* character in a single case. A faulty method is responsible (see above, p. 255 n. 3).

30. Cf. the relevant comments on this by Luz, "Logienquelle," 529. But cf. differently Laufen, *Doppelüberlieferungen*, 237ff., 511ff.

31. Dungan, *Sayings*, 7, assumes with no evidence that the brothers of the Lord had been in Corinth.

32. Barrett, *First Corinthians*, ad loc., concludes from the mention of Barnabas in this passage that Barnabas had again joined the Pauline mission after the incident in Antioch. In my opinion, the reference to Barnabas is better explained by seeing Paul's terminology as here influenced by the traditional formula (=the agreement settled on at the conference); cf. the explanation given above in the text.

33. Cf. Roloff, *Apostolat*, 62, and n. 80, whose interpretation approximates this.

34. With Lietzmann, *An die Korinther* 1, ad loc.

35. Lietzmann, *An die Korinther* 1, ad loc.

36. But cf. Kümmel, *Kirchenbegriff*, 35 n. 13: "The question of the inclusion of the brothers of Jesus in the apostolic circle must . . . remain open."

37. Paul lists himself "as a matter of course in the number of all the apostles, as the *hoi loipoi* shows" (Klein, *Apostel*, 57).

38. With the text here compare *Paul, Apostle to the Gentiles*, 46, and n. 80.

39. See the examples in von der Osten-Sacken, "Apologie," 246.

40. Cf. correctly Klein, *Apostel*, 40f.; von der Osten-Sacken, "Apologie," 249.

41. So Schmithals, *Gnosticism in Corinth*, 92 (cf. also p. 333).

42. Cf. Holl, "Kirchenbegriff," 153; and Blank, *Jesus*, 188. In any case, *ektrōma* is not an insulting term coined by his opponents, but Paul's own self-description (cf. von der Osten-Sacken, "Apologie," 249).

43. Wilckens, "Ursprung," 65 n. 21, 66 n. 23.

44. Cf. von der Osten-Sacken, "Apologie," 256 (bib.).

45. A certain difficulty for understanding this text apparently arises from the history of its tradition. For if vv. 6–7 were first added by Paul himself to this traditional formula which he had delivered to them at the time of the founding of the church, it still appears that the formula which goes back to a separate tradition ("Christ appeared to James, then to all the apostles") *alone* excludes Paul's apostleship. On the other hand, the apostleship of Cephas and the Twelve is to be presupposed (probably also that of the five hundred brethren), and it is to

be understood that the old group of the Twelve (with Cephas) has been included in the group of apostles.

46. Cf. Wellhausen, *Einleitung*, 143: "Paul distinguishes the Twelve, as the first to be granted an appearance of the Risen One, from the apostles in general (1 Cor. 15:7; cf. 9:5). He regarded them too, of course, as belonging to the apostolic group—in fact, as the leading apostles."

47. The oral character of the report that came to Paul makes the difficulty of its reconstruction even more difficult. In any case, it is necessary to keep in mind the tension that exists between the oral information conveyed to Paul and the letter of the Corinthians to Paul. The letter expressed the loyalty of the congregation of its founder (1 Cor. 11:2: the general opinion is that Paul is here quoting from the letter of the Corinthians [Hurd, *Origin*, 67f., 90f.]). That means that the anti-Paulinism can at the most have been advocated only by a minority.

48. In my opinion, a "Christ party" never existed. It is thus not discussed in the following. Cf. Pfleiderer, *Paulinismus*, 36 n. *; Reitzenstein, *Mystery-Religions*, 426–27; Hurd, *Origin*, 101–3 (survey); and Ollrog, *Paulus*, 163 n. 4.

49. The Corinthian parties are subgroups of the whole congregation; cf. Dobschütz, *Church*, 72ff., and, by the application of the methods of the social sciences (often well done), Schreiber, *Gemeinde*, 154ff. and passim (cf. further in this regard Serkland, "Dissension").

50. Cf. Munck, *Paul*, 135–67 ("The Church Without Factions"); and the survey in Hurd, *Origin*, 106ff. In my opinion, Munck falls into error when he denies any party spirit in the sense described in n. 49.

51. We are still lacking a form-critical investigation of the slogans found in 1 Cor. 1:12.

52. Weiss, *Der erste Korintherbrief*, xxxi (I am not able to understand the protest against this by Schreiber, *Gemeinde*, 157). "As long as no influence but Paul's was felt in Corinth such a slogan [i.e., "I am of Paul"] would have been meaningless" (Barrett, "Christianity," 272).

53. Thus the arguments of Ollrog, *Paulus*, 164, are seen to be rather frail, for he—like many others before him (cf. Hurd, *Origin*, 97ff.)—strives to show that the Apollos group were anti-Paulinists.

54. In my opinion, it is impossible to discover beneath the surface of 4:1ff. any sort of concrete attacks against Paul. In any case, the occurrence of the same expression (*anakrinein*) hardly suffices to identify the critics of 4:3 with those of 9:3 (in response to Weiss, *Der erste Korintherbrief*, 233, cf. Betz, *Apostel*, 103).

55. Schreiber, *Gemeinde*, 168, should have seen this passage as a challenge to his interpretation. Instead, he offers the following convoluted explanation: "Perhaps we may see here [i.e., in the inquiry con-

cerning Apollos reflected in 1 Cor. 16:12] a Corinthian compromise which is expressed in the fact that on the one hand the 'Apollos group' tolerates the letter [i.e., of the Corinthians to Paul] because it expresses their concern for a visit by Apollos to Corinth." Similarly, Sellin ("Rätsel") regards the Apollos party as the fertile soil for the anti-Paulinism in Corinth. However, he introduces the doubtful presupposition that 1 Corinthians 1—4 is a separate letter (p. 72) and puts Apollos close to the argument behind 1 Cor. 9:1ff. Apollos is "the first of the pneumatic apostles that go from one community to another" (ibid., 71). See above, p. 255, n. 3, concerning my rejection of mirror-reading which also applies to Sellin's method.

56. Cf. the survey in Hurd, Origin, 99–101.

57. Cf. now Vielhauer, "Kephaspartei," 343.

58. Cf. Vielhauer, "Kephaspartei," 351: "The claim of the Cephas group was the catalytic agent in the process of the formation of parties" (to which Theissen in ThLZ 105 [1980], col. 514, agrees).

59. Partly, this observation was already made by Lietzmann, An die Korinther, 1:16. On vv. 6–15, cf. also Ollrog, Paulus, 216ff., although, to be sure, he does not get beyond paraphrasing the text.

60. Lietzmann, An die Korinther, 1:16.

61. The function of 1 Corinthians 1—4 within 1 Corinthians is thus (unfortunately) no "apology for the Pauline apostleship" (Vielhauer, "Kephaspartei," 343, with F. C. Baur and Dahl, "Church"). Such a thesis would propose "to downplay the degree to which Paul is critical of his own adherents as well as of his opponents" (Dahl, "Church," 61 n. 50 = Appendix to reprinted essay).

62. But cf. Vielhauer, "Kephaspartei," 347: Paul had been informed by Chloe's people concerning the concept of church polity held by the Cephas party.

63. Conzelmann, First Corinthians, 32–33, and in conversation.

64. Cf. Colpe, "Religionsgeschichtliche Interpretation paulinischer Texte?" 487–94 (review article on Wilckens, Weisheit).

65. An anti-Pauline attitude of the Corinthian advocates of Cephas is best explained as the effect of external influences.

66. Cf. Conzelmann, First Corinthians, 153: the anakrinontes (still) stand outside the congregation. That is correct to the extent that it is seen that the provocation for criticism of Paul in this passage comes from outside the congregation.

67. Cf. Vielhauer, "Kephaspartei," 351: "The opposition to Paul in Corinth appears at the time of 1 Corinthians to have been limited to the Cephas party."

68. Cf. correctly Zahn, Introduction, 288–89: "It was impossible for anyone to boast with pride that he was a follower of Peter in a Church

founded by Paul, without at the same time belittling Paul. . . . These followers of Peter were responsible, at least primarily, for the aspirations against which Paul defends his apostolic dignity, even in i. 1, more clearly in ix. 1–3, and in somewhat different tone in xv. 8–10. . . . One observes that Paul knows more than he writes, and fears more than he knows."

69. Lietzmann, An die Korinther 1, ad loc.

70. Contra Conzelmann, First Corinthians, 155: "It is best not to specify the alloi, 'others,' too closely." Why not?

71. The critique of Paul was apparently not connected with the introduction of legal ritual obligations, as is postulated by Barrett, "Things," 146, and Manson, Studies, 200, with reference to the debate between the "strong" and the "weak". (The argument is supposed to have been ignited when the Cephas party wanted to introduce the Apostolic Decree.) Theissen has rightly argued against such hypotheses in "The Strong and Weak in Corinth" in Social Setting, 121–43.

72. On 1 Corinthians 12—14, cf. Wischmeyer, Weg, 27–38; and esp. Lührmann, Offenbarungsverständnis, 27–44, whose exegesis is illuminating if one takes account of the need to revise his view of assuming that there were opponents of Paul (–"Corinthian spiritualists," p. 38) behind 1 Corinthians 12—14.

73. This represents the birth of Paulinism on Gentile soil (on this, see my forthcoming volume on the theology of Paul).

74. Cf. the survey in Kümmel, Introduction, 287. Cf. now Betz, 2 Corinthians 8 and 9, 3–36.

75. It is here only presupposed that 2 Corinthians 10—13 is not a fragment of the tearful letter which comes from the period between 1 and 2 Corinthians (2 Cor. 2:3ff.; 7:8, 12). This thesis was first proposed by Hausrath, Vier-Capitel-Brief (cf. the survey in Windisch, Der zweite Korintherbrief, 12ff.; and Kümmel, Introduction, 289 n. 22). The decisive counterarguments are found in Kümmel, Introduction, 290; cf. in addition Betz, Apostel, 13f., who introduces form-critical evidence against this hypothesis.

76. Cf. Barrett, "Adikēsas," where the different interpretations are noted almost exhaustively.

77. For the evidence and arguments supporting the course of events here presupposed, cf. Paul, Apostle to the Gentiles, 93ff.

78. Barrett, "Adikēsas", 153: "Paul's narrative of the event, or rather his allusion to it, is full of obscurities, most of which arise because he knew what had happened, and knew that his readers knew what had happened, and could therefore allude rather than narrate." Barrett's hypothesis, that the "offender" was not a Corinthian, is, in my opinion, not demonstrable and in fact quite doubtful, since the congregation

could punish him. In my opinion, Barrett understands this event too much in the light of the opposition to Paul visible in 2 Corinthians 10ff. (cf. "Adikēsas", 156f.).

79. So Hausrath, *Vier-Capitel-Brief, 7f.*; and, more recently, Dobschütz, *Church,* 46–49.

80. For details, cf. *Paul, Apostle to the Gentiles,* 193–95.

81. 2 Cor. 12:17f. stands in an apologetic context (cf. the remark in 2 Cor. 12:19: "Have you been thinking all along that we have been defending ourselves before you?"). The appended list of vices (vv. 20–21) may not be used for describing the Corinthian opposition to Paul (contra Schmithals, *Gnosticism in Corinth,* 222ff.). In the first place, the (rhetorical) form, a vice catalogue, speaks against it. Thus the enumerated sexual offenses are to be considered "as particularly pagan, and hardly have any special connection with the spirituality in Corinth. Otherwise, Paul would have attacked his opponents' teaching much earlier and in quite different fashion. He thus intends to say, 'I fear I must take action against many who are still stuck fast in heathenism'" (Bultmann, *Second Corinthians,* 240); cf. his further evidence for this exegetical decision, ibid.). On 2 Cor. 12:20, cf. also *Paul, Apostle to the Gentiles,* 85f.

82. Cf. Ollrog, *Paulus,* 79–84; and above, p. 150.

83. In agreement with Lietzmann, *An die Korinther 2,* ad loc.

84. Cf. Lietzmann, *An die Korinther 2,* ad loc. Contra Bultmann, *Stil,* 67; Blass and Debrunner[14] §130$_3$ (p. 72) indicates that *phēsin* in this passage is not, as in the diatribe, an objection of the projected imaginary opponent but refers to the attack of one or more opponents in Corinth. Cf. correctly Stowers, "Reassessment," 269. The same situation obtains in Rom. 3:8 (cf. below, pp. 110f.).

85. The issues present in this text as a whole cannot be discussed here; cf. the commentaries, and Betz, "Christus-Aretalogie" (with bib.).

86. Contra Windisch, *Der zweite Korintherbrief,* who thinks the "lack of the article (namely, before *optasias*) makes it unlikely that Paul here turns to a subject that already plays an ominous role in Corinth" (p. 368). Against this view we may mention first the context (Paul "compares" himself with opponents in 2 Cor. 10:12—12:18 [see below]); against Windisch's position, cf. further Schmithals, *Gnosticism in Corinth,* 209. Thus precisely the lack of the article and the plural, "visions and revelations," speak against Windisch's view. "The subject of this paragraph is not only a certain vision of and revelation to Paul but visions and revelations in general" (Georgi, *Opponents,* 281).

87. Cf. Lührmann, *Offenbarungsverständnis,* 57.

88. This includes 1 Cor. 7:40, which cannot be taken as such evidence: "Is it a subtle thrust at the pneumatics in Corinth? An adequate

explanation is to assume that Paul is appealing to the idea of office (v. 25) and Spirit. It is not necessary to adopt the special assumption (derived from 2 Corinthians) that his possession of the Spirit had been denied in Corinth already at the time of the composition of 1 Corinthians" (Conzelmann, *First Corinthians*, 136). Cf. also pp. 79f. above.

89. Lietzmann, *An die Korinther*, 1:22.

90. In my opinion, it is not possible to accept the view of Lührmann, *Offenbarungsverständnis*, 46–48, and others, that in the adjoining passage 2 Cor. 3:7–18 Paul polemically takes up a piece of the opponents' own preaching. Cf. what is said above in the text concerning the method to be used in reconstructing the doctrine of the opponents, and for a criqitue of the particulars of Lührmann's thesis, cf. Luz, *Geschichtsverständnis*, 127–31 (bib.).

91. On the "signs of an apostle," cf. Betz, *Paulus*, 70ff. (bib.). Contra Betz, however, it should still be maintained that Paul worked miracles; cf. Rom. 15:19 as commentary on 2 Cor. 12:12; and Jervell, "Charismatiker," esp. p. 189.

92. Contra Schmithals, *Gnosticism in Corinth*, 207ff., *diakonia Christou*, "servants of Christ," was a self-designation of the opponents (with Georgi, *Opponents*, 27).

93. Cf. Georgi, *Opponents*, 41–60.

94. Cf. Georgi, *Opponents*, 41–60.

95. I am grateful to Prof. G. Klein, Münster (letter of 27 November 1980), for referring me to this important passage. His letter also led me to a revision of my earlier understanding of *hoi huperlian apostoloi* (see below, n. 98) and to a deeper engagement with Vielhauer, "Kerphaspartei,"

96. As argued by the older exegesis. Hausrath, *Vier-Capitel-Brief*, 19, e.g., assumed: 2 Corinthians 11:4 "accordingly . . . is talking about one of the twelve apostles, whom the Judaists had invited to Corinth to straighten out the confusion." Cf. further Käsemann, "Legitimität," 480ff.; and Betz, *Apostel*, 9.

97. Kümmel, in Lietzmann, *An die Korinther*, 1:210.

98. Contra Luedemann, "Antipaulinismus," 452, and, in addition to those listed there, contra Drane, *Paul*, 106; and Reitzenstein, *Mystery-Religions*, 466–67. With most recent interpreters: Hahn, "Apostolat," 58; Klein, *Apostel*, 58 n. 248; Georgi, *Opponents*, 32; Betz, *Apostel*, 121; Bultmann, "Probleme," 320; and Furnish, *II Corinthians*, 502–05. In an earlier period the correct understanding was already advocated by Pfleiderer, *Paulinismus*, 320; Wrede, *Paul*, 71 n. 1; Dobschütz, *Apostolic Age*, 106 n. 2; and Zahn, *Introduction*, 1:301. Thrall, "Super-apostles," has recently argued that the expression "superlative apostles" describes, on the one hand, the Jerusalem apostles, but that, on the other

hand, Paul used the expression for the opponents because they claimed to be apostles sent from Jerusalem. This suggestion only complicates a matter already confused.

99. Cf. Betz, *Paulus*, 100ff. (bib.).

100. The Matthean parallel (Matt. 10:8) appears to be secondary to the Lukan passage cited above (Schulz, *Q*, 406f.).

101. Cf. Lührmann, *Offenbarungsverständnis*, 59.

102. On the analysis of Matt. 11:25–27 and the understanding of revelation of the Q community, cf. Hoffmann, *Studien*, 106ff.

103. According to Friedrich, "Gegner," 193, the view argued in the text above that the opponents are from Palestine is opposed by "the appeal to miracles and visions. The rabbinic Jewish Christianity from Jerusalem was not interested in visions but in keeping the written law." The alternative "visions/keeping the law" is false. In addition, the supposition that the Jerusalem Christianity at the time of Paul was rabbinic is anachronistic.

104. Georgi, *Opponents*, 166, also discusses the interest in miracles of the missionary discourse in the Gospels are parallel to that of the anti-Paulinists of 2 Corinthians. But in my opinion he falls into error in characterizing the opponents as entirely unapocalyptic. What he supposes to be evidence for this, the nonapocalyptic missionary discourse tradition found in Mark (*Opponents*, 167), is inadequate, for the Q tradition reflected in Luke 10:2–12 is more original than the Markan form (6:7–13): cf. Schulz, *Q*, 408 n. 32. For critique of Georgi, cf. Theissen, *Social Setting*, 65 n. 53.

105. Schmithals, *Gnosticism in Corinth*, 168. On this passage (2 Cor. 11:4), cf. also Oostendorp, *Jesus*, 7–16.

106. Cf. Borse, *Standort*, 84–91.

107. Cf. Strecker, "Evangelium," 524ff. (=*Eschaton*, 204ff.). Windisch considers the triad to be rhetorical (*Der zweite Korintherbrief*, 326f.).

108. So Georgi, *Opponents*, 273.

109. Cf. Irenaeus's identification of Valentinians, Marcionites, and Ebionites, whom he conceived as a unity in his struggles with heresy.

110. It may be noted incidentally that I consider the alleged connection between the *allos Iēsous* and 2 Cor. 5:16—namely, that the opponents appealed to their contacts with the historical Jesus—to be uncertain and thus do not go into that matter further here. On the problem, cf. Georgi, *Opponents*, 252f., 273; Blank, *Paulus*, 304–26 (bib.); and Oostendorp, *Jesus*, 52–58 (bib.).

111. On the interpretation of this passage, cf., in addition to the standard commentaries, Barrett, "Christianity," 291–94; idem, "Opponents," 237f.; and Holmberg, *Paul*, 203 n. 31.

112. In my opinion, the longer reading should still be preferred: with Kümmel in Lietzmann, *An die Korinther I.II*, 208f.; Oostendorp, *Jesus*, 22f. n. 13; contra Windisch, *Der zweite Korintherbrief*, ad loc.; and Käsemann, "Legitimität," 503f., among others.

113. Cf. esp. Blank, *Paulus*, 203 n. 31.

114. Theissen, *Social Setting*, 52. The geographical understanding of *kanōn* (so Windisch, *Der zweite Korintherbrief*, 310) is to be examined critically, with Beyer, art. *"kanōn"* in *TDNT*, 3:598ff.

115. So Barrett, "Opponents," 238. Differently, Furnish, *II Corinthians*, 471f.

116. Lietzmann, *An die Korinther 2*, ad loc. Cf. also Betz, *Apostel*, 130–36.

117. Cf. esp. Lütgert, *Freiheitspredigt*, 41–47.

118. Vielhauer, *Geschichte*, 149 (followed by Kümmel, *Introduction*, 285; cf. already Windisch, *Der zweite Korintherbrief*, 26). In any case, "legalism" is not an appropriate expression for the historical description of a group and its convictions, since it is already a value judgment. Vielhauer means observance of laws of Jewish origin.

119. Cf. the argument of Davies (details of which may be disputed), *Paul*, 111ff.; and Seeberg, *Katechismus*, 1–44.

120. On proselytes and God-fearers, cf. Luedemann, *Early Christianity*, 155–56. Note that "God-fearers" is not a *terminus technicus* ("technical term") but an umbrella term to denote people interested in Judaism.

121. Further discussion of the theological and historical delineation of the anti-Paulinist position is developed below, pp. 112–15.

122. The following considerations are intended to continue the previous discussions in Luedemann, *Paul, Apostle to the Gentiles*, 44–45 and passim, from a different point of view and with different questions in mind.

123. Cf. Lührmann, "Tage."

124. Paul probably alludes here to the Jewish festival calendar (cf. the commentaries: Burton, Lagrange, Lietzmann, Oepke). In my opinion, it is inadequate to say that "the cultic activities described in v. 10 are not typical of Judaism" (Betz, *Galatians*, ad loc.). On this, cf. already Lührmann, *Galater*: "A connection between the law and the elements of the cosmos and the course of the world dependent on the stars is . . . thoroughly documented in Judaism and thus readily conceivable in the new doctrines taught at Galatia, without the need to consider foreign influences. Precisely here was found an attractive feature of the Jewish mission in behalf of the law over against paganism, because basic human questions about the nature of the cosmos were addressed—

Paul is the first to defame this by equating it with idol worship" (pp. 72f.).

125. With Burton, *Galatians*, 2; Lietzmann, *An die Galater*, 3 (Lietzmann refers, in the context of this statement made with reference to Gal. 1:1, to his exegesis of Gal. 1:13ff. but does not in fact pursue the matter in this latter passage); Lagrange, *Galates*, xxxi; and Schlier, *Der Brief an die Galater*, 28: "In Pauline terminology, he would have been in their [i.e., the opponents'] eyes something like the *apostoloi ekklēsiōn* mentioned in Rom. 16:17; 2 Cor. 8:23; and Phil. 1:25."

126. That this context is concerned with apostleship (namely, Paul's) is also indicated by Gal. 1:17: Paul did not go to those who before him had already become *apostles*.

127. In Galatians 1—2, Paul defends the independence of his apostleship and his gospel. The arguments of Howard, *Paul*, against such a thesis are not persuasive. Howard describes the function of Galatians 1—2 as follows: "Paul's account of the belatedness and infrequency of his Jerusalem visits, in our view, was to inform the Galatians that he did not tell the Jerusalem apostles of the uniqueness of his apostolic call until his fourteen-year visit. During the first three years he told them absolutely nothing" (*Paul*, 21). On this view, the Galatian opponents would have supposed that for Paul, of course, circumcision had been an essential element of his preaching (ibid., 44) and would not have attacked Paul. Paul withheld his call to be apostle to the Gentiles from the Christian congregations of Palestine and from Cephas, and first informed the congregations in Jerusalem thereof during his visit pictured in Gal. 2:1ff. (Gal. 2:2 *kata apokalypsin* is translated by Howard "on account of my initial revelation of Jesus Christ," ibid., 38). The Galatian opponents would not have known of the arrangement worked out in Jerusalem: "It no doubt took time after the initial disclosure of the revelation for the apostles to inform the church (*sic*) of the new developments in the Gentile mission" (ibid., 44).

128. So Schmithals, *Paul and the Gnostics*, 25f.

129. Cf. Luedemann, *Paul, Apostle to the Gentiles*, 45ff. (bib.).

129a. Differently Walter, "Gegner," who identifies Paul's opponents as non-Christian Jews. Why, then, does Paul take so much space to deal with his relationship to the Jerusalem Jewish *Christians* (Galatians 1—2)?

Differently also, Martyn, who in a stimulating article ("Law-Observant Mission") argues that Paul's opponents in Galatia had nothing to do with the Jerusalem Christian community but were carrying out an independent, "law-observant mission" among Gentiles. However, Martyn fails to offer a historical hook for this "law-observant mission" to the Gentiles. Unfortunately, he also lacks specificity for the "virgin fields" (ibid., 323ff.) in which Paul's opponents in Galatia are supposed to have worked.

130. The motivation for the demand of circumcision is of course disputed. Suhl, *Paulus*, 15–20, considers it to be a result of political-tactical motives: the opponents advocate circumcision so that they could boastfully present themselves in a favorable light before the Jerusalem authorities and so that they could receive the collection (similarly Jewett, "Agitators," 204ff., but without reference to the collection. On Jewett's view, see Suhl, *Paulus*, 17 n. 9). Suhl sees a parallel in the situation at Antioch. That could be correct. But since in Antioch there was no collection as an issue in the debate, some other explanation for the intervention of the people from James must be proposed (see above, pp. 38f.). So too in Galatia the determining factors for the intervention of the opponents were primarily theological. Suhl's argument (*ibid.*, 72), that Paul's reference in Gal. 2:11ff. to the common basic elements of the faith shared by Peter and Paul proves that there were no differences between Jerusalem and Paul, is to no avail. If one follows Suhl's logic, all the influential Jerusalem leaders would be Paulinists. But already at the Jerusalem Conference, Paul had to defend himself against the demand for circumcision of Gentile converts. Which political factors were brought into play there? When Paul could successfully resist the demand for circumcision, why would he still be asked to take a collection at all? Marxsen, *Einleitung*, 70, adopts the view of Suhl with regard to the position of the opponents in Galatia. He writes: "Now it was forbidden to the Jews to accept gifts from the Gentiles (as Suhl, 18ff., shows—in dependence on M. Hengel, *Zeloten* [1961], 204–11)" (ibid.). A risky retrojection of a law from immediately before the outbreak of the Jewish War has resulted in a generalization that is certainly false.

131. Lütgert, *Gesetz*. His view was adopted by Ropes, *Problem*.

132. Contra Lütgert, *Gesetz*, 12ff. Cf. Betz, "Geist," 80.

133. In response to Lutgert, *Gesetz*, 17ff.

134. Schmithals, *Paul and the Gnostics*, adopts Lütgert's thesis but in contrast to Lütgert wants to see only one opposing front. Since he follows Lütgert on the question of libertinism as discussed above, the objections mentioned there also apply to Schmithals. Drane too (in *Paul*, 78–94) gives an extensive argument rightly rejecting the view of Galatians advocated by Lütgert, Ropes, and Schmithals (although with a line of argument that is in part problematical). But Drane's reconstruction is still unsatisfactory, because then the Judaists in Galatia are still seen as false *brethren* (in the most true sense of the word) who had

no support from the Jerusalem leaders. In addition, Drane regards Galatians—misguidedly—as the oldest Pauline letter (ibid., 116ff., 140ff.; Gal. 2:1–10 = Acts 11:27–30).

135. Plato, *Apol.* 21B; 21C; 35A. Cf. further passages in Barrett, "Paul," 2f.

136. Euripides, *Hec.* 294f.

137. 1 Cor. 3:18; 8:2; 10:2; 2 Cor. 10:9; 12:19. The best parallel is found in Gal. 6:3: *ei gar dokei tis einai ti mēden ōn, phrenapata heauton.* Cf. also Phil. 3:4.

138. For the translation of *esan* with the present tense, cf. Luedemann, *Paul, Apostle to the Gentiles,* 69, 120 n. 78.

139. Contra Lietzmann, *An die Galater,* 10.

140. For a similar view, cf. Oepke, *Galater,* 212f. Slightly different, Watson, *Paul,* 58–61: Paul's opponents in Galatia are to be identified with the "men from James" (Gal. 2:12).

141. Luedemann, *Paul, Apostle to the Gentiles,* 86.

142. The decision advocated by Ritschl is thus too hasty. Cf. idem, *Entstehung,* 128 n. 1: "The interpretation of the standpoint of the original apostles depends on the dilemma: we evaluate them either from the standpoint of the Judaizing Christian party which regards them as authorities or from the standpoint of the New Testament scriptures. I choose the latter basis . . . precisely because the Epistle of the Galatians proves that the opponents of Paul in Galatia knew they were lying when they appealed to the original apostles."

143. Important textual witnesses read *peritetmēmenoi.* The translation would then be unambiguous: "those who have been circumcised" = Jews. For text-critical grounds for the originality of the present tense, cf. Richardson, *Israel,* 84ff.

144. Hirsch, "Fragen," 193. For a criqitue of Hirsch, cf. Holtzmann, "Hirsch"; and Goguel, "Apôtre, 483–88. Previously de Wette, *Lehrbuch,* 222, had expressed the same opinion as Hirsch with regard to Gal. 6:13 (and 5:12).

145. Hirsch, "Fragen," 194.

146. Cf. Jewett, "Agitators," 202f.; and Smith, "Problems," 119f. n. 20. For further discussion, cf. Howard, *Paul,* 17ff. In my opinion, Betz, *Galatians,* 316, is too skeptical with regard to the question here broached.

147. Cf. Gal. 2:3; Josephus, *Vita* 113.

148. Lührmann, *Offenbarungsverständnis,* 67 n. 1.

149. Jewett, "Agitators," 202.

150. Cf. correctly Holtzmann, "Hirsch," 78.

151. Schmithals, *Paul and the Gnostics,* 33.

152. Cf. the survey in Kümmel, *Introduction*, 324-32.

153. Cf. the survey in Kümmel, *Introduction*, 332-95.

154. Gnilka, *Philippians*, 21.

155. Dibelius, *An die Philipper*, ad loc.

156. Contra Dibelius, *An die Philipper*, ad loc., who sees Paul as speaking here of experiences he has had in different places with different groups of Christian preachers.

157. Cf. *phthonos*: Rom. 1:29; Gal. 5:21; *eris*: Rom. 1:29; 13:13; 2 Cor. 12:20; *eritheia*: 2 Cor. 12:20; Gal. 5:20. The three terms are standard elements in Paul's vice catalogues and thus provide no information concerning the concrete views of his opponents in particular cases. *Prophasis* is likewise a polemical slogan word in 1 Thess. 2:5.

158. On the following, cf. Gnilka, *Philippians*, ad loc.

159. The majority (Phil. 1:14) remained loyal to Paul.

160. A survey of the different interpretations is found in Gnilka, *Philippians*, 55f. It is worthy of note that Vincent, *Philippians*, ad loc., considers Paul's critics in this passage to be Paulinists themselves. On this, cf. the following note.

161. The most recent attempt, by Ollrog, *Paulus*, 194-96, to understand the controversy reflected in Phil. 1:14-18 as one going on among Paul's own fellow missionaries (Paul supposedly alluding to the critics among them in 2:21) is, in my opinion, not probable. *Hoi pantes* (2:21) can hardly be identified with *hoi pleiones* (1:14: the majority still loyal to Paul), despite Ollrog, *Paulus*, 196.

162. It is still to be noticed, however, that in this "conciliatory" conclusion Paul characterizes the activity of his opponents polemically with *en prophasei*.

163. In any case, it is certain that the opponents in this passage were *not* Jews, who had sought to cause Paul trouble by preaching Christ (so Suhl, *Paulus*, 173; against this thesis, cf. Müller in ThLZ 101 [1976], col. 927).

164. The arguments against the hypothesis that the opponents were Jews are convincingly given by Gnilka, *Philippians*, ad loc. (cf. already Vincent, *Philippians*, ad loc.), contra Lütgert, *Vollkommenen*, 7ff., and others. At the time of Paul, a Gentile Christian congregation was hardly in danger of converting to Judaism but rather to a Jewish Christianity. But to the extent that Paul attacks Jewish Christians, he also of course attacks Jews (response to Lütgert, *Vollkommenen*, 8).

165. In addition, there are even other verses or expressions that are claimed as evidence for reconstructing the views of the opponents: e.g., Koester, "Purpose," 324 (with appeal to Bultmann's article "*ginō-skō*" in *TDNT*, 1:689ff.), regards the terms *gnōsis* (v. 8) and *ginōskein* (v.

10) as reflections of the opponents' teaching. But these terms appear in other passages as well (2 Cor. 1:14 and often) and thus should, rather, be regarded as Pauline.

166. Gnilka, *Philipperbrief*, 214. Cf. Betz, *Nachfolge*, 151 and often.

167. Koester, "Purpose," 331.

168. Here one sees the relative correctness of Lohmeyer's martyr hypothesis, *Philipper*, passim.

169. Dibelius, *An die Philipper*[2], 71.

170. Schmithals, *Gnosticism in Corinth*, 224.

171. Koester, "Purpose," 324, 327.

172. So Dibelius, *An die Philipper*, ad loc., correctly.

173. Cf. Beare, Philippians, 109f.; and Collange, *Philippiens*, 28–30.

174. Cf. Matt. 10:10/Luke 10:7, a tradition that also stands in the background in 1 Cor. 9:6ff. (see above, p. 69).

175. On this, cf. Georgi, *Opponents*, 40: "Although the functional designation is consistent with 2 Cor. 11:13, it is a mistake to assume the same circle of opponents in both cases. Today not all questionable ministers belong to the same movement or group either." Unfortunately Georgi does not take into account that additional parallels are also present (see above). Contra Georgi, correctly, Ellis, *Prophecy*, 120 n. 21.

175a. Similarly, Watson, *Paul*, 74–80: Paul's opponents are Judaizers and are to be equated with the "men from James" (Gal. 2:12) who had already invaded the Galatian congregation.

176. Cf. the standard introductions and commentaries; Suhl, *Paulus*, 264–82; and K. P. Donfried, ed., *The Romans Debate* (Minneapolis: Augsburg, 1977).

177. Cf. Bultmann, *Stil*, and the important work of Stowers, *Reassessment*, which developes Bultmann's work further.

178. Bornkamm, "Römerbrief," 125; cf. idem, *Paul*, 89–90.

179. Cf. Rom. 3:1, 3, 5 (2x), 7, 8, 9, 31; 6:1, 15; 7:7, 13; 9:14, 19; 11:1, 11, 19; cf. also Stowers, *Reassessment*, 181–234.

180. Bultmann, *Stil*, 67.

181. Cf., e.g., Vielhauer, *Geschichte*, 183ff., and Kümmel, *Introduction*, 314f., who with most scholars see an attack against Paul reflected here. It is, however, methodologically unsatisfactory that Rom. 3:8 is both mixed in with the other objections conditioned by the style of the diatribe (see above, n. 179) and that concrete attacks against Paul are seen to be reflected here.

182. On this, cf. Bornkamm, "Theologie"; Jeremias, "Gedankenführung," 146f. (=*Abba*, 269f.); and the commentaries. The most recent contribution that I have seen in Räisänen, *Torah*, 185–203, who does not pay special attention to Rom. 3:8.

183. "Most commentaries understand *kai mē* as a continuation of the question *ti kagō . . . krinomai:* but then it would have to continue *kai ouchi* (namely, *poioumen) kathōs blasphēmoumetha . . .*" (Lietzmann, *An die Römer,* ad loc.).

184. Cf. Moxnes, *Theology in Conflict,* 58ff.

185. Contra Smith, *Clement,* 259: Rom. 3:8 "looks from the context as if it were said by libertines who claimed that Paul's teaching agreed with theirs; cf. also Rom. 6:1, 15-23." Cf. the similar views expressed previously by Lütgert, *Römerbrief,* on which see H. Pachali.

186. This view is still advocated by Weizsäcker, *Apostolic Age,* 2:108f., with the reworking of his earlier essay, "Über die älteste Römische Christengemeinde," in *JDTh* 21 (1876), 248–310. Similarly, still M. Kettunen, *Der Abfassungszweck des Römerbriefes* (Helsinki, 1979), 182–89.

187. In response to Schmithals, *Römerbrief,* 44: "Where and by whom these charges were spoken, Paul does not say." Schmithals considers them to be Jewish objections (ibid., 90). A Jewish-Christian origin does not come in question for him, because "a Judaist countermission among the Gentile Christians never existed" (ibid., 44). For the contrary view, see above, chapters 3 and 4.

CHAPTER 5. ANTI-PAULINISM IN JERUSALEM AND IN THE PAULINE CHURCHES

1. Cf. most recently Manson, *Studies,* 216; and Barrett, "Controversies," 232f. Such a construction attracts criticism in that it "is willing to admit less direct and more problematic evidence, and to proceed by hypothesis and even conjecture. It is probably better, however, to operate with a general identification of Paul's rivals based on relatively clear and unambiguous evidence—and which is therefore reasonably certain—than with a more specific but essentially hypothetical identification which must tease details out of difficult and ambiguous texts" (Furnish, *II Corinthians,* 54). I fear lest Furnish's "genera identification" is too broad to be of help for identifying the issues at Corinth as far as Paul's relationship of his opponents is concerned. Equally unsatisfactory are Meeks's sporadic remarks on Paul's opponents: Meeks complains that the "ghost of Baur had been raised again recently" (*Urban Christians,* 223 n. 41) and that his "assumption of a single, unified, Jewish Christian, antipauline movement in the first century [is] an unnecessary inference from the sources, and not the most economical way of accounting for what little evidence we have" (ibid.). According to Meeks, the "original apostles of Jerusalem . . .

seem to have had little or no direct authority so far as the Pauline churches were concerned" (ibid., 132). "The reformers who followed him [i.e., Paul] into Galatia must have been independent of Jerusalem too, or Paul's counterarguments in Galatians 1—2 would make little sense" (ibid.). "What the Corinthians meant who called themselves Cephas's (1 Cor. 1:12; 3:21f.) we cannot know, but there is no evidence of any attempt by Peter or agents of his to claim authority over Pauline congregations" (ibid.). Where the rivals of 2 Corinthians "came from we do not know, for there is nothing in the text to connect them with Jerusalem" (ibid., 132). My first point of criticism is that Meeks's statements are not argued at all. Therefore, I have not dealt with them in the text and trust that the reader will detect these inadequacies. Second, I find it disappointing that Meeks, in a work that purports to be historical (cf., e.g., ibid., 132) hardly ever asks the classic historical questions of why, whence, and when and simply refuses to reconstruct a historical sequence. That is to say, Meeks's brilliant analysis of the social world of Paul has to be supplemented by a necessary hypothetical reconstruction of the whereabouts of Paul's opponents. Otherwise, unless embedded in the history of early Christianity, it becomes theory and not history.

2. But note what was said above with regard to anti-Paulinism as an inner-Corinthian phenomenon (pp. 79f., 84f.).

3. Although it is not demonstrable (and thus is not utilized in this study), the lack of the demand for circumcision could have been determined by the following factors, e.g.: "At Corinth precisely this ritual [i.e., baptism] had been accepted with such approval that here the Judaists did not dare to come out with the demand for circumcision at the same time that the Corinthians were even beginning to introduce . . . a posthumous vicarious baptism for believers who had died without being baptized" (Holtzmann, Lehrbuch, 1:451).

4. Contra Schmithals, Gnosticism in Corinth, 378, who comes to this conclusion only on the basis of questionable methodological bases in his reconstruction of the opponents (for critique, see chapter 4, above). Cf. further Georgi, Opponents, 238, 290 n. 72.

5. This point is often overlooked in discussions of the Gentile mission of Peter or the like; cf., e.g., Hengel, "Mission," 52, 170 n. 24.

6. But cf. now Betz, "2 Cor"; idem, Galatians, 329f.; and Betz's works on the Sermon on the Mount (see Bib.) Because of the method adopted in this study, I will not here discuss Betz's results, since the sources reconstructed by him are not explicitly anti-Pauline (cf. also p. 30, above, with p. 233, n. 247). In addition, the Sermon on the Mount is not a source but Matthean composition.

7. It is nevertheless sometimes assumed that the Corinthian anti-

Paulinists—differently than in the case of the Galatian opponents—had at first been hesitant concerning the demand for circumcision (thus, e.g., Pfleiderer, *Paulinismus*, 317; and Goguel, "Apôtre," 480f. [and cf. above, n. 3].

8. Cf. above, chapter 4, n. 142.

9. Cf. Goguel, "Apôtre," 500. The same applies to the question of support for the Corinthian anti-Paulinists in Jerusalem.

10. Cf. Holl, "Kirchenbegriff," 162.

11. Holl, "Kirchenbegriff," 174.

12. Luz now supports this view. Cf. his essay in R. Smend and U. Luz, *Gesetz* (Stuttgart, 1981), 75–79.

CHAPTER 6. ANTI-PAULINISM
OF THE *DESPOSYNOI*

1. On the term *desposynoi*, cf. Weiss, *Earliest Christianity*, 2:716ff. n. 15, who renders it with "sons of the house" (cf. similarly Achelis, *Christentum*, 1:226, "children of the house"). Differently Knopf, *Zeitalter*, 27, who translates the concept with "those belonging to the Lord" (which was already rejected by Weiss, ibid.).

2. On the *desposynoi*, cf. Schlatter, *Synagoge*, 111ff., but ho is to bo read with critical caution, since he knows too much; Réville, *Origines*, 214–25 (the critique by Loofs in ThLZ 21 [1896], col. 207, against Réville's thesis that a "legitimist conception" had been advocated in Jerusalem is not persuasive: the Réville and Loofs controversy is strongly reminiscent of that between Stauffer and von Campenhausen—see above, pp. 119f.); McGiffert, *History*, 563ff.; Goguel, *Birth*, 133ff.; and Achelis, *Christentum*, 1:226f.

3. Zahn, *Forschungen*, 6:236, prefers to translate "an uncle of James," which does not affect the sense of the passage.

4. Trans. by M. Eugene Boring from the German; a paraphrase of this text, from Eusebius's own pen, is found in *Hist. Ecc.* 3.11.

5. We are here speaking in general terms: after James, Simeon was the leading figure in the Jerusalem church.

6. Cf. Zahn, *Forschungen*, 281–301; Turner, "Lists"; and Andresen, *Kirchen*, 214.

7. Cf. Strecker, "Christentum," 463f. n. 47 (bib.) (=*Eschaton*, 296f. n. 47).

8. One example is presented by Eusebius, *Hist. Ecc.* 5.24.6, as an exception: seven of the relatives of Polycrates of Ephesus had been bishops. He was the eighth. Cf. the commentary by Stauffer, "Kalifat," 200.

9. This family connection with Jesus is the only basis for his being chosen: contra von Campenhausen, "Nachfolge," 143: Hegesippus underscores "the appropriateness of the choice of Simeon by the fact that . . . the unanimous choice was in addition [!] a relative of Jesus, just as James had been."

10. Cf. Zahn, *Forschungen*, 241–43. The summaries composed by Eusebius himself (32.1–3a4) here remain out of consideration.

11. Cf. below, pp. 164ff.

12. Cf. below, p. 120.

13. This is the tendency of von Campenhausen, "Nachfolge," 143.

14. Cf. the illustrations in Stauffer, "Kalifat," 194ff.

15. Lines 3–6 are a summary composed of Eusebius himself: see Zahn, *Forschungen*, 240ff.

16. Translation here and in the following is from the Loeb Classical Library. On the text, cf. Pöhlmann, *Opposition*, 416–25.

17. Our procedure has, of course, the methodological weakness of considering the *tradition* to be largely historical. But in view of the paucity of sources, we must give this one due consideration. On this problem, cf. also Gustafsson, "Sources."

18. I am presupposing that the anecdote was not composed at the same time as the summons to appear before Domitian (between 81 and 96 C.E.).

19. Cf. Wrede, *Vorträge*, 155 n. 1; Meyer, *Ursprung*, 73 n. 2; Burger, *Jesus*, 123–27; and Vermes, *Jesus*, 156f. Hahn, *Titles*, 229, 266 n. 5, expresses a different point of view on the episode discussed in the text above.

20. Burger, *Jesus*, 165.

21. Stauffer, "Kalifat," 199, defends the Davidic descent of Judas' grandsons with the consideration that they would "hardly [namely, have claimed their own Davidic descent] . . . if they had not in fact been convinced of it in all seriousness. An ancient Palestinian Jew and small farmer would come forth with pious fiction only *in conspectu mortis* at the latest." But Stauffer errs in a one-sidedly historicizing direction. The first task is to determine the redactional meaning of the text before the question of the (reliable) historical kernel in the tradition can be raised.

22. In Palestine and possibly Galilee, although that does not stand explicitly in the text: cf. Lohmeyer, *Galiläa*, 54.

23. On Domitian's political policies with regard to Jews and Christians, cf. Conzelmann, *Gentiles*, 31ff. (bib.); and Keresztes, "Jews," 1–28.

24. The next sentence proves that reliable reports are being presented here: "I recall being present in my youth when the person of a

man ninety years old was examined before the procurator and a very crowded court, to see whether he was circumcised."

25. Cf. Conzelmann, *Gentiles*, p. 31, n. 89; and Grant, *Christianity*, 51.

26. *tous proēgoumenous hēmōn aidesthōmen*. On this passage, cf. Weidinger, *Haustafel*, 55.

27. I cannot understand how von Campenhausen, "Nachfolge," 135 n. 17, can argue that this is not a technical term.

28. *Pas* without a following article is so to be translated (cf. Blass and Debrunner[14] § 275₂); in response to von Campenhausen, "Nachfolge," 135.

29. Thus Weiss's suggestion in *Earliest Christianity* 2:721 n. 23, that an article after *pasē* had been omitted from the text of Hegesippus, is unnecessary.

30. Contra Zahn, *Forschungen*, 300 (followed by von Campenhausen, "Nachfolge," 135, with n. 17): "The meaning is only that they immediately enjoyed respect and influence in every church in which they visited, since they had offered their testimony before the authorities and were relatives of the Lord." This is mistaken, since it does not take account, among other things, of the expression *proēgeomai*.

31. Although it cannot be proved, one can at least ask whether the emphasis on their role as witnesses belonged at all to the tradition that came to Hegesippus.

32. *Te* belongs to the original text (cf. Schwartz's edition). I have here translated it with "also" in order to bring out its associative sense. The meaning is obviously: They explained the previously mentioned genealogy (of the evangelists), and referred to the books of Chronicles in a supplementary way.

33. Edition: W. Reichardt, TU 34.3 (Leipzig, 1909). For our purposes we will henceforth quote from the excerpt in Eusebius.

34. The basis for this is the Jewish institution of levirite marriage (cf. Deut. 25:5f.).

35. Cf. *Hist. Ecc.* 1.7.15: "In any case, the gospel speaks the truth."

36. It is given in detail in *Hist. Ecc.* 1.7.11.

37. Cf. Johnson, *Purpose*, 103.

38. Knopf, *Zeitalter*, 7 (Weiss, *Earliest Christianity*, 599 n. 1). Knopf continues: "all of these being things which are not particularly significant for the history of Jewish Christianity itself." This observation is correct and should have made Knopf wonder whether the "daily log" of Jesus' relatives had in fact ever existed at all.

39. Cf. M. Sachs, *Beiträge zur Sprach- und Alterthumsforschung* (Berlin, 1854), 156, as well as the translation in the edition of Eusebius in the LCL by Lake: "They traversed the rest of the land and ex-

pounded the preceding genealogy of their descent, and from the book of Chronicles so far as they went." Cf. furtehr Schwartz, *Eusebius*, 58 n. 2.

40. Cf. Jeremias, *Jerusalem*, 281f., who is inclined to consider the report historical anyway.

41. So correctly Johnson, *Purpose*, 103. Contra Kraft, *Entstehung*, 75, who even thinks that in the period between 44 c.e. and 66 c.e. Jesus' family had restored their family records from Herod's destruction. (Kraft considers Africanus's report to be historically reliable.)

42. Cf. Jeremias, *Jerusalem*, 270ff., and the critical examination of Jeremias's theses by Johnson, *Purpose*, 99–108, esp. p. 105: "Our conclusions regarding the references to genealogical records of the laity must . . . be somewhat negative."

43. On the significance and use of Chronicles in the Judaism contemporary with Jesus, cf. Jeremias, *Jerusalem*, 281f. Luke, and especially Matthew, had already latched on to these OT books.

44. The historical value of Africanus's Cochaba tradition is enhanced by the fact "that Julius Africanus does not know where one would try to locate Cochaba: he simply describes it as a Jewish . . . city" (Knopf, *Zeitalter*, 14).

45. Harnack, *Mission*, 2:102 n. 3; trans. by M. Eugene Boring from the German. Also Bagatti, *Church*, 21, 25, distinguishes a Cochaba in Galilee from the one in east Jordan (and further distinguishes this one from a Cochaba near Damascus; see below, n. 53).

46. Cf. Zahn, *Forschungen*, 1:333f.

47. Cf. Schmidtke, *Fragmente*, 234.

48. On the concept "Ebionites," cf. chapter 12 below. In the following, it is used in the sense of "anti-Pauline Jewish Christians."

49. In response to Zahn, *Forschungen*, 1:334f.: "The decisive objection against this is, namely, the clear distinction between Kokab (Choba), which is located near Damascus, and the Cochaba of Epiphanius in the *Onomasticon* of Eusebius, the residence of the Ebionites. The abbreviated writing of the name, and the vagueness in describing its location, may be an indication that Eusebius was less precisely informed on this matter than Epiphanius. But according to this passage he must have known enough about the residence of the Ebionites, which he did not locate in the neighborhood of Damascus, to distinguish it from a place of the same name near Damascus."

50. Cf. the commentaries on Gen. 14:15. The point of orientation was eastward.

51. Cf., e.g., Kneucker, in the Schenkel *Bibellexikon*, 519: "The small village Kokab [Choba], 2 3/4 hours southwest of Damascus, has

been confused with the old Choba; but this contradicts the prevailing linguistic convention ('left'='north')".

52. I have not found a single instance in the preserved writings of Eusebius in which the expression "left of" is used with reference to a point of the compass.

53. So, e.g., Bagatti, Church, 25; and Lipsius, Quellenkritik, 136f. According to Schoeps, Theologie, 273, Eusebius locates it west of Damascus. Guthe, Bibelatlas, no. 14, locates Kokab about ten km southwest of Damascus.

54. Cf. Plutarch, Moralia 363 E. 729B. I am grateful for these references to Larry L. Welborn, McCormick Theological Seminary. Cf. already Sophocles, Lexicon, entry "aristera."

55. Cf. further Avi-Yonah, Land, 167f., who refers to a village in Batanaea called Kaukab mentioned in the rabbinic literature.

56. In response to Bagatti, Church, 26, who distinguishes the Cochaba of Epiphanius from that of Eusebius.

57. The traditional character of this text is not sufficiently noticed even by Freyne, Galilee, 353. In the context of a discussion of Eusebius, Hist. Ecc. 1.7.14f., he asks whether connections existed between Galilean and Transjordan Jewish Christians, but responds negatively: "Admittedly, it is precarious evidence upon which to build an hypothesis about the situation a century earlier." But where does Freyne get his information that the Nazareth tradition derives from the second century?

58. On this, cf. Gelzer, Sextus Julius Africanus und die byzantinische Chronographie, vol. 1: Die Chronographie des Julius Africanus, 1–19.

59. "In any case, Cochaba, along with Pella, was a very old settlement of Transjordanian Jewish Christianity" (Knopf, Zeitalter, 14).

60. Cf. correctly Brandt, Elchasai, 52.

61. "Apostolum Paulum recusant, apostatam eum legis dicentes" ("They repudiate the apostle Paul, maintain that he was an apostate from the law").

CHAPTER 7. THE ANTI-PAULINISM OF THE ELKESAITES

1. Strecker, "Elkesai," has assembled the best collection of sources. Cf. further Irmscher, "Elchasai"; Klijn and Reinink, Evidence, 54–67; Rudolph, Mandäer, 233–52; idem, Baptisten, 13–17; Thomas, Mouvement, 140–56; Waitz, "Buch"; and Elsas, Weltablehnung, 34–39 (his-

tory-of-religions approach); an article by Harnack from 1877 is still worthy of note, which he published later as an appendix to his history of dogma (Harnack, *Lehrbuch*, 2:529–38, esp. 534ff. [Islam and Jewish Christianity, esp.Elkesaitism]). A classic older work is Brandt, *Elchesai* (on which see Harnack in ThLZ 37 [1912], cols. 638f.), which offers a history of research on pp. 155–66; cf. already Brandt, *Baptisten*, 99–112. Cf. now the comprehensive study, Luttikhuizen, *Revelation*. In my opinion, despite its interesting history of research (pp. 1–37) and its detailed analysis of all the possible texts, Luttikhuizen's work is a step back behind Strecker. (Cf. the critical review by F. Stanley Jones in JAC 30[1987]: 200–209.) Since, in addition, Luttikhuizen does not deal with an anti-Paulinism of the Elkesaites, I have not entered into a discussion with him.

2. English translation by Lake in LCL, 2:91–93.

3. The novelty argument served in the ancient church's struggle against heresy to disqualify the opponents: cf. only two illustrations, Tertullian, *Adv. Val.* 4; *Can. Mur.* 73–80. Thus the statement in the preceding text, "which has lately come into opposition with the churches," is to be considered historically worthless polemic (in response to Schoeps, *Theologie* 326). The final sentence can be recognized even more easily as polemic, for every heresy brings "a forgiveness other than that which Jesus Christ has bestowed."

4. Since Epiphanius's report of the Sampsaei, who are certainly connected to the Elkesaites (*Heresies* 53.1.7: *oute prophētas dechontai hoi tououtoi oute apostolous* . . . [315.22f., Holl's edition]), has the plural *apostolous*, it can hardly be regarded as rejection of *Paul*.

5. Cf. Klijn and Reinink, *Evidence*, 61; and Koester, *Introduction*, 2:205. That Hippolytus did not report anything about anti-Paulinism among the Elkesaites is insiginificant, since in contrast to Irenaeus (*Heresies*, 1.26.2) he also suppresses the Ebionites' rejection of Paul (*Ref.* 7.34.1–2).

6. We know no anti-Paulinism from Jewish sources. One possible exception (*Aboth* 3:12) is discussed by Kittel, "Paulus im Talmud"; cf. Billerbeck, *Kommentar*, 2:753ff.; and Urbach, *Sages*, 295f. Even less certain allusions to Paul are discussed by Hirschberg, "Paulus im Midrasch."

7. In general, this hypothesis is advocated by those scholars who consider Elkesai to be a non-Christian prophetic figure and regard Alcibiades as belonging to the second (Christian) layer of the Elkesaite religion. So, e.g., Brandt, *Elchasai*, chap. 6: "The Mission in the West and the Christianization of the Book of Elchasai" (pp. 76–100).

8. We may incidentally note that the relevant chapters are found in the sections of the *Refutation* which are not suspect (=those passages

which do not stand out because of their noticeable similarity to each other; on this, cf. Staehelin, *Quellen*).

9. The text of Hippolytus (including the numbering system and emphases) used here is *ANF*, vol. 5. The numbers in parentheses represent the page and line numbers of the edition of the *Refutation* by Paul Wendland (GCS 26) (compare the edition of Miroslav Marcovich, PTS 25 [1986]).

10. Shortly after this it is reported that the book had been revealed through an angel (13.2: *chrēmatistheisan hypo angelou* [p. 251.14]). Klijn and Reinink, *Evidence*, think that "two different observations about the origin of this book have been confused. One of them probably spoke of it originating among the Seres, a legendary people, and the other about it having been inspired by an angel" (p. 55). To the contrary: the two descriptions of the origin of the book are to be understood cumulatively and not as alternatives. In apocalyptic thought, a book inspired by an angel has a mysterious origin. Apocalyptic motifs can thus provide no criteria for decisions that must be made on the basis of literary criticism and tradition criticism. As a point of comparison, note the different transmitters of the summons to flee to Pella (cf. above, pp. 203f.). Here no one would suppose that this is a basis for presupposing that different sources of traditions must have been used. The discussion by Reinink, "Land," 84f., is more appropriate to the issue.

11. Translation from *ANF* 5.132.

12. Translation from *ANF* 5.132.

13. Contra Klijn and Reinink, *Evidence*, 56, who see Alcibiades's preaching reflected in chap. 13, which is to be distinguished from the Book of Elkesai. Although they made good efforts in the right direction, the authors did not analyze Hippolytus's report with enough precision. They proceed on the basis of the doubtlessly correct assumption: "We are certain however that the particular situation in Rome at that time influenced his [i.e., Alcibiades's] preaching" (ibid.). But this still says nothing at all concerning the literary form of the text, even if Hippolytus later mentions that Alcibiades had been an amazing translator (*hermeneus*) of Elkesai (17.2 [p. 253.16]). On the contrary, it is important to emphasize that in 17.3 (unfortunately not cited by the authors) Hippolytus comes back to his intention of quoting excerpts from the revelatory book: *dokei toinyn hikana einai pros epignōsin ta eirēmena tēs toutōn manias* (p. 255.17f.).

14. It is in any case entirely to be expected that already at the beginning Hippolytus partly quotes from the Book of Elkesai, although he was at first concerned only to describe Alcibiades's manner of life, and nevertheless in the summary comment above (9.13.6) does not

refer to this citation with a single word, for it is hardly conceivable that the appearance of Alcibiades in Rome could have occurred without some reference to the contents of the revelatory book.

15. On this, cf. Peterson, *Frühkirche*, 221–35 ("Die Behandlung der Tollwut bei den Elchasaiten nach Hippolyt").

16. Translations of both citations from *ANF*, 5.131–32.

16a. Hippolytus's report contains the following additional quotations: 9.10 (p. 253.26—254.15); 9.11 (p. 254.21—255.5); 9.12 (p. 255.6–11).

17. Cf. Strecker, "*Elkesai*," *col. 1179* [=*Eschaton*, 327], against Schmidtke, *Fragmente*, 188 n. 1.

18. Contra Klijn and Reinink, *Evidence*, 58. In case the demand for circumcision should not after all go back to the earliest stage of the Elkesaites (the mother church of Mani appears not to have practiced it, and no report of Mani known to me affirms his circumcision; see below, p. 285 n. 51), the Jewish Christian character of the Elkesaites would still of course remain unchanged. Cf. above, p. 136, on their Jewish Christian praxis.

19. On this, cf. already Lipsius, *Quellenkritik*, 145ff.

20. It is here presupposed that Epiphanius is not simply copying Hippolytus. This is not assumed by Klijn and Reinink, *Evidence*, 63.

21. Strecker, "Elkesai," col. 1184 [=*Eschaton*, 331].

22. Strecker, "Elkesai," col. 1184 [=*Eschaton*, 331].

23. Cf. Strecker, "Elkesai," col. 1184 [=*Eschaton*, 331]. In addition, the description of Elkesai as *dikaios* (Hippolytus, *Ref.* 9.8 [p. 251.13]) is analogous to the description of James as "the Just."

24. It is also clear that the Elkesaites practiced a kind of dynastic principle. We read in Epiphanius, *Pan.* 19.2.12 and 53.1.2, 5ff., of two sisters who were venerated because they came from the family of Elkesai. This fits in with the previous chapter's discussion of the *desposynoi* with regard to a dynastic Jewish Christianity and can thus only strengthen the case for the Jewish Christian character of the Elkesaites.

25. It is a completely different issue whether this Jewish Christianity, evaluated in phenomenological terms, is also to be considered Judaism. But an affirmative answer is also to be given to this question.

26. This is also the original direction in which Mohammed instructed that prayer should be made. Cf. the texts in Jefferey, *Islam*, 172–74.

27. Cf. also Brandt, *Elchasai*, 11f.; and Urbach, *Sages*, 61. In my opinion, the quotation from the Book of Elkesai, which Epiphanius has formulated in indirect speech, does not begin until the sentence "In whatever place one is praying, one must turn the face toward Jerusalem." The beginning of *Pan.* 19.3.5 ("For he forbids praying in the

direction of the East, saying that one has to turn one's face from all regions to Jerusalem") corresponds well to the redaction of the church father who had seen a contradiction in the prayer instructions of the Book of Elkesai and the Christian custom of praying while facing east. This "contradiction" is, however, chronologically impossible, since at the beginning of the second century there was not yet any prescribed direction for posture in prayer. In addition, that this "contradiction" goes back to the church father Epiphanius himself may also be seen from the continuation of the citation quoted above: "those in the East have to turn to the West and those in the West to the East in the direction of Jerusalem, in the same way those in the North to the South and those in the South to the North in order that a man in all regions faces Jerusalem" (trans. from Klijn and Reinink, *Evidence*).

28. This datum hardly justifies the chronological conclusions drawn by Waitz, *Pseudoklementinen*: "The book's prescription, that prayer should not be made to the east but always in the direction of Jerusalem, presupposes that Jerusalem had not yet been profaned by the abomination perpetrated against the Holy City by the erection of the statue of Jupiter Capitolinus by Hadrian (135). All of this proves that the Book of Elkesai was written while Trajan was still emperor, in any case before 135" (pp. 158f.; so also Waitz, "Buch," 101). Against this view: The Jews continued to pray toward Jerusalem even after its profanation, and the oldest synagogues known to us from the third and fourth centuries are so constructed that the worshipers face Jerusalem while praying. Cf. *Enc. Jud.*, vol. 15, cols. 597f.; and on the question of the direction faced during prayer in Judaism, Christianity, and Islam, cf. Peterson, *Frühkirche*, 1–14 ("Die geschichtliche Bedeutung der jüdischen Gebetsrichtung" [bib.]). Cf. further Schürer, *History* 2.441f.

29. Cf. Lohse, art. "Siōn" in *TDNT*, 7:324; Urbach, *Sages*, 57ff.; and Bill. I:852f.; II:246f. Cf. Dan. 6:11; Ezek. 8:16ff.; m. Ber. 4:5f.

30. "Hierosolymam adorent, quasi domus sit Dei" ("They even adore Jerusalem as if it were the house of God").

31. The work of S. Bacchiocchi, *From Sabbath to Sunday* (Rome, 1977) is useful only for the collection of materials it contains (cf. the review by Ferguson, "Sabbath," 172–81).

32. Cf. Flusser, "Salvation," 147.

33. Clemen, "Abhängigkeit," 239; cf. already Kessler, *Mani*, 8 n. 3: "The Elkesaites are pre-Manichean Manicheans."

34. The question of whether permission to deny one's faith in times of persecution was ever a basic element of Elkesaite doctrine must, in my opinion, remain an open question. Both Origen (see above) and Epiphanius (*Pan.* 19.1.8) affirm that this was indeed the case Klijn and Reinink, *Evidence*, dispute this, but on inadequate grounds: "This

practice was confined to the Gnostics and had little in common with Elkesaite teaching" (p. 61). In fact, Gnostics and Elkesaites had much in common with regard to syncretistic inclinations, and the Gnostics had a very different attitude toward martyrdom than Klijn and Reinink obviously believe them to have had (cf. Koschorke, *Polemik*, 134ff.). Brandt, *Elchasai*, considers the permission to *arneisthai* to be original with the Elkesaites but attributes it to the later time of the prophet. It was "the vote of a man who was no longer young. . . . On the great day of judgment it will depend on *his* witness. There he, Elkesai, wanted to testify in behalf of those who belonged to him that their denial had been merely superficial, not meant seriously" (p. 64). In any case it is clear that the permission to deny did not originate in the polemics of the heresy fighters but was developed sometime (during the Hadrianic persecution?) within the Elkesaite congregations. The datum that the figure of Phinehas was used as scriptural proof (Epiphanius, *Pan.* 19.1.9) speaks in favor of this. This can best be understood in contrast to a rival Jewish interpretation which used the figure of Phinehas as a call to violent resistance. Cf. Hengel, *Zeloten*, 152ff. (bib.), on Phinehas as a symbolic figure of resistance.

35. Ritschl, *Entstehung*, 247 (last third of the second century [Hilgenfeld already protested against this, in *ZWTh* 1 (1858): 418]); Harnack, *Geschichte*, II.1, p. 625; Hort, *Notes*, 85f.; Chapman, "Date"; and Schoeps, *Theologie*, 326f.

36. But on this, cf. Klijn and Reinink, *Evidence*, 56 n. 1.

37. "The scale of the war points to apocalyptic dimensions; the events of the end of the world are intended" (Strecker, "Elkesai," col. 1182 [=*Eschaton*, 329]). The same Last Day is in view in the mysterious formulation: "I will be your witness in the Day of the Great Judgment" (Epiphanius, *Pan.* 19.4.3; cf. Levy, "Bemerkung," 712. Cf. Rohde, *Roman*, 391 n. 1: The war against the Parthians produced many similar apocalyptic predictions.

38. Cf. Brandt, *Elchesai*, 13.

39. On the following, cf. Strecker, "Elkesai," col. 1173 (=*Eschaton*, 321f.).

40. Cf. Reinink, "Land," 84f.

41. Differently Irmscher, "Elkesai," 745f.; Waitz, "Buch," 90; and Luttikhuizen, *Revelation*, 192–94. The command not to seek the meaning of the secret formulation (see above, n. 37) is mainly "meaningful for Greek-speaking believers" (Strecker, "Elkesai," col. 1184 [=*Eschaton*, 330] and an argument for a Greek original of the book, ibid.).

42. Klijn and Reinink, *Evidence*, 60 consider the Elkesaites to be "a movement that tried to show its allegiance to the Parthian nation." The

opposite view is given in Flusser, "Salvation," 150; and Elsas, *Welt-ablehnung*, 37. It is not clear to me *how* the Elkesaites wanted (or did not want) to show their "allegiance."

43. The codex confirms the testimony of the librarian al-Nadim from the tenth century that Mani's father belonged to an Elkesaite congregation (cf. Fihrist, pp. 773f.), which has found little credence among scholars (but cf. already Chwolsohn, *Ssabier*, 123ff.; and in more recent times Strecker, "Elkesai," cols. 1177ff. [=*Eschaton*, 325f.]). Klijn and Reinink, *Evidence*, 66, are skeptical concerning the possible value of the codex for the study of Elkesaitism; cf. idem, "Elchasai," 289; and J. K. Coyle. Similarly, Luttikhuizen, *Revelation*, 153–64. On the other side, cf. Henrichs, "Cologne," 366, with n. 51. Pages 1–99 of the codex are now conveniently available in the original language and in an English translation: see R. Cameron and A. J. Dewey, *The Cologne Mani Codex (P. Codex, inv. nr. 4780): "Concerning the Origin of His Body."* A. Henrichs and L. Koenen have edited, translated (German), and provided a (splendid!) commentary for the first 120 pages of the codex; see bibliography for details.

44. Cf. Koenen, "Augustine," 187–90; Henrichs, "Cologne," 354–67; and Rudolph, *Baptisten*, 14–16, 32–34.

45. The translation follows Henrichs and Koenen in *ZPE* 32 (1978): 101. Cf. the parallel passages in CMC 87, pp. 19f., and 89, pp. 13f.

46. Cf. Henrichs, "Cologne," 365f. and passim.

47. Cf. Henrichs, "Cologne," 365: The Elkesaite Baptists of CMC 80:6ff. "seem to acknowledge the *entolai tou sōtēros* but implicitly reject Paul as Greek."

48. Epiphanius, *Pan.* 30.16.8f. For the text, see below, pp. 180ff.

49. For the evidence, cf. Henrichs, "Mani," 52f.; and Koenen, "Augustine," 190ff. Cf. further Aland, "Mani und Bardesanes—Zur Entstehung des manichäischen Systems," in *Synkretismus im syrisch-persischen Kulturgebiet*, ed. Dietrich, pp. 123–43; and Böhlig, *Der Synkretismus des Mani*, idem, 144–169, esp. pp. 158f. (Mani and Marcion).

50. For the expression, cf. John 7:35. Cf. Strecker, "Das Judenchristentum und der Manikodex," 95, who deals with Jewish Christianity and the Mani codex in general. Also, Betz, "Paul in the Mani Biography."

51. On distinguishing this group from the groups of Elkesaites familiar to us, cf. Henrichs, "Cologne," 365f. Mani's mother congregation appears not to have practiced circumcision (this as a supplementary comment to the balanced discussion of Henrichs).

CHAPTER 8. ANTI-PAULINISM IN JAMES

1. In my opinion, the most important evidence against the authenticity of James is the theological position of the Lord's brother which becomes visible in Gal. 2:11ff. For additional arguments against authenticity, cf. Aland, "Herrenbruder"; Dibelius, *James*, 11ff.; Ropes, *James*, 43ff.; Kümmel, *Introduction*, 411ff.; Schenke and Fischer, *Einleitung*, 2:237ff.; and Laws, *Epistle*, 40f. The opposite hypothesis, that James was written by the brother of the Lord, is again increasingly advocated by modern scholars: cf. Mussner, *Jakobusbrief*, 1ff.; Wuellner, "Jakobusbrief," 38; and Stuhlmacher, *Verstehen*, 234f.

2. Most of the recent literature to 1977 has been worked over by Lindemann, *Paulus*, 240–52. For older works, cf. the unsurpassed treatment in Holtzmann, *Lehrbuch*, 2:368–90.

3. The following could also count as points of contact: PEIRASMOIS/THLIPSESIN, GINŌSKONTES HOTI/ EIDOTES HOTI.

4. Barnett, *Paul*, 187.

5. Cf. Dibelius, *James*, passim.

6. Cf. Lindemann, *Paulus*, 242f.

7. For arguments against a literary dependence of James 1:2ff. on Rom. 5:3ff., cf. also Hoppe, *Hintergrund*, 20ff.

8. On the concept, "the whole law", cf. Hübner, "Das ganze und das eine Gesetz," 239–56.

9. But cf. Matt. 5:18f.

10. Cf. Sanders, "Law," 109–26. Sanders distinguishes three different types of answers to the question of the extent to which the law must be fulfilled: (a) It is required that at least 51 percent of the law be fulfilled; (b) one violation is sufficient for condemnation; and (c) the keeping of one commandment is sufficient for salvation (ibid., 109). Although the three types appear to exclude one another, "all three statements could be made without intellectual embarrassment by anyone but a systematic theologian. Each type of saying is an effective way of urging people to obey the commandments as best they can and of insisting upon the importance of doing so" (ibid., 119).

11. A detailed exegesis can be dispensed with here because of the question we are pursuing and the method we are using. For exegetical studies, cf. the commentaries, and now Burchard, "Jakobus," who, however, contributes nothing to the question of anti-Paulinism in James, apart from a supplementary excursus (p. 43 n. 77, and p. 44), which is not clear to me.

12. In addition, it should be noted that the question form in James already indicates a polemical stance.

13. Cf. Wilckens, *Römer*, 262 (bib.).

14. Cf. Lindemann, *Paulus*, 245.

15. Cf. the commentaries. 4 Ezra 13:23; 7:24; and 8:31ff. come closest to Paul, but these passages likewise do not know faith and works as polar opposites.

16. Cf. Wilckens, *Römer*, 247 (bib.).

17. Lindemann, *Paulus*, 249.

18. On this, cf. esp. Schrage, "Jakobusbrief," 34.

19. So Trocmé, "Églises." The author of James answers in 2:14ff. "echos of Paul's preaching" (p. 664) which he had obtained by his own visits to Pauline churches or through reports of such from others.

20. On the sapiential background of James, cf. the splendid study of Hoppe, *Hintergrund*.

21. Cf. e.g., Schrage, "Jakobusbrief," 35: a coarsened Paulinism that had lost all of its original subtlety or had simply gone to seed; Stuhlmacher, *Gerechtigkeit*, 193 n. 1: a Paulinism developed by enthusiasts or Gnostics; similarly also Dassmann, *Stachel*, 112f. Lührmann, *Glaube*, 83, on the other hand, speaks of the opposition as an orthodox Paulinism.

22. Since the Nag Hammadi discoveries, one should hesitate before adopting the general thesis of a libertine gnosticism.

23. To be sure, misunderstandings of Paul are documented in the Corinthian correspondence. But they do not concern the theological polarities "faith/works of the law." In response to Schrage, "Jakobusbrief," 35, who points to the Corinthian enthusiasts as candidates for a misuse and misunderstanding of Paul, cf. the discussion of enthusiasm above, pp. 79f., 84.

24. Cf. Eph. 2:10; Col. 1:10; 1 Tim. 2:10; Titus 2:7, 14.

25. Holtzmann, *Lehrbuch*, 2:379.

26. Schrage, "Jakobusbrief" 35, also considers the hypothesis advocated in the above text. He then rejects it on the following basis: "But such a degree of distortion which would then have to be presupposed is not to be attributed to this author, who does not live by cheap shots" (ibid.). Response: The first issue to be clarified is still whether James in fact has understood Paul at all. If it should turn out to be that this is not the case, the degree of distortion is considerably reduced.

27. The term "ceremonial law" is a modern Christian formulation. A Jew would say: Laws that regulate the relationship between God and human beings. Cf. Sanders, "Law," 125; and Moore, *Judaism*, 2:6f. The phenomenon of the nullification of the ceremonial law had already been essentially anticipated in Hellenistic Judaism (with the exception of the prohibition against idolatry): cf. Philo, *Migr.* 89f.

28. On both expressions, cf. Hoppe, *Hintergrund*, 87ff.

29. The expression is from Walker, "Allein," 177.

30. Bousset, *Kyrios*, 367, describes the Christianity of *1 Clement* together with that of James, Barnabas, Hermas, and *2 Clement* "as a Diaspora-Judaism opened up to a complete universalism." Bousset's view of the history-of-religions context of James was accepted by Windisch, "Jakobusbrief," in idem, *Die katholischen Briefe*, 36; Dibelius, *James*, 43; and Lohse, "Glaube," 305. Laws, *Epistle*, 36–38, implicitly agrees.

31. One must not go so far as to label it "law piety", as does Walker, "Allein," 177.

32. Cf. Lührmann, *Glaube*, 79. On James 3:13ff., cf. still Hoppe, *Hintergrund*, 44ff.

33. Lührmann, *Glaube*, 80.

34. So also Strecker, "Strukturen," 130. On the nature of the saving event presupposed in James, see also Lührmann, *Glaube*, 83f.

35. Cf. only *1 Clem.* 30:3: *ergois dikaioumenoi [kai] mē logois* ("being justified by deeds, [and] not by words").

36. On this, cf. Lindemann, *Paulus*, 177ff.; and Dassmann, *Stachel*, 79ff.

37. On these further differences, cf. Lindemann, *Paulus*, 186.

38. So Lindemann, *Paulus*, 185ff.; and Dassmann, *Stachel*, 86ff.

39. This would lead one, with Schulz, *Mitte*, passim, to associate anti-Paulinism and early catholicism. That would be an unhistorical way of regarding the matter.

40. Like Paul, the author of James has been emancipated from the ceremonial law.

41. Vielhauer, *Geschichte*, 576.

42. Responding to Schulz, *Mitte*, 287, and Lindemann, *Paulus*, 249f., according to whom James's theology is in fact (essentially) anti-Pauline. But one must make a distinction between what the author attempted and what he really presents.

43. From the above it is clear that I cannot, in contrast to Holtzmann, *Lehrbuch*, 2:368–90, assign James to the deutero-Pauline tradition (cf. ibid., 262–390).

44. Differently Laws, *Epistle*, 17f. According to her, Paul enjoyed respect in the environment in which James was written. (However, she does not explicitly say whether she is referring to the author of James or its readers.) But in contrast to 2 Peter, to which Laws refers in this connection, a positive picture of Paul is difficult to make convincing. In addition, Laws's assumption is also unlikely, because James uses letters of Paul (see above in text) and not merely oral tradition (so Laws, *Epistle*).

45. According to Harnack, *Geschichte*, II. 1, p. 489, the prescript of James comes from the hand of a later redactor.

46. Cf. Lindemann, *Paulus*, 249 n. 109.

47. The attribution of the document to James and its legal piety both speak against the other theoretical possibility, that the author of James comes from a Gentile Christian community.

48. Weiss, *Earliest Christianity*, 2:751, thinks of the place of composition as a small urban congregation in Syria; cf. now also Schenke and Fischer, *Einleitung*, 2:240, who consider Syria to be the place of origin. Recently Laws, *Epistle*, 25f., considers a Roman origin to be probable.

CHAPTER 9. THE ANTI-PAULINISM OF JUSTIN'S JEWISH CHRISTIANS

1. Bibliography: Schliemann, *Clementinen*, 553–56; Otto, *Apparat*, ad loc.; Purves, *Testimony*, 104–11; Harnack, *Judentum* (the most important contribution); and Simon, *Israel*, 243–45. For some unknown reason, this text is omitted from the treatment of similar texts by Klijn and Reinink, *Evidence* (cf. the critique of Wilken, in *ThSt* 36 [1975]: 538f.). Betz, *Galatians*, 334f., helpfully prints the Greek text and English translation of *Dial.* 46f. in parallel columns. Editions of the text of Justin's works: J. K. T. Otto, *CorpAp* and Goodspeed, *Die ältesten Apologeten*.

2. On the concept *ennomos politeia*, cf. the inscription from Stobi: *CIJ* 694, lines 6–9: (the founder of the synagogue) *poleiteusamenos pasan poleiteian kata ton 'Ioudaïsmon* ("he has oriented all his conduct to the Jewish way of life"); this is an English version of the German translation by Lietzmann in *ZNW* 32 [1933]: 93f.). Cf. further Hengel, "Die Synagogeninschrift von Stobi," 176–81: "Der Vater der Synagoge und sein Wandel im Judentum."

3. The sacrificial rules of course no longer apply, since the temple is destroyed (*Dial.* 46.2).

4. Such Christians will perhaps (*isōs*) be saved (*Dial.* 47.4). On the translation of *isōs* with "perhaps," cf. Harnack, *Judentum*, 87. But the translation "probably" is just as possible. Cf. Engelhardt, *Christenthum*, 262; Otto, *Apparat*, ad loc. and on *Dial.* 85; and Stylianopoulos, *Justin*, 8 n. 4.

5. These have forfeited their salvation.

6. Sometimes it is assumed that Justin's Jewish Christians had an adoptionistic Christology. Cf. *Dial.* 48.4 (Justin:) *kai gar eisi tines, ō philoi, elegon, apo tou hēmeterou genous homologountes auton Christon einai, anthrōpon de ex anthrōpōn genomenon apophainomenoi: hois ou syntithemai* ("For these are some, my friends,' I said, 'of our race, who admit that He is Christ, holding Him to be man of men, with

whom I do not agree." But the advocates of such a hypothesis (e.g., Hort, *Christianity*, 196; Harnack, *Judentum*, 94, on par. 164:1 of Otto's edition; Weiss, *Earliest Christianity* 2:732 n. 47; and Zahn, *Geschichte*, 2:671 n. 2) are compelled to alter the *hēmeterou* of the text to a *hymeterou*. If this is correct (contra: Nitzsch, *Grundriss*, 40, among others), this would still document adoptionistic Christology for only one part of Jewish Christianity, not for Jewish Christianity as a whole. Cf. further discussion of the problem in Simon, *Israel*, 477, n. 2; and Strecker, in Bauer, *Orthodoxy*, 273–75.

7. Response to Wilken, in *ThSt* 36 (1975): 538, who, however, correctly joins with Simon, *Israel*, 237, in pleading that Jewish Christianity (like Judaism) had an ethnic *and* religious significance. This argument (against Harnack [see above, pp. 15f.] was already made by Lüdemann in ThJber 6 (1887), 115ff.; and Holtzmann, *Lehrbuch*, 1:565f. n. 2.

8. It is to be noted that *Trypho* links the "conversation" to the problem of Jewish Christianity.

9. We do not know enough about mixed congregations after 70 C.E. to introduce them into the present discussion.

10. On the life of Justin, cf. Barnard, *Justin*, 1–13.

11. Justin does not draw what would seem to be the logical inferences of his position, as did Irenaeus a generation after him (see below, p. 196) and contemporary Gentile Christians, with whom Justin is not able to concur in their rejection of fellowship with Jewish Christians (*Dial.* 47.2).

12. According to Harnack, *Judentum*, 86 and n. 1, these Gentile Christians occupied the majority position, since Justin gives no indication that this was only a minority point of view.

13. In agreement with Harnack, *History*, 1:294ff.

14. Lindemann, *Paulus*, passim, has correctly pointed this out.

15. Cf. Lindemann's summary, *Paulus*, 396f.

16. Contra Keck, "Saints," 57: Keck passes entirely too quickly over the problems of *Dial.* 47. His statements in this connection deserve to be cited here, since they are representative: "Justin Martyr . . . knew of Jewish Christians (*Dial.*) but did not name them. As long as they did not 'Judaize' the Gentile Christians, he tolerated them. He had an entirely different attitude toward the Gnostics (*Dial.* 35, 80) and toward Marcion (*Apol.* 1.26, 58) This means that Justin did not regard them as heretics but as a peculiar kind of Christian; he certainly did not know of their anti-Pauline polemics" (ibid.). Response: (1) Keck does not make clear *which* Jewish-Christian type Justin tolerates. (2) He forgets that even the rigorist Jewish-Christian type was presented by Justin. On the apodictic declaration that Justin knew nothing of an anti-Paulinism among Jewish Christians, see above in the text.

17. Cf. Zahn, *Geschichte*, 563ff., who of course gives an exaggerated list of Justin's points of contact with Pauline letters; Barnett, *Paul*, 231ff.; Lindemann, *Paulus*, 353–67; and Dassmann, *Stachel*, 244–48.

18. Overbeck, "Verhältnis," 343f. Opposed by Engelhardt, *Christenthum*, 59–64, 352–65; and Purves, *Testimony*, 111–15.

19. There would have been plenty of opportunity to do this, had Justin wanted: cf. correctly Harnack, *Judentum*, 51. Justin does name John (*Dial.* 81.4), the sons of Zebedee (*Dial.* 106.3), or Peter (*Dial*, 106.3). (This lack is overlooked by Verweijs, *Evangelium*, 239ff., in his critique of Harnack.)

20. Lindemann, *Paulus*, 366.

21. In addition, Lindemann wrongly presupposes that only Paulinists used Paul. That was not the case in the second century (1 *Clement!*).

22. On this, cf. Stylianopoulos, *Justin* (bib.).

23. It should not be disputed that Justin had contact with Jewish theologians (cf. *Dial.* 50.1: [Trypho] *Eoikas moi ek pollēs prostripseōs tēs pros pollous peri pantōn tōn zētoumenōn gegonenai* ["You seem to me to have come out of a great conflict with many persons about all the points we have been searching into"]), and that these served as a foil in tho composition of tho *Dialoguo.* Juotin'o knowlodgo of pootbiblioal Iudaism (cf. Barnard, *Iustin*, 44–52) sneaks in favor of this assumption. But one need nonetheless have no doubt that Gentiles too were included in the addressees of the *Dialogue* [in response to Stylianopoulos, *Justin*, 169–95].)

24. The "treatise" (*syntagma*) against all heresies mentioned in *Apol.* 1.26.7 is identical with the *syntagma* against Marcion. See Luedemann, "Geschichte," 87 n. 3.

25. Cf. Bauer, *Orthodoxy*, 216; and Dassmann, *Stachel*, 247f.

26. Contra Lindemann, *Paulus*, 357: "If the hypothesis is supposed to be correct, that Justin did not mention Paul because he was 'exhibit A' for Marcion . . . then it would be expected that in the sections of the *Apology* which deal with Marcion there would at least be allusions to Marcion's 'Paulinism.'" I cannot share this opinion, already because of the nature of the genre "apology." Political denunciation (chap. 26, on which see Seeberg, "Geschichtstheologie," 73) fits better in this genre. In addition, charging him with ditheism was more effective among Christian readers than debates over Marcion's Paulinism.

27. Harnack, *Judentum*, 50f. (cf. also n. 19, above). Such a procedure was of course possible only as long as Paul did not yet stand in a canon in which he had equal rank with "the Lord"—as was the case with Marcion (cf. Harnack, *Judentum*, 51).

28. In addition, in contrast to Irenaeus (*Heresies* 1.26.2), Justin does

not express himself systematically concerning the Jewish Christians, with the result that he in fact describes the Jewish-Christian phenomenon more correctly than Irenaeus (see above, p. 26).

29. There is hardly anything definite that can be said concerning a possible rejection of Paul by the tolerant group of Jewish Christians. According to Knopf, *Zeitalter*, 30 they would have "condemned Paul, personally renouncing him as a traitor." Similarly Wagenmann, *Stellung*, 143. I share this opinion, though it cannot be proven.

CHAPTER 10. THE ANTI-PAULINISM
OF HEGESIPPUS

1. Older literature on Hegesippus is listed in Weizsäcker, art. "Hegesipp," in *RE*[3]; a thorough commentary on the extant fragments is given by Zahn, *Forschungen*, 6:228–50. We are lacking a more modern treatment. Nevertheless, cf. Kemler, *Herrenbruder*.

2. On the chronology, cf. Harnack, *Geschichte*, II.1, pp. 311ff.

3. Cf., e.g., Blum, *Tradition*, 78f.

4. Cod. 232, par. 70:8–16, Henry (translator's English rendition of author's German translation).

5. Cf. cod. 232 (par. 67:16f., Henry): *Tauta de dittai doxai katemerizonto, kai ou dittai monon alla kai antikeimenai* ("These things were divided up into two opinions, and they were not only different but contradictory" [translator]).

6. So also Eusebius, *Hist. Ecc.* 2.23.3. He obviously sees the matter differently in *Hist. Ecc.* 4.8.2 and 11.7.

7. Lightfoot, *Clement*, 115: "Stephanus Gobarus himself, writing some centuries later and knowing the text only as it occurs in S. Paul, is not unnaturally at a loss to know what Hegesippus means by this condemnation."

8. For evidence of the use of the saying or a similar formulation in apocalyptic literature, cf. the commentaries on 1 Cor. 2:9 and Berger, "Diskussion." Cf. also Stone and Strugnell's translation of the collection in *The Books of Elijah*, 41–73.

9. Rensberger, "Apostle," 207, is inclined toward this possibility, without wanting completely to exclude a reference to 1 Cor. 2:9.

10. Cf. Lindemann, *Paulus*, 295f.; and Dassmann, *Stachel*, 243.

11. Cf. above, n. 8. The possibility of Christian influence is, however, to be seriously examined. Cf. below, n. 12.

12. This is the only explanation for the fact that they were preserved in the tradition.

13. Early Catholic: *1 Clem.* 34:8; *2 Clem.* 11:7; 14:5; *Mart. Pol*, 2:3;

Gnostic: *Gospel of Thomas* 17; the *Book of Baruch of the Gnostic Justin* (in Hippolytus, *Ref.* 5.19, 22). Examples could be multiplied.

14. I have never found the third line of 1 Cor. 2:9 in gnostic texts. For individual apocalyptic texts that contain the three stichs, see Berger, "Diskussion." The most important text is a passage from the Ethiopic *Apocalypse of Ezra* (text and French translation by J. Halévy), which offers an almost verbatim parallel to 1 Cor. 2:9 (cf. the German translation of the relevant passage by Berger, 271). Independent of the question of whether the Ezra Apocalypse is purely Jewish (on which see Berger, 272 and n. 1), one can hardly regard the text in it which is parallel to 1 Cor. 2:9 as the target of Hegesippus's critique, because the Ezra Apocalypse was not composed before the fifteenth century (information from Prof. Walter Harrelson, Vanderbilt University).

15. 2 *Clem.* 11:7 and 14:5 more likely derive the citation from *1 Clem.* 34:8 than from 1 Cor. 2:9. Cf. Lindemann, *Paulus*, 266f., for details.

16. Cf. Knopf, *Väter*, ad loc., who ventures the further possibility that *1 Clement* derives the saying from the congregation's liturgy which had been influenced by 1 Cor. 2:9.

17. Cf. what was said above concerning Gobarus's compositional procoduro.

18. Lindemann, *Paulus*, 187 n. 98 expresses the attractive hypothesis that the third line of 1 Cor. 2:9 derives from Paul himself.

19. Prigent, "Oeil," 418f., points out that the order of the lines present in Hegesippus is also found in other early Christian texts which have, of course, been influenced by 1 Cor. 2:9.

20. With Hilgenfeld, *Judenthum*, 43–46; and Holtzmann, in *ZWTh* 21 (1878): 292. Opposed by Zahn, *Geschichte*, 791ff., 801ff. Lindemann, *Paulus*, argues against the view that there is a polemic against Paul in Hegesippus and refers to Kemler, *Herrenbruder*. He writes: "If Hegesippus had in fact been an obvious critic of Paul, then there would be no explanation for Eusebius's having 'included him in his *Ecclesiastical History* in such a significant way'" (Lindemann, *Paulus*, 295).

My response: (1) For better or worse, Eusebius had no choice but to use Hegesippus, if he wanted to carry out the program of his church history. This has really nothing to do with acknowledging his significance. (2) It is not a matter of whether or not Hegesippus had been an *obvious* critic of Paul. An obvious critique is not to be expected, in any case (James too avoids mentioning Paul by name). The question must, rather, be whether Eusebius could have used an author who expresses a somewhat masked criticism of Paul. This is to be answered affirmatively. Anyway, Eusebius ascribes to Hegesippus his *idia gnōmē* ("own opinion") (4.22.1), an expression that contains a mild critique, and he does not hesitate to make corrections to Hegesippus, without noting that he has done so. (3) It is very probable that Eusebius had only a badly damaged copy of Hegesippus's work at his disposal (so Schwartz, *Eusebius Werke*, 2:cliii. The counterargument of Gustafsson, "Sources," 228, is, in my opinion, not convincing).

21. Cf. further the unclear report in *Hist. Ecc.* 3.16.

22. Cf. similarly Schneemelcher, "Paulus," 9.

23. Cf. Vielhauer, *Geschichte*, 773f.; and Abramowski, "*Diadoche*," 323f.

24. Cf. the parallels in the Ps.-Clem. *Hom.* 18.19 (see below, p. 187).

25. Vielhauer, *Geschichte*, 774; and Rensberger, "Apostle," 202.

26. Cf., however, Ritschl, *Entstehung*, 268: "The Law, the Prophets, and the Lord are *the authorities of the Catholic Church*, which it used against the Gnostics precisely in the time of Hegesippus" (cf. similarly Lightfoot, *Galatians*, 333f., n. 3). In the same place, Ritschl refers to the following passages: *Ap. Const.* 2.39; Tertullian, *Praescr.* 36; Irenaeus, *Heresies* 2.35.4; *Diogn.* 11. Against this it to be said: In every place the concept "apostle" also appears (except for the *Ap. Const.*, where it is presupposed, since the apostle Matthew is the speaker).

27. Contra Telfer, "Hegesippus," 153, who throughout places Hegesippus in the vicinity of Irenaeus.

28. Cf. Bauer, *Orthodoxy*, 196f.

29. For the following, cf. esp. Kemler, *Herrenbruder*, 1–15; and Abramowski, "*Diadoche*." Most recently, also Conzelmann, *Gentiles*, pp. 258f.

30. Cf. Völker, "Tendenzen." Grant, "Origins," 201ff., provides an analysis of the (various) uses of Hegesippus by Eusebius.

31. Cf. Grant's commentary, "Eusebius," 16f.

32. Cf. further 2.23.6 and 4.21.

33. On this, cf. Lawlor, *Eusebiana*, 21ff., whose view is opposed in what follows. Eusebius uses this expression in several passages of the *Hist. Ecc.* (cf. e.g., 3.18.1; 3.19.1). Zahn, *Forschungen*, 6:238, comments: "This phrase used often by Eusebius, which in § 2 is continued with *hōs phasi* ["as they say"], does not exclude the possibility that he found the basis for this story in a written document or several such, and the style of the narrative seems to require it."

34. The method here pursued is fundamentally different from that of Lawlor, *Eusebiana*, 18–26, who weaves both reports together. Kraft, *Entstehung*, 288, does not recognize the doublet character of *Hist. Ecc.* 3.11 and considers the report as historically reliable.

35. *Epi tō autō logō* also appears in the citation of Hegesippus concerning the martyrdom of Symeon (*Hist. Ecc.* 3.32.6). On the expression, cf. Zahn, *Forschungen*, 6:236; and Kemler, *Herrenbruder*, 8.

36. Cf. Acts 25:11f.; 27:1.

37. Cf. Josephus, *Ant.* 20.201ff.

38. Cf. *Hist. Ecc.* 2.23.8–18.

39. Cf. *Hist. Ecc.* 2.1.5.

40. For another reference, cf. *Hist. Ecc.* 7.32.29. On the Jerusalem relics cult, cf. Harnack, *Mission*, 2.106 n. 2.

41. Cf. the same conception in the Ps.-Clem. *Recg.* 1.43.3; *Ap. Const.* 8.35.

42. Cf. also Abramowski, "*Diadoche*," 325.

43. The reading *meta tōn apostolōn* is also testified by Rufinus, who reads *cum apostolis*. The Syrian, on the contrary, has "from the apostles"; cf. also the survey by Zahn, *Forschungen*, 6:229. In my opinion, *meta tōn apostolōn* is, as the *lectio difficilior*, the original reading. Eusebius uses it to express his view that the leadership of the Jerusalem church was also instituted by the apostles, although *pros tōn apostolōn* would probably have been more fitting. On the problem, cf. further Ehrhard, *Succession*, 65 and n. 3; Abramowski, "*Diadoche*," 325f.; and Kemler, *Herrenbruder*, 12f.

44. Cf. Kemler, *Herrenbruder*, 14.

45. Zahn, *Forschungen*, 6.252.

46. One may think concretely of the reading of Scripture which regularly occurred during the worship services, which included Law, Prophets, and the Lord; cf. Abramowski, "*Diadoche*," 326f.

47. Cf. Cohen, "A Virgin Defiled," 1–11.

48. Zahn, *Forschungen*, 6:240f.

49. Cf. Andresen, *Kirchen*, 268 n. 280.

50. Cf. Hilgenfeld, "Hegesippus," 198.

51. On the apologetic motifs in this narrative, cf. Hyldahl, "Hypomnemata," 86ff.

52. Cf. Andresen, *Kirchen*, 134f.

53. The statement of Lawlor, *Eusebiana*, that Hegesippus had expressed himself just as extensively on the history of the Roman church ("the scope of his dissertation on the Roman Church was similar to that of his dissertation on the Church of Jerusalem", p. 89) has properly been ignored or rejected by scholarship. Cf. Holl on Epiphanius, *Pan.* 27, in the *Apparat*, in which chapter Lawlor sees Hegesippus's report reflected and used.

54. Cf. esp. his description as a lifelong Nazirite (*Hist. Ecc.* 2.23.5; on this, cf. most recently Zuckschwerdt, "Naziräat").

55. English translation from LCL.

56. Contra Hilgenfeld, "Noch einmal Hegesippus," 301–8; and Zahn, *Forschungen*, 6:252.

57. Cf. Telfer, "Hegesippus," 146.

58. Cf. Zahn, *Forschungen*, 6:252f. n. 1, who seems to have the same view.

59. Eusebius knew the *Gospel of the Hebrews*; cf. the documentation of the passages in Schmidtke, *Fragmente*, 33f.

60. Vielhauer, "Gospels," 163.

61. Cf. Vielhauer, "Gospels," 159.

62. Bauer, *Orthodoxy*, 52. In my opinion, one can infer a Jewish-Christian praxis from this.

63. Against the latter possibility the opinion of Hegesippus could be brought forward that the church had remained a pure virgin until the time of the death of James (see above, p. 164). But on this, cf. already Baur, *Paul*, 1:226 n. 3.

CHAPTER 11. ANTI-PAULINISM
IN THE PSEUDO-CLEMENTINES

1. This chapter attempts no more than to treat the Pseudo-Clementines in a general way. For the current state of research, the reader is referred to the comprehensive survey of the literature by F. Stanley Jones, "The Pseudo-Clementines: A History of Research," *The Second Century* 2 (1982): 1–33 (Part I), 63–96 (Part II). On the theme "Paul in the Pseudoclementines," of the older literature H. R. Offerhaus, *Paulus in de Clementinen* (Groningen, 1894), is still valuable (history of research, pp. 1–32).

2. The date of composition was probably during the first two decades of the fourth century C.E. Cf. Strecker, *Judenchristentum*, 267f. Standard edition: B. Rehm, GCS 42^2.

3. The date of composition was about 350 C.E.; cf. Strecker, *Judenchristentum*, 268ff. Rufinus translated it into Latin after 406 C.E. Standard edition: B. Rehm, GCS 51.

4. One manuscript comes from the year 411 C.E. The edition used in this work: W. Frankenberg, TU 48.3. Sound methodology requires that the Syriac always be compared with Rufinus's Latin translation. This has in fact been done in the following work, although the results were not significant.

5. In addition, there are two Greek *Epitomes* that are based on H, as well as various other epitomes and fragments of epitomes. Cf. Paschke, *Die beiden griechischen Klementinen-Epitomen und ihre Anhänge*.

6. Although at opposite poles on other issues, this is affirmed by both Rehm, "Entstehung," and Strecker, *Judenchristentum*.

7. Strecker, *Judenchristentum*, 35ff. (bib.).

8. Rehm, "Entstehung", 98ff. (bib.)

9. Waitz, *Pseudoclementinen*, 78–250; and Strecker, *Judenchristentum*, 137–254.

10. Cf. Rehm, "Entstehung," 139ff.; idem, GCS 42, pp. viif.; Irmscher, "Pseudo-Clementines," in *New Testament Apocrypha*, 2:533–34.

10a. But cf. Rius-Camps, "Pseudoclementinas." Rius-Camps questions the existence of a KP source (the corresponding texts are due to Ebionite interpolation) and distinguishes two slightly different corpora of G: the orthodox edition R and the original *Periodoi Petrou* (=G). H, unlike R, inserts again what the orthodox edition of R had cut out. I am currently preparing a commentary on H and will then discuss Rius-Camps's noteworthy suggestions in detail.

11. Cf. only Brown, "James," 192ff.; Martyn, "Gospel," 57ff.; Lindemann, *Paulus*, 104ff.; and Dassmann, *Stachel*, 283ff.

12. In NT scholarship, this would be analogous to reconstructing a source of Q. Stötzel, "Darstellung," 25f., completely misrepresents Strecker's source-critical position.

13. Cf. J. Wehnert, "Literarkritik," He was able to support his conclusions with Strecker, *Konkordanz*. Cf. already Thomas, "Ebionites," 278, on the problem dealt with here.

14. Strecker, *Judenchristentum*, 220.

15. Wehnert, "Literarkritik," 297. Cf. also Rohde, *Roman*, 289–309, 618f

16. Cf. e.g., Schwartz, "Beobachtungen," on the Elkesaites: "But since the so-called Elkesaites are again and again brought up in connection with the Clementines, the most important thing must be said about that overrated (*sic*) 'prophet' who has been blown up into the founder of a religion" (p. 194). The Book of Elkesai "for over a hundred years attracted no notice beyond the little sectarian nook (*sic*) in which it was used. . . . The 'Elkesaites' were never a sect of any significance" (ibid., 195). Cf. also Harnack, *Geschichte*, 2.1, p. 625.

17. The only presupposition that we are here making is that this section is based on some kind of traditions. One thing among others that suggests this is the different chronology: R 1.7 is set still during the earthly ministry of Christ, while in R 1.43,3 we find ourselves already seven years after the resurrection.

18. Edition: Funk, *Apokalypse*, 10–49; C. Hedrick, in *Nag Hammadi Studies* 11, pp. 110–49. Cf. also Brown, "James," 295–315. First edition by Böhlig and Labib, *Apokalypsen*, 66–85. On the literary-critical problems of our document, which do not lie in the center of my attention, cf. in addition to the editions mentioned above, Brown, "Elements." I also found J. A. Brashler and M. Meyer, "James in the Nag Hammadi Library," to be instructive.

19. Response to Funk, *Apokalypse*, 196f., and often, according to

whom only the report of the martyrdom in the *Second Apocalypse of James* has a genetic connection to Hegesippus.

20. That of course does not mean that the *Second Apocalypse of James* is directly dependent on the report in Hegesippus; see above, p. 177.

21. The charge of error is located in a logical context in Hegesippus. As James gives his testimony for Jesus, the scribes and Pharisees respond with this charge (cf. Funk, *Apokalypse*, 177 and n. 2). But in the *Second Apocalypse of James*, it is forced into the account of the stoning.

22. Funk, *Apokalypse*, 144f., considers it "hardly imaginable that there is any connection between the statements (i.e., par. 55:6ff.: cf. the synopsis above) and the strange question addressed to James in Hegesippus . . . *tis he thura tou Iesou*. A setting in the tradition for this note which is hardly understandable in itself could only be supposed if we could be sure that this passage, at least originally, had something to do with the role of James as mediator." That is not convincing. In the first place, the question is whether there was literary connection. Precisely, the previously unexplained question of the meaning of *tis he thura tou Iesou* is a strong argument for a literary connection.

23. On issues related to the history of the tradition, cf. further Lipsius, *Apostelgeschichten*, 238ff., who provides an extensive discussion of the relation of R 1 to Hegesippus.

24. This discussion presupposes the correctness of the results of the literary analysis of the account of the martyrdom of James in Hegesippus by Schwartz, "Eusebius", 56f.

25. Cf. the Mishnah tractate *Sanh.*; and Little, "Death," 83ff.

26. Hegesippus is not himself guilty of this combination. Cf. correctly Schwartz, "Eusebius," 56f.

27. Cf. Schwartz, "Eusebius," 56f.

28. For additional doublets in the text of Hegesippus on the martyrdom of James, cf. Schwartz, "Eusebius," 55f.

29. In the quotation cited above, Clement of Alexandria appears to be dependent on the original form of the text in Hegesippus; cf. also Turner, "Lists," 533. n. 4.

30. Cf. Beyschlag, "Jakobusmartyrium," 150ff. (bib.)

31. Schmidt, *Studien*, 325.

32. Schoeps, *Theologie*, 413ff.

33. Strecker, *Judenchristentum*, comments laconically, "The text before us [i.e., R 1] has in common with Hegesippus's report . . . of the martyrdom of James . . . only the plunge of James" (p. 249f.). Cf. further Schoeps, *Theologie*, 413ff.; Schmidt, *Studien*, 325; and Brown, "James," 214ff. (a detailed examination of Schmidt's argument).

34. Brown, "James," 220.

35. In the following it is presupposed that R 1.44.3—53.4a does not all belong to the same level of tradition (cf. Strecker, *Judenchristentum*, 236). Additional clearly secondary elements in R 1.33–71 are 63.1–9 (cf. Strecker, *Judenchristentum*, 42) and 69.5b–7 (cf. Rehm, "Entstehung," 96f.).

36. On the parallels with Acts 7, cf. Martyn, *Gospel*, 59 (=idem, "Recognitions," 269).

37. R 1.36.1: "immolare quidem eis concessit." On this complex of motifs, cf. Hübner, "Mark VII.1–23 und das 'jüdisch-hellenistische' Gesetzesverständnis," 319–45, esp. 327ff.

38. In fact, the Prophet also eliminated the sacrifice presented to God alone.

39. The understanding of the law which becomes visible here has a parallel in Justin, *Dial.* 19:6 (incorporation of the sacrificial system into the goal of preventing idolatry [cf. similarly, *Dial.* 22.1; 11]); cf. in addition Justin's understanding that portions of the OT law had been issued because of the hardness of the peoples' hearts (on which see Stylianopoulos, *Justin*, 147 and often; and Luedemann, "Geschichte," 110). In the Syriac *Didascalia*, similarly as in R 1, the ceremonial law was provided secondarily (*deuterosis*) after the worship of the golden calf (Exodus 32) (cf. also Schmidt, *Studien*, 262ff.). Of course the differences are also considerable: the *Didascalia* understands the laws given after the Exodus 32 incident to be a *punishment* (pars. 130:32ff. Achelis-Flemming), while in R 1 they are provided as concessions to the Jews (see above in text). A genetic relationship between the Syriac *Didascalia* and R 1.33–71 is thus unlikely (contra Schmidt, *Studien*, 290f.). On the problem, cf. further Strecker in Bauer, *Orthodoxy*, 256 n. 44. In addition, *Barn.* 4:7f. and 14:1–4 show how widespread the use of Exodus 32 was in the discussion of the law—a further argument against the assumption of a genetic connection in the case discussed above.

40. The question of the origin of this list may remain out of consideration here.

41. The redactor is the author of the Recognitions and/or the author of the source document (*Grundschrift*).

42. Contra Martyn, *Gospel*, 69–77 (=idem, "Recognitions," 278–84), who follows Strecker in regarding our passage as a component of the *Anabathmoi* source. Cf. below, p. 300 n. 44.

43. [This is my rendition of Strecker's German translation, *Judenchristentum*, 251.—Translator.] Of course this horror story has no historical value for reconstructing the life of Paul (contra Windisch, *Paulus und Christus*, 133; and idem, *Paulus und das Judentum*, 5.)

44. Strecker, *Judenchristentum*, 252f. He thinks the *Anabathmoi*

Jakobou named by Epiphanius (=AJ I) and R 1.33–71 (=AJ II) go back to one archtype (=AJ). Previously Zahn (*Die Apostelgeschichte des Lukas*, vol. 1) had argued that the content of R 1.55–70 (and probably also 1.71–74; 2.7–13) had been taken from the *Anabathmoi Jakobou*. From him comes the suggestion (taken over by Strecker, *Judenchristentum*, 252) that *anabathmoi* is to be understood in the sense of *anabaseis*. For support he refers to Psalms 120—134, the (secondary) superscript of which in the LXX is translated as *ōdai tōn anabathmōn*. Zahn designates them "pilgrimage songs." But that is still no *proof* that *anabathmoi* can be translated by "ascents."

45. This statement is even possible on the basis of R 1, since here baptism, which abolishes sacrifice, is already spoken of. (This is in reponse to Strecker, *Judenchristentum*, 252: "The information given by Epiphanius concerning the content of the speech of James is completely different from the summary in R 1.69." This is also correctly opposed by Brown, "James," 202 n. 22. Cf. further Bacon, *Studies*, 489.)

46. The changes in the story of the martyrdom possibly go back even to the compiler of the tradition visible behind R 1.66–71, although the author of the basic source document (*Grundschrift*) and the author of the *Recognitions* also are possibilities.

47. In general, it is probable that many of the references to the NT are from the redactor, all the more so since most of the echoes of the NT are found in 1.33ff., a section that is strongly redactional in any case (the speakers are Peter/the twelve apostles). On the whole, echoes of Acts predominate. They belong predominantly to the core of the R 1 tradition; it is no accident that they are especially thick in 1.66ff.

48. Cf. 1.37.2 (Matt. 9:13); 1.54.6 (Matt. 23:13); 1.40.2 (Matt. 11:19); 1.55ff. (Matt. 10:2ff.); 1.64.2 (Matt. 24:2, 15).

49. Cf. 1.40.4 (Luke 6:13; 10:1).

50. Cf. Strecker, *Judenchristentum*, 253 (documentation). The source is especially dependent on Acts (so also Strecker, *Judenchristentum*). Strecker presents the following examples: 1.65.2 (Acts 5); 1.71.2 (Acts 4:4); 1.71.3f. (Acts 9:1ff.). The following passages may also be noted: 1.36.2 (Acts 3:22f); 1.60.5 (Acts 1:23, 26); 1.62.4 (Acts 5:34ff.); 1.69.8 (Acts 6:7). Additional noticeable parallels are the figure of Simon Magus (1.70.2; 72:3ff.—cf. Acts 8:9ff.) and the delineation of redemptive history (1.33–42—cf. Acts 7:2–53).

51. On R 1.39, cf. also Schmidt, *Studien*, 292f., who referred to this passage as a reflection of the Pella tradition prior to Schoeps and Strecker.

52. The report in 1.39.3, that the Jews were driven out of Jerusalem, fits better in the time of Hadrian than in the time of Vespasian. Cf. Strecker, *Judenchristentum*, 231.

53. Cf. above, pp. 205f.

54. With Strecker, *Judenchristentum*, 253; Martyn, *Gospel*, 63 (= idem, "Recognitions," 272); and Stötzel, "Darstellung," 32.

55. On the term "universalism," cf. Mensching, *Religion*, 71ff. It is here used in the manner of the discipline of comparative religions. Judaism at the time of Jesus did not belong to the category of universal religions but of national religions (cf. Hoheisel, *Das antike Judentum in christlicher Sicht*, 175ff.). Of course, it contained embryonic elements of a universalism which were developed further by Jewish and Gentile Christianity. On the history of the concept of universalism in the nineteenth century, cf. Smend, "Universalismus und Partikularismus"; cf. idem, *Arbeit*, 77–85.

56. Cf. R 1.43.1: "frequenter mittentes ad nos rogabant, ut eis de Iesu dissereremus, si ipse esset propheta quem Moyses praedixit, qui est Christus aeternus" ("Therefore they often sent to us, and asked us to discourse to them concerning Jesus, whether he were the prophet whom Moses foretold, who is the eternal Christ") (cf. R 1.44.2; 63.1).

57. Aristo read Gen. 1:1 as "in filio"; cf. the reprint of the extant fragments of Aristo by Routh, *Reliquiae Sacrae*, 1:95–97 (texts), 98–109 (commentary). On the christological interpretation of Gen. 1:1, cf. in addition Lorenz, *Arius judaizans?* 136–40.

58. On this, cf. esp. Verweijs, *Evangelium*, 117–242 (an analysis of the understanding of the law in the *Didache*, 1 Clement, Ignatius, Barnabas, Hermas, and Justin).

59. So Martyn, *Gospel*, 61 (= idem, "Recognitions," 270f.).

60. So Strecker in Bauer, *Orthodoxy*, 256 n. 44.

61. Cf. correctly Molland, "Circoncision," 32.

62. Thus the author of the R 1 source may belong to that group attacked by the rabbis because of their exclusive emphasis on the Decalogue; cf. Urbach, *Sages*, 361f. On the Decalogue in the first two centuries, cf. Vokes, "The Ten Commandments in the New Testament and in First Century Judaism; and Vermes, "The Decalogue and the Minim."

63. A passage such as Mark 12:9 (cf. Matt. 21:41; Luke 20:16) is somewhat reminiscent of R 1.64.2.

64. So explicitly Brown, "James," 233f., who of course uses the results of Munck with too much confidence (*Paul*, 55ff.), and argues against the view presented above.

65. Of course, the critique on the cult could go back to the influence of another group or the group's own inheritance from the period before 70 C.E. (on which cf. Simon, *Stephen*). But we know of no Jewish Christianity before 70 C.E. that was both critical of the cult and anti-

Pauline. Paul appears to have cooperated with the Hellenists (see above, pp. 58f.).

66. Schoeps, *Theologie*, 440ff.

67. The church of Matthew must have also experienced a similar development; cf. Luz, "Die Erfüllung des Gesetzes bei Matthäus (Matt. 5:17–20)," esp. 428ff.

68. Schoeps, *Theologie*, 453.

69. Martyn, *Gospel*, 63.

70. Cf. Martyn, *Gospel*, 62: The author of our source "would have his readers believe that had Paul and his churches never appeared, the mission of the Jewish church to its brethren would have been invincible."

71. Contra Lindemann, *Paulus*, 109 n. 44. But his report (ibid., 108f.) is done somewhat carelessly: e.g., the enemy does not at all *kill* James, as Lindemann states.

72. See what is said above in the text (p. 182) with regard to the validity of the Decalogue.

73. Whether the source contained a report of the conversion of Paul (so Martyn, *Gospel*, 61, in agreement with Schoeps, *Theologie*, 452f., and Strecker, *Judenchristentum*, 253) can, in my opinion, not be decided.

74. The fact that Saul rather than Paul is introduced as the opponent can change nothing with regard to the anti-*Paul*inism of the document (contra Schwartz, "Beobachtungen," 184f., whose delineation also shatters on the fact that R 1.69f. derives from tradition [Schwartz argues on the level of the narration of the author of the *Recognitions*]). Likewise, the original anti-Pauline character of particular sections is not altered by the fact that on the narrative level of the Homilist the argument is directed against Simon Magus (contra Chapman, "Date," 151).

75. Although the AJ presupposes the R 1 source and is thus later, its critique of Paul can be older than that of the R 1 source.

76. It is appropriate to say with regard to the R 1 source what Ulhorn, *Homilien*, 391, said concerning the *Homilies* more than 125 years ago: "We thus find forms of Jewish Christianity that have taken on a completely universal character, a universal outlook which has already given up the strict requirements, especially that of circumcision, and which still betray the fact that they have grown out of a more rigorous party. The *Homilies* have given up the demand for circumcision but retain the polemic against Paul, which appears to be the element that was held on to most tenaciously."

77. Nor can one affirm that the *Second Apocalypse of James* con-

tained an anti-Paulinism at an earlier level of tradition (contra Böhlig, "Hintergrund," 109).

78. The only recent attempt in this direction known to me is that of Beyschlag, "Jakobusmartyrium", 152: the homo inimicus of R 1.70.1 recurs in Hegesippus refracted in a threefold way: (1) in James, (2) in the Rechabite, and (3) "finally in the fuller." The hypothesis is based on a misunderstanding of the history of the tradition.

79. On anti-Paulinism in the Homilies, cf. esp. Waitz, Pseudoklementinen, 133–40 (bib.); and Strecker, Judenchristentum, 187–98; the older literature is listed by Cassels, Religion, 2: 34 n. 1.

80. Parallel texts in R, to the extent that they exist, will be indicated in parentheses.

81. The English translations of the Homilies in this section represent either the German translations of Strecker and Luedemann rendered into English by the translator or the English translation in ANF.

82. Cf. esp. the analysis of this section by Salles, "Diatribe," 518–25. (In the text mentioned above, Salles distinguishes—in my opinion by an incorrect methodology—two different anti-Pauline hands, that of the author of the Kerygmata Petrou and that of the author of an anti-Pauline pamphlet, the latter of which he considers a near contemporary of the historical Paul [cf. pp. 543f.]).

83. Cf. already chap. 5.6 (par. 231.18–21 Rehm).

84. Strecker, Judenchristentum, 192 n. 1: "This concept of revelation is not well chosen in the polemic against Paul. Really, the context demands the statement that—since no authentic instruction can be obtained through dreams (H XVII 14:5f.)—Peter was instructed in every way by his Master." That is doubtless correct with regard to the historical Paul and his opponents. But the combination of mysticism and reference to personal discipleship of Jesus in a later epoch has to be evaluated for the time of the anti-Pauline author.

85. Cf. Strecker's commentary on this, Judenchristentum, 193 n. 1 (bib.).

86. That the opponent is here called Simon Magus and not Paul does not change this in the least. The strength of what was said above in n. 74 against Schwartz and Chapman is here increased exponentially.

87. Strecker, Judenchristentum, 187.

88. To this would correspond the statement that Peter was kategnōsmenos (XVIII 19:6); see above, p. 187.

89. Cf. Strecker, Judenchristentum, 190.

90. But cf. on 2.17.4, Strecker, Judenchristentum, 126, 190, who considers the passage to be redactional and attributes it to H. A different view is found in Schmidt, Studien, 293ff.

91. Cf. correctly Schmidt, *Studien*, 293ff.

92. In my opinion (contra Strecker, *Judenchristentum*, 195), one should not consider par. 171.19 Rehm: *astrapē ex ouranou*, to be an allusion to Paul's call vision (Acts 9:3), since Luke 10:18 fully suffices as its background; cf. also Salles, "Diatribe," 539.

93. Cf. also Strecker, *Judenchristentum*, 195.

94. On the following, cf. Brandt, *Elchasai*, 15ff.

95. The series in Epiphanius, *Pan.* 19.1.6 and 30.17.4, are almost identical with the above and can thus here remain out of consideration.

96. Brandt, *Elchasai*, 20, who of course considers this to be an "author's joke." According to him, *EpPetr.* and *Cont.* derive "from the catholic editor of Romans, who demonstrates an outlandishly decorated bit of magic for his readers" (ibid., 21).

97. Of course this distinction is regarded positively by the Elkesaites (the Holy Spirit is the feminine partner of Christ), while in 17.3 it is regarded negatively.

98. Points of contact were noted, of course, in the older research; cf. Waitz, *Pseudoklementinen*, 155ff., and in more recent times, e.g., by Salles, "Diatribe," 545–50.

99. Paul is named in both "sources" as the enemy (cf. R 1.70.1 and *EpPetr.* 2.3). Strecker, *Judenchristentum*, 249f., of course thinks that G transplanted this expression from *EpPetr.* to the "AJ II source."

100. Schmidt, *Studien*, 318f., among others.

101. Brandt, *Elchasai*, 20f.

102. Cf., e.g, Strecker, *Judenchristentum*, 141, with the important reference to Walter Bauer in Schoeps, *Theologie*, 475 n. 1.

103. Molland, "Circoncision," 31–45, goes even farther (followed apparently by Strecker in Bauer, *Orthodoxy*, 252–53), by arguing that in the milieu of the Pseudo-Clementines baptism as an act of initiation generally had taken the place of circumcision.

104. The comments do not indicate any agreement with the literary analysis of Salles (see above, n. 82), however much the author is in fact correct that a genetic connection exists between the anti-Pauline sections of the Pseudo-Clementines and Paul's opponents. Strecker, *Judenchristentum*, speaks of the fact that the anti-Pauline polemic of our section enriches "the picture of the Pauline-Jewish discussion in earliest Christianity," although "the polemic, on the contrary, . . . [is] literarily determined" (p. 196).

CHAPTER 12. THE ANTI-PAULINISM OF IRENAEUS'S
JEWISH CHRISTIANS (HERESIES 1.26.2)

1. "Qui autem dicuntur Ebionaei consentiunt quidem mundum a Deo factum, ea autem, quae sunt erga dominum, (non) similiter ut Cerinthus et Carpocrates opinantur. solo autem eo, quod est secundum Matthaeum evangelio, utuntur et apostolum Paulum recusant, apostatam eum legis dicentes. quae autem sunt prophetica, curiosius exponere nituntur; et circumciduntur ac perseverant in his consuetudinibus, quae sunt secundum legem, et iudaico charactere vitae, uti et Hierosolymam adorent, quasi domus sit Dei" ("Those who are called Ebionites agree that the world was made by God; but their opinions with respect to the Lord are [not] similar to those of Cerinthus and Carpocrates. They use the Gospel according to Matthew only, and repudiate the apostle Paul, maintaining that he was an apostate from the law. As to the prophetical writings, they endeavor to expound them in a somewhat singular manner: they practice circumcision, persevere in the observance of those customs which were enjoined by the law, and are so Judaic in their style of life that they even adore Jerusalem as though it were the house of God").

2. Cf. Luedemann, Untersuchungen, 35f.

3. On the date of the composition of the Heresies, cf. Lipsius, Quellenkritik, 50f.; and Harnack, Geschichte, II.1, pp. 320f.

4. Cf. Heresies, 4.33.2–4.

5. "Not" is not to be considered a part of the original text (see n. 1 above), for the reasons given by Stieren, App., ad loc. Contra Klijn and Reinink, Evidence, p. 20. That the work is to be struck is seen from syntactical reasons: after the antecedent clause had emphasized the difference to the previously named groups, the following clause underscores what they have in common christologically despite the named differences. Thus on the presupposition of the correctness of the reading non similiter, one would have expected that the difference would be pointed out more exactly. For support for their view, the two authors appeal to the fact "that in this part of the book . . . Irenaeus is primarily interested not in doctrines about Christ but in ideas about God. Therefore there is no reason for him to go into details about the christological beliefs of the Ebionites" (Evidence, 20). Response: the comprehensive section in which the Ebionite reference is found begins in 23.1. The scope of this section, unless there is indication to the contrary, is the derivation of all heresy from Simon Magus. I do not see that the doctrine of God here plays a special role. At the same time it must be said that in 26.2 Irenaeus is copying a source and not himself composing, as the authors incorrectly assume.

6. Probably a shortened version of Matthew without the genealogy, cf. Harnack, *Geschichte*, II.1, pp. 630ff. But cf. differently Bacon, *Studies*, 519–27 ("Matthew and the Jewish Christian Gospels").

7. Greek: *periergoterōs*, which is translated by Klijn and Reinink with "diligently" or "carefully" (*Evidence*, 20). Cf. Strecker, *Judenchristentum*, 277; and in addition Harnack, *Geschichte*, II.1, p. 631: "They have a characteristic exposition of the prophets (so do not reject it)." In any case, the expression does not necessarily have anything to do with gnostic exegesis (contra Thomas, "Ebionites," 268).

8. We do not know whether the author of the *source* had a personal knowledge of these groups.

9. Our reflections in Part II incline us toward attributing considerable historical reliability to the report (especially with regard to its anti-Paulinism).

10. Cf. what was said above with regard to the *Desposynoi*.

11. On the adoption of the term "Ebionites" by the church fathers, see chapter 1 above, passim, and Strecker, "Ebioniten," col. 488. Strecker receives the credit for having called our attention to the heresiological understanding of the Ebionites by the church fathers.

12. Cf. Harnack, *Mission* 1:401.

13. Cf. Keck, "Saints," 56.

14. Cf. Pss. 86:1f.; 132:15f; Isa. 61:1ff.; and other such references; and Dibelius, *James*, 57ff.; and Michel, art. "Armut II" in *TRE*, 4:72–76.

15. Lietzmann, *An die Galater*, on Gal. 2:10; and Strecker, Ebioniten," col. 487.

16. Here Keck, "Poor," is convincing (with bibliography); cf. idem, art. "Armut III" in *TRE*, 4: 76–80. But in response to Keck, "Poor," cf. the questions raised by Stuhlmacher, *Evangelium*, 101f., which are worth pondering.

17. Whether the self-description may be connected with the event described by Epiphanius (see below, p. 000) seems at least uncertain.

18. Bauer, *Orthodoxy*, 236. Cf. also Kümmel, in *ThR* NF 14 (1942): 93: It was the Judaists in their struggle with Paul who first introduced the concept of heresy into the Christian framework of thought.

CHAPTER 13. SUMMARY

1. The Elkesaite mother church in southern Babylonia is only an apparent exception, since Elkesai worked in the *Syrian*-Parthian border area and the movement went forth from there.

2. Exception: Hegesippus.

3. What is said above suggests that also Justin's Jewish Christians *had already taken over* an anti-Paulinism.

4. Cf. the discussion above, p. 167, on Hegesippus's community.

5. I find myself here on the opposite side from most scholars, from Ritschl on. A few sample probes: Ritschl, *Entstehung*, 23: "We will rather have to emphasize the lack of Jewish Christianity's capacity for development even more sharply than previously"; Achelis, *Christentum*, 1:240: "We see that they [i.e., the Jewish Christians] have made a reverse development in the direction of Judaism" (similarly even Strecker, "Christentum," 469 [=*Eschaton*, 302]); Bauer, *Orthodoxy*, 236: "Because of their inability to relate to a development that took place on hellenized gentile soil, the Judaists soon became a heresy, rejected with conviction by the gentile Christians. Basically, they probably had remained what they had been in the time of James the Just." Cf. similarly Goppelt, *Christentum*, 167f.; Dunn, *Unity*, 244f.; and Drane, *Paul*, 121, 176, and elsewhere.

APPENDIX: THE SUCCESSORS
OF EARLIEST JERUSALEM CHRISTIANITY:
AN ANALYSIS OF THE PELLA TRADITION

1. On excavations in Pella, see R. H. Smith, *IDBSup*, (1976), 651f. (bib.); and idem, *RB* 75 (1968): 105ff. Cf. now Meyers and Strange, *Archaeology*, 104f.

2. From earlier studies, cf. McGiffert, *History*, 562f.; Hort, *Christianity*, 174ff.; Purves, *Christianity*, 163f.; and Ritschl, *Entstehung*, 152. From more recent scholarship, cf. Goppelt, *Christentum*, 164; Schoeps, *Theologie*, 262ff.; Elliott-Binns, *Christianity*, 65ff.; and Jocz, *People*, 165f. Most recently Pesch, *Markusevangelium*, 2:291f., has declared his support for the historicity of the Pella flight (different from his earlier view in *Naherwartungen*, 217 n. 29).

3. Cf. Schwartz, "Aeren," 376; idem, *Chronologie*," 150 n. 1; Farmer, *Maccabees*, 128 n. 2; Strecker, *Judenchristentum*, 229ff. and 283–86 (debate with Simon, "Migration"); Munck, "Jewish Christianity," 103f.; Gaston, *Stone*, 142; and Schneemelcher, *Urchristentum*, 11, 52, 164. In the older research, the historicity of the Pella flight was disputed only by Joël, *Blicke*, 83ff. (on substantial grounds); Conzelmann, *History*, 111, 137, leaves the question open.

4. Brandon, *Fall*, 168ff.; and idem, *Jesus*, 208ff. Unfortunately Brandon's critique of the historicity of the Pella flight is often rejected in the same breath with his understanding of the close association of Jesus and his disciples with the Zealot movement, an understanding that is in fact untenable. For a criqitue of this latter view, cf. Hengel, "Besprechung von Brandon, *Jesus*." It is remarkable how the Pella tradition is definitely accepted as historically reliable without a close look at the relevant texts. Cf., e.g., Kretschmar, "Bedeutung," 116 n. 1; and Kümmel, in *ThR* NF 22 (1954): 152ff. (responding to Brandon, *Fall*): "Again it is clear that this entire understanding of the historical event is based on a completely unfounded rejection of the later report of the flight of the Jerusalem Christians to east Jordan."

5. Sowers, "Circumstances."

6. Simon, "Migration."

7. Gunther, "Fate."

8. Gray, "Movements."

9. This corresponds to Munck's hypothesis that Paul's opponents in Galatia were Gentile Christians and in no way represent the views of the Jewish Christians in Jerusalem; cf. above, p. 24.

10. The general consideration that a flight might have taken place sometime leads some scholars to assume incorrectly that the whole church fled to Pella; cf. e.g, Theissen, *Studien*, 118. Is it really certain that the "Zealots for the law" (Acts 21:10) did not take up arms after all? On this problem, cf. the balanced remarks of Rhoads, *Israel*, 92; and Grant; *Jews*, 210. Cf. also above, p. 62.

11. The English translation is from LCL. Words that are identical or very similar to the report in Epiphanius are italicized.

12. The English translation of the passages from the *Panarion* are taken from Klijn and Reinink, *Evidence*, 169ff.

13. English translation from J. E. Dean, *Epiphanius' Treatise on Weights and Measures: The Syriac Version* (Chicago, 1935), 30f. Dean has indicated in the notes whenever the Greek original differs from the Syriac version. The translation above is from the Greek version.

14. The following statement by Gray, "Movements," 7, is an extreme example of the fact that in the interest of a historicizing exegesis the issue of literary relationships can simply be neglected. She writes: "Epiphanius is not the most trustworthy of historians, but the combined witness of himself, Eusebius, and Hegesippus makes it an almost undeniable fact that there was a Church in Jerusalem between C.E. 70 and 135, and that this Church was composed, at least in part, of those

who had made up its number prior to the first revolt." Gray leaves the question of the origin of Eusebius's note about Pella open and immediately explains why: "Our concern is in the trustworthiness of the statement that before the fall of Jerusalem in C.E. 70 the Christian community there had fled to Pella" (ibid., 2).

15. Lawlor, *Eusebiana*, 30, has collected these similarities and writes: "If according to Eusebius the Christians received a chrēsmos, in *De Mens.* 15 it is said proechrēmatisthēsan. We have in Eusebius the phrae metanastēnai tēs poleōs corresponding to metastēnai apo tēs poleōs in *De Mens.* 15 and reminding us of apo tōn Hierosolymōn metastasis in *Pan.* 29, metanastantes, in *Pan.* 30, and metanastai in *De Mens.* 15. Jerusalem is hē polis in Eusebius and *De Mens.* 15, and Pella is tis polis in Eusebius and *Pan.* 30. The word oikein is used in relation to Pella in Eusebius exactly as in the three passages of Epiphanius, hoi eis Christon pepisteukotes as in *Pan.* 30, arden of the destruction of Jerusalem as in *De Mens.* 15, Christou phēsantos as in *Pan.* 29, though in a different connexion. We may also note that polin . . . Pellan autēn onomazousin in Eusebius and Pellē . . . polei kaloumenē in *Pan.* 30 read very much like different paraphrases of the same words."

16. Klijn and Reinink, *Evidence*, 28 n. 3, arrive at the same results. Differently Lawlor, *Eusebiana*, 28ff., who like Zahn, *Forschungen*, 6:269f., and many others, advocates the view that Epiphanius obtained his Pella notice from Hegesippus. Although we will state our view below on the issue of whether Hegesippus's theology would have allowed him to report the Pella flight at all (see p. 204), the careful presentation of Zahn and Lawlor deserves a (preliminary) response here: Zahn, *Forschungen*, 6:270f. n. 3, concludes from the fact that Epiphanius used the ancient term "Decapolis" in association with Pella—while Eusebius supposedly does not use it—that Epiphanius was dependent on Hegesippus for this expression. That is not persuasive, since (cf. K. Holl, "Epiphanius I," in GCS 25 [Leipzig, 1915], 330) Eusebius does have this ancient term "Decapolis" in association with Pella in his *Onomasticon* (par. 80:16f., Klostermann). One may add that the expression "Decapolis" in Epiphanius may derive from his own reading of the NT (cf. *Pan.* 30.2.7; see above, p. 203). According to Lawlor, *Eusebiana*, 29f., Eusebius's *Ecclesiastical History* cannot have been Epiphanius's source, "for he states definitely that the Christians left Jerusalem in obedience to a command of Christ (*Pan.* 29) which was conveyed by an angel (*De Mens.* 15), while Eusebius merely says that they had 'some sort of (tina) divine intimation (chrēsmon) granted by revelation.'" In my opinion, these small variations cannot be used as

an argument for the dependence of Epiphanius upon Hegesippus, and all the less so since Lawlor himself already harmonizes the different versions of *De Mens.* and *Pan.* Rather, the difference between Eusebius and Epiphanius pointed out by Lawlor above must be credited to Epiphanius, who has characteristically elaborated the description of the flight to Pella which he had received from Eusebius. In addition: Lawlor's assumption that Epiphanius used Hegesippus's *Hypomnemata* at all is questionable: compare Holl's comments on *Pan.* 27.6.1 (GCS 25, 308f.) with Lawlor, *Eusebiana*, 9f. (bib.).

17. In *Demonstratio Evangelica* 6.18.14 Eusebius seems to leave no room for the Pella tradition when he says that the apostles, disciples, and believing Jews were carrying on missionary work outside Palestine and thus escaped the disaster that befell Jerusalem in the Jewish War.

18. Cf. Fascher, "Untergang" (bib.); and Brandon, *Fall*, 12ff. On the interpretation of the fall of Jerusalem in Judaism, cf. Schoeps, *Zeit*, 144–83.

19. Keck, "Saints," even thinks that it is "possible that the tradition goes back no farther than the Hadrianic war in A.D. 135, though for apologetic reasons such a group would encourage the belief that its lineage goes back to those who endured the great revolt of A.D. 66–70" (p. 65 n. 36). To be sure, this noteworthy suggestion must struggle with a chronological difficulty, if Aristo of Pella is taken as documentation for the Pella tradition. Should we think of him, who wrote shortly after the Bar Kochba war, as already having confused the two wars? Further, it is an established fact that many Jewish Christians already lived in Transjordan before the 135 C.E. war. So why should the Pella tradition have originated *after* 135 C.E.?

20. The form-critical question whether Eusebius's Pella tradition was part of a miracle story, an apocalypse, or a historical narrative cannot be answered because of the fragmentary character of the tradition. (All the same, we can say this much, that it is to be considered a kind of founding legend of the Pella church; see above, p. 204). It should, however, be clear, that the Pella tradition affirms the deliverance of the whole church.

21. Contra Jeremias, *Golgotha*, 11, who like many others (Bagatti, *Church*, 5–10, is an extreme case) simply combines and harmonizes the extant Pella texts instead of first examining the literary relation of the texts to each other.

22. On this expression, cf. Hyldahl, "Hypomnemata."

23. To be sure, we have no explicit reference to the place where the selection was held. Even the exact time of the selection (before or after the war) is unclear. It would thus be incorrect to say: "According to

tradition, when hostilities started in 66, the entire Christian church of Jerusalem, led by its chief Simon . . . , proceeded upon a single organized flight to Pella" (Grant, *Jews*, 210). Against this also is the observation that Symeon is not at all mentioned in Eusebius's Pella tradition.

24. Against this, Lawlor, *Eusebiana*, 32, states "that Eusebius introduces his account of the flight with a reference to the Memoirs" of Hegesippus. He is thinking of the sentence in the (preceding) context of the Pella report: "In addition to all, James, who was the first after the ascension of our saviour to be appointed to the throne of the bishopric in Jerusalem, passed away in the manner mentioned above" (*Hist. Ecc.* 3.5.2). This is not convincing. Certainly, Eusebius had taken the report of the martyrdom of James from the work of Hegesippus. But the sentence quoted above is only part of Eusebius's introduction to the flight to Pella in which the crimes of the Jews are listed. The killing of James is only one of many crimes. One should better say: Eusebius introduces the tradition of the Pella flight with a summary of his own in which there is reference to one of Hegesippus's stories. This of course cannot make it probable that the Pella tradition was also taken from Hegesippus's *Hypomnemata*.

25. Lawlor, *Eusebiana*, 33, however, believes that in Eusebius *Hist. Ecc.* 3.11 the expression *pantachothen* includes Pella and refers to the coming of the disciples from Pella to Jerusalem. By this assumption Lawlor reads into the text something that the passage simply does not contain unless, with Lawlor, one presupposes in advance that Hegesippus mentioned the exodus to Pella. Further, Eusebius *Hist. Ecc.* 3.11 is not a quotation from Hegesippus but a summary of a quotation that appears in its pure form in *Hist. Ecc.* 4.22.4f.; cf. Zahn, *Forschungen*, 6:235, and the appropriate comments of Kemler, *Herrenbruder*, 6ff.; cf. also pp. 159f., above.

26. Cf. Eusebius, *Hist. Ecc.* 4.22.4f. and the commentary of Zahn, *Forschungen*, 6:235ff.

27. Nevertheless Stevenson, *Eusebius*, 7, considers it certain that Hegesippus reports the flight to Pella. Conzelmann likewise considers it probable, *History*, 137.

28. Harnack, *Überlieferung*, 124f.

29. Schlatter, *Synagoge*, 154 (from idem, *Die Kirche Jerusalems vom Jahre 70 bis 130* [Gütersloh, 1898]).

30. On this, cf. Harnack, *Geschichte*, I.1, pp. 92ff. (bib.). Cf. further Harnack, *Die Altercatio Simonis Iudaei et Theophili Christiani*, 1–136; Zahn, *Forschungen*, 4:308–29; Corssen, *Die Altercatio Simonis Iudaei et Theophili Christiani auf ihre Quellen geprüft*, on which see Harnack in ThLZ 15 (1890), cols. 624–26. Scholarship has tried hard to recover the complete text of this dialogue, which was known to Celsus.

Probably Tertullian used it (in *Adv. Jud.*), probably also Justin (in *Dial.*) and Euagrius (*Altercatio Legis inter Simonem Iudaeum et Theophilum Christianum* [CSEL 45, ed. E. Bratke]). The following additional dialogues are supposed to have used Aristo's lost *Dialogue*: McGiffert, ed., *Dialogue Between a Christian and a Jew*; Conybeare, ed., *The Dialogues of Athanasius and Zacchaeus and of Timothy and Aquila*; on the latter, cf. Goodspeed, "'The Dialogue of Timothy and Aquila': Two Unpublished Manuscripts," 58–78; Robertson, "The Dialogue of Timothy and Aquila: The Need for a New Edition," 276–88; and Birdsall, "The Dialogue of Timothy and Aquila and the Early Harmonistic Traditions," 66–77. In addition, compare Bruns, "The Altercatio Jasonis et Papisci, Philo, and Anastasius the Sinaite," 287–94. The whole question deserves a new investigation. Judging from the extant fragments, it seems that Aristo had connections with Jewish Christianity. He probably used Aquila's translation of the OT. On this latter, cf. Williams, *Adversus Judaeos*, 29.

31. Marxsen, *Evangelist*, 209f.

32. On Galilee in early Christianity, cf. the thorough studies of Stemberger in Davies, *Gospel*, 409–38 ("Galilee—Land of Salvation?"): and Freyne, *Galilee*, 344–91. On the extent of Galilee, cf. Stemberger, in Davies, *Gospel*, 415ff.; and Freyne, *Galilee*, 3f.

33. Marxsen, *Evangelist*, 115f. n. 176.

34. Cf. the survey in Pesch, *Naherwartungen*, 19–47; and Hahn, "Rede," 240–66. Hahn thinks of a Christian tradition (from the years 66–70 C.E.) as the primary source, while on the other hand Pesch, *Naherwartungen*, 207–18, considers a Jewish text (from the year 40 C.E., when Caligula wanted to have his statue erected in the Jerusalem temple) to be the primary source. Pesch, *Markusevangelium*, 2:290ff., now sees the matter differently, understanding Mark 13:14 to be a prophecy current in Mark's time related to the Pella tradition.

35. Dodd, *Parables*, 46f.

36. Schoeps, *Studien*, 70f.

37. Cf. Beasley-Murray, *Jesus*, 242ff., for additional examples of this type of interpretation.

38. See rightly Hahn, "Rede," 259 n. 74.

39. Schoeps, *Studien*, 70.

40. Thus, e.g., Weiss, *Earliest Christianity*, 2:714f.

41. Cf. Zmijewski, *Eschatologiereden*, 59ff. (bib.); and Geiger, *Endzeitreden*, 149ff.

42. Contra Flückiger, "Zerstörung."

43. It is arbitrary to find in Luke 21:16 a possible reference to the martyrdom of James (so Simon, "Migration," 40 n. 10), since this verse presupposes Mark 13:12.

44. Sowers, "Circumstance," 307, writes: "Had not the flight from the city been an open possibility at some time during the war, it would have made no sense for Luke to have included an entreaty to flee directed to the folk in Jerusalem." Sowers ascribes to the author of the Third Gospel a knowledge of the Jewish War which he would have to demonstrate in advance; cf. the same author similarly: "Evidence that flight from Jerusalem was possible at least during the earlier period of the conflict is found" in Luke 21:20. Sowers thus considers it possible "that Luke may be thinking of the earlier encirclement by the Idumean troops" (War 4.282) (ibid., 320 n. 44).

45. Other NT texts that are sometimes considered to be indirect references to the Pella tradition are Matt. 10:23 (so Robinson, Jesus, 76 [opposed by Bammel, "Matthäus"]) and Rev. 12:6ff. (cf. Schoeps, Theologie, 267f. [bib.]).

46. Cf. above, pp. 18ff. We there make a critical appropriation of the analysis in Strecker, Judenchristentum, 221–54, and adopt the designation "R I source."

47. Cf. Strecker, Judenchristentum, 253; see above, p. 181.

48. It should be emphasized here that we are not concerned with the question of whether James was in fact the first and Symeon the second bishop of Jerusalem. We are, rather, seeking Hegesippus's understanding of the matter. But since this distinction is often overlooked, we may immediately add that Jacob was (of course) not the (first) bishop of Jerusalem; cf. McGiffert, History, 564f.; and Schwartz, Eusebius Werke, 2:ccxxvif. On the other hand, another question deserves more attention: To what extent does Hegesippus's account of the selection of Symeon reflect historical reality, in that it reflects a kind of caliphate in early Christianity? Cf. von Campenhausen, "Nachfolge," and Stauffer, "Kalifat," as well as our comments above, pp. 119f.

49. Cf. Andersen, Kirchen, 135: Hegesippus made "that tradition . . . which saw in James the Just the founder of the whole church and thus was primarily oriented to the continuity of the officeholders of the Jerusalem bishop's chair . . . and thus shows that he is a spokesman for a Jewish-Christian ecclesiology."

50. Cf. Eusebius, Demonstratio Evangelica 3.5.108: kai hē historia de katechei hōs kai megistē tis ēn ekklēsia Christou en tois Hierosolymois hypo Ioudaiōn sygkrotoumenē mechri tōn chronōn tēs kat' Adrianon poliorkias ("and the story goes that until the time of the siege by Hadrian there was an extremely significant church of Christ at Jerusalem which consisted of Jews"—trans. by author).

51. Cf. the appropriate comments of Jöel, Blicke, 84.

52. The fact that according to Eusebius (Hist. Ecc. 5.12) fifteen Gentile Christian bishops followed fifteen Jewish-Christian bishops (two

names have dropped out of the list in *Hist. Ecc.* 5.12) of course generates the suspicion that this parallelism (2 x 15) is artificial and goes back to the fifteenth Gentile Christian bishop, Narcissus, who in any case will be the creator of the present form of the list (response to Prigent, *Fin*, 81; cf. also Andresen, *Kirchen*, 214; and Carrington, *Church*, 1:418). On the other hand, Narcissus will have used material from older lists, since he probably was not the first monarchial bishop of Aelia.

53. Not the descendants of the disciples of the apostles, as Simon, "Migration," 53, presupposes. Simon obviously refers to the Syriac version (beginning of chap. 15), which is already a harmonization of the Aquila story and the Pella tradition. The Greek original reads "the disciples of the apostles."

54. It should be a priori clear that the escape of Johanan ben Zakkai is no analogy to the Pella flight, as is sometimes argued (so Richardson, *Israel*, 35 n. 4). Johanan escaped as an individual, the Jerusalem church is supposed to have escaped as a group. On Johanan, cf. Neusner, *Life*; and Saldarini, "Johanan". Saldarini, "Johanan," 203f., considers it possible that the story of Johanan's escape does not belong to the oldest layer of the tradition. Should that be correct, we would have an interesting analogy to the Pella tradition. On the flight of Johanan, cf. Schäfer, "Die Flucht Johanan b. Zakkais aus Jerusalem und die Gründung des 'Lehrhauses' in Jabne," 43–101.

55. Cf. Josephus, *Ant.* 20.256 and *War* 2.279: the end of 64 C.E., with the inauguration of Gessius Florus into office. Of course the passages from Josephus are *not* allusions to the Pella flight (response to Klausner, *Paul*, 599 n. 19).

56. But cf. Josephus, *War*, 2.556: the end of 66 C.E.

57. On this issue, Simon, "Migration," 43, and Brandon are in agreement.

58. Cf. Josephus, *War* 2.562: "The Jews who had pursued Cestius, on their return to Jerusalem, partly by force, partly by persuasion, brought over to their side such pro-Romans as remained."

59. Cf. Schürer, *Geschichte*, 2:173–76 (new English ed. 2:145–48).

60. Simon, "Migration," 42, however, thinks that the flight of the Essenes into the Gentile city of Damascus is a good parallel; so also Elliott-Binns, *Christianity*, 67. This suggestion does not sufficiently take into consideration that a literal understanding of "Damascus" in the Qumran documents is extremely unlikely; cf. Davies, *Gospel*, 223f. (bib.); and Charlesworth, *John*, 104f. (bib.); against Simon's understanding, cf. also Reinink, *JSJ* 5 (1974): 77f.

61. Gunther, "Fate," 91, affirms this, because "scout-messengers from the Jerusalem church must have prepared the way for the gath-

ering of Judaean and Galilean refugees," or "Jews and Christians had become distinguished since Nero's persecutions of A.D. 64" (ibid., 90). But would this distinction include *Jewish* Christians and Jews?

62. The statements of Kraft, *Entstehung*, 288, are to be corrected in the light of the passage from Josephus mentioned above.

63. Differently, Simon, "Migration," 43: "The fact that they were Jews, even when it was a matter of being Jewish Christians, probably sufficed to confer impunity." But would this apply to Jewish deserters?

64. This possibility must be seriously considered. Cf. Simon, "Migration," 46 (referring to a statement of Reinach); cf. also Gray, "Movements," 4. In favor of such a possibility, I would point out that cities such as Scythopolis, Ascalon, and others whose sacking (together with that of Pella) is reported in *War* 2.458f. are mentioned again in the immediate context (2.477). This would seem to indicate that they were not completely destroyed and opens the possibility that Pella also was not sacked (though there is no report on Pella afterward).

65. Gray, "Movements," writes: "If Pella was not pronationalist at the onset of the war, after this incident (i.e. as reported in *War* 2.458) it was probably even less so, and there is no reason to believe that it would have been hostile to others fleeing from the Jews." Against this conjecture one may note what the people of Scythopolis did to the Jews who had been living there before, although these wanted to join them in their fight against the rebellious Jews (Josephus, *War* 2.466ff., 477; *Life*, 26f.).

66. The following brief remarks are intended only to relate the phenomenon that lies behind the Pella tradition to other contemporary phenomena. An exhaustive treatment of the problem is found in von Campenhausen, *Ecclesiastical Authority*, 76–177; cf. also Blum, *Tradition* (on which see K. Beyschlag, in ThLZ 92 [1967], cols. 112–15).

67. On this, cf. Müller, *Theologiegeschichte*, 67–74.

68. Hebrews gives the impression that it is a Pauline letter by the way it concludes; cf. Wrede, *Rätsel*, 62f.

69. Cf. the collection by Brox, *Pseudepigraphie*.

70. Exceptions are the writings of Ignatius (on which see von Campenhausen, *Ecclesiastical Authority*, 103–05) and the *Didache*. Cf. in addition Grant, "Succession," 180f. Hegesippus, to be sure, does not know of the apostles as bearers of authority (see above, pp. 158ff.), but nevertheless a similar phenomenon may be observed in him, since for him (from "apostolic" times) the Jerusalem church and James the Lord's brother were of normative significance for his own time.

71. Irenaeus (and his source in *Heresies* 1.23ff.) on polemical grounds attributes the beginning of Gnosticism to apostolic times, namely, to Simon Magus. Cf. Luedemann, *Untersuchungen*, 36f.

72. Cf. Luedemann, "Geschichte," 97ff.

73. This is the reason it is unlikely that the Gnostics were impressed by Tertullian's declaration that their doctrine had no apostolic origin but was merely of recent origin (*Praescr.* 30).

74. We speak of "apostolicity in the broadest sense," because it is a matter of having bearers of authority from the earliest Christian times, whether or not they belonged to the apostles (cf. also n. 70, above).

75. On the Aelia church and its relation to other churches, cf. Harnack, *Mission*, 2:105ff., 113.

76. Brandon, *Fall*, 173, finds the transmitters of the Pella tradition among the Gentile Christians of Aelia who, after living in Pella, moved after 135 C.E. to Jerusalem and claimed to stem from the original Jerusalem mother church. In my opinion, a Jewish Christian context fits better, all the more so since Jewish Christians were living in the second century also in Pella. Furthermore, the elements of the Pella tradition do not presuppose a return. Finally, I doubt whether Gentile Christians would so early be proud of stemming from the Jerusalem mother church.

77. On the term "Jewish Christian," see above, pp. 29f.

78. It is to be noted that the R 1 source represents a partial correction to the canonical Acts.

79. Epiphanius enumerates several places not far away from Pella: Moabitis, Kokabe, Basanitis (30.18.1). From his statement that Ebion received the impetus (for his preaching) in Pella (30.2.7), one may conclude that these groups who claimed to be the "poor" of apostolic times also lived in Pella. Or were they even the founders of the Pella tradition?

80. Simon, *Israel*, rightly states against Munck: "Even if the evidence were to show that the migration was a myth, this would still not prove that the first Jewish Christianity became extinct in A.D. 70" (pp. 416f.).

81. Cf. our attempt in chapter 6.

82. Funk and Richardson, "Sounding," 87, state that "it is difficult to reject the tradition [i.e., on the flight to Pella] because there is no ostensible motive in the choice of Pella on the part of the early church." We have attempted to show why Pella was "chosen."

BIBLIOGRAPHY

SOURCES

Altercatio Legis inter Simonen Iudaeum et Theophilim Christianum. CSEL 45. Edited by E. Bratke.

The Apocrypha and Pseudepigrapha of the Old Testament. 2 vols. Translated by R. H. Charles. Oxford, 1913.

The Apostolic Fathers. 2 vols. Translated by Kirsopp Lake. LCL.

The Books of Elijah, ed. Michael Stone and John Strugnell. Missoula: Scholars Press, 1979.

Clement of Alexandria. *The Stromata.* Pp. 299–568 in *ANF*, vol. 2. Edited by A. Cleveland Coxe. Grand Rapids, 1962.

(Pseudo-)Clement. *Homilies.* Pp. 215–346 in *ANF*, vol. 8. Edited by Alexander Roberts and James Donaldson. Grand Rapids, 1951.

———. *Recognitions.* Pp. 75–211 in *ANF*, vol. 8. Edited by Alexander Roberts and James Donaldson. Grand Rapids, 1951.

The Cologne Mani Codex: "Concerning the Origin of His Body". Edited and translated by Ron Cameron and Arthur J. Dewey. Missoula, 1979. (Abbr.: CMC.)

Constitutions of the Holy Apostles. Pp. 385–508 in *ANF*, vol. 7. Edited by A. Cleveland Coxe. Grand Rapids, 1951.

Diogenes Laertius. *Lives of Eminent Philosophers.* 2 vols. Translated by R. D. Hicks. LCL. 1925.

Epiphanius. *Epiphanius' Treatise on Weights and Measures: The Syriac Version.* Edited and translated by J. E. Dean. Chicago, 1935.

Eusebius. *The Ecclesiastical History.* Vol. 1 translated by Kirsopp Lake. LCL. 1953. Vol. 2 translated by J. E. L. Oulton. LCL. 1957.

———. *A New Eusebius.* Edited by James Stevenson. London, 1974.

The Fihrist of al-Nadim. 2 vols. Translated and edited by Bayard Dodge. New York, 1970.

Hippolytus. *The Refutation of All Heresies.* Pp. 9–153 in *ANF*, vol. 5. Edited by Alexander Roberts and James Donaldson. Grand Rapids, 1981.

Irenaeus. *Contra Omnes Haereses Libri Quinque.* Edited by Adolphus Stieren. Leipzig, 1853.

———. *Against Heresies.* Pp. 309–567 in *ANF*, vol. 1. Edited by Alexander Roberts and James Donaldson. Grand Rapids, 1969.

Jerome. *Lives of Illustrious Men.* Pp. 359–84 in *NPNF²*, vol. 3. Edited by Philip Schaff. Grand Rapids, 1953.

Josephus, Flavius. *Antiquities.* Vols. 4–10 in *Josephus.* Translated by H. St. J. Thackeray, Ralph Marcus, and Louis H. Feldman. LCL. 1976–81.

———. *The Jewish War.* Vols. 2–3 in *Josephus.* Translated by H. St. J. Thackeray. LCL. 1976–79.

———. *The Life. Against Apion.* Translated by H. St. J. Thackeray. LCL. 1926.

Justin Martyr. *The First Apology.* Pp. 242–89 in *Early Christian Fathers.* Library of Christian Classics, vol. 1. Translated and edited by Cyril C. Richardson. Philadelphia, 1953.

———. *Dialogue with Trypho, a Jew.* Pp. 194–270 in *ANF*, vol. 1. Edited by Philip Schaff. Grand Rapids, 1953.

———. *Dialogus cum Tryphone.* Pp. 4–463 in *St. Justin. Philosophi et Martyris Opera*, 2. Edited by Joann. Carol. Theod. Otto. Jena, 1842.

The Mishnah. Translated by Herbert Danby. Oxford, 1958.

Philo of Alexandria. *Complete Works.* 12 vols. Translated by F. H. Colson, G. H. Whitaker, and R. Marcus. LCL. 1929–62.

Philostratus. *Life of Apollonius of Tyana.* 2 vols. Translated by Frederick Cornwallis Conybeare. LCL. 1912.

Plato. *Dialogues.* 12 vols. Translated by H. N. Fowler, P. Shorey, et al. LCL. 1914–29.

Plutarch. *Moralia.* 16 vols. LCL. 1927–76.

Stern, Menahem, ed. and trans. *Greek and Latin Authors on Jews and Judaism.* 3 vols. Jerusalem, 1974–84.

Suetonius. *The Lives of the Caesars and The Lives of Illustrious Men.* 2 vols. Translated by J. C. Rolfe. LCL. 1965.

Die syrische Didaskalia. TU 25. Edited by Hans Achelis and Johannes Flemming. Leipzig, 1904.

Tertullian. *On the Veiling of Virgins.* Pp. 27–38 in *ANF*, vol. 4. Edited by A. Cleveland Coxe. Grand Rapids, 1956.

———. *The Writings of Quintus Sept. Flor. Tertullianus*, 2. Ante-Nicene Christian Library, vol. 15. Translated by Peter Holmes. Edinburgh, 1870.

Xenophon. *Memorabilia and Oeconomicus.* Translated by E. C. Marchant. LCL. 1923.

SECONDARY LITERATURE

Abel, Félix-Marie. *Histoire de la Palestine depuis la conquête d'Alexandre jusqua'à l'invasion arabe.* 2 vols. EtB. Paris, 1952.

BIBLIOGRAPHY

Abramowski, Luise. "*Diadoche* und *Orthos Logos* bei Hegesipp." *ZKG* 87 (1976): 321–27.

Achelis, Hans. *Das Christentum in den ersten drei Jahrhunderten.* 2 vols. Leipzig, 1912. 2d ed. (abbr. in 1 vol.). Leipzig, 1925.

Aland, B. "Mani und Bardesanes—Zur Entstehung des manichäischen Systems." Pp. 144–69 in *Synkretismus im syrisch-persischen Kulturgebiet.* Edited by Albert Dietrich. Göttingen, 1975.

Aland, Kurt. "Der Herrenbruder Jakobus und der Jakobusbrief." In *ThLZ* 69 (1944), cols. 97–104. (= Pp. 233–45 in *Neutestamentliche Entwürfe.* ThB 63. Munich, 1979.)

Allen, Edgar Leonard. "Controversy in the New Testament." *NTS* 1 (1954–55): 143–49.

Allo, Ernest-Bernard. *Saint Paul: Première Epître aux Corinthiens.* EtB. Paris, 1956.

Alon, Gedalyahu. *Jews, Judaism and the Classical World.* Jerusalem, 1977.

Alsup, John E. *The Post Resurrection Appearance Stories of the Gospel Tradition.* CThM A.5. Stuttgart, 1975.

Andresen, Carl. *Die Kirchen der alten Christenheit.* RM 29.1/2. Stuttgart, 1971.

Avi Yonah, Michael. *Geschichte der Juden im Zeitalter des Talmud.* SJ 2. Berlin, 1962.

―――. *The Holy Land.* Grand Rapids, 1966.

Bacon, Benjamin W. *Studies in Matthew.* New York, 1930.

Bagatti, Bellamino. *The Church from the Circumcision.* Translated by Eugene Hoade. Jerusalem, 1971.

Bammel, Ernst. "Herkunft und Funktion der Traditionselemente in 1.Kor. 15,1–11." *ThZ* 11 (1955): 401–19.

―――. "Matthäus 10,23" *StTh* 15 (1961): 79–92.

Barnard, Leslie William. *Justin Martyr: His Life and Thought.* London, 1967.

Barnett, Albert E. *Paul Becomes a Literary Influence.* Chicago, 1941.

Barrett, Charles Kingsley. "Cephas and Corinth." Pp. 1–12 in *Abraham unser Vater. O. Michel Festschrift.* Edited by O. Betz, M. Hengel, and P. Schmidt. AGJU 5. Leiden, 1963.

―――. "Christianity at Corinth." *BJRL* 46 (1963–64): 269–97.

―――. *A Commentary on the Epistle to the Romans.* BNTC. London, 1957. (= HNTC. New York, 1958.)

―――. *A Commentary on the First Epistle to the Corinthians.* BNTC. London, 1971. (= HNTC. New York, 1968.)

―――. *A Commentary on the Second Epistle to the Corinthians.* BNTC. London, 1973. (= HNTC. New York, 1974.)

―――. "HO ADIKĒSAS (2 Cor. 7.12)." Pp. 149–57 in *Verborum Ver-*

itas. G. Stählin Festschrift. Edited by O. Böcher and K. Haacker. Wuppertal, 1970.

_____. "Jews and Judaizers in the Epistles of Ignatius." Pp. 220–44 in *Jews, Greeks, and Christians*. W. D. Davies Festschrift. Edited by R. Hamerton-Kelly and R. Scroggs. SJLA 21. Leiden, 1976.

_____. "Paul and the Pillar Apostles." Pp. 1–19 in *Studia Paulina*. J. de Zwaan Festschrift. Edited by J. N. Sevenster. Haarlem, 1953.

_____. "Pauline Controversies in the Post-Pauline Period." *NTS* 20 (1973–74): 229–45.

_____. "Paul's Opponents in II Corinthians." *NTS* 17 (1970–71): 233–54.

_____. "PSEUDAPOSTOLOI (2 Cor. 11.13)." Pp. 377–96 in *Mélanges bibliques*. B. Rigaux Festschrift. Edited by A. Descamps and A. de Halleux. Gembloux, 1970.

_____. "*Shaliah* and Apostle." Pp. 88–102 in *Donum Gentilicium*. D. Daube Festschrift. Edited by C. K. Barrett, E. Bammel, and W. D. Davies. Oxford, 1978.

_____. "Things Sacrificed to Idols." *NTS* 11 (1965-66): 138–53.

Barthélemy, Dominique. "Qui est Symmaque?" *CBQ* 36 (1974): 451–65.

Bartsch, Christian. *"Frühkatholizismus" als Kategorie historisch-kritischer Theologie*. Studien zu jüdischen Volk und christlicher Gemeinde, 3. Berlin, 1980.

Bartsch, Hans-Werner. "Die Argumentation des Paulus in I Kor 15,3–11." *ZNW* 55 (1964): 261–74.

Bauer, Johannes B. "Uxores circumducere (1 Kor 9,5)." *BZ* NF 3 (1959): 94–102.

Bauer, Walter. *A Greek-English Lexicon of the New Testament and Other Early Christian Literature*. Translated and edited by William R. Arndt and F. Wilbur Gingrich. Chicago, 1979.

_____. "Neues Testament: Das apostolische und nachapostolische Zeitalter." *ThR* 12 (1909); 459–69.

_____. *Orthodoxy and Heresy in Earliest Christianity*. Edited by Robert A. Kraft and Gerhard Krodel. Philadelphia, 1971.

Baumbach, Günther. "Die von Paulus im Philipperbrief bekämpften Irrlehrer." *Kairos* 13 (1971): 252–66. (= Pp. 293–310 in *Gnosis und Neues Testament*. Edited by K.-W. Tröger. Berlin, 1973.)

_____. "Der sadduzäische Konservatismus." Pp. 201–13 in *Literatur und Religion des Frühjudentums*. Edited by J. Maier and J. Schreiner. Würzburg, 1973.

Baur, Ferdinand Christian. *Die christliche Gnosis oder die christliche Religions-Philosophie in ihrer geschichtlichen Entwicklung*. Tübingen, 1835. (= Darmstadt, 1967.)

_____. "Die Christuspartei in der korinthischen Gemeinde, der

Gegensatz des petrinischen und paulinischen Christenthums in der alten Kirche, der Apostel Petrus in Rom." *TZTh (1831): 61–206. (= Pp. 1–146 in Ferdinand Christian Baur: Ausgewählte Werke in Einzelausgaben.* Vol. 1, *Historisch-kritische Untersuchungen zum Neuen Testament.* Edited by K. Scholder. With an introduction by E. Käsemann. Stuttgart–Bad Cannstatt, 1963.)

———. *The Church History of the First Three Centuries.* Translated by Allan Menzies, 2 vols. Ann Arbor, 1979.

———. *De Ebionitarum origine et doctrina, ab Essenis repetenda. Schulprogramm.* Tübingen, 1831.

———. *Kirchengeschichte des neunzehnten Jahrhunderts.* Edited by E. Zeller. Tübingen, 1862. (= *Ferdinand Christian Baur: Ausgewählte Werke in Einzelausgaben,* vol. 4. Edited by K. Scholder. With an introduction by H. Liebing. Stuttgart-Bad Cannstatt, 1970.)

———. *Lehrbuch der christlichen Dogmengeschichte.* Leipzig, 1867. (= Darmstadt, 1968.)

———. *De orationis habitae a Stephano Act. Cap. VII. consilio, et de Protomartyris hujus in christianae rei primordiis momento. Adduntur critica quaedam de loco Act. XXI.20. Schulprogramm.* Tübingen, 1829. (Abbr.: Baur, Consilio.)

——— *Paul, the Apostle of Jesus Christ: His Life and Work, His Epistles and His Doctrine.* Translated by A. Menzies. Edited by Eduard Zeller. 2 vols. London, 1978. (= London, 1876.)

———. *Die sogenannten Pastoralbriefe des Apostels Paulus aufs neue kritisch untersucht.* Stuttgart, 1835.

———. *Die Tübingen Schule und ihre Stellung zur Gegenwart.* Tübingen, 1860² (="Für und wider die Tübinge Schule," pp. 293–465 in *Ferdinand Christian Baur. Ausgewählte Werke in Einzelausgaben* 5. Stuttgart and Bad Cannstatt, 1975.

———. "Über Zweck und Veranlassung des Römerbriefs und die damit zusammenhängenden Verhältnisse der römischen Gemoinde." *TZTh (1836): 179–232. (= Pp. 147–200 in Ausgewählte Werke,* vol. 1. Edited by K. Scholder.)

Beare, Francis Wright. *A Commentary on the Epistle to the Philippians.* BNTC. London, 1973. (= HNTC. New York, 1959.)

Beasley-Murray, George R. *Jesus and the Future.* London, 1954.

Beckh, Heinrich. "Die Tübinger historische Schule." *ZPK* NF 47 (1864): 1–57, 69–95, 133–78, 203–44.

Berger, Klaus. "Almosen für Israel." *NTS* 23 (1977): 180–204.

———. *Die Auferstehung des Propheten und die Erhöhung des Menschensohnes.* StUNT 13. Göttingen, 1976.

———. *Exegese und Philosophie.* SBS 123/24. Stuttgart, 1986.

———. "Die impliziten Gegner: Zur Methode der Erschliessung von

'Gegnern' in neutestamentlichen Texten." Pp. 373–400 in *Kirche*. G. Bornkamm Festschrift. Edited by D. Lührmann and G. Strecker. Tübingen, 1980.

_____. "Zur Diskussion über die Herkunft von I Kor. II.9." *NTS* 24 (1978): 271–83.

Betz, Hans-Dieter. *Der Apostel Paulus und die sokratische Tradition*. BHTh 45. Tübingen, 1972.

_____. "Eine Christus-Aretalogie bei Paulus." *ZThK* 66 (1969): 288–305.

_____. "2 Cor 6:14—7:1, An Anti-Pauline Fragment?" *JBL* 92 (1973): 88–108.

_____. *2 Corinthians 8 and 9: A Commentary on Two Administrative Letters of the Apostle Paul*. Hermeneia. Philadelphia, 1985.

_____. "Eine Episode im Jüngsten Gericht (Mt 7,21–23)." *ZThK* 78 (1981): 1–30.

_____. *Essays on the Sermon on the Mount*. Philadelphia, 1985.

_____. *Galatians: A Commentary on Paul's Letter to the Churches in Galatia*. Hermeneia. Philadelphia, 1979.

_____. "Geist, Freiheit und Gesetz: Die Botschaft des Paulus an die Gemeinden in Galatien." *ZThK* 71 (1974): 78–93.

_____. "Die Makarismen der Bergpredigt (Matthäus 5,3–12)." *ZThK* 75 (1978): 3–19.

_____. *Nachfolge und Nachahmung Jesu Christi im Neuen Testament*. BHTh 35. Tübingen, 1967.

_____. "Paul in the Mani Biography (Codex Manichaicus Coloniensis)." Pp. 215–34 in *Codex Manichaicus Coloniensis*. Edited by Luigi Cirillo with Amneris Roselli. Marra, 1986.

_____. "The Sermon on the Mount: Its Literary Genre and Function." *JR* 59 (1979): 285–97.

Beyschlag, Karlmann. "Das Jakobusmartyrium und seine Verwandten in der frühchristlichen Literatur." *ZNW* 56 (1965): 149–78.

Billerbeck, Paul. *Kommentar zum Neuen Testament aus Talmud und Midrasch*. 4 vols. Munich, 1922–61. Several reprints. (Abbr.: Bill.)

Birdsall, J. N. "The Dialogue of Timothy and Aquila and the Early Harmonistic Traditions." *NovTest* 22 (1980): 66–77.

Black, Matthew. *The Scrolls and Christian Origins*. London, 1961. (= New York, 1961.)

Blank, Josef. *Paulus und Jesus*. StANT 18. Munich, 1968.

Blass, F., and A. Debrunner. *A Greek Grammar of the New Testament and Other Early Christian Literature*. Translated and revised by Robert W. Funk. Chicago, 1961.

Blinzler, Josef. *Aus der Welt und Umwelt des Neuen Testaments*. *Gesammelte Aufsätze*, vol. 1. SBB. Stuttgart, 1969.

Blum, Günther Georg. *Tradition und Sukzession*. Berlin, 1963.

Böhlig, Alexander. "Der judenchristliche Hintergrund in gnostischen Schriften von Nag Hammadi." Pp. 102–11 in *Mysterion und Wahrheit*. AGJU 6. Leiden, 1968.

_____, and Pahor Labib. *Koptisch-gnostische Apokalypsen aus Codex V von Nag Hammadi im Koptischen Museum zu Alt-Kairo*. Halle, 1963.

Bornkamm, Günther. "Besprechung zu Schoeps, Theologie und Geschichte des Judenchristentums." *ZKG* 64 (1952–53): 196–204.

_____. "Das missionarische Verhalten des Paulus nach 1Kor 9,19–23 und in der Apostelgeschichte (1966)." Pp. 149–61 in *Geschichte und Glaube*, II. *Gesammelte Aufsätze*, vol. 4. BEvTh 53. Munich, 1971.

_____. *Paul*. Translated by D. M. G. Stalker. New York, 1969.

_____. "Der Römerbrief als Testament des Paulus." Pp. 120–39 in *Geschichte und Glaube*, II. *Gesammelte Aufsätze*, vol. 4. BEvTh 53. Munich, 1971.

_____. "Theologie als Teufelskunst." Pp. 140–48 in *Geschichte und Glaube*, II. *Gesammelte Aufsätze*, vol. 4. BEvTh 53. Munich, 1971.

_____. "Die Vorgeschichte des sogenannten Zweiten Korintherbriefes (1961)." Pp. 162–94 in *Geschichte und Glaube*, II. *Gesammelte Aufsätze*, vol. 4. BEvTh 53. Munich, 1971.

Borse, Udo. "Paulus in Jerusalem." Pp. 43–64 in *Kontinuität und Einheit*. F. Mussner Festschrift. Freiburg, 1981.

_____. *Der Standort des Galaterbriefes*. BBB 41. Cologne, 1972.

Bousset, Wilhelm. *Kyrios Christos: A History of the Belief in Christ from the Beginnings of Christianity to Irenaeus*. Translated by John E. Steely. With a foreword by Rudolf Bultmann. Nashville, 1970.

_____. *Die Religion des Judentums in späthellenistischen Zeitalter*. Edited by H. Gressmann. HNT 21. Tübingen, 1966.

Brandon, Samuel G. F. "The Death of James the Just: A New Interpretation." Pp. 57–69 in *Studies in Mysticism and Religion*. G. G. Scholem Festschrift. Jerusalem, 1967.

_____. *The Fall of Jerusalem and the Christian Church*. London, 1957.

_____. *Jesus and the Zealots*. Manchester, 1967.

_____. *The Trial of Jesus of Nazareth*. London, 1968.

Brandt, Wilhelm. *Elchasai, ein Religionsstifter und sein Werk*. Leipzig, 1912. (= Amsterdam, 1971.)

_____. *Die jüdischen Baptismen oder das religiöse Waschen und Baden in Judentum mit Einschluss des Judenchristentums*. BZNW 18. Giessen, 1910.

Brashler, James A., and Marvin Meyer. "James in the Nag Hammadi Library." Unpublished paper. SBL Seminar: Jewish Christianity. San Francisco, 1979.

Braun, Herbert, *Qumran und das Neue Testament*, vol. 2. Tübingen, 1966.

Brown, Scott Kent. "James. A religio-historical study of the relations between Jewish, Gnostic, and Catholic Christianity in the early period through an investigation of the traditions about James the Lord's brother". Ph.D. diss. Brown University, 1972.

———. "Jewish and Gnostic Elements in the Second Apocalypse of James (CG V, 4)." *NovTest* 17 (1975): 225–37.

Brown, Schuyler. "The Matthean Community and the Gentile Mission." *NovTest* 22 (1980): 193–221.

Brox, Norbert, ed. *Pseudepigraphie in der heidnischen und jüdischchristlichen Antike*. WdF 484. Darmstadt, 1977.

Bruce, Frederick Fyvie. "The History of New Testament Study." Pp. 21–59 in *New Testament Interpretation*. edited by I. Howard Marshall. Exeter, 1977.

———. *Men and Movements in the Primitive Church: Studies in Early Non-Pauline Christianity*. Exeter, 1979.

———. *Paul, Apostle of the Free Spirit*. Exeter, 1977.

Bruns, E. "The Altercatio Jasonis et Papisci, Philo, and Anastasius the Sinaite." *ThSt* 34 (1973): 287–94.

Bultmann, Rudolf. "Besprechung zu Schoeps, Theologie und Geschichte des Judenchristentums." *Gn.* 26 (1954): 177–89.

———. "Exegetische Probleme des zweiten Korintherbriefes." Pp. 298–322 in *Exegetica*. Edited by E. Dinkler. Tübingen, 1967.

———. "*Ginōskō*." *TDNT*, 1:689–719.

———. "Ein neues Paulus-Verständnis?" *ThLZ* 84 (1959), cols. 481–86.

———. *The Second Letter to the Corinthians*. Translated by Roy A. Harrisville. Minneapolis, 1985.

———. *Der Stil der paulinischen Predigt und die kynisch-stoische Diatribe*. FRLANT 13. Göttingen, 1910.

Burchard, Christoph. "Gemeinde in der strohernen Epistel. Mutmassungen über Jakobus." Pp. 315–28 in *Kirche*. G. Bornkamm Festschrift. Edited by D. Lührmann and G. Strecker. Tübingen, 1980.

———. "Zu Jakobus 2,14–26." *ZNW* 71 (1980): 27–45.

Burger, Christoph. *Jesus als Davidssohn*. FRLANT 98. Göttingen, 1970.

Burkitt, Francis Crawford. *Christian Beginnings*. London, 1924.

Burton, Ernest de Witt. *A Critical and Exegetical Commentary on the Epistle to the Galatians*. ICC. Edinburgh, 1921.

Campenhausen, Hans von. *Ecclesiastical Authority and Spiritual Power in the Church of the First Three Centuries*. Translated by J. A. Baker. London: 1969.

———. *The Formation of the Christian Bible*. Translated by J. A. Baker. London, 1972.

————. "Die Nachfolge des Jakobus." *ZKG* 63 (1950): 133–44. (= Pp. 135–51 in *Aus der Frühzeit des Christentums*. Tübingen, 1963.)

Carrington, Philip. *The Early Christian Church*. Vol. 1, *The First Christian Century*. Vol. 2, *The Second Christian Century*. Cambridge, 1957.

Carroll, Kenneth L. "The Place of James in the Early Church." *BJRL* 44 (1961–62): 49–67.

Cassels, Walter R. *Supernatural Religion*. 2 vols. London, 1874.

Chadwick, Owen. *The Victorian Church*, vol. 2. New York, 1970.

Chapman, Dom John. "La date du livre d'Elchasai." *RBen* 26 (1909): 221–23.

————. "On the Date of the Clementines." *ZNW* 9 (1908): 21–34, 147–59.

Charlesworth, James H., ed. *John and Qumran*. London, 1972.

Chwolsohn, Daniel. *Die Ssabier und der Ssabismus*, vol. 1. Petersburg, 1856. (= Amsterdam, 1965.)

Clemen, Carl. "Mohammeds Abhängigkeit von der Gnosis." Pp. 249–62 in *Harnack-Ehrung*. Leipzig, 1921.

Cohen, S. J. D. "A Virgin Defiled: Some Rabbinic and Christian Views on the Origins of Heresey." *USQR* 35 (1980): 1–11.

————. *Josephus in Galilee and Rome*. Leiden, 1979.

Collange, Jean-François. *L'épître de Saint Paul aux Philippiens*. CNT(N) 10a. Paris, 1973.

Colpe, Carsten. "Religionsgeschichtliche Interpretation paulinischer Texte?" *MPTh* 52 (1963): 487–94.

Conybeare, Frederick Cornwallis, ed. *The Dialogues of Athanasius and Zacchaeus and of Timothy and Aquila*. Oxford, 1898.

————. *History of New Testament Criticism*. London, 1910. (= New York, 1910.)

Conzelmann, Hans. *Die Apostelgeschichte*. HNT 7. Tübingen, 1972.

————. *1 Corinthians: A Commentary on the First Epistle to the Corinthians*. Heremeneia. Translated by James W. Leitch. Bibliography and references by James W. Dunkly. Edited by George W. MacRae. Philadelphia, 1975.

————. *Der erste Brief an die Korinther*. KEK 5. Göttingen, 1981.

————. *Pagans–Jews–Christians*. Translated by M. Eugene Boring. Minneapolis. (Forthcoming.)

————. *History of Primitive Christianity*. Translated by John E. Steely. Nashville, 1973.

Corssen, P. *Die Altercatio Simonis Iudaei et Theophili Christiani auf ihre Quellen geprüft*. Jever, 1890.

Coyle, J. K. "The Cologne Mani-Codex and Mani's Christian Connections." *Eet* 10 (1979): 179–93.

Craig, Clarence Tucker. *The Beginning of Christianity.* New York, 1943.

Credner, Karl August. *Beiträge zur Einleitung in die biblischen Schriften.* Vol. 1, *Die Evangelien der Petriner oder der Judenchristen.* Halle, 1832.

_____. "Über Essäer und Ebioniten und einen theilweisen Zusammenhang derselben." *ZWTh* 1 (1829): 211–64, 277–328.

Cullmann, Oscar. "Courants multiples dans la communauté primitive. A propos du martyre de Jacques fils de Zébédée." *RSR* 60 (1972): 55–68.

_____. "Dissensions Within the Early Church." *USQR* 22 (1967): 83–92.

_____. "Ebioniten." *RGG³*, vol. 2, cols. 297–98.

_____. *Jesus and the Revolutionaries.* Translated by Gareth Putnam. New York, 1970.

_____. *Peter—Disciple, Apostle, Martyr: A Historical and Theological Study.* Translated by Floyd V. Filson. Philadelphia, 1953.

_____. *Petrus: Jünger—Apostel—Märtyrer.* Zurich, 1960. (= Siebenstern, TB 90/91. Munich, 1967.)

_____. *Le problème littéraire et historique du roman pseudo-clémentin.* EHPhR 23. Paris, 1930.

Dahl, Nils Alstrup. "Paul and the Church at Corinth." Pp. 40–61 in *Studies in Paul.* Minneapolis, 1977.

Daniélou, Jean. *The Development of Christian Doctrine Before the Council of Nicaea.* Vol. 1, *The Theology of Jewish Christianity.* Translated by John A. Baker. London, 1964.

Dannreuther, Henri. *Du témoignage d'Hégésippe sur l'Eglise Chrétienne.* Nancy, 1878.

Dassmann, Ernst. *Der Stachel im Fleisch: Paulus in der frühchristlichen Literatur bis Irenäus.* Münster, 1979.

Dautzenberg, Gerhard. "Der Verzicht auf das apostolische Unterhaltsrecht: Eine exegetische Untersuchung zu 1Kor 9." *Biblica* 50 (1969): 212–32.

Davies, William David. *The Gospel and the Land.* Berkeley, 1974.

_____. *Paul and Rabbinic Judaism.* 4th ed. Philadelphia, 1980.

Dibelius, Martin. *James: A Commentary on the Epistle of James.* Hermeneia. Revised by Heinrich Greeven. Translated by Michael A. Williams. Edited by Helmut Koester. Philadelphia, 1976.

_____. *An die Thessalonicher I.II. An die Philipper.* HNT 11. Tübingen, 1925², 1937³.

Dietzfelbinger, Christian. *Was ist Irrlehre?* TEH 143. Munich, 1967.

Dilthey, Wilhelm. "Ferdinand Christian Baur." Pp. 403–32 in *Ferdinand Christian Baur. Gesammelte Schriften*, vol. 4. Leipzig, 1921.

Dix, Gregory, *Jew and Greek.* London, 1955.

Dobschütz, Ernst von. *The Apostolic Age.* Translated by F. L. Pogson. Boston, 1910.

—————. *Christian Life in the Primitive Church.* Translated by George Bremer. Edited by W. D. Morrison. New York, 1904.

Dodd, Charles Harold. *The Parables of the Kingdom.* New York, 1961.

Drane, John William. *Paul: Libertine or Legalist?* London, 1975.

Drijvers, Hans J. W. "Mani und Bardaisan: Ein Beitrag zur Vorgeschichte des Manichäismus." Pp. 459–69 in *Mélanges d'histoire des religions.* H.-C. Puech Festschrift. Paris, 1974.

Duncan, George S. *St. Paul's Ephesian Ministry.* New York, 1930.

Dungan, David L. *The Saying of Jesus in the Churches of Paul.* Philadelphia, 1971.

Dunn, James D. G. "The Incident at Antioch (Gal. 2.11–18)." *JSNT* 18 (1983): 3–57.

—————. *Unity and Diversity in the New Testament.* Philadelphia, 1977.

Eckert, Jost. "Die Kollekte des Paulus für Jerusalem." Pp. 65–80 in *Kontinuität und Einheit.* F. Mussner Festschrift. Freiburg, 1981.

—————. *Die urchristliche Verkündigung im Streit zwischen Paulus und seinen Gegnern nach dem Galaterbrief.* BU 6. Regensburg, 1971.

Ehrhardt, Arnold. *The Apostolic Succession.* London, 1953.

Elliott-Binns, Leonard Elliott. *Galilean Christianity.* London, 1956. (= Chicago, 1956.)

Ellis, Edward Earle. *Prophecy and Hermeneutic in Early Christianity.* WUNT 18. Tübingen, 1978. (= Grand Rapids, 1978.)

Elsas, Christoph. *Neuplatonische und gnostische Weltablehnung in der Schule Plotins.* RVV 34. Berlin, 1975.

Engelhardt, Moritz von. *Das Christenthum Justins des Martyrers.* Erlangen, 1878.

Farmer, William Reuben. *Maccabees, Zealots, and Josephus.* New York, 1956.

Fascher, Erich. "Jerusalems Untergang in der urchristlichen und altkirchlichen Überlieferung." ThLZ 89 (1964), cols. 81–98.

Ferguson, Everett. "Sabbath: Saturday or Sunday? A Review Article." *RestQ* 23 (1980): 172–81.

Filson, Floyd V. *A New Testament History.* London, 1964.

Fitzmyer, Joseph A. "The Qumran Scrolls, the Ebionites and Their Literature." *TS* 16 (1955): 335–72. (=Pp. 435–80 in *Essays on the Semitic Background of the New Testament.* Missoula, 1974.)

Flückiger, Felix. "Luk. 21,20–24 und die Zerstörung Jerusalems." *ThZ* 28 (1972): 385–90.

Flusser, David. "Salvation: Present and Future." *Numen* 16 (1969): 139–55.

Foerster, Werner. "Die *dokountes* in Gal. 2." *ZNW* 36 (1937): 286–92.

Fraedrich, Gerhard. *Ferdinand Christian Baur der Begründer der Tübinger Schule als Theologe, Schriftsteller und Charakter*. Gotha, 1909.

Freyne, Sean. *Galilee from Alexander the Great to Hadrian—323 C.E. to 135 C.E.* University of Notre Dame Center for the Study of Judaism and Christianity, 5. Wilmington, 1980.

Friedrich, Gerhard. "Die Gegner des Paulus im 2. Korintherbrief." Pp. 181–215 in *Abraham unser Vater*. O. Michel Festschrift. Edited by O. Betz, M. Hengel, and P. Schmidt. AGJU 5. Leiden, 1963. (= Pp. 189–223 in *Auf das Wort kommt es an*. Edited by J. H. Friedrich. Göttingen, 1978.)

Fueter, Eduard. *Geschichte der neueren Historiographie*. HMANG.A 1. Munich, 1936.

Funk, Robert W., and H. Neil Richardson. "The 1958 Sounding at Pella." *BA* 21 (1958): 82–96.

Funk, Wolf-Peter. *Die zweite Apokalypse des Jakobus aus Nag-Hammadi-Codex V.* TU 119. Berlin, 1976.

Furnish, Victor Paul. *II Corinthians*. AB 32A. Garden City, 1984.

Gaechter, Paul. *Petrus und seine Zeit*. Innsbruck, 1958.

Gasque, W. Ward. *A History of the Criticism of the Acts of the Apostles*. BGBE 17. Tübingen, 1975.

Gaston, Lloyd. *No Stone on Another*. NovTestS. 23. Leiden, 1970.

Geiger, Ruthild. *Die Lukanischen Endzeitreden*. EHS.T 16. Frankfurt, 1976.

Geiger, Wolfgang. *Spekulation und Kritik: Die Geschichtstheologie Ferdinand Christian Baurs*. FGLP X.28. Munich, 1964.

Gelzer, H. *Sextus Julius Africanus und die byzantinische Chronographie*. Vol. 1, *Die Chronographie des Julius Africanus*. Leipzig, 1880.

Georgi, Dieter. *Die Geschichte der Kollekte des Paulus für Jerusalem*. ThF 38. Hamburg, 1965.

———. *The Opponents of Paul in Second Corinthians: A Study of Religious Propaganda in Late Antiquity*. Philadelphia, 1985.

Georgii, Ludwig. "Über den Charakter der christlichen Geschichte in den ersten zwei Jahrhunderten." Pp. 913–27 in *Deutsche Jahrbücher für Wissenschaft und Kunst*, 229. 1842.

Gieseler, Johann Karl Ludwig. "Über die Nazaräer und Ebioniten," *Archiv für Kirchengeschichte* 4 (1820): 279–330.

Gnilka, Joachim. *The Epistle to the Philippians*. Translated by R. A. Wilson. New York, 1981.

_____. *Der Philipperbrief.* HThK 10.3. Freiburg, 1980.

Goguel, Maurice. "L'apôtre Pierre a-t-il joué un rôle personnel dans les crises de Grèce et de Galatie?" *RHPhR* 14 (1934): 461–500.

_____. *The Birth of Christianity.* Translated by H. C. Snape. New York, 1954.

Goodspeed, Edgar Johnson, *Die ältesten Apologeten.* Göttingen, 1914.

_____. "'The Dialogue of Timothy and Aquila': Two Unpublished Manuscripts." *JBL* 24 (1905): 58–78.

Goppelt, Leonhard. *Apostolic and Post-Apostolic Times.* Translated by Robert A. Guelich. London, 1970.

_____. *Christentum und Judentum im ersten und zweiten Jahrhundert.* BFChTh II.55. Gütersloh, 1954.

Grässer, Erich. "Acta-Forschung seit 1960." *ThR* NF 41 (1976): 259–90.

_____. *Das Problem der Parusieverzögerung in den synoptischen Evangelien und in der Apostelgeschichte.* BZNW 22. Berlin, 1977.

Grant, Michael. *The Jews in the Roman World.* New York, 1973.

Grant, Robert M. *Early Christianity and Society.* New York, 1977.

_____. "Early Episcopal Succession." Pp. 179–84 in StPatr, XI. TU 108. Berlin, 1972.

_____. "Eusebius and Gnostic Origins." Pp. 195–205 in *Paganisme, Judaisme, Christianisme.* M. Simon Festschrift. Edited by A. Benoît, M. Philonenko, and C. Vogel. Paris, 1978.

_____. *Eusebius as Church Historian.* Oxford, 1980.

Grass, Hans. *Ostergeschehen und Osterberichte.* Göttingen, 1970.

Gray, Barbara C. "The Movements of the Jerusalem Church During the First Jewish War." *JEH* 24 (1973): 1–7.

Grillmeier, Aloys. "Hellenisierung—Judaisierung des Christentums als Deuteprinzipien der Geschichte des kirchlichen Dogmas." *Schol.* 33 (1958): 321–55, 528–58.

Güttgemanns, Erhardt. *Der leidende Apostel und sein Herr.* FRLANT 90. Göttingen, 1966.

Gunther, John J. "The Fate of the Jerusalem Church." *ThZ* 29 (1973): 81–94.

_____. *Paul: Messenger and Exile.* Valley Forge, 1972.

_____. *St. Paul's Opponents and Their Background.* NovTest. S 35. Leiden, 1973.

Gustafsson, Bengt. "Hegesippus' Sources and His Reliability." Pp. 227–32 in StPatr, III. Edited by F. L. Cross. TU 78. Berlin, 1961.

Guthe, Hermann. *Bibelatlas in 21 Haupt- und 30 Nebenkarten.* Leipzig, 1926.

Haacker, Klaus. "Exegetische Probleme des Römerbriefs." *NT* 20 (1978): 1–21.

Haenchen, Ernst. *The Acts of the Apostles: A Commentary*. Philadelphia, 1971.

_____. "Petrus-Probleme." *NTS* 7 (1960–61): 187–97. (= Pp. 55–67 in *Gott und Mensch. Gesammelte Aufsätze*, vol. 1. Tübingen, 1965.)

Hahn, Ferdinand. "Der Apostolat im Urchristentum." *KuD* 20 (1974): 54–77.

_____. *Mission in the New Testament*. Translated by Frank Clarke. SBT 47. London, 1965.

_____. "Die Rede von der Parusie des Menschensohnes Markus 13." Pp. 240–66 in *Jesus und der Menschensohn*. A. Vögtle Festschrift. Edited by R. Pesch, R. Schnackenburg, and O. Kaiser. Freiburg, 1975.

_____. *The Titles of Jesus in Christology: Their History in Early Christianity*. Translated by Harold Knight and George Ogg. London, 1969.

Hainz, Josef. "Gemeinschaft (*koinōnia*) zwischen Paulus und Jerusalem (Gal 2,9f.)." Pp. 30–42 in *Kontinuität und Einheit*. F. Mussner Festschrift. Edited by P.-G. Müller and W. Stenger. Freiburg, 1981.

_____. *Koinōnia: "Kirche" als Gemeinschaft bei Paulus*. BU 16. Regensburg, 1982.

Halévy, Joseph. *Te'ezaza Sanbat (Commandements du Sabbat) accompagné de six autres écrits pseudo-apostoliques admis par les falachas ou Juifs d'Abyssinie*. Paris, 1902.

Harnack, Adolf von. *Die Altercatio Simonis Iudaei et Theophili Christiani*. TU 1.3. Leipzig, 1883.

_____. *Entstehung und Entwicklung des Kirchenrechts in den zwei ersten Jahrhunderten*. Leipzig, 1910. (= Darmstadt, 1978.)

_____. *Geschichte der altchristlichen Literatur bis Eusebius*. Vol. 1, *Die Überlieferung und der Bestand*. Vol. 2, *Die Chronologie*. Leipzig, 1958.

_____. *History of Dogma*. Translated by Neil Buchanan. 2 vols. New York, 1958.

_____. *Judentum und Judenchristentum in Justins Dialog mit Trypho*. TU 39.1. Leipzig, 1913. Pp. 47–92.

_____. "Kritische Übersicht über die kirchengeschichtlichen Arbeiten der letzten Jahre I: Geschichte der Kirche bis zum Konzil von Nicäa." *ZKG* 2 (1878): 56–111.

_____. *Lehrbuch der Dogmengeschichte*. Vol. 1, *Die Entstehung des kirchlichen Dogmas*. Vol. 2, *Die Entwicklung des kirchlichen Dogmas*. Tübingen, 1909.

_____. *The Mission and Expansion of Christianity in the First Three Centuries*. Translated and edited by James Moffatt. 2 vols. New York, 1908.

————. "Die Neuheit des Evangeliums nach Marcion." Pp. 128–43 in *Aus der Werkstatt des Vollendeten*. Giessen, 1930.

————. *New Testament Studies*. Vol. 3, *The Acts of the Apostles*. Translated by J. R. Wilkinson. CTL 27. London, 1908.

————. *New Testament Studies*. Vol. 4, *The Date of Acts and of the Synoptic Gospels*. Translated by J. R. Wilkinson. CTL 33. London, 1911.

————. *Die Überlieferung der griechischen Apologeten des zweiten Jahrhunderts in der alten Kirche und im Mittelalter*. TU 1.1. Leipzig, 1883.

————. "Die Verklärungsgeschichte Jesu, der Bericht des Paulus (I. Kor. 15,3ff.) und die beiden Christusvisionen des Petrus." *SPAW.PH* (1922): 62–80.

Harris, Horton. *The Tübingen School*, Oxford, 1975.

Hausrath, Adolf. *Der Vier-Capitel-Brief des Paulus an die Korinther*. Heidelberg, 1870.

Hefner, Philip. "Baur versus Ritschl on Early Christianity." *ChH* 31 (1962): 259–78.

————. *Faith and the Vitalities of History*. New York, 1966.

Heinrici, C. F. Georg. *Der erste Brief an die Korinther*. KEK 5. Göttingen, 1896.

Hengel, Martin. *Acts and the History of Earliest Christianity*. Translated by John Bowden. Philadelphia, 1979.

————. "Besprechung von Brandon, *Jesus*." *JJS* 14 (1969): 231–40.

————. "Between Jesus and Paul." Pp. 1–29 in *Between Jesus and Paul: Studies in the Earliest History of Christianity*. Translated by John Bowden. Philadelphia, 1983.

————. *The Charismatic Leader and His Followers*. Translated by James Greig. New York, 1981.

————. "Jakobus der Herrnbruder—der erste 'Papst'?" Pp. 71–104 in *Glaube und Eschatologie*. W. G. Kümmel Festschrift. Edited by Erich Grässer and Otto Merk. Tübingen, 1985.

————. "Maria Magdalena und die Frauen als Zeugen." Pp. 243–256 in *Abraham unser Vater*. O. Michel Festschrift. Edited by O. Betz, M. Hengel, and P. Schmidt. AGJU 5. Leiden, 1963.

————. "The Origins of the Christian Mission." Pp. 48–64 in *Between Jesus and Paul: Studies in the Earliest History of Christianity*. Translated by John Bowden. Philadelphia, 1983.

————. "Die Synagogeninschrift von Stobi." *ZNW* 57 (1966): 145–83.

————. *Die Zeloten*. AGJU 1. Leiden, 1976.

————. "Der Jakobusbrief als antipaulinische Polemik." *Tradition and Interpretation in the New Testament: Essays in Honor of E. Earle Ellis*. Edited by G. F. Hawthorne with O. Betz. Tübingen, 1987.

Henrichs, Albert. "The Cologne Mani Codex Reconsidered." *HSCP* 83 (1979): 339–67.

_____. "Mani and the Babylonia Baptists." *HSCP* 77 (1973): 23–59.

_____, and Ludwig Koenen. "Ein griechischer Mani-Codex." *ZPE* 5 (1970): 97–216.

_____, and _____. "Der Kölner Mani-Codex (P. Colon, inv. nr. 4780) PERI TĒS GENNĒS TOU SŌMATOS AUTOU. Edition der Seiten 1-72[,7]." *ZPE* 19 (1975): 1–85. "Edition der Seiten 72.8–99,9." *ZPE* 32 (1978): 87–199. "Edition der Seiten 99,10–120." *ZPE* 44 (1981): 201–318. "Edition der Seiten 121–192 und Fragmente, nur Text." *ZPE* 48 (1982): 1–59 (=319–77).

Herzog, Eduard. "Die Gefangennehmung des Apostels Paulus in Jerusalem." *RITh* 13 (1905): 193–224.

Hilgenfeld, Adolf. "Baur's kritische Urgeschichte des Christenthums und ihre neueste Bearbeitung." *ZWTh* 7 (1864): 113–145.

_____. "Ferdinand Christian Baur nach seiner wissenschaftlichen Entwickelung und Bedeutung." *ZWTh* 36 (1893): 222–24.

_____. "Hegesippus." *ZWTh* 19 (1876): 177–229.

_____. *Historisch-kritische Einleitung in das Neue Testament.* Leipzig, 1875.

_____. *Judenthum und Judenchristenthum: Eine Nachlese zur Ketzergeschichte des Urchristenthums.* Leipzig, 1886. (= Hildesheim, 1966.)

_____. *Die Ketzergeschichte des Urchristenthums.* Leipzig, 1884. (= Hildesheim, 1963.)

_____. "Noch einmal Hegesippus." *ZWTh* 21 (1878): 297–321.

_____. "Die Theologie des neunzehnten Jahrhunderts nach ihrer Stellung zu Religion und Christenthum unter besonderer Berücksichtigung auf Baur's Darstellung." *ZWTh* 6 (1863): 1–40.

_____. *Das Urchristenthum.* Jena, 1855.

_____. "Das Urchristenthum und Ernst von Dobschütz." *ZWTh* 48 (1905): 260–304, 517–59.

_____. "Das Urchristenthum und seine neuesten Bearbeitungen von Lechler und Ritschl." *ZWTh* 1 (1858): 54–140, 377–440, 565–602.

_____. "Das Urchristenthum und seine neuesten Bearbeitungen durch G. V. Lechler und A. Harnack." *ZWTh* 29 (1886): 385–441.

Hirsch, Emanuel. *Geschichte der neuern evangelischen Theologie.* Vols. 3, 5. Gütersloh, 1968.

_____. "Petrus und Paulus." *ZNW* 29 (1930): 63–76.

_____. "Zwei Fragen zu Galater 6." *ZNW* 29 (1930): 192–97.

Hirschberg, Harris H. "Paulus im Midrasch." *ZRGG* 12 (1960): 252–56.

Hock, Ronald F. *The Social Context of Paul's Ministry.* Philadelphia, 1980.

Hodgson, Peter Crafts. *The Formation of Historical Theology*. New York, 1966.

Hoennicke, Gustav. *Das Judenchristentum im ersten und zweiten Jahrhundert*. Berlin, 1908.

Hoffmann, Paul. *Studien zur Theologie der Logienquelle*. NTA NF 8. Münster, 1972.

Hoheisel, Karl. *Das antike Judentum in christlicher Sicht*. Wiesbaden, 1978.

Holl, Karl. "Der Kirchenbegriff des Paulus in seinem Verhältnis zu dem Urgemeinde." *SPAW.PH* (1921): 920–47. (= Pp. 44–67 in *Gesammelte Aufsätze zur Kirchengeschichte*. Vol. 2, *Der Osten*. Tübingen, 1928 [= Darmstadt, 1964].) (= Pp. 144–78 in *Das Paulusbild in der neueren deutschen Forschung*. WdF 24. Darmstadt, 1969.)

Holmberg, Bengt. *Paul and Power: The Structure of Authority in the Primitive Church*. CB.NT 11. Lund, 1978.

Holsten, Carl. *Das Evangelium des Paulus dargestellt*. Vol. 1, *Die äussere Entwicklungsgeschichte des paulinischen Evangeliums*. Part 1: "Der Brief an die Gemeinden Galatiens und der erste Brief an die Gemeinde zu Korinth." Berlin, 1880.

Holtz, T. "Der antiochenische Zwischenfall (Galater 2,11–14)." *NTS* 32 (1986): 344–61.

Holtzmann, Heinrich Julius. "Baur und die neutestamentliche Kritik der Gegenwart." *PrM* 1 (1897): 177–88, 225–39.

―――. *Lehrbuch der historisch-kritischen Einleitung in das Neue Testament*. Freiburg, 1892.

―――. *Lehrbuch der neutestamentlichen Theologie*. 2 vols. Tübingen, 1911.

―――. "Zur neuesten Literatur über neutestamentliche Probleme." *ARW* 12 (1897): 382–408.

Holtzmann, Oscar. "Zu Emanuel Hirsch: Zwei Fragen zu Galater 6." *ZNW* 30 (1931): 76–83.

Hoppe, Rudolf. *Der theologische Hintergrund des Jakobusbriefes*. Würzburg, 1977.

Hort, Fenton John Antony. *Judaistic Christianity*. London, 1904.

―――. *Notes Introductory to the Study of the Clementine Recognitions*. London, 1901.

Howard, George. *Paul—Crisis in Galatia: A Study in Early Christian Theology*. SNTSMS 35. Cambridge, 1979.

Hübner, Hans. "Das ganze und das eine Gesetz." *KuD* 21 (1975): 239–56.

―――. "Mark VII.1–23 und das 'jüdisch-hellenistische' Gesetzesverständnis." *NTS* 22 (1976): 319–45.

Hurd, John Coolidge. *The Origin of I Corinthians.* London, 1965. (= New York, 1965.)

Hyldahl, Niels. "Hegesipps Hypomnemata." *StTh* 14 (1960): 70–113.

Irmscher, Johannes. "The Book of Elchasai." Pp. 745–50 in *NTApo,* vol. 2. Edited by E. Hennecke and W. Schneemelcher. Translated by R. McL. Wilson et al. Philadelphia, 1965.

Jackson, F. J. Foakes, and Kirsopp Lake, eds. *The Beginnings of Christianity,* I.1–5. London, 1920–33. (Abbr.: *Beg.*)

Jefferey, Arthur, ed. *Islam: Muhammed and his Religion.* The Library of Liberal Arts. Indianapolis, 1975.

Jeremias, Joachim. "Chiasmus in den Paulusbriefen." *ZNW* 49 (1958): 145–56. (= Pp. 276–90 in *Abba.* Göttingen, 1966.)

―――. *Golgotha.* Angelos Beih., 1. Leipzig, 1926.

―――. *Jerusalem in the Time of Jesus: An Investigation Into Economic and Social Conditions During the New Testament Period.* Translated by F. H. and C. H. Cave. Philadelphia, 1969.

―――. "Zur Gedankenführung in den paulinischen Briefen." Pp. 146–54 in *Studien Paulina.* J. de Zwaan Festschrift. Edited by J. N. Sevenster. Haarlem, 1953. (= Pp. 269–76 in *Abba.* Göttingen, 1966.)

―――. *The Eucharistic Words of Jesus.* London, 1966.

Jervell, Jacob. *Luke and the People of God.* Minneapolis, 1972.

―――. "Der schwache Charismatiker." Pp. 185–98 in *Rechtfertigung.* E. Käsemann Festschrift. Edited by J. Friedrich, W. Pöhlmann, and P. Stuhlmacher. Tübingen, 1976.

Jewett, Robert. "The Agitators and the Galatian Congregation." *NTS* 17 (1970–71): 198–212.

―――. *Paul's Anthropological Terms: A Study of Their Use in Conflict Settings.* AGJU 10. Leiden, 1971.

Jocz, Jacob. *The Jewish People and Jesus Christ.* London, 1954.

Joël, Manuel. *Blicke in die Religionsgeschichte zu Anfang des zweiten christlichen Jahrhunderts mit Berücksichtigung der angrenzenden Zeiten,* vol. 2. Breslau, 1883. (= Amsterdam, 1971.)

Johnson, Luke Timothy. *The Literary Function of Possessions in Luke-Acts.* SBLDS 39. Missoula, 1977.

Johnson, Marshall D. *The Purpose of the Biblical Genealogies with Special Reference to the Setting of the Genealogies of Jesus.* SNTSMS 8. Cambridge, 1988.

Jones, F. Stanley. "The Pseudo-Clementines: A History of Research." *The Second Century* 2 (1982): 1–33, 63–96.

Jülicher, Adolf. "Die jüdischen Schranken des Harnackschen Paulus." *PrM* 17 (1913): 193–224.

Käsemann, Ernst. *Commentary on Romans.* Translated by Geoffrey W. Bromiley. Grand Rapids, 1980.

————. "Die Legitimität des Apostels." *ZNW* 41 (1942): 33–71. (= Pp. 475–521 in *Das Paulusbild in der neueren deutschen Forschung*. WdF 24. Darmstadt, 1969.)

Kasting, Heinrich. *Die Anfänge der urchristlichen Mission*. BEvTh 55. Munich, 1969.

Kattenbusch, Ferdinand. "Die Vorzugsstellung des Petrus und der Charakter der Urgemeinde zu Jerusalem." Pp. 322-51 in *Festgabe von Fachgenossen und Freunden Karl Müller zum siebzigsten Geburtstag dargebracht*. Tübingen, 1922.

Keck, Leander. "Armut III." *TRE*, 4:76–80.

————. "The Poor Among the Saints in Jewish Christianity and Qumran." *ZNW* 57 (1966): 54–78. (Abbr.: Keck, "Saints.")

————. "The Poor Among the Saints in the New Testament." *ZNW* 56 (1965): 100–29.

Kemler, Herbert. *Der Herrenbruder Jakobus bei Hegesipp und in der frühchristlichen Literatur*. Theol. diss. Göttingen, 1966.

Keresztes, Paul. "The Jews, the Christians, and the Emperor Domitian." *VigChr.* 27 (1973): 1–28.

Kertelge, Karl. *"Rechfertigung" bei Paulus*. NTA NF 3. Münster, 1967.

Kessler, Konrad, *Mani: Forschungen über die manichäische Religion*, Vol. 1, Voruntersuchungen und Quellen. Berlin, 1889.

Kittel, Gerhard. "Der geschichtliche Ort des Jakobusbriefes." *ZNW* 41 (1942): 71–105.

————. "Der Jakobusbrief und die Apostolischen Väter." *ZNW* 43 (1950–51): 54–112.

————. "Paulus im Talmud." Pp. 1–16 in *Rabbinica*. Leipzig, 1920.

————. "Die Stellung des Jakobus zu Judentum und Heidenchristentum." *ZNW* 30 (1931): 145–57.

Klausner, Joseph. *From Jesus to Paul*. London, 1943.

————. *Jesus of Nazareth*. London, 1929.

Klein, Günter. "Galater 2,6–9 und die Geschichte der Jerusalemer Urgemeinde." *ZThK* 57 (1960): 275–95. (= Pp. 99–118 in *Rekonstruktion und Interpretation*. BEvTh 50. Munich, 1969. [with postscript, 118–28].)

————. "Die Verleugnung des Petrus." *ZThK* 58 (1961): 285 328. (= Pp. 49–90 in *Rekonstruktion und Interpretation*. BEvTh 50. Munich, 1969. [With postscript, 90–98].)

————. *Die zwölf Apostel*. FRLANT 77. Göttingen, 1961.

Klijn, Albertus Frederik Johannes. "The Study of Jewish Christianity." *NTS* 20 (1973–74): 419–31.

————, and Reinink, G.J. "Elchasai and Mani." *VigChr* 28 (1974): 277–89.

_____, and G. J. Reinink. *Patristic Evidence for Jewish-Christian Sects.* NovTest. S 36. Leiden, 1973.

Kneucker, Johann Jacob. P. 519 in *Bibellexicon*, vol. 1. Edited by Daniel Schenkel. Leipzig, 1869.

Knopf, Rudolf. *Die Apostolischen Väter.* Vol. 1, *Die Lehre der Zwölf Apostel. Die zwei Clemensbriefe.* HNTSup. Tübingen, 1920.

_____. *Das nachapostolische Zeitalter.* Tübingen, 1905.

Knox, John. *Chapters in a Life of Paul.* New York, 1950. (= Leiden, 1954.)

Knox, Wilfred L. *St. Paul and the Church of Jerusalem.* Cambridge, 1925.

Koch, Glenn Alan. "A Critical Investigation of Epiphanius' Knowledge of the Ebionites". Ph.D. diss. University of Pennsylvania, 1976.

Koch, Hugo. "Zur Jakobusfrage Gal 1,19." *ZNW* 33 (1934): 204–9.

Koenen, Ludwig. "Augustine and Manichaeism in Light of the Cologne Mani Codex." *Illinois Classicial Studies* 3 (1978): 154–95.

Koester, Helmut. *Introduction to the New Testament.* Vol. 1, *History, Culture, and Religion of the Hellenistic Age.* Vol. 2, *History and Literature of Early Christianity.* Hermeneia: Foundation and Facets. Philadelphia, 1982.

_____. "The Purposse of the Polemic of a Pauline Fragment." *NTS* 8 (1961–62): 317–32.

Köstlin, Karl Reinhold. "Zur Geschichte des Urchristenthums." In ThJb (T) 9 (1850), 1–62, 235–302.

Koschorke, Klaus. *Die Polemik der Gnostiker gegen das kirchliche Christentum.* Nag Hammadi Studies, 12. Leiden, 1978.

Kraft, Heinrich. *Die Entstehung des Christentums.* Darmstadt, 1981.

Kraft, Robert A. "In Search of 'Jewish Christianity' and Its 'Theology.'" *RSR* 60 (1972): 81–92.

Kremer, Jacob. *Das älteste Zeugnis von der Auferstehung Christi.* SBS 17. Stuttgart, 1966.

_____, ed. *Les Actes des Apôtres: Traditions, rédaction, théologie.* BEThL 48. Gembloux, 1979.

Kretschmar, Georg. "Die Bedeutung der Liturgiegeschichte für die Frage nach der Kontinuität des Judenchristentums in nachapostolischer Zeit." Pp. 113–37 in *Aspects du Judéo-Christianisme.* Paris, 1965.

Krüger, Gustav. *Das Dogma vom neuen Testament.* Giessen, 1896.

Kümmel, Werner Georg. *Introduction to the New Testament.* Translated by Howard C. Kee. Nashville, 1975. (Abbr.: Kümmel, *Introduction.*)

_____. *Kirchenbegriff und Geschichtsbewusstsein in der Urgemeinde und bei Jesus.* SyBu 1. Zurich, 1943.

————. *Das Neue Testament im 20. Jahrhundert: Ein Forschungsbericht*. SBS 50. Stuttgart, 1970.

————. *The New Testament: The History of the Investigation of Its Problems*. Translated by S. McLean Gilmour and Howard C. Kee. Nashville, 1972. (Abbr.: Kümmel, *Testament*.)

————. "Theologie und Geschichte des Judenchristentums." *StTh* 3 (1949): 188–94.

————. "Das Urchristentum." *ThR* NF 14 (1942): 81–95, 155–73. 17 (1948–49): 3–50, 103–42. 18 (1950): 1–53. 22 (1954): 138–70, 191–211.

Lagrange, Marie-Joseph. *Saint Paul, Epître aux Galates*. EtB. Paris, 1925.

Lake, Kirsopp. *The Earlier Epistles of St. Paul*. London, 1927.

Lange, Johann Peter. *Die Geschichte der Kirche*. Vol. 1, *Das apostolische Zeitalter*. Braunschweig, 1853.

Laufen, Rudolf. *Die Doppelüberlieferungen der Logienquelle und des Markusevangeliums*. BBB 54. Königstein, 1980.

Lawlor, Hugh Jackson. *Eusebiana*. Oxford, 1912.

————, and John Ernest Leonhard Oulton. *Eusebius, The Ecclesiastical History and the Martyrs of Palestine, translated, with introduction and notes. Vol. 1, Translation. Vol. 2, Introduction, Notes, and Index*. London, 1928.

Laws, Sophie. *A Commentary on the Epistle of James*. BNTC. London, 1980. (= HNTC. New York, 1980.)

Lechler, Gotthard Victor. *The Apostolic and Post-Apostolic Times: Their Diversity and Unity in Life and Doctrine*. Translated by A. J. K. Davidson. 2 vols. Edinburgh, 1886.

————. *Das apostolische und das nachapostolische Zeitalter*. Stuttgart, 1885.

Lehmann, Karl. *Auferweckt am dritten Tag nach der Schrift*. Freiburg, 1968.

Le Moine, Jean. *Les Sadducéens*. EtB. Paris, 1972.

Levy, M. A. "Bemerkung zu den arabischen Analekten des Herrn Prof. Hitzig." *ZDMG* 12 (1858): 712.

Lietzmann, Hans. *An die Galater*. HNT 10. Tübingen, 1971.

————. *An die Korinther I.II*. Revised by W. G. Kümmel. HNT 9. Tübingen, 1969.

————. *An die Römer*. HNT 8. Tübingen, 1971.

————. "Die Synagogeninschrift in Stobi/Ausgrabungen in Doura-Europos." *ZNW* 32 (1933): 93–95.

Lightfoot, Joseph Barber. *Dissertations on the Apostolic Age*. London, 1892.

————. *Essays on the Work Entitled "Supernatural Religion."* London, 1889.

_____. *S. Clement of Rome: The Two Epistles to the Corinthians.* London, 1869.

_____. *Saint Paul's Epistle to the Galatians.* London, 1890.

Lindemann, Andreas. *Paulus im ältesten Christentum: Das Bild des Apostels und die Rezeption der paulinischen Theologie in der frühchristlichen Literatur bis Marcion.* BHTh 58. Tübingen, 1979.

Lipsius, Richard Adelbert. *Die apokryphen Apostelgeschichten und Apostellegenden,* II.2. Braunschweig, 1884.

_____. "Ferdinand Christian Baur und die Tübinger Schule." *Unsere Zeit* 6 (1862): 229–54.

_____. *Zur Quellenkritik des Epiphanios.* Wien, 1865.

Little, Donald Henry. "The Death of James, the Brother of Jesus". Ph.D. diss. Rice University, 1971.

Lohmeyer, Ernst. *Galiläa und Jerusalem.* FRLANT 52. Göttingen, 1936.

_____. *Kultus und Evangelium.* Göttingen, 1942.

Lohse, Eduard. "Glaube und Werke. Zur Theologie des Jakobusbriefes." Pp. 285–306 in *Die Einheit des Neuen Testaments.* Göttingen, 1973.

_____, and Anton Vögtle. "Geschichte des Urchristentums." Pp. 3–69 in *Ökumenische Kirchengeschichte.* Vol. 1, *Alte Kirche und Ostkirche.* Edited by R. Kottje and B. Moeller. Munich, 1970.

Longenecker, Richard N. *The Christology of Early Jewish Christianity.* London, 1970.

_____. *Paul, Apostle of Liberty.* New York, 1964.

Loofs, Friedrich. "Review of Jean Réville, *Les origines de l'épiscopat.*" In ThLZ 21 (1896), cols. 206–10.

Lorenz, R. *Arius judaizans?* FKDG 31. Göttingen, 1979.

Luedemann, Gerd. *Early Christianity according to the Traditions in Acts.* Minneapolis: Fortress Press, 1989.

_____. *Paul, Apostle to the Gentiles.* Vol. 1, *Studies in Chronology.* Translated by F. Stanley Jones. Foreword by John Knox. Philadelphia, 1984.

_____. *Untersuchungen zur simonianischen Gnosis.* GTA 1. Göttingen, 1975.

_____. "Zum Antipaulinismus im frühen Christentum." *EvTh* 40 (1980): 437–55.

_____. "Zur Geschichte des ältesten Christentums in Rom. I. Valentin und Marcion; II. Ptolemäus und Justin." *ZNW* 70 (1979): 86–114.

Lüdemann, Hermann. "Kirchengeschichte bis zum Nicänum." In ThJber 4 (1885), 88–106.

_____. "Kirchengeschichte bis zum Nicärun." In ThJber 6 (1887), 107–32.

———. "Kirchengeschichte bis zum Nicärun." In ThJber 14 (1895), 165–91.

Lührmann, Dieter. *Der Brief an die Galater*. ZBK.NT 7. Zurich, 1978.

———. *Glaube im frühen Christentum*. Gütersloh, 1976.

———. *Das Offenbarungsverständnis bei Paulus und in paulinischen Gemeinden*. WMANT 16. Neukirchen-Vluyn, 1965.

———. "Tage, Monate, Jahreszeiten, Jahre (Gal 4,10)." Pp. 428–45 in *Werden und Wirken des Alten Testaments*. C. Westermann Festschrift. Edited by R. Albertz et al. Göttingen, 1980.

Lütgert, Wilhelm. *Amt und Geist im Kampf: Studien zur Geschichte des Urchristentums*. BFChTh, XV.4–5. Gütersloh, 1911.

———. *Freiheitspredigt und Schwarmgeister in Korinth: Ein Beitrag zur Charakteristik der Christuspartei*. BFChTh, XII.3. Gütersloh, 1908.

———. *Gesetz und Geist: Eine Untersuchung zur Vorgeschichte des Galaterbriefes*. BFChTh, XXII.6. Gütersloh, 1919.

———. *Die Irrlehrer der Pastoralbriefe*. BFChTh, XIII.3. Gütersloh, 1909.

———. *Der Römerbrief als historisches Problem*. Gütersloh, 1913.

———. *Die Vollkommenen im Philipperbrief und Die Enthusiasten in Thessalonich*. BFChTh, XIII.6. Gütersloh, 1909.

Lutterbeck, Johann Anton Bernhard. *Die Neutestamentlichen Lehrbegriffe*. Vol. 2, *Die nachchristliche Entwicklung*. Mainz, 1852.

Luttikhuizen, Gerard P. *The Revelation of Elchasai*. TSAJ 8. Tübingen, 1985.

Luz, Ulrich. "Die Erfüllung des Gesetzes bei Matthäus (Matt. 5:17–20)." ZThK 75 (1978): 398–435.

———. *Das Geschichtsverständnis des Paulus*. BEvTh 49. Munich, 1968.

———. "Die Jünger im Matthäusevangelium." ZNW 62 (1971): 141–71.

———. "Die wiederentdeckte Logienquelle." EvTh 33 (1973): 527–33.

Mackay, Robert William. *The Tübingen School and Its Antecedents*. Edinburgh, 1863.

Maier, Johann, and Josef Schreiner, eds. *Literatur und Religion des Frühjudentums*. Würtzburg, 1973.

Maier, Johann, and Kurt Schubert. *Die Qumran-Essener*. UTB 224. Munich, 1982.

Malina, Bruce J. "Jewish Christianity: A Select Bibliography." AJBA 2 (1973): 60–65.

———. "Jewish Christianity and Christian Judaism." JSJ 7 (1976): 46–57.

Mancini, I. *Archaeological Discoveries Relative to the Judaeo-Christians*. SBFA 10. Jerusalem, 1970.

Manns, F. *Essais sur le Judéo-Christianisme*. SBFA 12. Jerusalem, 1977.

Manson, Thomas Walter. *Studies in the Gospels and Epistles*. Manchester, 1962 (= Philadelphia, 1962).

Martyn, J. Louis. "Clementine Recognitions 1,33–71, Jewish Christianity, and the Fourth Gospel." Pp. 265–95 in *God's Christ and His People*. N. A. Dahl Festschrift. Edited by J. Jervell and W. A. Meeks. Oslo, 1977.

_____. *The Gospel of John in Christian History*. New York, 1978.

_____. "A Law-Observant Mission to Gentiles: The Background of Galatians." *SJTh* 38 (1985): 307–24.

Marxsen, Willi. *Einleitung in das Neue Testament*. Gütersloh, 1978.

_____. *Introduction to the New Testament: An Approach to Its Problems*. Translated by G. Buswell. Philadelphia, 1970.

_____. *Mark the Evangelist: Studies on the Redaction History of the Gospel*. Translated by James Boyce et al. Nashville, 1969.

Mattill, Andrew Jacob. "Luke as a Historian in Criticism Since 1840". Ph.D. diss. Vanderbilt University, 1959.

_____. "The Purpose of Acts. Schneckenburger Reconsidered." Pp. 108–22 in *Apostolic History and the Gospel*. F. F. Bruce Festschrift. Edited by W. W. Gasque and R. P. Martin. Exeter, 1970.

Mayor, Joseph B. *The Epistle of St. James*. London, 1910. (= Grand Rapids, 1978.)

McGiffert, Arthur Cushman, ed. *Dialogue Between a Christian and a Jew*. New York, 1889.

_____. *A History of Christianity in the Apostolic Age*. New York, 1914.

Meeks, Wayne A. *The First Urban Christians: The Social World of the Apostle Paul*. New Haven, 1983.

_____, and Fred O. Francis, eds. *Conflict at Colossae*. Missoula, 1975.

Mensching, Gustav. *Die Religion: Erscheinungsformen, Stukturtypen und Lebensgesetze*. Stuttgart, 1959.

Merklein, Helmut. "Die Einheitlichkeit des ersten Korintherbriefes." *ZNW* 75 (1984): 153–83.

Meyer, Eduard. *Ursprung und Anfänge des Christentums*. Vol. 3, *Die Apostelgeschichte und die Anfänge des Christentums*. Stuttgart, 1923.

Meyers, Eric M., and James F. Strange. *Archaeology, the Rabbis, and Early Christianity*. Nashville, 1981.

Michaelis, Wilhelm. "Judaistische Heidenchristen." *ZNW* 30 (1931): 83–89.

Michel, D. "Armut II." *TRE*, 4:72–76.

Molland, Einar. "La circoncision, le baptême et l'autorité du décret apostolique (Actes XV,28 sq.) dans les milieux judéo-chrétiens des

Pseudo-Clémentines." *StTh* 9 (1955): 1–39. (= Pp. 25–59 in *Opuscula Patristica*. Oslo, 1970.)

Momigliano, Arnaldo. *Studies in Historiography*. London, 1966.

Moore, George Foot. *Judaism in the First Centuries of the Christian Era: The Age of the Tannaim*, vol. 2. New York, 1971.

Morgan, Robert. "Biblical Classics II: F. C. Baur: Paul." *ET* 90 (1978–79): 4–9.

_____. "F. C. Baur's Lectures on New Testament Theology." *ET* 88 (1976–77): 202–6.

Moxnes, Halvor. *Theology in Conflict*. Leiden, 1980.

Müller, Karl. *Kirchengeschichte*. GThW 4.1. Freiburg, 1892.

Müller, Ulrich B. *Zur frühchristlichen Theologiegeschichte: Judenchristentum und Paulinismus in Kleinasien an der Wende vom ersten zum zweiten Jahrhundert*. Gütersloh, 1976.

Munck, Johannes. "Jewish Christianity in Post-Apostolic Times." *NTS* 6 (1959–60): 103–16.

_____. "The New Testament and Gnosticism." Pp. 224–38 in *Current Issues in New Testament Interpretation*. O. A. Piper Festschrift. Edited by W. Klassen and G. F. Snyder. New York, 1962.

_____. *Paul and the Salvation of Mankind*. Translated by Frank Clarke. London, 1959.

_____. "Primitive Jewish Christianity and Later Jewish Christianity: Continuation or Rupture?" Pp. 77–93 in *Aspects du Judéo-Christianisme*. Paris, 1965.

Murphy-O'Connor, Jerome. "The Essenes and Their History." *RB* 81 (1974): 215–44.

_____. "Tradition and Redaction in 1 Cor 15:3–7." *CBQ* 43 (1981): 582–89.

Murray, Robert. "Defining Judaeo-Christianity." *HeyJ* 15 (1974): 303–10.

_____. "On Early Christianity and Judaism: Some Recent Studies." *HeyJ* 13 (1972): 441–51.

_____. "Recent Studies in Early Symbolic Theology." *HeyJ* 6 (1965): 412–33.

Mussner, Franz. *Der Galaterbrief*. HThK 9. Freiburg, 1981.

_____. *Der Jakobusbrief*. HThK 13.1. Freiburg, 1981.

Neander, August. *Genetische Entwickelung der vornehmsten gnostischen Systeme*. Berlin, 1818.

_____. *History of the Planting and Training of the Christian Church by the Apostles*, vol. 2. Translated by J. E. Ryland. New York, 1867.

Neill, Stephen. *The Interpretation of the New Testament 1861–1961*. London, 1964.

Neusner, Jacob. *A Life of Yohanan Ben Zakkai ca. 1–80 C.E.* SPB 6. Leiden, 1970.

Nickle, Keith Fullerton. *The Collection: A Study in Paul's Strategy.* London, 1966.

Nitzsch, Friedrich. *Grundriss der Christlichen Dogmengeschichte.* Vol. 1, *Die patristische Periode.* Berlin, 1870.

Oepke, Albrecht. *Der Brief des Paulus an die Galater.* Revised by J. Rohde. ThHK 9. Berlin, 1979.

Ollrog, Wolf-Henning. *Paulus und seine Mitarbeiter.* WMANT 50. Neukirchen-Vluyn, 1979.

Oostendorp, Derk William. *Another Jesus: A Gospel of Jewish-Christian Superiority in II Corinthians.* Kampen, 1967.

Osten-Sacken, Peter von der. "Die Apologie des paulinischen Apostolats in 1 Kor 15,1–11." *ZNW* 64 (1973): 245–62.

von Otto, Johann Karl Theodore, ed. *Corpus apologetarum Christianorum saeculi secundi.* 2 vols. Weisbaden, 1876, 1877. (= 1969.)

Overbeck, Franz. *Kurze Erklärung der Apostelgeschichte von Dr. W. M. L. de Wette.* Fourth edition revised and expanded by Franz Overbeck. Leipzig, 1870.

_____. "Über das Verhältnis Justins des Märtyrers zur Apostelgeschichte." *ZWTh* 15 (1872): 305–49.

_____. *Über die Auffassung des Streits des Paulus mit Petrus in Antiochien (Gal. 2.11ff.) bei den Kirchenvätern.* Basel, 1877. (= Libelli, 183. Darmstadt, 1968.)

Pachali, H. "Der Römerbrief als historisches Problem. Bemerkungen zu W. Lütgert's gleichnamiger Abhandlung." *ThStKr* 88 (1914): 481–505.

Panikulam, George. *Koinonia in the New Testament: A Dynamic Expression of Christian Life.* AnBib 85. Rome, 1979.

Paschke, Franz. *Die beiden griechischen Klementinen-Epitomen und ihre Anhänge: Überlieferungsgeschichtliche Vorarbeiten zu einer Neuausgabe der Texte.* TU 90. Berlin, 1966.

Peake, Arthur Samuel. "Paul and the Jewish Christians." *BJRL* 13 (1929): 31–62.

Penzel, Klaus. "Church History in Context: The Case of Philip Schaff." Pp. 217–60 in *Our Common History.* A. C. Outler Festschrift. Edited by J. Deschner, L. T. Howe, and K. Penzel. New York, 1975.

Perlitt, Lothar. *Vatke und Wellhausen.* BZAW 94. Berlin, 1965.

Pesch, Rudolf. *Das Markusevangelium,* vol. 2. HThK 2.2. Freiburg, 1980.

_____. *Naherwartungen.* KBANT. Düsseldorf. 1968.

Peterson, Erik. *Frühkirche, Judentum und Gnosis.* Rome, 1959.

Pfleiderer, Otto. *Christian Origins*. Translated by D. A. Huebsch. New York, 1906.

―――. *The Development of Theology in Germany Since Kant and Its Progress in Great Britain Since 1825*. Translated by J. Frederick Smith. London, 1890.

―――. *Die Entstehung des Christentums*. Munich, 1907².

―――. *Die Entwicklung der protestantischen Theologie in Deutschland seit Kant und in Grossbritannien seit 1825*. Freiburg, 1891.

―――. "Paulinische Studien 2. Der Apostelkonvent." In JPTh 9 (1883), 78–104, 241–62.

―――. *Paulinism: A Contribution to the History of Primitive Christian Theology*. 2 vols. Translated by Edward Peters. London, 1877.

―――. *Der Paulinismus: Ein Beitrag zur Geschichte der urchristlichen Theologie*. Leipzig, 1890.

―――. *Primitive Christianity: Its Writings and Teachings in Their Historical Connections*. 4 vols. Translated by W. Montgomery. Edited by W. D. Morrison. Clifton, 1965.

―――. "Theologie und Geschichtswissenschaft (1894)." Pp. 222–42 in *Reden und Aufsätze*. Munich, 1909.

Pieper, Karl. *Die Kirche Palästinas bis zum Jahre 135: Ihre äussere Geschichte und ihr innerer Zustand. Ein Beitrag zur Erkenntnis des Urchristentums*. PUVHL 16. Cologne, 1938.

Planck, Karl. "Judenthum und Urchristenthum." ThJb(T) 6 (1847), 258–93, 409–34, 448–506.

―――. "Das Princip des Ebionitismus." ThJb(T) 2 (1843), 1–34.

Pöhlmann, Wolfgang. *Die heidnische, jüdische und christliche Opposition gegen Domitian*. D.theol. diss. Erlangen, 1966.

Pölcher, Helmut. *Adolf Hilgenfeld und das Ende der Tübingen Schule: Untersuchungen zur Geschichte der Religionswissenschaft im 19. Jahrhundert*. D.phil. diss. Erlangen, 1961.

Pratscher, Wilhelm. "Der Verzicht des Paulus auf finanziellen Unterhalt durch seine Gemeinden: Ein Aspekt seiner Missionsweise." NTS 25 (1979): 284–98.

―――. *Der Herrenbruder Jakobus und die Jakobustradition*. FRLANT 139. Göttingen, 1987.

―――. "Der Herrenbruder Jakobus und sein Kreis." EvTh 47 (1987): 228–44.

Prigent, Pierre. "Ce que l'oeil n'a pas vu, I Cor. 2,9." ThZ 14 (1958): 416–29.

―――. *La fin de Jérusalem*. Archéologie Biblique, 17. Neuchâtel, 1969.

Purves, George Tybout. *Christianity in the Apostolic Age*. New York, 1900.

_____. The Testimony of Justin Martyr to Early Christianity. London, 1888.

Quispel, Gilles. "The Discussion of Judaic Christianity." Pp. 146–58 in Gnostic Studies II. Istanbul, 1975.

Radl, Walter. Paulus und Jesus im lukanischen Doppelwerk. EHS.T 49. Bern, 1975.

Räisänen, Heikki. The Torah and Christ. Helsinki, 1986.

Rehm, Bernhard. "Zur Entstehung der pseudoclementinischen Schriften." ZNW 37 (1938): 77–184.

Reicke, Bo. The New Testament Era: The World of the Bible from 500 B.C. to A.D. 100. Translated by D. E. Green. Philadelphia, 1968.

Reinink, G. J. "Das Land 'Seiris' (Sir) und das Volk der Serer in jüdischen und christlichen Traditionen." JSJ 6 (1975): 72–85.

Reitzenstein, Richard. Hellenistic Mystery-Religions. Translated by John E. Steely. Pittsburgh Theological Monograph Series, 15. Pittsburgh, 1978.

Rensberger, David K. "As the Apostle Teaches: The Development of the Use of Paul's Letters in the Second Century". Ph.D. diss. Yale University, 1981.

Réville, Jean. Les origines de l'épiscopat. Paris, 1894.

Rhoads, David M. Israel in Revolution 6–74 C.E. Philadelphia, 1976.

Richardson, Peter. Israel in the Apostolic Church. SNTSMS 10. Cambridge, 1969.

Riegel, Stanley K. "Jewish Christianity: Definitions and Methodology." NTS 24 (1978): 410–15.

Ritschl, Albrecht. Die christliche Lehre von der Rechtfertigung und Versöhnung. 3 vols. Bonn, 1895.

_____. Die Entstehung der altkatholischen Kirche. Bonn, 1857.

Ritschl, Otto. Albrecht Ritschls Leben. Vol. 1, 1822–1864. Freiburg, 1892.

Rius-Camps, Josep. "Las Pseudoclementinas: Bases filológicas para una nueva interpretación." Revista Catalana de Teologia 1 (1976): 79–155.

Robertson, Archibald, and Alfred Plummer. A Critical and Exegetical Commentary on the First Epistle of St. Paul to the Corinthians. ICC. Edinburgh, 1914.

Robertson, R. G. "The Dialogue of Timothy and Aquila: The Need for a New Edition." VigChr 32 (1978): 276–88.

Robinson, John A. T. Jesus and His Coming. London, 1957.

Rohde, Erwin. Der griechische Roman und seine Vorläufer. Leipzig, 1914.

Roloff, Jürgen. "Apostel." TRE, 3:430–45.

_____. Apostolat—Verkündigung—Kirche. Gütersloh, 1965.

Ropes, James Hardy. *The Apostolic Age in Light of Modern Criticism.* New York, 1912.

_____. *A Critical and Exegetical Commentary on the Epistle of St. James.* ICC. New York, 1916.

_____. "The Epistle to the Romans and Jewish Christianity." Pp. 353–65 in *Studies in Early Christianity.* Edited by S. J. Case. New York, 1928.

_____. *The Singular Problem of the Epistle to the Galatians.* HThSt 14. Cambridge, 1929.

Routh, M. J. *Reliquiae Sacrae,* vol. 1. Oxford, 1846.

Rudolph, Kurt. *Antike Baptisten: Zu den Überlieferungen über früh-jüdische und -christliche Taufsekten.* SSAW.PH 121.4. Berlin, 1981.

_____. "Die Bedeutung des Kölner Mani-Codex für die Manichäis-musforschung. Vorläufige Anmerkungen." Pp. 471–86 in *Mélanges d'historie des Religions.* H.-C. Puech Festschrift. Paris, 1974.

_____. *Die Mandäer.* Vol. 1, *Das Mandäerproblem.* FRLANT 74. Göttingen, 1960.

Saldarini, Anthony J. "Johanan's Escape from Jerusalem: Origin and Development of a Rabbinic Story." *JSJ* 6 (1975): 189–204.

Salles, A. "La diatribe anti paulinienne dans le 'roman pseudo-clémentin' et l'origine des 'kérygmes de Pierre.'" *RB* 64 (1957): 516–51.

Sandelin, Karl-Gustav. *Die Auseinandersetzung mit der Weisheit in 1. Korinther 15.* Åbo, 1976.

Sanders, Ed P. "On the Question of Fulfilling the Law in Paul and in Rabbinic Judaism." Pp. 103–26 in *Donum Gentilicium.* D. Daube Festschrift. Edited by C. K. Barrett, E. Bammel, and W. D. Davies. Oxford, 1978.

Schäfer, P. "Die Flucht Johanan b. Zakkais aus Jerusalem und die Gründung des 'Lehrhauses' in Jabne." Pp. 43–101 in *ANRW,* II.19.2. Edited by W. Haase. Berlin, 1979.

Schaff, Philip. *History of the Christian Church.* Vols. 1-2. New York, 1886.

Schenke, Hans-Martin, and Karl Martin Fischer. *Einleitung in die Schriften des Neuen Testaments.* Vol. 1, *Die Briefe des Paulus und Schriften des Paulinismus.* Berlin, 1978. (= Gütersloh, 1978.) Vol. 2, *Die Evangelien und die anderen neutestamentlichen Schriften.* Berlin, 1979.

Schille, Gottfried. "Anfänge der christlichen Mission." *KuD* 15 (1969): 320–39.

_____. *Anfänge der Kirche.* BEvTh 43. Munich, 1966.

_____. *Osterglaube.* Berlin, 1973.

_____. *Das vorsynoptische Judenchristentum.* Stuttgart, 1970.

Schlatter, Adolf. *Die Geschichte der ersten Christenheit*. BFChTh, II.11. Stuttgart, 1971.

———. *Synagoge und Kirche bis zum Barkochba-Aufstand*. Stuttgart, 1966.

Schliemann, Adolph. *Die Clementinen nebst den verwandten Schriften und der Ebionitismus*. Hamburg, 1844.

Schlier, Heinrich. *Der Brief an die Galater*. Göttingen, 1965[4].

Schmahl, Günther. *Die Zwölf im Markusevangelium*. TThSt 30. Trier, 1974.

Schmidt, Carl. *Studien zu den Pseudo-Clementinen*. TU 46.1. Leipzig, 1929.

Schmidtke, Alfred. *Neue Fragmente und Untersuchungen zu den judenchristlichen Evangelien: Ein Beitrag zur Literatur und Geschichte der Judenchristen*. TU 37.1 Leipzig, 1911.

Schmithals, Walter. *Gnosticism in Corinth: An Investigation of the Letters to the Corinthians*. Translated by John E. Steely. Nashville, 1971.

———. "Judaisten in Galatien?" *ZNW* 74 (1983): 27–58.

———. *Neues Testament und Gnosis*. Darmstadt, 1984.

———. *The Office of the Apostle in the Early Church*. Translated by John E. Steely. Nashville, 1969.

———. *Paul and James*. Translated by Dorthea M. Barton. SBT 46. Naperville, 1965.

———. *Paul and the Gnostics*. Translated by John E. Steely. Nashville, 1972.

———. *Der Römerbrief als historisches Problem*. StNT 9. Gütersloh, 1975.

Schnackenburg, Rudolf. "Das Urchristentum." Pp. 284–309 in *Literatur und Religion des Frühjudentums*. Edited by J. Maier and J. Schreiner. Würtzburg, 1973.

Schneckenburger, Matthias. *Ueber den Zweck der Apostelgeschichte*. Bern, 1841.

Schneemelcher, Wilhelm. "Paulus in der griechischen Kirche des zweiten Jahrhunderts." *ZKG* 75 (1964): 1–20.

———. "Das Problem des Judenchristentums." *VF* 5 (1949–50): 229–38.

———. *Das Urchristentum*. UB 336. Stuttgart, 1981.

Schoeps, Hans-Joachim. *Aus frühchristlicher Zeit*. Tübingen, 1950.

———. *Jewish Christianity: Factional Disputes in the Early Church*. Translated by Douglas R. A. Hare. Philadelphia, 1969.

———. *Paul: The Theology of the Apostle in Light of Jewish Religious History*. Translated by Harold Knight. Philadelphia, 1961.

———. *Studien zur unbekannten Religions- und Geistesgeschichte*.

Veröffentlichungen der Gesellschaft für Geistesgeschichte, 3. Göttingen, 1963.

———. *Theologie und Geschichte des Judenchristentums.* Tübingen, 1949.

———. *Urgemeinde, Judenchristentum, Gnosis.* Tübingen, 1956.

Scholder, Klaus. "Ferdinand Christian Baur als Historiker." *EvTh* 21 (1961): 435–58.

Schrage, Wolfgang. "Der Jakobusbrief." Pp. 5–58 in *Die katholischen Briefe.* 11th ed. NTD 10. Göttingen, 1980.

Schreiber, Alfred. *Die Gemeinde in Korinth: Versuch einer gruppendynamischen Betrachtung der Entwicklung der Gemeinde von Korinth auf der Basis des ersten Korintherbriefes.* NTA NF 12. Munich, 1977.

Schürer, Emil. *Geschichte des jüdischen Volkes im Zeitalter Jesu Christi.* 3 vols. Leipzig, 1901–11. (= Hildesheim, 1964; 1970.)

———. *The History of the Jewish People in the Age of Jesus Christ (175 B.C.—A.D. 135): A New English Version* revised and edited by G. Vermes, F. Millar, M. Black. 2 vols. Edinburgh, 1973–1979.

Schulz, Siegfried. *Die Mitte der Schrift.* Stuttgart, 1976.

———. *Q—Die Spruchquelle der Evangelisten.* Zurich, 1972.

Schwartz, Eduard. "Die Aeren von Gerasa und Eleutheropolis." *NGWG.PH* (1906), 340–95.

———. *Eusebius Werke. Vol. 2, Die Kirchengeschichte, 3.Teil.* GCS 9.3. Leipzig, 1909.

———. *Ueber den Tod der Söhne Zebedaei.* AAWG.PH NF 7.5. Berlin, 1904. (= Pp. 48–123 in *Zum Neuen Testament und zum frühen Christentum. Gesammelte Schriften,* vol. 5. Berlin, 1963.)

———. "Unzeitgemässe Beobachtungen zu den Clementinen." *ZNW* 31 (1932): 151–99.

———. "Zu Eusebius Kirchengeschichte." *ZNW* 4 (1903): 48–66.

———. *Zur Chronologie des Paulus.* *NGWG* (1907): 262–99. (= Pp. 124–69 in *Zum Neuen Testament und zum frühen Christentum. Gesammelte Schriften,* vol. 5. Berlin, 1963.

Schwegler, Albert. *Der Montanismus und die christliche Kirche des zweiten Jahrhunderts.* Tübingen, 1841.

———. *Das Nachapostolische Zeitalter in den Hauptmomenten seiner Entwicklung.* 2 vols. Tübingen, 1847. (= Graz, 1977.)

———. "Ueber den Charakter des nachapostolischen Zeitalters." In *ThJb* 2 (1843), 176–94.

Scott, J. Julius. "Parties in the Church of Jerusalem as Seen in the Book of Acts." *JETS* 18 (1975): 217–27.

Seeberg, Alfred. *Der Katechismus der Urchristenheit*. Leipzig, 1903. (= TB 26. Munich, 1966. With an introduction by F. Hahn.)

Seeberg, Bengt. "Die Geschichtstheologie Justins des Märtyrers." *ZKG* 58 (1939): 1–81.

Sellin, Gerhard. "Das 'Geheimnis' der Weisheit und das Rätsel der 'Christuspartei' (zu 1 Kor 1–4)." *ZNW* 73 (1982): 69–96.

_____. *Der Streit um die Auferstehung der Toten*. FRLANT 138. Göttingen, 1986.

Serkland, John D. "The Dissension at Corinth: An Exploration." *LexTQ* 8 (1973): 27–36.

Siegert, Folker. "Gottesfürchtige und Sympathisanten." *JSJ* 4 (1973): 109–64.

Simon, Marcel. "La migration à Pella: Légende ou réalité?" *RSR* 60 (1972): 37–54.

_____. "Problèmes du Judéo-Christianisme." Pp. 1–17 in *Aspects du Judéo-Christianisme*. Paris, 1965.

_____. "Réflexions sur le Judéo-Christianisme." Pp. 53–76 in *Christianity, Judaism, and Other Greco-Roman Cults*. Vol. 2, *Early Christianity*. Edited by J. Neusner. SJLA 12.2. Leiden, 1975.

_____. *St. Stephen and the Hellenists in the Primitive Church*. London, 1958.

_____. *Verus Israel: A Study of the Relations Between Christians and Jews in the Roman Empire (135–425)*. Translated by H. McKeating. Oxford, 1986.

_____, and André Benôit. *Le Judaïsme et le Christianisme antique d'Antiochus Epiphane à Constantin*. NC(C) 10. Paris, 1968.

Slenczka, Reinhard. *Geschichtlichkeit und Personsein Jesu Christi*. FSÖTh 18. Göttingen, 1967.

Slingerland, H. Dixon. *The Testaments of the Twelve Patriarchs: A Critical History of Research*. SBLMS 21. Missoula, 1977.

Smend, Rudolf. "Universalismus und Partikularismus in der Alttestamentlichen Theologie des 19. Jahrhunderts." *EvTh* 22 (1962): 169–79.

_____. *Wilhelm Martin Leberecht de Wettes Arbeit am Alten und am Neuen Testament*. Basel, 1958.

Smith, Morton. *Clement of Alexandria and a Secret Gospel of Mark*. Cambridge (Mass.), 1973.

_____. "Early Christianity and Judaism." Pp. 41–61 in *Great Confrontations in Jewish History*. Edited by S. Wagner and W. Breck. Denver, 1977.

_____. *Jesus the Magician*. New York, 1978.

_____. "Pauline Problems." *HThR* 50 (1957): 107–31.

_____. "The Reason for the Persecution of Paul and the Obscurity of

Acts." Pp. 261–68 in *Studies in Mysticism and Religion*. G. G. Scholem Festschrift. Jerusalem, 1967.

Sophocles, Evangelinus Apostolides. *Greek Lexicon of the Roman and Byzantine Periods*. New York, 1900. Several reprints.

Sorley, William Ritchie. *Jewish Christians and Judaism*. Cambridge, 1881.

Sowers, Sydney. "The Circumstances and Recollection of the Pella Flight." *ThZ* 26 (1970): 305–20.

Staehelin, Hans. *Die gnostischen Quellen Hippolyts in seiner Hauptschrift gegen die Häretiker*. TU 6.3. Leipzig, 1890.

Stauffer, Ethelbert. "Petrus und Jakobus in Jerusalem." Pp. 361–72 in *Begegnung der Christen*. Edited by M. Roessel and O. Cullmann. Stuttgart, 1960.

――――. "Zum Kalifat des Jakobus." *ZRGG* 4 (1952): 193–214.

Stern, Menahem. *Greek and Latin Authors on Jews and Judaism*. 3 volumes. Leiden, 1980-84.

Stevenson, James, ed. *A New Eusebius*. London, 1974.

Stone, Michael E., and John Strugnell, eds. and trans. *The Books of Elijah, Parts 1–2*. Missoula, 1979.

Stötzol, Arnold. "Dio Darstollung dor ältoston Kirchengeschichte nach den Pseudo-Clementinen." *VigChr* 36 (1983): 24–37.

Stolle, Volker. *Der Zeuge als Angeklagter*. BWANT 102. Stuttgart, 1973.

Stowers, Stanley Kent. "A Critical Reassessment of Paul and the Diatribe: The Dialogical Element in Paul's Letter to the Romans." Ph.D. diss. Yale University, 1979.

Strecker, Georg. "Christentum und Judentum in den ersten beiden Jahrhunderten." *EvTh* 16 (1956): 458–77. (= Pp. 291–310 in *Eschaton und Historie*. Göttingen, 1979.)

――――. "Ebioniten." Cols. 487–500 in *RAC*, vol. 4.

――――. "Elkesai." Cols. 1171–86 in *RAC*, vol. 4. (= Pp. 320–33 in *Eschaton und Historie*. Göttingen, 1979.)

――――. "Eine Evangelienharmonie bei Justin und Pseudoklemens?" *NTS* 24 (1978): 297–316.

――――. "Das Evangelium Jesu Christi." Pp. 183–228 in *Eschaton und Historie*. Göttingen, 1979.

――――. "Judenchristentum," *TRE* 17 (1988): 310–25.

――――. *Das Judenchristentum in den Pseudoklementinen*. TU 70. Berlin, 1981.

――――. "Das Judenchristentum und der Manikodex." Pp. 81–96 in *Codex Manichaicus Coloniensis*. Edited by Luigi Cirillo with Amneris Roselli. Marra, 1986.

――――. "Judenchristentum und Gnosis." Pp. 261–82 in *Altes Testa-*

ment—Frühjudentum—Gnosis. Edited by K.-W. Tröger. Gütersloh, 1980. (Abbr.: Strecker, *Gnosis.*)

———. "The Kerygmata Petrou." Pp. 102–27 in *NTApo*, vol. 2. Edited by E. Hennecke and W. Schneemelcher. Translated by R. McL. Wilson et al. Philadelphia, 1965.

———. *Konkordanz zu den Pseudoklementinen.* 2 vols. Berlin, 1986.

———. "Die sogenannte Zweite Jerusalemreise des Paulus (Acts 11,27–30)." *ZNW* 53 (1962): 67–77. (= Pp. 132–41 in *Eschaton und Historie.*)

———. "Strukturen einer neutestamentlichen Ethik." *ZThK* 75 (1978): 117–46.

Strobel, August. "Das Aposteldekret als Folge des antiochenischen Streites." Pp. 81–104 in *Kontinuität und Einheit.* F. Mussner Festschrift. Edited by P.-G. Müller and W. Stenger. Freiburg, 1981.

———. *Die Stunde der Wahrheit.* WUNT 21. Tübingen, 1980.

Stuhlmacher, Peter. "Das Evangelium von der Versöhnung in Christus." Pp. 13–54 in *Das Evangelium von der Versöhnung in Christus.* Edited by P. Stuhlmacher and H. Class. Stuttgart, 1979.

———. *Gerechtigkeit Gottes bei Paulus.* FRLANT 87. Göttingen, 1966.

———. *Das paulinische Evangelium.* Vol. 1, *Vorgeschichte.* FRLANT 95. Göttingen, 1968.

———. *Vom Verstehen des Neuen Testaments.* GNT 6. Göttingen, 1979.

Stylianopoulos, Theodore. *Justin Martyr and the Mosaic Law.* SBLDS 20. Missoula, 1975.

Suhl, Alfred. *Paulus und seine Briefe.* StNT 11. Gütersloh, 1975.

Surkau, Hans-Werner. *Martyrien in jüdischer und frühchristlicher Zeit.* FRLANT 54. Göttingen, 1938.

Telfer, William. *The Office of a Bishop.* London, 1962.

———. "Was Hegesippus a Jew?" *HThR* 53 (1960): 143–53.

Theissen, Gerd. "Review of Schreiber, Alfred. *Die Gemeinde in Korinth.*" *ThLZ* 105 (1980), cols. 513–14.

———. *The Social Setting of Pauline Christianity: Essays on Corinth.* Translated by John H. Schütz. Philadelphia, 1982.

———. *Sociology of Early Palestinian Christianity.* Translated by John Bowden. Philadelphia, 1978.

———. *Studien zur Soziologie des Urchristentums.* WUNT 19. Tübingen, 1979.

Thomas, Joseph. "Les Ebionites baptistes." *RHE* 30 (1934): 257–96.

———. *Le mouvement baptiste en Palestine et Syrie.* Gembloux, 1935.

Thrall, Margaret E. "Super-Apostles, Servants of Christ, and Servants of Satan." *JSNT* 6 (1980); 42–57.

Trilling, W. "Zur Entstehung der Zwölferkreises: Eine geschichts-kritische Überlegung." Pp. 201–22 in *Die Kirche des Anfangs.* H.

Schürmann Festschrift. Edited by Rudolf Schnackenburg. Leipzig, 1977.

Trocmé, Etienne. "Les églises pauliniennes vues du dehors, Jacques 2,1 à 3,13." Pp. 660–69 in StEv, II. Tu 87. Berlin, 1964.

Trudinger, L. Paul. HETERON DE TŌN APOSTOLŌN OUK EIDON EI MĒ IAKŌBON: A Note on Gal i 19." NovTest 17 (1975): 200–02.

Turner, Cuthbert Hamilton. "The Early Episcopal Lists, II." JThS 1 (1900): 529–53.

Uhlhorn, Gerhard. "Die älteste Kirchengeschichte in der Darstellung der Tübinger Schule." JDTh 3 (1858), 280–349. (= Pp. 222–91 in Ferdinand Christian Baur, Ausgewählte Werke in Einzelausgaben. Vol. 5, Für und wider die Tübinger Schule. Edited by K. Scholder. Stuttgart–Bad Cannstatt, 1975.

————. Die Homilien und Recognitionen des Clemens Romanus. Göttingen, 1854.

Urbach, Ephraim E. The Sages: Their Concepts and Beliefs. 2 vols. Jerusalem, 1975.

Vermès, Géza. "The Decalogue and the Minim." Pp. 169–77 in Post-Biblical Jewish Studies. SJLA 8. Edited by F. L. Cross. Leiden, 1975.

————. Jesus the Jew. Oxford, 1974.

Verweijs, Pieter Godfried. Evangelium und neues Gesetz in der ältesten Christenheit bis auf Marcion. Utrecht, 1960.

Vielhauer, Philipp. Geschichte der urchristlichen Literatur. Berlin, 1975.

————. "Jewish-Christian Gospels." Pp. 117–65 in NTApo, vol. 1. Edited by E. Hennecke and W. Schneemelcher. Translated by R. McL. Wilson et al. Philadelphia, 1963.

————. "Paulus und die Kephaspartei in Korinth." NTS 21 (1975): 342–52. (= Pp. 169–82 in Oikodome. Edited by G. Klein. ThB 65. Munich, 1969.)

Vincent, Marvin R. A Critical and Exegetical Commentary on the Epistles to the Philippians and to Philemon. ICC. Edinburgh, 1955.

Völker, Walther. "Von welchen Tendenzen liess sich Euseb bei der Abfassung seiner 'Kirchengeschichte' leiten? "VigChr 4 (1950): 157–80.

Vokes, F. E. "The Ten Commandments in the New Testament and in First Century Judaism." Pp. 146–54 in StEv, vol. 5. Edited by F. L. Cross. TU 103. Berlin, 1968.

Wagenmann, Julius. Die Stellung des Apostels Paulus neben den Zwölf in den ersten beiden Jahrhunderten. BZNW 3. Giessen, 1926.

Wagner, Harald. An den Ursprüngen des frühkatholischen Problems: Die Ortsbestimmung des Katholizismus im ältern Luthertum. FTS 14. Frankfurt, 1973.

Wagner, Siegfried. *Die Essener in der wissenschaftlichen Diskussion.* BZAW 79. Berlin, 1959.

Waitz, Hans. "Das Buch des Elchasai, das heilige Buch der judenchristlichen Sekte der Sobiai." Pp. 87–104 in *Harnack-Ehrung.* Leipzig, 1921.

_____. *Die Pseudoklementinen.* TU 25.4. Leipzig, 1904.

Walker, Rolf. "Allein aus Werken: Zur Auslegung von Jakobus 2,14–26." *ZThK* 61 (1964): 155–92.

Walter, Nikolaus. "Paulus und die Gegner des Christusevangeliums in Galatien." Pp. 351–56 in *L'apôtre Paul: Personnalité, style et conception du ministère.* Edited by A. Vanhoye. Louvain, 1986.

Ward, Roy Bowen. "James of Jerusalem" *RestQ* 16 (1973): 174–90.

Watson, Francis. *Paul, Judaism and the Gentiles.* SNTSMS 56. Cambridge, 1986.

Wehnert, Jürgen. "Literarkritik und Sprachanalyse: Kritische Anmerkungen zum gegenwärtigen Stand der Pseudoklementinen-Forschung." *ZNW* 74 (1983): 268–301.

Weidinger, K. *Die Haustafel: Ein Stück urchristlicher Paränese.* UNT 14. Leipzig, 1928.

Weiss, Johannes. *Earliest Christianity: A History of the Period A.D. 30–150.* Translated by Frederick C. Grant. 2 vols. New York, 1959.

_____. *Der erste Korintherbrief.* KEK 5. 9th ed. Göttingen, 1910. (= 1970.)

Weizsäcker, Carl von. *The Apostolic Age of the Christian Church.* 2 vols. Translated by James Millar. London, 1907.

Wellhausen, Julius. *Einleitung in die drei ersten Evangelien.* Berlin, 1911.

Wette, Wilhelm Martin Leberecht de. *Lehrbuch der historisch-kritischen Einleitung in die kanonischen Bücher des Neuen Testaments,* vol. 2. Berlin, 1842.

Wilckens, Ulrich. *Der Brief an die Römer,* vol. 1. EKK 6.1. Neukirchen-Vluyn, 1978.

_____. *Resurrection: Biblical Testimony to the Resurrection: An Historical Examination and Explanation.* Translated by A. M. Stewart. Atlanta, 1977.

_____. "*Stylos.*" *TDNT,* 7:732–36.

_____. "Der Ursprung der Überlieferung der Erscheinungen des Auferstandenen." Pp. 59–95 in *Dogma und Denkstrukturen.* E. Schlink Festschrift. Edited by W. Joest and W. Pannenberg. Göttingen, 1963.

Wilken, Robert L. "Review of *Patristic Evidence for Jewish-Christian Sects.* By A. F. J. Klijn and G. J. Reinink." *ThSt* 36 (1975): 538–39.

Williams, A. L. *Adversus Judaeos.* Cambridge, 1935.

Windisch, Hans. *Die katholischen Briefe*. HNT 15. Tübingen, 1951.

――――. *Paulus und Christus: Ein biblisch-religionsgeschichtlicher Vergleich*. UNT 24. Leipzig, 1934.

――――. *Paulus und das Judentum*. Stuttgart, 1935.

――――. "Urchristentum." *ThR* NF (1933): 186–200, 239–58, 289–301, 319–34.

――――. *Der zweite Korintherbrief*. 9th ed. KEK 6. Göttingen, 1924. (= 1970. Edited by G. Strecker.)

Winter, Martin. *Pneumatiker und Psychiker in Korinth*. MThSt 12. Marburg, 1975.

Winter, Paul. "I Corinthians XV 3b–7." *NovTest* 2 (1957–58): 142–50.

Wischmeyer, Oda. *Der höchste Weg: Das 13. Kapitel des 1. Korintherbriefes*. StNT 13. Gütersloh, 1981.

Wisse, Frederik. "The 'Opponents' in the New Testament in Light of the Nag Hammadi Writings." Pp. 99–120 in *Colloque international sur les textes de Nag Hammadi*. Edited by B. Barc. Quebec, 1981.

Wrede, William. *Das literarische Rätsel des Hebräerbriefes*. FRLANT 8. Göttingen, 1906.

――――. *Paul*. Translated by Edward Lummis. Lexington, 1962.

――――. *Vorträge und Studien*. Edited by A. Wrede. Tübingen, 1907.

Wuellner, Wilhelm H. "Der Jakobusbrief im Licht der Rhetorik und Textpragmatik." *LingBibl* 43 (1978): 5–66.

Zahn, Theodor. *Die Apostelgeschichte des Lukas*, vol. 1. Leipzig, 1919.

――――. *Forschungen zur Geschichte des neutestamentlichen Kanons und der altkirchlichen Literatur*. Vol. 1, *Tatian's Diatessaron*. Erlangen, 1881. Vol. 4, Erlangen, 1891. Vol. 6, 1. *Apostel und Apostelschüler in der Provinz Asien; 2. Brüder und Vettern Jesu*. Leipzig, 1900.

――――. *Geschichte des neutestamentlichen Kanons*, vol. 2. 2. Erlangen, 1892.

――――. *Introduction to the New Testament*, vol. 1. Translated by John Moore Trout et al. Grand Rapids, 1953.

Zeller, Eduard. "Albert Schwegler." Pp. 329–63 in *Vorträge und Abhandlungen*, vol. 2. Leipzig, 1877.

――――. *Die Apostelgeschichte nach ihrem Inhalt und Ursprung kritisch untersucht*. Stuttgart, 1854.

――――. "Die Tübinger historische Schule." *HZ* 4 (1860): 90–173. (= Pp. 294–389 in *Vorträge und Abhandlungen*, vol. 1. Leipzig, 1875.)

Ziesler, John A. "Luke and the Pharisees." *NTS* 25 (1979): 146–57.

Zmijewski, Josef. *Die Eschatologiereden des Lukas-Evangeliums*. BBB 40. Bonn, 1972.

Zuckschwerdt, Ernst. "Das Nazyräat des Herrenbruders Jakobus nach Hegesipp (Euseb, h.e. II 23,5–6)." *ZNW* 68 (1977): 276–87.

INDEX OF AUTHORS

INDEX OF AUTHORS

INDEX OF BIBLICAL REFERENCES

OTHER ANCIENT SOURCES